D0961168

New York Times BESTSELLING AUTHOR

JOHN C. MAXWELL

THREE BOOKS IN ONE VOLUME

The Winning Attitude

~

Developing the Leaders Around You

~

Becoming a Person of Influence

THOMAS NELSON PUBLISHERS®
Nashville

All rights reserved. Written permission must be secured from the publisher to use or reproduce any part of this book, except for brief quotations in critical reviews or articles.

Published in Nashville, Tennessee, by Thomas Nelson, Inc.

The individual book in this omnibus edition were originally published in hardcover as follows: *Developing the Leaders Around You* © 1995 by InJoy Inc. *Becoming a Person of Influence* © 1997 by Maxwell Motivation, Inc. a California Corporation and Dornan International, Inc. *The Winning Attitude* © 1993 by John C. Maxwell

Scripture quotations noted NIV are taken from the HOLY BIBLE, NEW INTERNATIONAL VER-SION ®. Copyright © 1973, 1978, 1984 by International Bible Society. Used by permission of Zondervan Bible Publishing House. All rights reserved.

The "NIV" and "New International Version" trademarks are registered in the United States Patent and Trademark Office by International Bible Society. Use of either trademark requires the permission of International Bible Society.

Scripture quotations noted NASB are taken from THE NEW AMERICAN STANDARD BIBLE ®, © Copyright The Lockman Foundation 1960, 1962, 1963, 1968, 1971, 1972, 1973, 1975, 1977. Used by permission. (www.Lockman.org)

Scripture quotations noted TLB are from THE LIVING BIBLE (Wheaton, Illinois: Tyndale House Publishers, 1971) and are used by permission.

Library of Congress Control Number: 00-134116
ISBN 0-7852-6840-5

Printed in the United States of America
1 2 3 4 5 6 7 - 06 05 04 03 02 01 00

The Winning Attitude

JOHN C. MAXWELL

THOMAS NELSON PUBLISHERS
Nashville

"Ability is what you're capable of doing.
Motivation determines what you do.
Attitude determines how well you do it."

Lou Holtz
Notre Dame Football Coach

The Winning Attitude is dedicated to
Dr. Tom Phillippe, Sr.

He is my friend, a co-laborer in the gospel and
an example of proper attitude living.

Contents

Acknowledgments

Thanks for this book must be expressed to my parents, Melvin and Laura Maxwell, for providing a home life that was accented with healthy attitudes for living. Positive attitudes which are more caught than taught surrounded me from the day I was born.

My wife, Margaret, provided wise counsel, and our children, Elizabeth and Joel Porter, gave me many illustrations. The Maxwell family is trying to live the principles of this book.

Appreciation is also to be given to my staff at Skyline Wesleyan Church for their input into this book. Their insights, questions and suggestions highlighted many Tuesday staff meetings. Barbara Brumagin, my administrative assistant, especially followed through on this project.

Thank you to Paul Nanney for his friendship and exciting flying experiences that added to this book.

Section I

The Consideration of Your Attitude

1

It's a Bird...
It's a Plane...
No, It's an Attitude!

Have this attitude in yourselves which was also in Christ Jesus (Philippians 2:5).

It was a beautiful day in San Diego, and my friend Paul wanted to take me for a ride in his airplane. Being new to Southern California, I decided to see our home territory from a different perspective. We sat in the cockpit as Paul completed his instrument checks. Everything was A-Okay, so Paul revved the engines and we headed down the runway. As the plane lifted off, I noticed the nose was higher than the rest of the airplane. I also noticed that while the countryside was truly magnificent, Paul continually watched the instrument panel.

Since I am not a pilot, I decided to turn the pleasure ride into a learning experience. "All those gadgets," I began, "what do they tell you? I notice you keep looking at that one instrument more than the others. What is it?"

"That's the attitude indicator," he replied.

"How can a plane have an attitude?"

"In flying, the attitude of the airplane is what we call the position of the aircraft in relation to the horizon."

By now my curiosity had been aroused, so I asked him to explain more. "When the airplane is climbing," he said, "it has a nose-high attitude because the nose of the airplane is pointed above the horizon."

"So," I jumped in, "when the aircraft is diving, you would call that a nose-down attitude."

"That's right," my instructor continued. "Pilots are concerned about attitude of the airplane because that indicates its performance."

"Now I can understand why the attitude indicator is in such a prominent place on the panel," I replied.

Paul, sensing I was an eager student, continued, "Since the performance of the airplane depends on its attitude, it is necessary to change the attitude in order to change the performance."

He demonstrated this by bringing the aircraft into a nose-high attitude. Sure enough, the plane began to climb and speed decreased. He changed the attitude, and that changed the performance.

Paul concluded the lesson by saying, "Since the attitude of the airplane determines its performance, instructors now teach 'attitude flying.' "

That conversation triggered my thinking concerning people's attitudes. Doesn't an individual's attitude dictate his performance? Does he have an "attitude indicator" that continually evaluates his perspective and achievements in life?

What happens when the attitude is dictating undesirable results? How can the attitude be changed? And, if the attitude changes, what are the ramifications to other people around him?

My friend Paul had an instructor's manual on "Attitude Flying," the relationship between the aircraft's attitude and its performance. We, too, have been given a handbook to attitude living . . . the Bible.

The apostle Paul, when writing to the church at Philippi, placed before those Christians an attitude indicator. "Have this attitude in yourselves which was also in Christ Jesus" (Philippians 2:5).

Christ gives us a perfect example to follow. His high standard was not given to frustrate us but to reveal areas in our lives that need improvement. Whenever I study Philippians 2:3-8, I am reminded of the healthy attitude qualities that Jesus possessed.

He was selfless. "Do nothing from selfishness or empty conceit, but with humility of mind let each of you regard one another as more important than himself; do not merely look out for your own personal interests, but also for the interests of others" (verses 3,4).

He was secure. "Who, although He existed in the form of God, did not regard equality with God a thing to be grasped, but emptied Himself, taking the form of a bond-servant, and being made in the likeness of men" (verses 6,7).

He was submissive. "And being found in appearance as a man, He humbled Himself by becoming obedient to the point of death, even death on a cross" (verse 8).

Paul says that these qualities were exhibited in the life of Christ because of His attitude (verse 5). He also says that we can have this same attitude in our lives. We have a visual example of a Christian attitude and we are also encouraged to attain it.

Paul states in Romans 12:1,2:

I urge you therefore, brethren, by the mercies of God, to present your bodies a living and holy sacrifice, acceptable to God, which is your spiritual service of worship. And do not be conformed to this world, but be transformed [How?] by the *renewing of your mind,* that you may prove what the will of God is, that which is good and acceptable and perfect (emphasis mine).

The result of a renewed mind or a changed attitude is to prove and fulfill God's will. Again we see that the attitude dictates performance.

I once preached a message from Psalm 34 entitled "How to Face Fear." David was lonely, fearful and frustrated in a cave surrounded by the enemy when he wrote this comforting message. The opening of the chapter enables the reader to see the reason for David's success even when surrounded by problems.

David's Three-Fold Process of Praise

1. Praise begins with the will (verse 1).

"*I will bless the* LORD at all times; His praise shall continually be in my mouth." His attitude reflects a determination to rejoice regardless of the situation.

2. Praise flows to the emotion (verse 2).

"*My soul shall make its boast* in the LORD." Now David is praising the Lord not only because it's right but also because he feels like it.

3. Praise spreads to others (verses 2,3).

"*The humble shall hear it and rejoice. O magnify the* LORD *with me, and let us exalt His name together.*" David demonstrates that the desired performance — "praise" — begins with an attitude that is determined to do it. The conclusion of the chapter records David's triumphant "The LORD redeems the soul of His servants, and none of those who take refuge in Him will be condemned."

Attitude living, like attitude flying, says "my attitude dictates my performance." That canopy represents a lot of ground to cover in one book. We'll need to examine:

- What is an attitude, and why is it important?
- What are the necessary ingredients for a high-performance attitude?
- What causes an attitude to become negative, disappointing?
- How can a wrong attitude that is working against us be turned around to work for us?

Along the way we will discover the attitude indicators revealed in persons described in the Bible, the best handbook on attitude performance available since God Himself gave it to us. Obviously, this book will not be the last word on this critical subject. But I hope it will be an enlightening word to those who understand the importance of the attitude. I pray it will be helpful to those who want to change.

Attitude Application:

Take a few minutes before proceeding and ask yourself the following questions:

Have I checked my attitude lately?

How would I rate my attitude?

Never been better	☐
Never been worse	☐
Nose-high	☐
Nose-down	☐

What is an attitude indicator (something which reflects my perspective) in my life?

2

The Attitude—
What Is It?

A person cannot travel within and stand still without.

—James Allen

The high school basketball team I played for was not having a good season, and one day the coach had one of those team meetings in which every player was quiet and listening. The coach continually stressed the relationship between the team's attitude and the win-loss record. I can still hear his words, "Fellows, your abilities say 'win,' but your attitudes say 'lose.'"

Parents are called to school for a conference concerning their child. The issue? Timmy, a fifth-grader, has failing grades and is causing a disturbance among his classmates. His aptitude tests show he is intellectually capable, yet he is failing miserably. The teacher suggests he has a "bad attitude."

A member of the congregation is being discussed in a

pastoral staff meeting. Constantly recurring in the conversation is the phrase, "She has a 'terrific attitude.' "

Hardly a day passes without the word "attitude" entering a conversation. It may be used as a complaint or a compliment. It could mean the difference between a promotion or a demotion. Sometimes we sense it, other times we see it. Yet it is difficult to explain.

The attitude is an inward feeling expressed by behavior. That is why an attitude can be seen without a word being said. Haven't we all noticed "the pout" of the sulker, or "the jutted jaw" of the determined? Of all the things we wear, our expression is the most important.

My daughter Elizabeth has brought much joy to our family, yet her personality at times tends to be melancholic. When she feels that way, her face does not express happiness. My wife Margaret bought Elizabeth a figurine that says, "Put on a happy face." It is a reminder that our expressions usually reflect our inward feelings.

The Bible teaches us that "God sees not as man sees, for man looks at the outward appearance, but the Lord looks at the heart" (1 Samuel 16:7). "The heart is more deceitful than all else and is desperately sick; who can understand it?" (Jeremiah 17:9). These statements express our inability to know for sure what emotions are going on inside someone else. Yet while we refrain from judging others by their outward expressions, many times the outward actions become a "window to the soul." A person who gives "a look that kills," probably is not inwardly singing, "Something Good Is Going to Happen to You."

Acts 20 gives the account of Paul stopping at Miletus and calling for the Ephesian elders. These men gathered and listened to Paul's farewell address. The future was uncertain and their leader declared, "And now, behold, bound in spirit, I am on my way to Jerusalem, not knowing what will happen to me there, except that the Holy Spirit solemnly testifies to me in every city, saying that bonds and afflictions await me" (verses 22,23).

Paul exhorted these church leaders to watch over the work that he had begun. Inwardly they were moved with compassion for the man who had discipled them. Their attitudes of love resulted in a touching display of affection. "And when he had said these things, he knelt down and prayed with them all. And they began to weep aloud and embraced Paul, and repeatedly kissed him, grieving especially over the word which he had spoken, that they should see his face no more. And they were accompanying him to the ship" (verses 36-38).

Since an attitude often is expressed by our body language and by the looks on our faces, it can be contagious. Have you noticed what happens to a group of people when one person, by his expression, reveals a negative attitude? Or have you noticed the lift you receive when a friend's facial expression shows love and acceptance?

David's music and presence encouraged a troubled King Saul. Scripture tells us "the spirit of the LORD departed from Saul, and an evil spirit from the LORD terrorized him" (1 Samuel 16:14). The king's men were told to find someone who could lift their ruler's spirit. They brought David into the palace and "Saul loved him greatly. . . . And Saul sent to Jesse, saying, 'Let David now stand before me; for he has found favor in my sight.' So it came about whenever the evil spirit from God came to Saul, David would take the harp and play it with his hand; and Saul would be refreshed and be well, and the evil spirit would depart from him" (verses 21-23).

Sometimes the attitude can be masked outwardly and others who see us are fooled. But usually the cover-ups will not last long. There is that constant struggle as the attitude tries to wiggle its way out.

My father enjoys telling the story of the four-year-old who had one of those trouble-filled days. After reprimanding him, his mother finally said to him, "Son, you go over to that chair and sit on it now!" The little lad went to the chair, sat down and said, "Mommy, I'm sitting on the outside, but I'm standing up on the inside."

Have you ever said that to God? We have all experienced the inner conflict similar to the one expressed by Paul in Romans 7:

> For the good that I wish, I do not do; but I practice the very evil that I do not wish . . . but I see a different law in the members of my body, waging war against the law of my mind, and making me a prisoner of the law of sin which is in my members. Wretched man that I am! Who will set me free from the body of this death? Thanks be to God through Jesus Christ our Lord! So then, on the one hand I myself with my mind am serving the law of God, but on the other, with my flesh the law of sin (Romans 7:19,23-25).

Sound familiar? Whenever a sincere Christian asks me to help him with his spiritual walk I always talk about obedience. The simplicity of "Trust and Obey," that great hymn by James H. Sammis, points to the importance of our obedient attitude to our spiritual growth.

> When we walk with the Lord in the light of His Word,
> What a glory He sheds on our way!
> While we do His good will He abides with us still,
> And with all who will trust and obey.
> Trust and obey, for there's no other way,
> to be happy in Jesus, but to trust and obey.

During a time of congregational renewal at Skyline Wesleyan Church, where I am the senior pastor, my heart was challenged with the words of Mary, the mother of Jesus, who said, "Whatever He [Jesus] says to you, do it." I shared with my congregation this thought of obedience drawn from the story of Jesus' miracle at the wedding in Cana (John 2:1-8).

Whatever Jesus says to you, do it, even though

1. You are not in the "right place" (verse 2).

They were at a wedding and not a church when Jesus performed the miracle. Some of God's greatest blessings will be at "other places" if we will be obedient to Him.

2. You have a lot of problems (verse 3).

They had run out of wine. Too many times our problems drive us away from Jesus instead of to Him. Christian renewal begins when we focus on God's power and not our problems.

3. You are not encouraged (verse 4).

Jesus said to those at the wedding, "My hour has *not yet* come." Instead of being discouraged by these words, Mary laid hold of the possibility of a miracle.

4. You have not walked with Him very long (verse 5).

The servants who obeyed Jesus had just met Him, and the disciples had just started following the Lord, yet they were expected to obey Him.

5. You have not seen Him work miracles in your life.

This was our Lord's first miracle. The people in this situation had to obey Him without His having a previous track record.

6. You don't understand the entire process.

From this biblical story we can draw out a definition for obedience. It is listening to the words of Jesus and doing His will. Inward obedience provides outward growth.

Psychologist/philosopher James Allen states, "A person cannot travel within and stand still without." Soon what is happening within us will affect what is happening without. A hardened attitude is a dreaded disease. It causes a closed mind and a dark future. When the attitude is positive and conducive to growth, the mind expands and the progress begins.

What is an attitude?

It is the "advance man" of our true selves.
Its roots are inward but its fruit is outward.
It is our best friend or our worst enemy.
It is more honest and more consistent than our words.
It is an outward look based on past experiences.
It is a thing which draws people to us or repels them.
It is never content until it is expressed.
It is the librarian of our past.
It is the speaker of our present.
It is the prophet of our future.

Attitude Application:

Choose a friend and evaluate his attitude. Write down several words that describe it. What is his performance indicator as a result of that attitude? Now do this for yourself.

3

The Attitude— Why Is It Important?

Do you feel the world is treating you well? If your attitude toward the world is excellent, you will receive excellent results. If you feel so-so about the world, your response from that world will be average. Feel badly about your world and you will seem to have only negative feedback from life.

—John Maxwell

We live in a world of words. Attached to these words are meanings that bring varied responses from us Words such as *happiness, acceptance, peace* and *success* describe what each of us desires. But there is one word that will either heighten the possibility of our desires being fulfilled or prevent them from becoming a reality within us.

While leading a conference in South Carolina, I tried the following experiment. To reveal the significance of this word, I read the previous paragraph and asked, "What word describes what will determine our happiness, acceptance, peace and success?" The audience began to express words such as job, education, money, time. Finally someone said *attitude*. Such an important area of their lives was a second thought. Our attitude is the primary force that will determine whether we succeed or fail.

For some, attitude presents a difficulty in every opportunity; for others it presents an opportunity in every difficulty. Some climb with a positive attitude, while others fall with a negative perspective. The very fact that the attitude "makes some" while "breaking others" is significant enough for us to explore its importance. Studying the major statements listed in this chapter will highlight this truth to us.

Attitude Axiom #1:
Our attitude determines our approach to life.

The story of the two buckets underlines this truth. One bucket was an optimist, and the other was a pessimist.

"There has never been a life as disappointing as mine," said the empty bucket as it approached the well. "I never come away from the well full but what I return again empty."

"There has never been such a happy life as mine," said the full bucket as it left the well. "I never come to the well empty but what I go away again full."

Our attitude tells us what we expect from life. If our "nose" is pointed up, we are taking off; if it is pointed down, we may be headed for a crash.

One of my favorite stories is about a grandpa and grandma who visited the grandchildren. Each afternoon Grandpa would lie down for a nap. One day, as a practical joke, the kids decided to put Limburger cheese in his moustache. Quite soon he awoke sniffing. "Why, this room stinks," he exclaimed as he got up and went out into the kitchen. He wasn't there long until he decided that the kitchen smelled too, so he walked outdoors for a breath of fresh air. Much to Grandpa's surprise, the open air brought no relief, and he proclaimed, "The whole world stinks!"

How true that is to life! When we carry "Limburger cheese" in our attitudes, the whole world smells bad.

One of the valid ways to test your attitude is to answer this question: "Do you feel your world is treating you well?" If your attitude toward the world is excellent, you will receive excellent results. If you feel so-so about the world, your response from the world will be average. Feel badly about your world, and you will seem to have only negative feedback from life. Look around you. Analyze the conversations of people who lead unhappy, unfulfilled lives. You will find they are crying out against a society which they feel is out to get them and to give them a lifetime of trouble, misery and bad luck. Sometimes the prison of discontent has been built by their own hands.

The world doesn't care whether we free ourselves from this prison or not. It marches on. Adopting a good, healthy attitude toward life does not affect society nearly so much as it affects us. The change cannot come from others. It must come from us.

The apostle Paul had a terrible background to overcome. He told Timothy that he was the "chief of sinners." But after his conversion he was infused with desire to know Christ in a greater way. How did he fulfill this desire? Not by waiting for someone else to assist him. Neither did he look backward and whine about his terrible past. Paul diligently "pressed on to lay hold of Jesus." His singleness of purpose caused him to state, "But one thing I do: forgetting what lies behind and reaching forward to what lies ahead, I press on toward the goal for the prize of the upward call of God in Christ Jesus" (Philippians 3:13,14).

We are individually responsible for our view of life.

The Bible says, "Whatever a man sows, this he will also reap" (Galatians 6:7). Our attitude and action toward life help determine what happens to us.

It would be impossible to estimate the number of jobs which have been lost, the number of promotions missed, the number of sales not made and the number of marriages ruined by poor attitudes. But almost daily we witness jobs that are held but hated and marriages that are tolerated but unhappy, all because people are waiting for others, or the world, to change instead of realizing that they are responsible for their behavior. God is sufficient to give them the desire to change, but the choice to act upon that desire is theirs.

It is impossible for us to tailor-make all situations to fit our lives perfectly. But it is possible to tailor-make our attitudes to fit. The apostle Paul beautifully demonstrated this truth while he was imprisoned in Rome. He certainly had not received a "fair shake." The atmosphere of his confinement was dark and cold. Yet he writes to the church at Philippi brightly declaring, "Rejoice in the Lord *always*; again I will say rejoice!" (Philippians 4:4, emphasis mine). Notice that the confined man was telling carefree people to rejoice! Was Paul losing his mind? No. The secret is found late in the same chapter. Paul states:

> Not that I speak from want; for I have *learned* to be content in whatever circumstances I am. I know how to get along with humble means and I also know how to live in prosperity; in any and every circumstance I have *learned* the secret of being filled and going hungry, both of having abundance and suffering need (verses 11,12, emphasis mine).

The ability to tailor-make his attitude to his situation in life was learned behavior. It did not come automatically. The behavior was learned and a positive outlook became natural. (I will talk more about this learned behavior in

Section IV, "The Changing of Your Attitude.") Paul repeatedly teaches us by his life that man helps create his environment—mental, emotional, physical and spiritual—by the attitude he develops.

Attitude Application:

Circle the number that most closely reveals your attitude toward life:

1. "Make the World Go Away"

2. "Raindrops Keep Falling on my Head"

3. "I Did It My Way"

4. "Oh, What a Beautiful Morning"

Attitude Axiom #2:
Our attitude determines our relationships with people.

The Golden Rule: "Therefore, however you want people to treat you, so treat them" (Matthew 7:12).

This axiom takes on a higher significance when, as Christians, we realize that effective ministry to one another is based on relationships.

The model of ministry (as I understand ministry) is best captured in John 13. Christ and His disciples are gathered in the upper room.

The components of Christ's model of ministry are:

1. men with whom He had shared all areas of life;

2. an attitude and demonstration of servanthood;

3. an all-encompassing command of relational love. ("By this all men will know you are My disciples.")

An effective ministry of relating to others must include all three of these biblical components. No single methodology (preaching, counseling, visitation) will effectively minister to all the needs all the time. It takes a wise combination of many methods to reach the needs of people. And the bridge between the gospel remedy and people's needs is leadership based on relationship.

John 10:3-5 gives a view of relational leadership:

1. Relationship to the point of instant *recognition* (He calls His own sheep by name);

2. Established relationship built on *trust* (His sheep hear his voice and come to Him);

3. *Modeled* leadership (He walks ahead of them and they follow Him).

Yet establishing such relationships is difficult. People are funny. They want a place in the front of the bus, the back of the church and the middle of the road. Tell a man there are 300 billion stars, and he will believe you. Tell that same man that a bench has just been painted, and he has to touch it to be sure.

People are frustrating at times. They show up at the wrong place at the wrong time for the wrong reason. They are always interesting but not always charming. They are not always predictable because they have minds of their own. You can't get along with them, and you can't make it without them. That's why it is essential to build proper relationships with others in our crowded world.

The Stanford Research Institute says that the money you make in any endeavor is determined only 12.5 percent by knowledge and 87.5 percent by your ability to deal with people.

87.5% people knowledge

$$+ \qquad = \qquad \textbf{Success}$$

12.5% product knowledge

That is why Teddy Roosevelt said, "The most important single ingredient to the formula of success is knowing how to get along with people."

"I will pay more for the ability to deal with people than any other ability under the sun," asserted John D. Rockefeller.

J. Paul Getty, when asked what was the most important quality for a successful executive, replied, "It doesn't make much difference how much other knowledge or experience an executive possesses; if he is unable to achieve results through people, he is worthless as an executive."

When the attitude we possess places others first and we see people as important, then our perspective will reflect their viewpoint, not ours. Until we walk in the other person's shoes and see life through another's eyes, we will be like the man who angrily jumped out of his car after a collision with another car. "Why don't you people watch where you're driving?" he shouted wildly. "You're the fourth car I've hit today!"

A few years ago I was traveling in the South and stopped at a service station for some fuel. It was a rainy day, yet the station workers were diligently trying to take care of the customers. I was impressed by the first-class treatment and fully understood the reason when I read this sign on the front door of the station:

WHY CUSTOMERS QUIT

1% die
3% move away
5% other friendships
9% competitive reasons (price)

14% product dissatisfaction
BUT . . .
68% quit because of an attitude of indifference
toward them by some employee!

In other words, 68 percent quit because the workers did not have a customer mindset working for them.

Usually the person who rises within an organization has a good attitude. The promotions did not give that individual an outstanding attitude, but an outstanding attitude resulted in promotions. A recent study by Telemetrics International concerned those "nice guys" who had climbed the corporate ladder. A total of 16,000 executives were studied. Observe the difference between executives defined as "high achievers" (those who generally have a healthy attitude) and "low achievers" (those who generally have an unhealthy attitude):

High achievers tended to care about people as well as profits; low achievers were preoccupied with their own security.

High achievers viewed subordinates optimistically; low achievers showed a basic distrust of subordinates' abilities.

High achievers sought advice from their subordinates; low achievers didn't.

High achievers were listeners; low achievers avoided communication and relied on policy manuals.

In 1980-81 I took on a rather ambitious project, which included teaching and leading fifteen pastors and their congregations to become growing, vibrant churches. One of my favorite responsibilities was to speak in a Sunday service and recruit workers for that particular church. Right before the "enlisting service," I would ask the pastor how many people he thought would come forward, sign a card and enlist in evangelism and discipleship. I would watch the pastor slowly calculate the "who woulds" and the "who would nots." After receiving the carefully chosen number, I would announce, "More than that number will sign up."

Why could I say that? Did I know his people better than he did? Of course not. What I did know was that the pastor had mentally placed his people into slots and "knew" how they would react during the service. Since I did not know the congregation, my attitude was open and positive toward all of them. I treated the listeners as if they all would respond, and most did! All fifteen pastors guessed lower than the actual laity response.

A negative past experience sometimes paralyzes our thinking and our attitude. A man unable to find his best saw suspected his neighbor's son who was always tinkering around with woodworking. During the next few days everything that the young man did looked suspicious—the way he walked, the tone of his voice and his gestures. But when the older man found the saw behind his own workbench, where it had fallen when he accidentally knocked it off the bench, he no longer saw anything suspicious in his neighbor's son.

Attitude Application:

Challenge: For one week treat every person you meet, without a single exception, as the most important person on earth. You will find that they will begin treating you the same way.

Attitude Axiom #3:
Often our attitude is the only difference between success and failure.

History's greatest achievements have been made by men who excelled only slightly over the masses of others in their fields.

This could be called the principle of the slight edge. Many times that slight difference was attitude. The former Israeli Prime Minister Golda Meir underlined this truth in one of her interviews. She said, "All my country has is spirit. We don't have petroleum dollars. We don't have mines or great wealth in the ground. We don't have the support of a worldwide public opinion that looks favorably on us. All Israel has is the spirit of its people. And if the people lose their spirit, even the United States of America cannot save us." This great lady was saying,

Resources - Right Attitude = Defeat

Right Attitudes - Resources = Victory

Below I've listed resources that enable a person to achieve success. Beside this list write down some of your other blessings. Read them when you are losing that slight edge.

health	experiences	connections
friends	family	aptitude
money	attitude	goals

Certainly aptitude is important to our success in life. Yet success or failure in any undertaking is caused more by mental attitude than by mere mental capacities. I remember times when Margaret, my wife, would come home from teaching school frustrated because of modern education's emphasis on aptitude instead of attitude. She wanted the kids to be tested on A.Q. (attitude quotient) instead of just the I.Q. (intelligence quotient). She would talk of kids whose I.Q. was high yet their performance was low. There were others whose I.Q. was low, but their performance was high.

As a parent, I hope my children have excellent minds and outstanding attitudes. But if I had to choose in an "either-or" situation, without hesitation I would want their

A.Q. to be high.

A Yale University president some years ago gave this advice to a former president of Ohio State: "Always be kind to your A and B students. Someday one of them will return to your campus as a good professor. And also be kind to your C students. Someday one of them will return and build a two-million dollar science laboratory."

A Princeton Seminary professor discovered that the spirit of optimism really does make a difference. He made a study of great preachers across past centuries. He noted their tremendous varieties of personalities and gifts. Then he asked the question, "What do these outstanding pulpiteers all have in common besides their faith?" After several years of searching he found the answer. It was their cheerfulness. In most cases they were happy men.

There is very little difference in people, but that little difference makes a big difference. The little difference is attitude. The big difference is whether it is positive or negative. Nowhere is this principle better illustrated than in the story of the young bride from the East who, during wartime, followed her husband to a U.S. Army camp on the edge of the desert in California.

Living conditions were primitive at best, and her husband had advised against her move, but she wanted to be with him. The only housing they could find was a run-down shack near an Indian village. The heat was unbearable in the daytime—115° in the shade. The wind blew constantly, spreading dust and sand all over everything. The days were long and boring. Her only neighbors were Indians, none of whom spoke English. When her husband was ordered farther into the desert for two weeks of maneuvers, loneliness and the wretched living conditions got the best of her. She wrote to her mother that she was coming home. She couldn't take it anymore.

In a short time she received a reply which included these two lines, "Two men looked through prison bars; one saw mud, the other saw stars." She read the lines over and over again and began to feel ashamed of herself. She didn't really want to leave her husband. All right, she thought, she'd *look* for the stars. In the following days she set out to make friends with the Indians, asking them to teach her weaving and pottery. At first they were distant, but as soon as they sensed her genuine interest, they returned her friendship. She became friendly with their culture and history—in fact, everything about them. As she began to study the desert, it too changed from a desolate, forbidding place to a marvelous thing of beauty.

She had her mother send her books. She studied the forms of the cacti, the yuccas and the Joshua trees. She collected sea shells that had been left there when the sands had been an ocean floor. Later, she became such an expert on the area that she wrote a book about it.

What had changed? Not the desert; not the Indians. Simply by changing her own attitude she had transformed a miserable experience into a highly rewarding one.

Attitude Application:

There is very little difference in people, but that little difference makes a big difference. That difference is attitude. Think of something that you desire. What attitude will you need to get it or achieve it?

Attitude Axiom #4:
Our attitude at the beginning of a task will affect its outcome more than anything else.

Coaches understand the importance of their teams having the right attitude before facing a tough opponent. Surgeons want to see their patients mentally prepared before going into surgery. Job-seekers know that their prospective employer is looking for more than just skills when they apply for work. Public speakers want a conducive atmosphere before they communicate to their audience. Why? Because the right attitude in the beginning insures success at the end. You are acquainted with the saying, "All's well that ends well." An equal truth is "All's well that begins well."

One of the key principles I teach when leading evangelism conferences is the importance of our attitude when witnessing to others. Most of the time it is the way we present the gospel rather than the gospel itself that offends people. Two people can share the same news with the same person and receive different results. Why? Usually the difference is in the attitude of the person sharing. The eager witness says to himself, "People are hungry for the gospel and desirous of a positive change in their lives." The reluctant witness says to himself, "People are not interested in spiritual things and don't want to be bothered." Those two attitudes will not only determine the number of attempts made in witnessing (can you guess which one will witness?) but also will determine the results if they both share the same faith.

The American statesman Hubert H. Humphrey was admired by millions. His bubbly enthusiasm was contagious. When he died I cut out one of his quotes from a newspaper article about him. It was written to his wife on his first trip to Washington, D.C., in 1935: "I can see how someday, if you and I just apply ourselves and make up our minds for bigger things, we can someday live here in Washington and probably be in government, politics or service. Oh gosh, I hope my dream comes true; I'm going to try anyhow." With that type of attitude he couldn't fail!

Most projects fail or succeed before they begin. A young mountain climber and an experienced guide were ascending a high peak in the Sierras. Early one morning the young climber was suddenly awakened by a tremendous cracking sound.

He was convinced that the end of the world had come. The guide responded, "It's not the end of the world, just the dawning of a new day." As the sun rose, it was merely hitting the ice and causing it to melt.

Many times we have been guilty of viewing our future challenges as the sunset of life rather than the sunrise of a bright new opportunity.

For instance, there's the story of two shoe salesmen who were sent to an island to sell shoes. The first salesman, upon arrival, was shocked to realize that no one wore shoes. Immediately he sent a telegram to his home office in Chicago saying, "Will return home tomorrow. No one wears shoes."

The second salesman was thrilled by the same realization. Immediately he wired the home office in Chicago saying, "Please send me 10,000 shoes. Everyone here needs them."

Attitude Application:

Why not write down a project that you have neglected because of an unhealthy attitude toward it? Read axiom #4 again and again, then list all the positive benefits that will be received from the completion of your project. Remember, "All's well that begins well." Raise the level of your attitude!

Attitude Axiom #5:
Our attitude can turn our problems into blessings.

In *Awake, My Heart,* my friend J. Sidlow Baxter writes, "What is the difference between an obstacle and an opportunity? Our attitude toward it. Every opportunity has a difficulty and every difficulty has an opportunity."[1]

When confronted with a difficult situation, a person with an outstanding attitude makes the best of it while he gets the worst of it. Life can be likened to a grindstone. Whether it grinds you down or polishes you depends upon what you are made of.

While attending a conference of young leaders, I heard this statement: "No society has ever developed tough men during times of peace." Adversity is prosperity to those who possess a great attitude. Kites rise against, not with, the wind. When the adverse wind of criticism blows, allow it to be to you what the blast of wind is to the kite—a force against it that lifts it higher. A kite would not fly unless it had the controlling tension of the string to tie it down. It is equally true in life.

When Napoleon's school companions made sport of him because of his humble origin and poverty, he devoted himself entirely to his books. Quickly rising above his classmates in scholarship, he commanded their respect. Soon he was regarded as the brightest in the class.

If the germ of the seed has to struggle to push its way up through the stones and hard sod, to fight its way up to the sunlight and air and then to wrestle with the storm, snow and frost, the fiber or its timber will be all the tougher and stronger.

Few people knew Abraham Lincoln until the great weight of the Civil War showed his character.

Robinson Crusoe was written in prison. John Bunyan wrote *Pilgrim's Progress* in the Bedford jail. Sir Walter Raleigh wrote *The History of the World* during a thirteen-year imprisonment. Luther translated the Bible while confined in the castle of Wartburg. For ten years Dante, author of *The Divine Comedy,* worked in exile and under the sentence of death. Beethoven was almost totally deaf and burdened with sorrow when he produced his greatest works.

When God wants to educate a man, He does not send him to the school of graces but to the school of necessities. Through the pit and the dungeon Joseph came to the throne. Moses tended sheep in the desert before God called him for service. Peter, humbled and broken by his denial of Christ, heeded the command to "Feed My sheep." Hosea loved and cared for an unfaithful wife out of obedience to God.

In the Chinese language, whole words are written with a symbol. Often when two completely unlike symbols are put together, they have a meaning different from their two separate components. An example is the symbol of "man" and that of "woman." When combined, they mean "good."

The same is true of dreams and problems. As the answers always lie in the questions, so the opportunities of life lie directly in our problems. Thomas Edison said, "There is much more opportunity than there are people to see it."

Great leaders emerge when crises occur. In the lives of people who achieve, we read repeatedly of terrible troubles which force them to rise above the commonplace. Not only do they find the answers, but they discover a tremendous power within themselves. Like a ground swell far out in the ocean, this force within explodes into a mighty wave when circumstances seem to overcome. Then out steps the athlete, the author, the statesman, the scientist or the businessman. David Sarnoff said, "There is plenty of security in the cemetery; I long for opportunity."

We will know our attitude is on the right track when we are like the small businessman whose clothing store was threatened with extinction. A national chain store had moved in and acquired all the properties on his block. This one particular businessman refused to sell. "All right then, we'll build around you and put you out of business," the new competitors said. The day came when the small merchant found himself hemmed in with a new department store stretching out on both sides of his little retail shop. The competitors' banners announced, "Grand Opening!" The merchant countered with a banner stretching across the entire width of his store. It read, "Main Entrance."

Attitude Application:

List two problems that are presently a part of your life. Besides the two problems write down your present reactions to them. Are they negative? Your challenge: Discover at least three possible benefits from each problem. Now attack the problem with your eyes on the benefits, not the barriers.

Attitude Axiom #6:
Our attitude can give us an uncommonly positive perspective.

The result of that truth: the accomplishment of uncommon goals. I have keenly observed the different approaches and results achieved by a positive thinker and by a person filled with fear and apprehension.

Example: When Goliath came up against the Israelites, the soldiers all thought, *He's so big we can never kill him.* David looked at the same giant and thought, *He's so big I can't miss.*

Example: When you go to a shopping mall or any public place that contains a lot of cars and people, do you start at the farthest point of the parking lot and work your way toward the building, or drive to the front, assuming someone will be pulling out so you can pull in? If you operate from a positive perspective in life you will always go to the front. One time I had a friend ask me why I always assumed a close parking space would be available. My answer: "The odds are that a person coming out of the store has been in there the longest. Since that individual arrived at the store the earliest, he parked the closest." When they pull out, I drive in and give them a friendly wave. It's the least I can do for a person who has saved my parking space.

Moody Bible Institute President George Sweeting, in his sermon entitled "Attitude Makes the Difference," tells about a Scotsman who was an extremely hard worker and expected all the men under him to be the same. His men would tease him, "Scotty, don't you know that Rome wasn't built in a day?" "Yes," he would answer, "I know that. But I wasn't foreman on that job."

The ind'vidual whose attitude causes him to approach life from an entirely positive perspective is not always understood. He is what some would call a "no-limit person." In othe words, he doesn't accept the normal limitations of life like most people. He is unwilling to accept "the accepted" just because it is accepted. His response to self-limiting conditions will probably be a "Why?" instead of an "Okay." He has limitation in his life. His gifts are not so plentiful that he cannot fail. But he is determined to walk to the very edge of his potential or the potential of a project before he accepts a defeat.

He is like the bumblebee. According to a theory of aerodynamics, as demonstrated through the wind tunnel tests, the bumblebee should be unable to fly. Because of the size, weight and shape of his body in relationship to the total wing spread, flying is scientifically impossible. The bumblebee, being ignorant of scientific theory, goes ahead and flies anyway and makes honey every day.

This mindset allows a person to start each day with a positive disposition, like the elevator operator on Monday morning. The elevator was full and the man began humming a tune. One passenger seemed particularly irritated by the man's mood and snapped, "What are you so happy about?" "Well, sir," replied the man happily, "I ain't never lived this day before!"

Asked which of his works he would select as his masterpiece, architect Frank Lloyd Wright, at the age of 83, replied, "My next one."

The future not only looks bright when the attitude is right, but also the present is much more enjoyable. The positive person understands that the journey is as enjoyable as the destination.

One day a man was watching two masons working on a building. He noticed that one worker continually frowned, groaned and cursed his labors. When asked what he was doing, he replied, "Just piling one stone on top of another all day long until my back is about to break." The other mason whistled as he worked. His movements were swift and sure and his face was aglow with satisfaction. When asked what he was doing, he replied, "Sir, I'm not just making a stone wall. I'm helping to build a cathedral."

A friend of mine in Ohio drove for an interstate trucking company. Knowing the hundreds of miles he logged weekly, I once asked him how he kept from getting extremely tired. "It's all in your attitude," he replied. "Some drivers 'go to work' in the morning but I 'go for a ride in the country,' " That kind of positive perspective gives him the "edge" on life.

Attitude Application:

Notice the limitation that you or your friends accept today. With each limitation example ask the question, Why? Example: "Why did I choose a parking space far away without checking up close first?" Make a mental note to become a "no limit person" each time you ask the question, Why?

Attitude Axiom #7:
Our attitude is not automatically good just because we are Christians.

It is noteworthy that the seven deadly sins (pride, covetousness, lust, envy, anger, gluttony and sloth) are all matters of attitude, inner spirit and motives. Sadly, many carnal Christians carry with them inner spirit problems. They are like the elder brother of the prodigal son, thinking they do everything right. He chose to stay home with the father. No way was he going to spend his time sowing wild oats. Yet, when the younger brother came back home, some of the elder brother's wrong attitudes began to surface.

First came a feeling of self-importance. The elder brother was out in the field doing what he ought to do, but he got mad when the party began at home. He didn't get mad because he didn't like parties. I know he liked parties, because he complained to his father that he would never let him throw one!

That was followed by a feeling of self-pity. The elder brother said, "Look! For so many years I have been serving you, and I have never neglected a command of yours; and yet you have never given me a kid, that I might be merry with my friends; but when this son of yours came, who has devoured your wealth with harlots, you killed the fatted calf for him" (Luke 15:29,30).

Often we overlook the true meaning of the story of the prodigal son. We forget that we have not one but two prodigals. The younger brother is guilty of the sins of the flesh, whereas the elder brother is guilty of the sins of the spirit (attitude). When the parable closes, it is the elder—the second prodigal—who is outside the father's house.

In Philippians 2:3-8, Paul talks about the attitudes we should possess as Christians:

> Do nothing from selfishness or empty conceit, but with humility of mind let each of you regard one another as more important than himself; do not merely look out for your own personal interests, but also for the interests of others. Have this attitude in yourselves which was also in Christ Jesus, who, although He existed in the form of God, did not regard equality with God a thing to be grasped, but emptied Himself, taking the form of a bond-servant, and being made in the likeness of man. And being found in appearance as a man, He humbled Himself by becoming obedient to the point of death, even death on a cross.

Paul tells us five things about the proper Christian attitude:

1. Do things for the right reasons (verse 3).

2. Regard others as more important than yourself (verse 3).

3. Look out for the interests of others (verse 4).

4. Christ recognized His sonship and therefore was willing to serve God and others (verse 6).

5. Possess the attitude of Christ, who was not power hungry (verse 6) but rather emptied Himself (verse 7), demonstrated obedience (verse 8) and fulfilled God's purpose (verse 8).

When our emphasis of lifestyle is focused on verse 4, looking out for our own personal interests, we become like the elder brother. We nurture attitudes of jealousy, pity and selfishness. Christians who possess no greater cause than themselves are not as happy as those who do not know Christ as Savior, yet have a purpose greater than themselves.

This "elder brother" attitude has three possible

results, none of which is positive.

First, it is possible for us to assume the place and privilege of a son while refusing the obligations of a brother. The elder brother outwardly was correct, conscientious, industrious and dutiful, but look at his attitude. Also note that a wrong relationship with the brother brought a strained relationship with the father (Luke 15:28).

Second, it is possible to serve the Father faithfully yet not be in fellowship with Him. A right relationship will usually cultivate similar interests and priorities. Yet the elder brother had no idea why the father would rejoice over his son's return.

Third, it is possible to be an heir of all our Father possesses yet have less joy and liberty than one who possesses nothing. The servants were happier than the elder son. They ate, laughed and danced while he stood on the outside demanding his rights.

A wrong attitude kept the elder brother away from the heart's desire of the father, the love of his brother and the joy of the servants. Wrong attitudes in our lives will block the blessings of God and cause us to live below God's potential for our lives.

Attitude Application:

When our attitude begins to erode like the elder brother's we should remember two things:

1. *Our privilege:* "My child, you have always been with me" (verse 31).

2. *Our possessions:* "All that is mine is yours" (verse 31).

Take a moment to list your privileges and possessions in Christ. How rich we are!

Section II

The Construction of Your Attitude

4

It's Hard to Soar With the Eagles When You Have to Live With the Turkeys

The last of the human freedoms is to choose one's attitude in any given set of circumstances.
—Victor Frankl

Our surroundings control our soaring. Turkey-thinking + turkey-talk = turkey-walk. We quickly blend into the color of our surroundings. Similarities in thinking, mannerisms, priorities, talk and opinions are very common within individual cultures. We all know married people who grow to look more alike as the years pass. Many times family members exhibit similar physical traits.

A man who had not seen his brother for many years went to the airport to pick him up. After a period of waiting, one of the brothers began walking across the terminal. Without hesitation the other brother called out his name and a happy reunion followed. When asked how he recognized the other brother, he replied quickly, "I knew he was my brother because he walked like my father."

It is true: We easily change to fit our environment. Our children, Elizabeth and Joel Porter, are both adopted. Although they possess their own unique identities, they also have become very similar to their adoptive parents. People who know the children are adopted continually remark about the similarities. In fact, my mother, who was recently visiting us from back east, began talking about the physical likenesses between Elizabeth and my wife Margaret. Suddenly she exclaimed, "I forgot she is adopted!"

Unquestionably our surroundings help construct our attitudes, too.

The word "choices" rises on the opposite side of environment in the attitude construction issue. Speaking more logically than emotionally, the voice of this word says, "We are free to choose our attitudes." This logic becomes more convincing with the additional voice of Victor Frankl, survivor of a Nazi concentration camp, who said, "The last of the human freedoms is to choose one's attitude in *any* given set of circumstances."

Job, ill, bereaved and poverty-stricken, refused to listen to the advice of his wife, who told him, "Curse God and die!" He rebuked her, saying, "You speak as one of the foolish women speaks. Shall we indeed accept good from God and not accept adversity?" (Job 2:10). These two viewpoints concerning how attitudes are constructed raise the question, "Which comes first, the condition or the choice?" The following chart will help us answer that question.

Which Comes First?

Conditions Early life Involuntary Others choose We react	Later life Voluntary We choose We initiate **Choice**

Age Increases ⟶

In our early years, our attitudes are determined mainly by our conditions. A baby does not choose his family or his environment. But as his age increases, so do his options.

A while ago I conducted a leadership seminar in Columbus, Ohio. For an entire day I talked about the importance of our attitudes and about how many times they make the difference in our lives. During one of the breaks, a man told me the following story.

> From my earliest recollections I do not remember a compliment or affirmation from my father. His father also had thought it unmanly to express affection or even appreciation. My grandfather was a perfectionist who worked hard and expected everyone else to do the same without positive reinforcement. And since he was neither positive nor relational, he had constant turnover in employees.
>
> Because of my background, it has been difficult for me to encourage my family. This critical and negative attitude has hindered my work. I raised five children and lived a Christian life before them. Sadly, it is easier for them to recognize my love for God than my love for them. They are all starved for positive affirmation. The tragedy is that they have received the bad attitude trait, and now I see them passing it down to my precious grandchildren.
>
> Never before have I been so aware of "catching an attitude" from surrounding conditions. Obviously, this wrong attitude has been passed along for five generations. It is now time to stop it! Today I made a conscious decision to change. This will not be done overnight, but it will be done. It will not be accomplished easily, but it will be accomplished!

That story contains both the conditions that mold our thinking and the choice to change. Both play a vital part in the construction of our attitude. Neither can be held solely responsible for forming our mindset.

Attitude Application:

List the conditions that have had positive and negative influences on your life (i.e., in a particular situation, you chose to find the good in the circumstance or you viewed the matter with humor).

Conditions:		Choices:	
Positive:	Negative:	Positive:	Negative:

5

Foundational Truths About the Construction of the Attitude

The air currents of life jolt us out of line and try to keep us from achieving our goals. Unexpected weather can change our direction and strategy. We must adjust our thinking continually so we can live right.

—John Maxwell

Before we look at specific things that help construct attitudes, we must understand some basic principles about attitude formation.

1. A child's formative years are the most important for instilling the right attitudes.

Child specialists generally agree that early development in a positive setting is a main reason for the child's future successes. Attitudes we accept as children are usually the attitudes we embrace as adults. It is hard to get away from our early training. Proverbs 22:6 states, "Train up a child in the way he should go, even when he is old he will not depart from it." Why? Because the feeling and attitudes we form early in life become a part of us. We feel comfortable with them even though they may be wrong. Even if our attitudes make us uncomfortable, they are still difficult to change.

During my senior year of high school I decided to teach myself to play golf. For months I played incorrectly but with enthusiasm. One day on the golf course a friend told me, "John, your problem is that you are too close to the ball *after* you hit it." I had developed a slice that streaked like a banana through the sky. No problem; I just compensated for my slice. To land the ball on the fairway, I aimed for the woods on the left.

Then one day I played with an excellent golfer. The ball went straight and his swing was slow. After observing a few of my boomerang shots, he offered to help. "What is wrong with my game?" I asked. "Everything!" he replied.

So the lessons began. I found out after a few weeks that it is more difficult to learn something wrong, unlearn it and re-learn it, than to learn it correctly the first time. That is certainly true about our attitudes. Those things which we feel and accept at an early age have a tendency to hang on tenaciously even when we know better and desire to change. The first impressions upon our lives are not the only impressions, but many times they are the most lasting.

2. An attitude's growth never stops.

Our attitudes are formed by our experiences and how we choose to react to them. Therefore, as long as we live, we are forming, changing or reinforcing attitudes. There is no such thing as an unalterable attitude. We are like the little girl who was asked by her Sunday school teacher,

"Who made you?" She replied, "Well, God made part of me." "What do you mean, God made part of you?" asked the surprised teacher. "Well, God made me real little, and I just growed the rest myself."

How true! The attitudes formed in our early years do not necessarily remain the same through later years. Many times marriages go through "deep waters" because of a mate's attitude change. People sometimes even switch spouses in the middle of life because of an attitude change.

My father has always been a positive influence in my life. Once, while visiting my parents back east, I noticed he was reading Norman Vincent Peales's book, *The Power of Positive Thinking*. When I noted that he had read this book previously, he replied enthusiastically, "Of course! I must keep building my attitude."

3. The more our attitude grows on the same foundation, the more solid it becomes.

Reinforcement of our foundational attitudes, whether positive or negative, makes them stronger. My father realized this truth in his commitment to read his positive-thinking books again. One of his attitude-growing practices was to write a positive thought on a 3 x 5 card and read it repeatedly throughout the day. Often I have seen him pull out the card during fifteen-second breaks and read the positive phrase. I have decided to make this a habit of mine also. I find that the more I reinforce my mind with excellent reading the stronger I become.

4. Many builders (specialists) help construct our attitudes at a certain time and place.

In building a home, certain specialists are needed to make the structure complete. Their time may be minimal and their contribution small, yet they are a part of the construction of that home. In the same way, certain people come into our lives at various times who help make or break our perspective.

One lady wrote to me, "In my senior year of high school my English teacher took an essay that I wrote and put it on the chalkboard. She then proceeded to tear it apart in front of the class. I was humiliated and felt dumb. Then she told me that I wouldn't last one year in college. I have never forgotten that incident." One teacher, in one day, affected a self-image for an entire lifetime.

5. There is no such thing as a perfect, flawless attitude.

In other words, we all have attitudes that need remodeling. When he taught me about airplanes, my friend Paul stated, "An aircraft hasn't been made that did not have to be trimmed." The word *trim* means to "balance in flight." Airplanes need continual adjustment in order to perform effectively. This is true of our attitudes also. The air currents of life jolt us out of line and try to keep us from achieving our goals. Unexpected weather can change our direction and strategy.

Our attitudes need adjustment with every change that comes into our lives. We need to be like the old mule owned by a Missouri farmer. One day the mule fell backward into a dry well. The farmer, fond of the animal, tried everything he could possibly think of to rescue his mule from the well. Finally, deciding rescue was impossible, he began to bury the mule. As he dumped a truckload of dirt down the well, dust began to fly and the mule began to stomp and snort. Soon old "sad face" was on top of the dirt, two feet higher than before. After a few dumped truckloads of dirt, the mule rose triumphantly to the top and walked out.

Everyone encounters storms and dry wells in his life

which threaten to wreck his attitude. The secret to safe arrival is to continually adjust your perspective.

Attitude Application:

Our attitude does not remain stagnant. A balloon half blown up is full of air but is not filled to capacity. A rubber band pulls the object it holds together and is effective only when stretched. What are you encountering that demands the stretching of your attitude? Are you adjusting? Write a statement that identifies what you feel will be your next "storm." Now think through the strategy you'll use to counter a possible bad attitude regarding that situation.

6

Materials That Are Used in Constructing an Attitude

People don't care how much you know until they know how much you care.
—John Maxwell

A s you're probably aware by this time, attitudes aren'
formed automatically, and they are not shaped in ;
vacuum. This chapter will deal with the main influence
that make our attitude what it is today. Although thes
"materials," listed below in chronological order, overlaɪ
their influence is greater at some times than at others.

Personality/Temperament

BIRTH:	Environment
AGES 1-6:	Word expression
	Adult acceptance/affirmation
AGES 6-10:	Self-image
	Exposure to new experiences
AGES 11-21:	Associations with peers

AGES 21-61:

Physical appearance
Marriage, family, job
Success
Adjustments
Assessment of life

All these factors play an important part in our lives and cannot really be "boxed" into age zones. Yet, as indicated above, there are certain ages these factors are most influential.

Attitude Application:

Take time to think through the materials that have constructed your attitudes. Write down your answers.

PERSONALITY/TEMPERAMENT: I was born into this world with a _____ personality. It affected my attitude when _____.

ENVIRONMENT: As a child, my environment was generally (a) secure, (b) unstable, (c) intimidating.

WORD EXPRESSION: I remember a situation when someone said something positive or negative to me that affected my attitude. Explain the comment and the circumstances.

_____

_____

ADULT ACCEPTANCE/AFFIRMATION: From my earliest recollection I felt (a) accepted, (b) rejected by my parents.

SELF-IMAGE:	Poor				Outstanding
My self-image as a child was:	1	2	3	4	5
My self-image as an adult is:	1	2	3	4	5

EXPOSURE TO NEW EXPERIENCES: One negative and one positive experience that helped cultivate my current attitude:

_____

ASSOCIATION WITH PEERS: _____
was the first person who had a strong influence in my life. Now
_____is most important and affects my
attitude the most.

PHYSICAL APPEARANCE: What do I like best about my appearance? What would I change? Why?

_____

_____

MARRIAGE, FAMILY, JOB: (These three areas of your life can determine your attitude to a large degree.) Which area affects me positively? Do any affect me negatively? What am I going to do about the negative influences?

SUCCESS: (Complete this sentence.) Success is:

_____

Am I a success in the eyes of those who love me most?

ADJUSTMENTS–PHYSICAL AND EMOTIONAL: Three difficult adjustments that I have faced within the last five years:

_____

_____

_____

How has my attitude changed because of them?

ASSESSMENT OF YOUR LIFE: Up until now, my life has been (a)unfulfilled, (b) fulfilled. Life begins at _____.

Now that you've assessed how your perspective was affected in various phases of life, let's look at the specific materials that form your attitude.

Personality—Who I Am

For Thou didst form my inward parts; Thou didst weave me in my mother's womb. I will give thanks to Thee, for I am fearfully and wonderfully made; wonderful are Thy works, and my soul knows it very well (Psalm 139:13,14).

We are born as distinct individuals. Even two children with the same parents, same environment and same training are totally different from each other. These differences contribute to the "spice of life" we all enjoy. Like tract homes that all look alike, if all people had similar personalities, our journey through life would certainly be boring.

I love the story of two men who, while fishing together, began discussing their wives. One said, "If all men were like me they would all want to be married to my wife." The other man quickly replied, "If they were all like me, none of them would want to be married to her."

A set of attitudes accompanies each personality. Generally people with certain temperaments develop specific attitudes common to that temperament. A few years ago, pastor and counselor Tim LaHaye made us aware of four basic temperaments. Through observation, I have noticed that a person with what he calls a Choleric personality often exhibits attitudes of perseverance and aggressiveness. A Sanguine person will be generally positive and look on the bright side of life. The introspective Melancholy can be negative at times while the Phlegmatic says, "Easy come, easy go." An individual's personality is composed of a mixture of these temperaments, and there are exceptions to these examples. However, a temperament follows a track that can be identified by tracing a person's attitudes.

Environment—What's Around Me

> Therefore, just as through one man sin entered into the world, and death through sin, and so death spread to all men, because all sinned (Romans 5:12).

I believe that our environment is a greater controlling factor in our attitude development than our personality or other inherited traits. Before Margaret and I began our family we decided to adopt our children. We wanted to give a child who might not normally have the benefit of a loving Christian home an opportunity to live in that environment. Although our children may not physically resemble us, they certainly have been molded by the environment in which we have reared them.

It is the environment of early childhood that develops the "belief system." The child continually picks up priorities, attitudes, interest and philosophies from his environment. It is true that *what I really believe affects my attitude!* But what I believe may be untrue. What I believe may be unhealthy. It may hurt others and destroy me. Yet an attitude is reinforced by a belief, right or wrong.

Environment is the first influencer of our belief system. Therefore the foundation of an attitude is laid in the environment to which we were born. Environment becomes even more significant when we realize that *the beginning attitudes are the most difficult to change.*

Because of this, when we look at society, we have a tendency to panic over the thought of bringing a child into this world. One person said, depressingly:

The litter is unbearable;
the bottles aren't returnable;
the empty cans aren't burnable;
the sonic booms incredible;
the tuna isn't edible;
the off-shore rigs are leakable;

the billboards are unspeakable;
the slums are incurable;
the smog is unendurable;
the phosphates aren't dissovable;
the problems seem unsolvable;
the people unforgivable;
and life has become intolerable.
  —Author unknown

A Christian should not view society so negatively. With Jesus, life becomes incredible! Knowing this gives hope in every environment. The apostle Peter said that the mercy of Christ has caused us to be born to "a living hope" (1 Peter 1:3).

Still, age and Christianity do not make us immune to the influences of our environment. I pastored Faith Memorial Church in Lancaster, Ohio, for more than seven years. I remember 1978 as the year central Ohio received many baptisms of snow and cold weather. It was then that I realized most weathermen have a bad attitude—they begin giving not only the temperature but also the wind chill factor. For more than thirty days the temperature never rose above freezing. Utility bills hit an all-time high. People became claustrophobic as they were "snowed in" for days. The result: depression. I averaged thirty hours a week counseling people who battled attitude problems because of bad weather. In fact, at times I would close my eyes in prayer and listen hopefully for God to say, "Son, go to Hawaii!" Even the weather can "ice our wings" and cause us to lose altitude in our attitude.

Word Expression—What I Hear

Faith comes from hearing . . . (Romans 10:17).

"Sticks and stones may break my bones
but names will never hurt me."

Don't you believe that! In fact, after the bruises have disappeared and the physical pain is gone, the inward pain of hurtful words remains. During one of our staff meetings I asked the pastors, secretaries and custodians to raise their hands if they could remember a childhood experience that hurt deeply because of someone's words. Everyone raised his hand.

One pastor recalled the time when he sat in a reading circle at school. (Do you remember how intimidating those sessions were?) When his time came to read, he mispronounced the word "Photography." He read it *photography* instead of *pho-tog'-ra-phy*. The teacher corrected him and the class laughed. He still remembers . . . forty years later. One positive result of that experience was Chuck's desire from that moment on to pronounce words correctly. Today he excels as a speaker because of that determination.

Another pastor on my staff told the group about his beginning days at seminary. He felt overwhelmed and intimidated by his new experience. The workload seemed impossible. There were thousands of pages to read, Greek words to learn, Scripture verses to memorize and papers to write. Although he hadn't told anyone about the pressure he was feeling, it was obvious to those around him.

Noticing his distress, an upperclassman walked up, put his arm around his shoulder and said, "Friend, I want to share something with you. It doesn't matter how big the rock is. If you just keep pounding, it's gonna bust." The pastor said, "Suddenly, my huge rock became manageable and I started pounding steadily, little by little. And sure enough, right on schedule—three years later—the rock 'busted' and they called it graduation." That time, words brought encouragement instead of hurt.

Words are powerful . . . yet meaningless until they are attached to a context. The same words coming from two different people are very seldom received in the same way. The same words phrased differently seldom have the same impact. The same words coming from the same person will usually be interpreted in light of the speaker's attitude. One father tried to teach his son this truth. One day the boy came home and said, "Dad, I think I flunked my arithmetic test." His dad said, "Son, don't say that; that's negative. Be positive." So the boy said, "Dad, I am positive I flunked my arithmetic test."

Words can encourage either the stretching or shrinking of our lives. If most of our conversations contain a negative bent, I am convinced it is better to say nothing. Years ago new engineers in General Electric's lamp division were assigned, as a joke, the impossible task of frosting the bulbs on the inside. Eventually, however, an undaunted newcomer named Marvin Papkin not only found a way to frost bulbs on the inside, but also developed an etching acid which left minutely rounded pits on the surface instead of sharp depressions. This strengthened each bulb. No one had told him it *couldn't* be done, so he did it!

Adult Acceptance/Affirmation — What I Feel

God demonstrates His own love toward us, in that while we were yet sinners, Christ died for us (Romans 5:8).

Often when I am speaking to leaders, I tell them about the importance of acceptance/affirmation of the ones they are leading. The truth is, *people don't care how much you know until they know how much you care!*

Think back to your school days. Who was your favorite teacher? Why? Probably your warmest memories are of someone who accepted and affirmed you. We seldom remember what our teacher said to us, but we do remember how they loved us. Long before we understand teaching we reach out for understanding. Long after we have forgotten the teachings we remember the feeling of acceptance or rejection.

Many times I have asked people if they enjoyed their pastor's sermon the previous week. After a positive response I ask, "What was his subject?" Seventy-five percent of the time they cannot give me the sermon title. They do not remember the exact subject but they do remember the atmosphere and attitude in which it was delivered.

My three favorite Sunday school teachers are beautiful examples of this truth. First came Katie, my second grade teacher. When I was sick and missed her class, she would come and visit me on Monday. She would ask how I was feeling and give me a five-cent trinket that was worth a million dollars to me. Katie would say, "Johnny, I always teach better when you are in the class. When you come next Sunday morning would you raise your hand so I can see you are in attendance? Then I will teach better."

When next Sunday morning dawned I would be up, preparing to go to Sunday school. Not even the German measles, the Asian flu and the Mediterranean fruit fly combined could keep me from getting some of Katie's acceptance and affirmation! I can still remember raising my hand and watching Katie smile at me from the front of the class.

I also remember other kids raising their hands when Katie began to teach and her class grew rapidly. The Sunday school superintendent wanted to split the class and start a new one across the hall. He asked for volunteers for the new class and no one raised his hand. That day the second grade held the church's first sit-down strike. Our theme: "We shall not be moved." Why? No kid was about to go across the hall with a new teacher and miss Katie's continual demonstration of love.

My second-favorite teacher was Roy Rogers (not Trigger's master). I had him in the fourth grade. Again, I don't remember much about what he said, but I do remember what he did. He conveyed love and acceptance to a group of fourth-grade boys by giving us his time. He took us to Ted Lewis Park and taught us to play baseball. We learned how to field grounders and make double plays. We laughed together, sweated together and got dirty together. Then, following an afternoon on the diamond, Roy would load us into his station wagon and take us to the Dairy Queen for a foot-long hot dog and a chocolate milk shake. I loved Roy Rogers!

Glen, who taught the junior boys class, was my third favorite. Did you ever teach a group of ten-wiggles-per-minute boys? Usually those teachers go straight from the class to their heavenly reward! Any teacher of this class who read about Daniel and the den of lions would say, "Big deal . . . if they really wanted to test Daniel's faith, they should have stuck him in a junior boys class!"

Well, Glen was stuck with us. More accurately, he was stuck on us. He taught this class for twenty years. Every ornery, wiggly, inattentive boy felt Glen's love. At times, tears trickled down his face as he saw how God's love could transform junior boys.

One day Glen stopped in the middle of his lesson and said, "Boys, I pray for you every day. Right after class I need to see Steve Banner, Phil Conrad, Junior Fowler and John Maxwell." After class the four of us huddled in the corner with Glen, and he said, "Last night while I was praying for you, I sensed that the Lord was going to call each of you into full-time Christian service. I want to be the first to encourage you to obey God." Then he wept as he prayed, asking the Lord to use us for His glory.

Today we all pastor churches—Steve Banner in Ohio, Phil Conrad in Arizona, Junior Fowler in Oklahoma and I in California. These Sunday school teachers made a positive mark on my life because of their acceptance and affirmation.

Recently I talked with Mary Vaughn who was once the head of counseling in the Cincinnati elementary school system. I asked her to pinpoint the main problem she noticed in counseling situations. "John," she said immediately, "most children's psychological problems stem from their lack of acceptance and affirmation from parents and peers." Mary continually emphasized that economic level, professional or social strata and other factors in which society puts so much value were insignificant.

Then she told me a story about Dennis, aged ten. This third-grader was always fighting, lying and causing disturbances with his classmates. He believed "no one likes me, the teacher just picks on me." He would not respond to the people who really cared for him and tried to help the most. His problem? He wanted his mother's affirmation and love so much that he lived in a fantasy world, always talking of his mother's love. In reality, his mother did nothing to affirm him. Dennis's need for care was so great that he fantasized about his mother's love and directed his bad attitude toward others.

Unlike Dennis, I was privileged to grow up in a very affirming family. I never questioned my parents' love and acceptance. They were continually affirming their love through action and words. Now Margaret and I have tried to create this same environment for our children. The other day we were talking about the importance of showing love to our children. We concluded that our kids see or sense our acceptance and affirmation at least thirty times a day. That's not too much! Have you ever been told too many times that you are important, loved and appreciated? Remember, *people don't care how much you know until they know how much you care.*

Self-Image — How I See Myself

For as he thinks within himself, so he is (Proverbs 23:7).

It is impossible to perform consistently in a manner inconsistent with the way we see ourselves. In other words, we usually act in direct response to our self-image. Nothing is more difficult to accomplish than changing outward actions without changing inward feelings. As we realize our performance is based on our perception of ourselves, we should also remember God's unconditional love and acceptance. He thinks more of us than we do of ourselves. The disciples may not have been high achievers in the sight of the world but the call of Christ turned their lives around.

One of the best ways to improve those inward feelings is to put some "success" under your belt. My daughter Elizabeth has a tendency to be shy and wants to hold back on new experiences. But once she has warmed up to a situation, it's "full steam ahead." When she was in the first grade, her school had a candy bar sale to help lift its financial burden. Each child was given thirty candy bars and was challenged to sell every one of them. When I picked up Elizabeth from school she was holding her "challenge" and needed some positive encouragement. It was time for a sales meeting with my new salesgirl.

All the way home I taught her how to sell candy bars. I surrounded each teaching point with a half dozen "You can do it — your smile will win them over — I believe in you" phrases. By the end of our fifteen-minute drive, the young lady sitting beside me had become a charming, committed saleslady. Off she went to the neighborhood with little brother Joel eating one of the candy bars and declaring that it was truly the best he had ever devoured.

At the end of the day, all thirty bars had been sold and Elizabeth was feeling great. I will never forget the words she prayed as I tucked her into bed that night: "O God, thanks for the candy sale at school. It's great. O Lord, help make me a winner! Amen."

This prayer is at the heart's desire of every person. We want to be winners. Sure enough, Elizabeth came home the next day with another box of candy bars. Now the big test! She'd exhausted the supply of friendly neighbors, and she was thrust out into the cruel world of the unknown buyer. Elizabeth admitted fear as we went to a shopping center to sell our wares. Again I offered encouragement, a few more selling tips, more encouragement, the right location, *more* encouragement. She did it. The experience amounted to two days of selling, two sold-out performances, two happy people and one boosted self-image.

I like the self-esteem demonstrated by the little fellow who excitedly pulled a cornstalk out by its roots. When his father congratulated him, he beamed. "And just think," he said, "the whole world had hold of the other end of it!"

Compare him with Shauna, a sixth grader. She usually behaved like a smart aleck and remained cocky, even when she had been caught stealing. When confronted about the theft, she said she did it to get revenge on her parents. She was not remorseful.

Counseling sessions revealed that Shauna rarely saw her father, and he did not love her. When they were together, she seldom received acceptance or a feeling of importance. She saw herself as she thought her father saw her. Shauna's counselor continually gave her sincere compliments and modeled to the parents the necessary ingredients for creating a proper self-image. In time, Shauna's sense of self-worth improved.

The principle works in reverse, too. How we see ourselves reflects how others see us. If we like ourselves it increases the odds that others will like us. *Self-image is the parameter to the construction of our attitude.* We act in response to how we see ourselves. We will never go beyond the boundaries that stake out our true feelings about ourselves. Those "other countries" can be explored only when our self-image is strong enough to give permission.

Exposure to New Experiences— Opportunities for Growth

> Brethren, I do not regard myself as having laid hold of it yet; but one thing I do: forgetting what lies behind and reaching forward to what lies ahead, I press on toward the goal for the prize of the upward call of God in Christ Jesus (Philippians 3:13,14).

Voltaire likened life to a game of cards. Each player must accept the cards dealt to him. But once those cards are in the hand, he alone decides how to play them to win the game.

We always have a number of opportunities in our hand. We must decide whether to take a risk and act on them. Nothing in life causes more stress, yet at the same time provides more opportunity for growth, than new experiences. The familiar poem,

> My life may touch a dozen lives
> Before this day is done;
> Leave countless marks for good or ill
> E'er sets the evening sun.

speaks of the power of influence.

That first line, with one word changed, can illustrate the effect of new experiences on a life.

> My life may *experience* a dozen lives
> Before this day is done;
> Leave countless marks for good or ill
> E'er sets the evening sun.

My parents recognized the value of new experiences and did their best to expose each child to positive ones. Some of my fondest memories are of times when I traveled with my father. Many times he would say to my teacher, "You are doing an excellent job teaching my son, but for the next week I am going to take him with me and open up some new experiences for him." Off we would go to another state, and my awareness of people, nature and culture would be heightened.

I will always be especially grateful for those pre-arranged new experiences. I'll never forget the time I met the great missionary statesman, E. Stanley Jones. After listening to this spiritual giant speak, my father took me to a side office to meet him! I can still remember the room, his attitude and, most important, his words of encouragement to me.

As a parent, it is impossible for you to shield your children from the new experiences that might be negative. So it is essential to prepare positive encounters that will build self-image and confidence. Both positive and negative experiences should be used as tools in preparing children for life.

Elizabeth's story didn't end after two successful selling days. Later she went door-to-door again, encouraging people to buy the "world's most delicious chocolate bar." I followed her in the car. Repeatedly she smiled, told her story and had no luck. Repeatedly I smiled and encouraged her not to quit. I was careful to stress that winning is trying. We set a goal (the end of a very long block) and determined not to quit until that goal was reached.

With each "no sale" visit her steps became slower and my enthusiasm greater. Finally, she made a sale at the next to the last house. She came running back to the car, waving money and wanting to go one more block. I said, "Fine," and off she ran.

The lesson is obvious. Children need continual reassurance and praise when their new experiences are less than positive. In fact, the worse the experience, the more encouragement they need. But sometimes we become discouraged when they are discouraged. This is a good formula to adopt:

New experiences + teaching applications x love = growth.

Association With Peers — Who Influences Me

> A man of many friends comes to ruin, but there is a friend who sticks closer than a brother (Proverbs 18:24).

What others indicate about their perceptions of us affects how we perceive ourselves. Usually we respond to the expectations of others. This truth becomes evident to the parent when his child goes to school. No longer can the parent control his child's environment. Any elementary teacher understands that kids very quickly develop a "pecking order" for the class. Students acquire labels and children relate to each other with sometimes cruel honesty. Peer pressure becomes a problem.

Mary Vaughn, in one of her case studies involving a first grader, wrote: "A very poor environment physically (little clothing, shelter or food) does not necessarily produce negative attitudes in the child. It is the lack of acceptance by peers that form scars deep within the child." Her example: A first grader who was stealing.

Terry looked pale and sickly. The teacher was concerned about his stealing. Missing things were usually found in his desk. After counseling with Terry, a home visit was arranged with his parents. Their dwelling contained four rooms and housed nine people. The rooms were scarcely furnished and poverty was evident. The parents were grateful for the offer of assistance and clothing. They were also willing to help Terry. Assessment of problem: Terry stole only because peer pressure made him aware of his poverty. He wanted the same cute erasers and lunch boxes his friends had.

No doubt this experience helped Terry's parents realize that others exercised a sizable amount of control over their son's behavior. My parents understood this fact also and determined to watch and control our peer relationships as much as possible.

Their strategy: Provide a climate in the Maxwell home that was appealing to their two boys' friends. This meant sacrificing their finances and time. They provided us with a shuffleboard game, Ping Pong table, pool table, pinball machine, chemistry set, basketball court and all the sports equipment that had been invented. We also had one mother who was spectator, referee, counselor, arbitrator and fan.

And the kids came, often twenty to twenty-five at a time. All sizes, shapes and colors. Everyone had fun and my parents observed our friends. Sometimes, after the gang had gone, my parents would ask about one of our friends. They would openly discuss his language or attitudes and encourage us not to act or think that way. I realize now that most of my major decisions as a young boy were influenced by my parents' teaching and observation of my associations.

My folks didn't limit the observations to my youth. When my father realized that Margaret and I were dating steadily, he spent a day driving to her home town and talking with her parents, pastor and schoolteachers to better understand the kind of girl his son was dating. Although he never told me this story until we were married, I know the reports he received were very favorable. He encouraged me to marry her! Now, I wouldn't recommend such close observation to every parent, but his interest demonstrated love to me.

Casey Stengel, a successful manager of the New York Yankees baseball team, understood the power of associations on a ball player's attitude. Billy Martin remembers Stengel's advice to him when Martin was a rookie manager. "Casey said there would be fifteen players on your team who will run through a wall for you, five who will hate you and five who are undecided," Martin said. Stengel added, "When you make out your rooming list, always room your losers together. Never room a good guy with a loser. Those losers who stay together will blame the manager for everything, but it won't spread if you keep them isolated."

At one meeting a man came up to me after I had spoken about attitudes and associates. He wanted me to clarify the concept of isolating ourselves from others who can drag us down. His question was, "How can we help others who have attitude problems if we stay away from them?" My answer: "There is a difference between helping those with perpetual attitude problems and enlisting them as our close friends. The closer our relationship, the more influential the attitudes and philosophies of our friends become to us."

Charles "Tremendous" Jones, author of *Life is Tremendous,* said, "What you will become in five years will be determined by what you read and who you associate with." That's good advice for us all.

Physical Appearance — How We Look to Others

> Man looks at the outward appearance, but the Lord looks at the heart (1 Samuel 16:7).

Our looks play an important part in the construction of our attitude. Incredible pressure is placed upon people to possess that "in look" which is the standard of acceptance. For one day, while you're watching television, notice how the commercials emphasize looks. Notice the percentage of ads dealing with clothing, diet, exercise and overall physical attractiveness. Hollywood says, "Homeliness is out and handsomeness is in." This influences our perception of our worth, based on physical appearance. What can make it even more difficult is the realization that others judge our worth also by our appearance. Recently I read a business article which stated, "Our physical attractiveness helps determine our income." The research reported in that article showed the discrepancies between the salaries of men 6'2" and 5'10". The taller men consistently received higher salaries.

Marriage, Family and Job—
Our Security and Status

God is our refuge and strength, a very present help in trouble (Psalm 46:1).

New influences begin to affect our attitude as we approach our middle twenties. It is during this time of our lives that most of us marry. That means another person influences our perspective.

When I speak on attitudes, I always emphasize the need to surround ourselves with positive people. One of the saddest comments that I often receive comes from one mate who tells me the other marriage partner is negative and doesn't want to change. To a certain extent, when the negative mate does not want to change, the positive one is imprisoned by negativism. In such situations, I advise the couple to remember and return to patterns they followed in their courtship days.

Observe a couple during courtship. They are illustrating two beautiful ideas. They are building on strengths and expecting the best.

This is when a girl tends to see the guy as a knight in shining armor. She's been looking for his best. She's been expecting his best. She ignores anything that seems to be a weakness. The man sees a beautiful girl with noble feelings and fine qualities. Then they get married, and each one sees the reality of the other—both strengths and weaknesses. The marriage will be good and reinforcing if the weaknesses are not emphasized. But many end up in divorce court because the strengths are ignored. The partners go from expecting the best to expecting the worst, from building on strengths to focusing on weaknesses.

Whether you are eleven, forty-two, or sixty-five, your attitude toward life is still under construction. By understanding the materials that are part of your attitude structures, you and those you influence can maintain a healthier perspective.

7

The Costliest Mistake People Make in Constructing an Attitude

---

Many intelligent adults . . . are restrained in thoughts, actions and results. They never move further than the boundaries of their self-imposed limitations.

—John Maxwell

It happens to us the moment we are born. Excited family members press their noses against the nursery window in the hospital and begin playing the game, "Who does he look like?" After much discussion, it is decided that their red-faced, wrinkly, toothless, bald baby looks like "Uncle Harry."

The labeling of the little child increases as his personality develops. That is a normal human reaction. We all do it. It becomes hurtful, however, when we start placing limitations on our child because he is a "C" student, a "fair" runner or a "plain" child. Unless parents exercise care, their children will grow up selling themselves short because of the "box" parents have put them in, the expectations parents have placed upon them.

One "boxed in" child was Adam Clarke, who was born in the eighteenth century in Ireland. When Adam was a schoolboy, his father told the teacher that Adam wouldn't do well.

The teacher said, "He looks bright. "

That statement changed his life—let him out of the box his father had put him in. He lived to be seventy-two, and he became a great scholar, an English Methodist preacher and an author of commentaries and a book called *Christian Theology*. When Adam Clarke preached, it was said, people listened.[1]

What are a person's capabilities? No one knows. Therefore, no one should be consciously instilling life-limiting thoughts into others. Thirty years ago, Johnny Weissmuller, also known as Tarzan to movie viewers, was called the greatest swimmer the world had ever known. Doctors and coaches around the world said, "Nobody will ever break Johnny Weissmuller's records." He held more than fifty of them! Do you know who is breaking Tarzan's records today? Thirteen-year-old girls! The 1936 Olympic records were the *qualifying* standards for the 1972 Olympics.

For decades, track enthusiasts declared boldly that nobody would break the four-minute mile. For decades their prediction looked secure. Roger Bannister did not listen to such limiting assumptions. Result: He broke the "impossible" four-minute mile. Today at least 336 men have accomplished this feat. They did not let themselves be limited by others' expectations.

Remember: Others can stop you temporarily, but you are the only one who can do it permanently.

An elephant can easily pick up a one-ton load with his

trunk. But have you ever visited a circus and watched these huge creatures standing quietly tied to a small wooden stake?

While still young and weak, an elephant is tied by a heavy chain to an immovable iron stake. He discovers that, no matter how hard he tries, he cannot break the chain or move the stake. Then, no matter how large and strong the elephant becomes, he continues to believe he cannot move as long as he sees the stake in the ground beside him.

Many intelligent adults behave like the circus elephant. They are restrained in thought, action and results. They never move further than the boundaries of self-imposed limitation.

Often when lecturing on limitations, I talk about what I call the "sap strata."

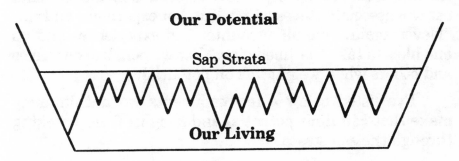

In this illustration, the sap strata line represents our self-imposed, limiting barrier. The jagged line that keeps rising and falling pictures our actual living. The effort it would take to break through that sap strata level takes the "sap" out of us. Every time we make an attempt to break through the line, there is accompanying pain. We pay a physical and emotional price when we actually break through our perceived limitations and enter into a new area of further potential.

Later, in Sections III and IV of this book, we will take

a closer look at this process. Sadly, many people accept their sap strata and never reach their potential. They are like the trained fleas that jump up and down in a canister. The observant bystander will notice that the jar has no lid to keep the fleas inside. So why don't those fleas jump out of the container to their freedom? The answer is simple. The flea trainer, when first placing the fleas into the canister also puts the lid on top. The fleas jump high and continually bash their little flea brains on the lid. After a few "Excedrin headaches" the fleas quit jumping so high and enjoy their new-found comfort. Now the lid can be removed and the fleas are held captive; not by a real lid, but by a mindset that says, "So high and no more."

Mark Twain once said, "If a cat sits on a hot stove, that cat will never sit on a *hot* stove again." He continued, "That cat will never sit on a *cold* stove either." Conclusion: That cat will associate stoves with a bad, hot experience and say, "Never again." We all encounter bad experiences and no one likes to take the "medicine." Yet we penalize ourselves and others when we put lids on potential.

I've listed below a few comments we unthinkingly make that can limit potential and keep us from breaking through the sap strata.

> "It's never been done before."
> "I'll never try that again."
> "Take it easy."

Now it's your turn. Make a list of statements that have limited your potential.

If someone tries to saddle you with a sap strata, here's a poem that can counter the attack. Read it from time to time.

> Somebody said that it couldn't be done,
> But he with a chuckle replied

That maybe it couldn't, but he would be one
Who wouldn't say no 'till he tried.
So he buckled right in with the trace of a grin
On his face. If he worried, he hid it.
He started to sing as he tackled the thing
That couldn't be done, and he did it.

Somebody scoffed: "Oh, you'll never do that;
At least no one ever has done it;"
But he took off his coat and took off his hat
And the first thing he knew he'd begun it.
With the lift of his chin and a bit of a grin,
Without any doubting or quiddit,
He started to sing as he tackled the thing
That couldn't be done, and he did it.

There are thousands to tell you it cannot be done,
There are thousands to prophesy failure;
There are thousands to point out to you, one by one,
The dangers that wait to assail you.
But just buckle right in with a bit of a grin,
Then take off your coat and go to it;
Just start in to sing as you tackle the thing
That "cannot be done," and you'll do it.

—Edgar A. Guest

Section III

The Crashing
of Your Attitude

8

Mayday! Mayday! My Attitude Is Losing Altitude

Therefore, since we have so great a cloud of witnesses surrounding us, let us also lay aside every encumbrance, and the sin which so easily entangles us, and let us run with endurance the race that is set before us, fixing our eyes on Jesus (Hebrews 12:1,2).

One of the first things I discovered during my ride in a small airplane was that turbulence often makes the ride a little rough. Just as flying has its "rough" weather, so does life. A smooth day is the exception, not the norm. Flying straight and level usually comes as a *recovery* from climbs, descents and turns. It is the exception, not the rule.

Have you ever had a day like the small boy had in *Alexander and the Terrible, Horrible, No Good, Very Bad Day* by Judith Viorst?

I went to sleep with gum in my mouth and now there's gum in my hair and when I got out of bed this morning I tripped on the skateboard and by mistake I dropped my sweater in the sink while the water was running and I could tell it was going to be a terrible, horrible, no good, very bad day.

At breakfast Anthony found a Corvette Stingray car kit in his breakfast cereal box and Nick found a Junior Undercover Agent code ring in his breakfast cereal box, but in my breakfast box all I found was breakfast cereal.

I think I'll move to Australia.

In the car pool Mrs. Gibson let Becky have a seat by the window. Audrey and Elliot got seats by the window too. I said I was being scrunched, I said I was being smushed. I said, "If I don't get a seat by the window I am going to be carsick." No one even answered.

I could tell it was going to be a terrible, horrible, no good, very bad day.

At school Mrs. Dickens liked Paul's picture of the sailboat better than my picture of the invisible castle.

At singing time she said I sang too loud. At counting time she said I left out sixteen. Who needs sixteen? I could tell it was going to be a terrible, horrible, no good, very bad day.

I could tell because Paul said I wasn't his best friend anymore. He said that Philip Parker was his best friend, and that Albert Moyo was his next best friend and that I was only his third best friend.

"I hope you sit on a tack," I said to Paul. "I hope the next time you get a double-decker strawberry ice cream cone the ice cream part falls off the cone part and lands in Australia."

There were two cupcakes in Philip Parker's lunch bag and Albert got a Hershey bar with almonds and Paul's mother gave him a piece of jelly roll that had little coconut sprinkles on the top. Guess whose mother forgot to put in dessert?

It was a terrible, horrible, no good, very bad day.

That's what it was because after school my mom took us all to the dentist and Dr. Fields found a cavity just in me. "Come back next week and I'll fix it," said Dr.

Fields. "Next week," I said, "I'm going to Australia."

On the way downstairs the elevator door closed on my foot and while we were waiting for my mom to go get the car, Anthony made me fall where it was muddy and when I started crying because of the mud, Nick said I was a crybaby and while I was punching Nick for saying crybaby my mom came back with the car and scolded me for being muddy and fighting.

"I am having a terrible, horrible, no good, very bad day," I told everybody. No one even answered.

So then we went to the shoe store to buy some sneakers. Anthony chose white ones with blue stripes. Nick chose red ones with white stripes. I chose blue ones with red stripes, but then the shoe man said, "We're all sold out." They made me buy plain old white ones, but they can't make me wear them.

When we picked up my dad at his office he said I couldn't play with his copying machine, but I forgot. He also said to watch out for the book on his desk, and I was careful as could be except for my elbow. He also said, "Don't fool around with the phone," but I think I called Australia. My dad said please don't pick him up anymore. It was a terrible, horrible, no good, very bad day.

There were lima beans for dinner and I hate limas. There was kissing on TV and I hate kissing.

My bath was too hot, I got soap in my eyes, my marble went down the drain, and I had to wear my railroad pajamas. I hate my railroad pajamas.

When I went to bed Nick took back the pillow he said I could keep and the Mickey Mouse night light burned out and I bit my tongue. The cat wants to sleep with Anthony, not with me.

It has been a terrible, horrible, no good, very bad day. My mom says some days are like that. Even in Australia.[1]

Here are some rules to remember when you have one of those terrible, horrible, no good, very bad days and your attitude starts to plummet:

Rule 1:
Maintain the right attitude
when the "going gets tough."

Our natural reaction is to bail out of the right attitude to compensate for our problems. During our flight of life our attitude is most critical during the "tough times." That is when we are tempted to panic and make bad attitude decisions. When we crash, it comes from a wrong reaction, not the turbulence. How often have we seen the "making a mountain out of a molehill" response become more dangerous than the problem itself?

Remember, the difficulty really becomes a problem when we internalize unfortunate circumstances. Another thing to remember when the weather gets rough is that *what really matters is what happens in us, not to us!* When the external circumstances lead to wrong internal reactions, we really have problems. I once talked to a man who was having financial difficulty. He faced the prospect of losing everything. I offered prayer and encouragement during this difficult time. His reaction: "I've never been closer to God!" He told how this trial was making him stronger in his walk with God. Paul told Timothy that Christians would be persecuted. He also said that not only had he endured persecution, but also that God had always delivered him (2 Timothy 3:11,12). Paul allowed the storms of life to strengthen him. How different from those who yell "I quit" every time difficulty arises.

James even tells us that those problems are good:

> Consider it all joy, my brethren, when you encounter various trials [Why?], knowing that the testing of your faith produces endurance. And let endurance have its perfect result, that you may be perfect and

complete, lacking in nothing (James 1:2-4).

Rule 2:
Realize that the "rough weather" will not last forever.

When you're caught in the middle of touchy situations, it is often difficult to remember this truth. We become consumed with the problems. Our entire outlook is colored by the present. A drowning man is not concerned about tomorrow's schedule.

There is an expression I use quite often when I sense that the difficulties of the day are overwhelming me. At the moment when I have "had enough" I say, "This too shall pass!" That brief statement really works. It helps me gain perspective on my situation.

Still, "rough weather" wears us down. Many times it is not the size of the problem but the length of it that weighs heavily on us. That is why Paul teaches the church at Galatia, "Let us not lose heart in doing good, for in due time we shall reap if we do not grow weary" (Galatians 6:9). Many times preachers will say, "What we sow we reap." Paul says that it is possible to sow and not reap the benefits. How? By not holding steady and being patient enough to wait.

Many times I have heard runners talk about the "highs" they receive in running. (It is hard to convince me of their claim when I observe the grimaces on their faces as they run.) Once they receive their "second wind," they feel like they could run all day. Their secret? Run until you get your second wind. The first part is difficult and painful. The last part is easier and fruitful.

Therefore, since we have so great a cloud of witnesses surrounding us, let us also lay aside every encumbrance, and the sin which so easily entangles us, and let us run with endurance the race that is set before us, fixing our eyes on Jesus, the author and perfecter of faith, who for the joy set before Him endured the cross, despising the shame, and has sat down at the right hand of the throne of God. For consider Him who has endured such hostility by sinners against Himself, so that you may not grow weary and lose heart (Hebrews 12:1-3).

Rule 3:
Try to make major decisions
before the storm.

Many storms can be avoided by thinking and planning ahead. A pilot will check the weather in his planned flight before he makes his decision to proceed. When flying, he will check his radar, or call ahead to anticipate weather conditions.

Obviously, not all storms can be avoided. Yet I wonder how many we encounter because we fail to check all the resources available to us. Too many times our troubles are a result of our own poor planning and not the conditions that surround our lives.

One of my college professors became a campus conversation piece because of his horrible driving. Kids would say things like, "I left class early so I could get home safely before Professor Gladstone got on the road." After the professor had three accidents in six weeks, a student said to his wife sympathetically, "The devil sure has been causing your husband problems in his driving." Her reply, "Honey, don't blame the devil. George never could drive."

To avoid some potential storms in life we need to know and rely on tough weather indicators. I've listed some possible "eyes" that can help us foresee trouble, and questions we should ask before proceeding toward solving the problem:

ROUGH WEATHER INDICATORS:	QUESTIONS TO ASK MYSELF:
Lack of experience	Do I know someone with *successful* experience in this area?
Lack of knowledge	Have I studied sufficiently to direct my course effectively?
Lack of time	Did I allow the process of time to work on me as well as the storm?
Lack of facts	Are all the facts gathered to allow a proper decision?
Lack of prayer	Is this idea God's or mine? If mine, does God bless it and back it through the Word?

Even after all weather indicators have been checked, we will still probably encounter some storms. Life's difficulties have a crazy way of sneaking up on us. When that happens, try to delay as many major decisions as possible. Our life is a series of "ups and downs." (See illustration.) There is one major difference between people who jump from one major problem to another and those who go from one major success to the next. The difference is timing.

Those who make one bad decision after another make their major decisions during the "lows" of life. Those who exhibit the "Midas touch" have learned to wait until the "lows" pass and they feel on top of things.

When do you make the big "D"?

The right time to make a decision

The wrong time to make a decision

I cringe when I hear seminar speakers say, "It is more

important to make the wrong decision immediately than to make no decision." Don't you believe it! The key to success in decision-making is as much timing as making the right choice.

> The wrong decision at the wrong time = disaster.
> The wrong decision at the right time = mistake.
> The right decision at the wrong time = unacceptance.
> The right decision at the right time = success.

Usually wrong decisions are made at the wrong time and right decisions are made at the right time. The reason? We let our environment control our thinking, which controls our decisions. Therefore the more decisions that are made in the calm of life, the fewer times storms can bring us down. God can use the fruit of our bad decisions for good, but we can avoid compounding our problems by making decisions at the best time.

Rule 4:
Keep in contact with the control tower.

Every pilot knows the value of communicating with knowledgeable men during times of trouble. The natural reaction when having difficulty in the sky is to radio for help. We do not always do this in our daily living.

Our tendency is often to try to make it on our own. We admire that rugged, independent individual who "pulled himself up by his bootstraps." That is the American way. At times we are all little Frank Sinatras belting out for all to hear, "I did it my way."

Jesus sings another song. Its words speak about fullness of joy and fruitfulness. The thesis of His song states, "Apart from Me you can do nothing" (John 15:5). The title of His song is "Abide in Me and I in You" or, more modernly stated, "You'll Be Fine If You're Connected to the Vine."

Stanza 1 says, "Abide in Me, and I in you. As the branch cannot bear fruit of itself, unless it abides in the vine, so neither can you unless you abide in Me" (John 15:4).

Stanza 2 says, "I am the Vine, you are the branches; he who abides in Me, and I in him, he bears much fruit; for apart from Me you can do nothing" (John 15:5).

Stanza 3 says, "If anyone does not abide in Me, he is thrown away as a branch, and dries up; and they gather them and cast them into the fire, and they are burned" (John 15:6).

Stanza 4 says, "If you abide in Me, and My words abide in you, ask whatever you wish, and it shall be done for you" (John 15:7).

During a time of revival at my church, God began dealing with me about Jesus' statements, "Apart from Me you can do nothing." I have always been prone to think, "Apart from God I can only do some things." I would quickly admit my need for Him to do "Exceeding abundantly beyond all that we ask or think," but that which was less than extraordinary I felt sufficient to accomplish by myself. I learned that I can fly solo in my world no longer. Whether I'm in rough weather or in calm, blue skies, I must keep in contact with Christ.

Attitude Application:

I've made the following statements in this chapter. Take a moment to apply these truths to your present attitude.

1. "What really matters is what happens in us, not to us."

Which is more important—wrong action directed at me or wrong reaction within me?

Why?

2. "What we sow, we always reap."

   Is that true?

   If not, why?

3. "The difference between success and failure in decision-making is often timing."

   When does a winner make his decisions?

   When do I make mine?

4. "We admire that rugged, independent individual who 'pulled himself up by his bootstraps' and made it on his own. That is the American way."

   What is God's way? Read 1 Corinthians 1:18-31; 2:1-5.

We talked about factors that cause us to lose altitude. The following chapters of Section Three are "crash causers." These are either the things that cause us to crash or the things we blame when we make uncomfortable landings.

9

The Crash From Within

There is no security on this earth. There is only opportunity.

—Douglas MacArthur

There are certain storms within a person's life that contribute to an altitude crash. The three storms I'm discussing in this chapter are predominantly inward, not outward. They are part of us and must be constructively dealt with to bring inner peace and a wholesome attitude.

The Fear of Failure

The first inward storm is: *The Fear of Failure.*

We have had many ways of dealing with it. Some people determine, "If at first you don't succeed, destroy all the evidence that you've tried."

Failure—We hide it,
        deny it,
        fear it,

ignore it, and
hate it.

We do everything but accept it. By acceptance, I don't mean resignation and apathy. I mean understanding that failure is a necessary step to success. The man who never made a mistake never did anything.

I enjoy reading about the lives of great men. One consistent fact I notice is all successful people experienced failure. In fact, most of them began as failures.

When the great Polish pianist Ignace Paderewski first chose to study the piano, his music teacher told him his hands were much too small to master the keyboard.

When the great Italian tenor Enrico Caruso first applied for instruction, the teacher told him his voice sounded like the wind whistling through the window.

When the great statesman of Victorian England, Benjamin Disraeli, attempted to speak in Parliament for the first time, members hissed him into silence and laughed when he said, "Though I sit down now, the time will come when you will hear of me."

Henry Ford forgot to put a reverse gear in his first car.

Thomas Edison spent two million dollars on an invention which proved to be of little value.

Very little comes out right the first time. Failures, repeated failures, are fingerprints on the road to achievement. Abraham Lincoln's life could demonstrate that the only time you don't fail is the last time you try something and it works. We can "fail forward" toward success.

ABRAHAM LINCOLN — Biography of a failure:

Difficult childhood

Less than one year formal schooling

Failed in business in 1831

Defeated for legislature, '32

Again failed in business, '33

Elected to legislature, '34

Fiancee died, '35

Defeated for Speaker, '38

Defeated for Elector, '40

Married, wife a burden, '42

Only one of his four sons lived past age 18

Defeated for Congress, '43

Elected to Congress, '46

Defeated for Congress, '48

Defeated for Senate, '55

Defeated for Vice-President, '56

Defeated for Senate, '58

Elected President, '60

Accepting failure in the positive sense becomes effective when you believe that the right to fail is as important as the right to succeed. I enjoy the weather in San Diego more than the Southern California natives. Why? Because I lived in Ohio and experienced the winter of '78, not to mention a few others. Most people seldom value their good health until they become ill. Exposure to the problems gives greater joy in our progress if we can accept failure as an important process in reaching our goal.

It is impossible to succeed without suffering. If you are successful and have not suffered, someone has suffered for you and if you are suffering without succeeding, perhaps someone may succeed after you. But there is not success without suffering.

A few years ago while speaking in Dallas, I took a poll among church leaders, asking this question: "What keeps you from building a great work for God?" The number one answer: "Fear of failure." Immediately I began speaking to leaders about failure. My closing message at a large conference where pastors had seen and heard success stories was on "Flops, Failures and Fumbles." The total content of that forty-five-minute address consisted of all my programs that had fizzled. The crowd laughed hysterically as I openly confessed my many mistakes. Why? I had just admitted failure and given them permission to do the same.

I once listened to Reuben Welch, author of *We Really Do Need Each Other,* speak the same liberating truth. He talked about how, when we're merely concerned about survival and maintaining the status quo, we strive for a reputation that stifles progress and becomes self-limiting. After hearing that message I had a plaque made that said, "I don't have to survive."

Our Lord not only taught this truth but He also demonstrated it. He said that dying, not living, was the key to effectiveness:

> Truly, truly, I say to you, unless a grain of wheat falls into the earth and dies, it remains by itself alone; but if it dies, it bears much fruit. He who loves his life loses it; and he who hates his life in this world shall keep it to life eternal (John 12:24,25).

A few chapters later we read how Christ demonstrated this truth at Calvary. He became a visual example of His words, "Greater love has no one than this, that one lay down his life for his friends" (John 15:13). Certainly the "survival syndrome" was not a part of Jesus' life.

The apostle Paul understood this teaching by saying of himself:

> I have been crucified with Christ; and it is no longer I who live, but Christ lives in me; and the life which I now live in the flesh, I live by faith in the Son of God, who

loved me, and delivered Himself up for me (Galatians 2:20).

Tertullian, a second-century apologist, addressed this survival issue early in the history of the church. Some of the Christians were making idols as their profession. When faced with the issue of Christians working in the idol-making business, their reply was, "We must live." Tertullian retorted with the question, "Must you live?" His point: It is more important to be obedient to God than to be concerned with survival.

Perhaps the words of William Arthur Word will encourage us to quit "surviving" and therefore lose our fear of failure:

> If you are wise, you will forget yourself unto greatness. Forget your rights, but remember your responsibilities. Forget your inconveniences, but remember your blessings. Forget your own accomplishments, but remember your debts to others. Forget your privileges, but remember your obligations. Follow the examples of Florence Nightingale, of Albert Schweitzer, of Abraham Lincoln, of Tom Dooley, and forget yourself into greatness.

> If you are wise, you will empty yourself into adventure. Remember the words of General Douglas MacArthur: "There is no security on this earth. There is only opportunity." Empty your days of the search for security; fill them with a passion for service. Empty your hours of the ambition for recognition; fill them with the aspiration for achievement. Empty your moments of the need for entertainment; fill them with the quest for creativity.

> If you are wise, you will lose yourself into immortality. Lose your cynicism. Lose your doubts. Lose your fears. Lose your anxiety. Lose your unbelief. Remember these truths: A son must soon forget himself to be long remembered. He must empty himself in order to discover a fuller self. He must lose himself to find himself.

Forget yourself into greatness. Empty yourself into adventure. Lose yourself into immortality.

Take a risk. Climb out on a limb where the fruit is. Too many people are still hugging the tree trunk, wondering why they are not receiving the fruit of life. Many potential leaders never achieved because they stood back and let someone else take the risk. Many potential recipients never received because they didn't step out of the crowd and ask. James tells us "we have not because we ask not." Realistically, we ask not because we fear rejection. Therefore we take no risk.

> To laugh is to risk appearing the fool.
> To weep is to risk appearing sentimental.
> To reach out for another is to risk involvement.
> To expose feeling is to risk exposing your true self.
> To place your ideas, your dreams, before the crowd is
>   to risk their loss.
> To love is to risk not being loved in return.
> To live is to risk dying.
> To hope is to risk despair.
> To try is to risk failure.

> —Author unknown

But risk must be taken, because the greatest hazard in life is to risk nothing. The person who risks nothing, does nothing, has nothing and is nothing. He may avoid suffering and sorrow, but he simply cannot learn, grow, feel, change, love, live. Chained by his certitudes, he is a slave, he has forfeited freedom.

Fear of failure grips those who take themselves too seriously. While we were growing up, many of us spent a great deal of time worrying about what the world thinks of us. By the time we reach middle age we realize that the world wasn't paying much attention all the time we were worrying. Until we accept the fact that the future of the world does not hinge on our decisions, we will be unable to forget past mistakes.

In his autobiography, *The Tumult and the Shouting,* the great sports columnist Grantland Rice gives this advice about past mistakes:

> Because golf exposes the flaws of the human swing — a basically simple maneuver — it causes more self-torture than any game short of Russian Roulette. The quicker the average golfer can forget the shot he had dubbed or knocked off-line — and concentrate on the next shot — the sooner he begins to improve and enjoy golf. Like life, golf can be humbling. However, little good comes from brooding about mistakes we've made. The next shot, in golf or life, is the big one.

Attitude is the determining factor of whether our failures make or break us. The persistence of a person who encounters failure is one sign of a healthy attitude. Winners don't quit! Failure becomes devastating and causes our attitude to crash when we quit. To accept failure as final is to be finally a failure.

Everyone within range of the golden arches is aware of the success of McDonald's restaurants. The executives of this franchise followed a statement that said, "Press on. Nothing in the world can take the place of persistence. Talent will not; nothing in the world is more common than unsuccessful men with talent. Genius will not; the world is full of educated derelicts. Persistence and determination alone are omnipotent."

In times of failure a key is to look at our Creator and chief motivator.

WHEN IT LOOKS LIKE I HAVE FAILED

Lord, are you trying to tell me something?
For . . .
Failure does not mean I'm a failure;
   It does mean I have not yet succeeded.
Failure does not mean I have accomplished nothing;

It does mean I have learned something.
Failure does not mean I have been a fool;
  It does mean I had enough faith to experiment.
Failure does not mean I've been disgraced;
  It does mean I dared to try.
Failure does not mean I don't have it;
  It does mean I have to do something in a different way.
Failure does not mean I am inferior;
  It does mean I am not perfect.
Failure does not mean I've wasted my time;
  It does mean I have an excuse to start over.
Failure does not mean I should give up;
  It does mean I must try harder.
Failure does not mean I'll never make it;
  It does mean I need more patience.
Failure does not mean You have abandoned me;
  It does mean You must have a better idea. Amen.

Attitude Application:

Read these reinforcing thoughts about dealing with failure. Write them on 3 x 5 cards and keep them visible so you can read them often.

The man who never made a mistake never made anything.

Failures, repeated failures, are fingerprints on the road to achievement.

It is impossible to succeed without suffering.

"I don't have to survive."

Attitude is the determining factor of whether our failures make or break us.

To accept failure as final is to be finally a failure.

Failure is the line of least persistence.

The Dread of Discouragement

The second storm within us that causes attitude crash is: *The Dread of Discouragement.*

Elijah is one of my favorite Bible characters. Never has a man of God enjoyed a greater moment than his experience at Mt. Carmel. Boldness, faith, power, obedience and effective prayer describe Elijah as he stood with the worshippers of Baal. But deliverance in 1 Kings 18 was followed by discouragement in 1 Kings 19. His attitude went from boldness before God to blaming God for his trouble. Fear replaced faith. Power was drained by pity, and disobedience replaced obedience. How quickly things changed! Sound familiar? Turn to 1 Kings 19 and notice the four thoughts on discouragement.

First, discouragement hurts our self-image:

> But he himself went on a day's journey into the wilderness, and came and sat down under a juniper tree; and he requested for himself that he might die, and said, "It is enough; now, O Lord, take my life, for I am not better than my fathers" (verse 4).

Discouragement causes us to see ourselves as less than we really are. This fact becomes even more important when we realize that we cannot consistently perform in a manner that is inconsistent with the way we see ourselves.

Second, discouragement causes us to evade our responsibilities:

> Then he came there to a cave, and lodged there; and behold, the word of the Lord came to him, and He said to him, "What are you doing here, Elijah?" (verse 9)

The Elijahs of life are created for Mt. Carmels, not caves. Faith brings us to ministry. Fear hands us only misery.

Third, discouragement causes us to blame others for

our predicament:

> And he said, "I have been very zealous for the Lord,
> the God of hosts; for the sons of Israel have forsaken Thy
> covenant, torn down Thine altars and killed Thy
> prophets with the sword. And I alone am left; and they
> seek my life, to take it away" (verse 10).

Fourth, discouragement causes us to blur the facts:

> Yet I will leave 7,000 in Israel, all the knees that
> have not bowed to Baal and every mouth that has not
> kissed him (verse 18).

From only one to 7,000. No doubt about it: Discouragement had done a number on this great prophet. And if it can happen to great men, what about us? What about others? Discouragement is contagious.

You may have heard the story of the fellow who was about to jump from a bridge. An alert police officer slowly, methodically moved toward him, talking with him all the time. When the officer got within inches of the man he said, "Surely nothing could be bad enough for you to take your life. Tell me about it. Talk to me." The would-be jumper told how his wife had left him, how his business had gone bankrupt, how his friends had deserted him. Everything in life had lost meaning. For thirty minutes he told the sad story—then they both jumped!

We are all subject to the currents of discouragement that can sweep us into a danger zone. If we know some of the causes of discouragement we can more easily avoid it. Discouragement comes *when we:*

1. Feel that opportunity for success is gone.

The test of your character is seeing what it takes to stop you. We need the spirit of the boy in the Little League. A man stopped to watch a Little League baseball game. He asked one of the youngsters the score.

"We're behind eighteen to nothing," was the answer.

"Well," said the man, "I must say you don't look discouraged."

"Discouraged?" the boy asked. "Why should we be discouraged? We haven't come to bat yet."

2. Become selfish.

Usually people who are discouraged are thinking mainly about one thing—themselves.

3. Are not immediately successful in our attempts to do something.

A study conducted by the National Retail Dry Goods Association points out that unsuccessful first attempts lead almost half of all salesmen to certain failure. Note:

48 percent of all salesmen make one call and stop.
25 percent of all salesmen make two calls and stop.
15 percent of all salesmen make three calls and stop.
12 percent of all salesmen go back and back and back and back.
They make 80 percent of all sales.

I witnessed the reality of this while pastoring at Faith Memorial Church in Lancaster, Ohio. We had several bus routes and picked up hundreds of people for church on Sunday. Each bus had a captain that would call on regular and potential riders each Saturday. Designated boundaries marked the geographical area for each route. The captains were not allowed to leave their "territory" to find new riders.

Evelyn McFarland was a successful captain. She averaged more than fifty rides per Sunday! Her secret? She did not take no for an answer. Every Saturday she would call on each house to possibly secure another rider. Her visits were recorded in a diary. On one page she had written, "I have visited this home over ninety times. Finally today they said yes." Evelyn understood that we do not conquer through brilliance. We conquer by continuing.

4. Lack purpose and a plan.

Another characteristic of discouragement is inactivity. You seldom see a discouraged activist running to and fro trying to help others. When you are discouraged, you tend to withdraw. Many times discouragement comes right after a successful venture. Elijah found this to be true. Perhaps he needed another Mt. Carmel to lift his spirits. When we lack a purpose, many times we lack fulfillment.

Thomas Edison's life was filled with purpose. When he spoke about his success, he said:

> The most important factors of invention can be described in a few words. (1) They must consist of definite knowledge as to what one wishes to achieve. (2) One must fix his mind on that purpose with persistence and begin searching for that which he seeks, making use of all of the accumulated knowledge of the subject which he has or can acquire from others. (3) He must keep on searching no matter how many times he may meet with disappointment. (4) He must refuse to be influenced by the fact that somebody else may have tried the same idea without success. (5) He must keep himself sold on the idea that the solution of his problem exists somewhere, and that he will find it. . . .
>
> When a man makes up his mind to solve any problem, he may at first meet with dogged opposition, but if he holds on and keeps on searching he will be sure to find some sort of solution. The trouble with most people is that they quit before they start.[1]

By this time you may be totally discouraged, thinking there is little you can do to overcome those feelings of frustration and inadequacy. But here are some steps you can take.

1. Positive action

Take action on the problem. The moment you are certain of the source of the discouragement, get busy. Nothing delivers us from discouragement quicker than taking positive steps to solve the problem.

A poet tells of walking in his garden and seeing a bird's nest lying on the ground. The storm had swept through the tree and ruined the nest. While he mused sadly over the wreck of the bird home, he looked up and saw them building a new one in the branches.

2. Positive thinking

Recently I was reading a brief but stimulating biography of Thomas Edison written by his son. What an amazing character! Thanks to his genius, we enjoy the microphone, the phonograph, the incandescent light, the storage battery, talking movies and more than a thousand other inventions. But beyond all that, Edison was a man who refused to be discouraged. His contagious optimism affected all those around him.

His son recalled a freezing December night in 1914. Unfruitful experiments on the nickel-iron-alkaline storage battery, a ten-year project, had put Edison on a financial tightrope. He was still solvent only because of profits from movie and record production.

On that December evening the cry "Fire!" echoed through the plant. Spontaneous combustion had broken out in the film room. Within minutes all the packing compounds, celluloid for records and film and other flammable goods were burning. Fire companies from eight surrounding towns arrived, but the heat was so intense and the water pressure so low that attempts to douse the flames were futile. Everything was being destroyed.

When he couldn't find his father, the son became

concerned. Was he safe? With all his assets being destroyed, would his spirit be broken? Soon he saw his father in the plant yard running toward him.

"Where's Mom?" shouted the inventor. "Go get her, Son! Tell her to hurry up and bring her friends! They'll never see a fire like this again!"

Early the next morning, long before dawn, with the fire barely under control, Edison called his employees together and made an incredible announcement. "We're rebuilding!"

He told one man to lease all the machine shops in the area. He told another to obtain a wrecking crane from the Erie Railroad Company. Then, almost as an afterthought, he added, "Oh, by the way, anybody here know where we can get some money?"

Later he explained, "We can always make capital out of a disaster. We've just cleared out a bunch of old rubbish. We'll build bigger and better on the ruins." Shortly after that, he yawned, rolled up his coat for a pillow, curled up on a table and immediately fell asleep.

3. Positive example

It happened in Southwest Asia in the 14th century. The army of Asian conqueror Emperor Tamerlane (a descendant of Ghengis Khan) had been routed, dispersed by a powerful enemy. Tamerlane himself lay hidden in a deserted manger while enemy troops scoured the countryside.

As he lay there, desperate and dejected, Tamerlane watched an ant try to carry a grain of corn over a perpendicular wall. The kernel was larger than the ant itself. As the emperor counted, sixty-nine times the ant tried to carry it up the wall. Sixty-nine times he fell back. On the seventieth try he pushed the grain of corn over the top.

Tamerlane leaped to his feet with a shout! He, too, would triumph in the end! And he did, reorganizing his forces and putting the enemy to flight.

4. Positive persistence

Two frogs fell into a can of cream
—or so I've heard it told.
The sides of the can were shiny and steep,
the cream was deep and cold.
"Oh, what's the use?" said No. 1,
"'tis fate—no help's around—
Good-bye, my friend! Good-bye, sad world!"
And weeping still, he drowned.
But No. 2 of sterner stuff,
dog-paddled in surprise,
The while he wiped his creamy face
and dried his creamy eyes.
"I'll swim awhile, at least," he said
—or so it has been said—
"It wouldn't really help the world
if one more frog was dead."
An hour or two he kicked and swam—
not once he stopped to mutter,
But kicked and swam, and swam and kicked,
then hopped out, via butter.

—Author unknown

Too many times we become discouraged and accept defeat. One of the most famous race horses of all time was Man o'War. As a two-year-old, Man o'War won six consecutive races. Then in 1919, the champ came across a contender appropriately named Upset. For the first time in his life, Man o'War trailed another horse across the finish line.

As is often the case when a champion goes down in defeat, there were the unusual circumstances that affected the situation. On this occasion, an assistant starter was working the gate at the Saratoga race track, and the break from the barrier was delayed for about five minutes. The champ, always nervous at the post, was dancing and bobbing his head, and when the field broke, the big red horse was off sideways, fifth in a seven-horse race.

A champion does not give up easily, and Man o'War was no exception. He made a gallant try to close the gap. By the time the race reached the halfway mark, the champ had already moved up to the fourth position. He had gained the third position by the three-quarter mark. At the turn into the stretch, he moved clearly into second place. Ten lengths from home and he was "nodding at Upset's saddle girth." Given another two or three lengths, Man o'War would have been a clear winner. But Upset won by the narrowest possible margin.

When you read about that incident, you wish that the upset by Upset would have never happened.

You wish, too, that upsets some great men have experienced would have never happened, either. Abraham failed in an hour of emergency, and in weakness let a king think his wife, Sarah, was his sister. There is Jacob, who tricked his brother out of his own birthright; Moses, whose impatience lost him the right to enter the promised land; and David, that "man after God's own heart," who tarnished his name through adultery and murder. Elijah, too, was upset and prayed to die.

But—and this is what is most important of all—all of these men, after tragic upsets, went on to win great victories (as did Man o'War one year later, when he upset Upset).

Has some upsetting defeat or discouragement come your way recently? It's up to you to decide how you will handle the defeats of life. No man will go through all of life without meeting defeat from time to time. When it happens to you, don't quit! Missionary E. Stanley Jones said that he had adopted as his motto for life, "When life kicks you, let it kick you forward!" A wise resolve! Anyone can start, but only a thoroughbred will finish.

Attitude Application:

Harold Sherman, quite awhile ago, wrote a book entitled, *How to Turn Failure Into Success.* In it he gives a "Code of Persistence." If you give up too easily, write this down and read it daily:

1. I will never give up so long as I know I am right.

2. I will believe that all things will work out for me if I hang on until the end.

3. I will be courageous and undismayed in the face of odds.

4. I will not permit anyone to intimidate me or deter me from my goals.

5. I will fight to overcome all physical handicaps and setbacks.

6. I will try again and again and yet again to accomplish what I desire.

7. I will take new faith and resolution from the knowledge that all successful men and women have had to fight defeat and adversity.

8. I will never surrender to discouragement or despair no matter what seeming obstacles may confront me.

The Struggle of Sin

The third storm that rages within and causes our attitude to crash is: *The Struggle of Sin.*

For that which I am doing, I do not understand; for I am not practicing what I would like to do, but I am doing the very thing I hate. But if I do the very thing I do not wish to do, I agree with the Law, confessing that it is good. So now, no longer am I the one doing it, but sin which indwells me. For I know that nothing good dwells in me, that is, in my flesh; for the wishing is present in me, but the doing of the good is not. For the good that I wish, I do not do; but I practice the very evil that I do not wish. But if I am doing the very thing I do not wish, I am no longer the one doing it, but sin which dwells in me. I find then the principle that evil is present in me, the one who wishes to do good. For I joyfully concur with the law of God in the inner man, but I see a different law in the members of my body, waging war against the law of my mind, and making me a prisoner of the law of sin which is in my members. Wretched man that I am! Who will set me free from the body of this death? Thanks be to God through Jesus Christ our Lord! So then, on the one hand I myself with my mind am serving the law of God, but on the other, with my flesh the law of sin (Romans 7:15-25).

Paul is not a golfer describing his inconsistent game. Rather he is writing about the conflict of two natures within him. One says, "Do good" while the other drags him down.

A new Christian was sharing with me his frustration over not always doing what was right and what he intended. This disciplined individual asked, "Pastor, do you understand what I feel?" My reply, "Yes, and so did Paul." I turned to Romans 7 and started reading. He stopped me and asked, "Where is that Scripture? I will need to go back to it."

I hope he will also go to Romans 8 where Paul tells of deliverance. "There is therefore now no condemnation for those who are in Christ Jesus" (verse 1).

Psalm 51 is known as David's prayer for pardon after he became involved in the double sin of adultery and murder. In Psalm 32 David records how he felt during the time he was trying to cover up his sin. "When I kept silent about my sin, my body wasted away through my groaning all day long." For a year he tried to live with a bad conscience and a fallen attitude. Finally, after the prophet Nathan's confrontation, David prays to God for forgiveness. That prayer is rendered in Psalm 51:1,2:

> Be gracious to me, O God, according to Thy lovingkindness; according to the greatness of Thy compassion blot out my transgressions. Wash me thoroughly from my iniquity, and cleanse me from my sin.

He then lays hold of forgiveness by acknowledging his guilt, recognizing his sin and not blaming God (verses 3,4).

Forgiveness is one thing; however, overcoming sin is another. David prays for purifying power in verses 5 to 13. His prayer reveals eight steps to this deliverance and the power over sin.

1. "Help me to understand the truth about myself."

   "Behold, Thou dost desire truth in the innermost being, and in the hidden part Thou wilt make me know wisdom" (verse 6).

2. "Allow the blood sacrifice to be applied to my heart."

   "Purify me with hyssop, and I shall be clean; wash me, and I shall be whiter than snow" (verse 7).

3. "Fill me with joy and gladness."

   "Make me to hear joy and gladness, let the bones which Thou has broken rejoice" (verse 8).

4. "God, remember my sins no more. I can't always have them thrown up to me."

   "Hide Thy face from my sins, and blot out all my iniquities" (verse 9).

5. "Give me a new heart which naturally does good."

   "Create in me a clean heart, O God, and renew a steadfast spirit within me" (verse 10).

6. "Assure me of Your presence."

   "Do not cast me away from Thy presence, and do not take Thy Holy Spirit from me" (verse 11).

7. "Give me a will that wants to do what You want me to do."

   "Restore to me the joy of Thy salvation, and sustain me with a willing spirit" (verse 12).

8. "Allow me to teach others what I have experienced."

   "Then I will teach transgressors Thy ways, and sinners will be converted to Thee" (verse 13).

Susanna Wesley, mother of John and Charles, once used this striking sentence: "Whatever weakens your reason, impairs the tenderness of your conscience, obscures your sense of God, or removes your relish for spiritual things — that is sin to you."

Your attitude begins to falter when sin enters your life. A withdrawal, a hardness and a fleshly nature begin to invade us, all caused by sin. It is first appealing, then appalling; first alluring, then alienating; first deceiving, then damning; it promises life and produces death; it is the most disappointing thing in the world.

Understanding the problem is a good first step in correcting your perspective. If your attitude is threatening to crash, check the internal indications. See if you are afraid of failure, dealing with discouragement or struggling with sin.

10

The Crash From Without

*Murphy's Law — "Nothing is as easy as it looks;
everything takes longer than you expect; and if anything can go wrong, it will and at the worst possible
moment."*

*Maxwell's Law — "Nothing is as hard as it looks;
everything is more rewarding than you expect; and if
anything can go right it will and at the best possible
moment."*

Internal problems are not the only things that endanger
our perspective. Our attitude sometimes crashes when
the storms around us begin to take their toll. I have
pinpointed four of these outward causes.

The Closeness of Criticism

I call the first one *The Closeness of Criticism.*

I use the word *closeness* because the criticism that
hurts always comes close to where we live or what we love.

117

Others' criticism of us is like having someone "step on our blue suede shoes."

When speaking on this subject, many times I ask the audience if they can remember a critical statement that greatly affected their lives. I usually receive a unanimous "Yes."

I, too, have heard my share of critical comments. I grew up in a denomination that placed a high status on pastors who received yearly unanimous votes of confidence from their congregations. Conversation during summer church conferences centered on the most recent votes. This emphasis was firmly implanted in my mind, and my prayer for my first pastorate was, "Oh Lord, help me to please everybody." (That is definitely a prayer for failure.)

I did my best. I kissed the babies, visited the elderly, married the young, buried the dead, everything I thought I should do. Finally the annual vote was to be taken on my performance. Fifteen years later I still remember the results. Thirty-one yes, one no, and one abstention. Now what would you do? Not everyone was pleased with me. I rushed to the phone and called my father for his advice. Fortunately he reassured me that the church would make it through the "crisis." Unfortunately, for six months I wondered who voted "no."

From that early pastoral experience I learned the negative effect that criticism can have on a young church leader. A person entering his calling with a dream can easily be crushed unless he understands that the best fruit is the one the birds pick.

Jesus, perfect in love and motives, was criticized and misunderstood continually. People:

● called Him a glutton (Matthew 11:19);

● called Him a drunkard (Luke 7:34);

- criticized Him for associating with sinners (Matthew 9:11);

- accused Him of being a Samaritan and of having a demon (John 8:48).

In spite of experiencing misunderstanding, ingratitude and rejection, our Lord never became bitter, discouraged or overcome. Every obstacle was an opportunity. Broken-heartedness? An opportunity to comfort. Disease? An opportunity to heal. Hatred? An opportunity to love. Temptation? An opportunity to overcome. Sin? An opportunity to forgive. Jesus turned trials into triumphs.

Contrast that with the attitude of Amos on radio's old "Amos 'n' Andy" show. Amos was tired of Andy's constant criticism. Most irritating was Andy's finger continually thumping on Amos' chest. One day Amos could take it no more. He bought some dynamite, taped it to his chest and told his friend Kingfish, "The next time Andy starts criticizing and thumping his fingers on my chest, this dynamite is going to blow his hand off!" Of course he didn't stop to think of what it would do to his precious chest.

We always hurt ourselves when our reaction toward those who criticize us becomes negative. When such feelings arise, it is important to read the teachings of Jesus:

> You have heard that it was said, "You shall love your neighbor, and hate your enemy." But I say to you, love your enemies, and pray for those who persecute you in order that you may be sons of your Father who is in heaven; for He causes the sun to rise on the evil and the good, and sends rain on the righteous and the unrighteous. For if you love those who love you, what reward have you? Do not even the tax-gatherers do the same? And if you greet brothers only, what do you do more than others? Do not even the Gentiles do the same? Therefore you are to be perfect, as your heavenly Father is perfect (Matthew 5:43-48).

Attitude Application:

Here are some ways to keep criticism from sabotaging your attitude.

1. When possible, avoid people who belittle you. Small people try to tear you down, but big people make you feel worthwhile.

2. Ask yourself: What bothers me most when I am criticized? Who says it? Why was it said? What was the attitude that accompanied it? The place where it was shared? Is criticism coming from different people about the same subject? Is it valid? If so, am I doing anything about it?

3. Find a friend who has the gift of encouragement. Go to him and receive healing from his gift. But never receive his support without using your gift to minister in return.

The Presence of Problems

The second storm is *The Presence of Problems.*

A couple's only son had been sent away to college. Their expectations were high, but his grades were low. After a few months the collegian was kicked out of school. Knowing the disappointment that his parents would feel, he sent his mother a telegram that read: "Flunked all my courses—kicked out of school—coming home—prepare Pop."

The next day he received the following telegram: "Pop prepared—prepare yourself."

Life is full of such problems and we might as well be prepared for them. There is no such place as a trouble-free area and no such person as one who knows no problems. And Christians aren't exempt!

It is my responsibility and joy to disciple the key leaders of my congregation. A few years ago we studied 2

Timothy in a series I call "Time Out for Timothy." One subject was "Persecution of the Christian Leader." The central thought: "All who desire to live godly lives in Christ Jesus will be persecuted." The major question discussed in this study was, "Can you name a Bible character greatly used of God who did not endure trials?" Take a moment to try it. Almost without exception, the people we read about in God's Word encountered troubles.

> When Noah sailed the waters blue
> He had his troubles same as you;
> For forty days he drove the ark
> Before he found a place to park.

At times we all become "flooded" with problems. Perhaps it is the number of difficulties more than the size of any one trouble that wears us down. We all have moments when we "bite off more than we can chew."

There are moments when we feel like the lion tamer who had more than he could handle and put the following ad in a show business paper: "Lion tamer—wants lion tamer."

The ad underscores the feeling of the man in the following story. He was one of those persons who accepted everything that happened as a manifestation of a divine power. It was not for him, he said, to question the workings of a Divine Providence.

All his life misfortune had been his, yet never once did he complain. He married, and his wife ran away with the hired man. He had a daughter, and the daughter was deceived by a villain. He had a son and his son was lynched. A fire burned down his barn, a cyclone blew away his home, a hailstorm destroyed his crops, and the banker foreclosed on his mortgage, taking his farm. Yet at each fresh stroke of misfortune he knelt and gave thanks to God Almighty for His interminable mercy.

After a time, penniless, but still submissive to the decrees from on high, he landed in the county poorhouse. One day the overseer sent him out to plow a potato field. A thunderstorm came up but seemed to be passing over when, without warning, a bolt of lightning descended from the sky. It melted the plowshare, stripped most of his clothing from him, singed off his beard, branded his naked back with the initials of a neighboring cattleman and hurled him through a barbed wire fence.

When he recovered consciousness, he got slowly to his knees, clasped his hands and raised his eyebrow toward heaven. Then, for the first time, he asserted himself: "Lord," he said, "this is gettin' to be plumb ridiculous!"

When our attitude crashes, we have two alternatives. We can either alter the difficulty or alter ourselves. What can be changed for the best, we must change. When that is impossible, we must adjust to the circumstances in a positive way.

Before the days of antibiotics, Robert Louis Stevenson, the great Scottish novelist and author of *Treasure Island,* was bedridden with consumption a great deal. But the disease never stifled his optimism. Once when his wife heard him coughing badly, she said to him: "I expect you still believe it's a wonderful day."

Stevenson looked at the rays of sunshine bouncing off the walls of his bedroom, then replied: "I do. I will never permit a row of medicine bottles to block my horizon."

The apostle Paul possessed the same attitude. He said:

> We are pressed on every side by troubles, but not crushed and broken. We are perplexed because we don't know why things happen as they do, but we don't give up and quit. We are hunted down, but God never abandons us. We get knocked down, but we get up again and keep going (2 Corinthians 4:8,9, TLB).

Attitude Application:

What are problems?

PREDICTORS – They help mold our future.

REMINDERS – We are not self-sufficient. We need God and others to help.

OPPORTUNITIES – They pull us out of our rut and cause us to think creatively.

BLESSINGS – They open up doors that we usually do not go through.

LESSONS – Each new challenge will be our teacher.

EVERYWHERE – No place or person is excluded from them.

MESSAGES – They warn us about potential disaster.

SOLVABLE – No problem is without a solution.

The Conflict of Change

The third external storm that can cause our attitude to fall is *The Conflict of Change.*

We resist nothing more than change. Many times we enjoy the rewards of change but endure its process. We are creatures of habit. We first form habits, then our habits form us. We are what we repeatedly do. It is easy to see our world only from our perspective. When that occurs, we stagnate and become narrow.

Read the following statements. One is always true. The other is not.

"Change brings growth."

"Growth brings change."

The first statement, "Change brings growth," is true only if your attitude is right. With the proper attitude, all change, whether positive or negative, will be a learning experience which results in a growing experience.

Our inability to control changing situations has caused many attitudes to crash. Yet this does not have to happen. One Christmas I was walking through our church offices wishing everyone a merry Christmas. Stopping to speak to one of the volunteer secretaries, I asked, "Are you ready for Christmas?" With a smile she replied, "Almost. Just one more Care Bear to stuff." Figuring she was making the bears for her grandchildren, I asked, "How many grandchildren do you have?" "None," she replied. "But that's okay. I went out into my neighborhood and adopted some. I figured that if I'm going to have a family at Christmas, then I'd better go round them up!"

With a little coaxing from me, she began to explain some of the problems she'd had with her own family. The more she told me, the more I sensed that this remarkable lady refused to wallow in the pool of pity in which so many are drowning. Christmas to her would be lovely and not lonely only because she would not allow her attitude to crash over things she could not control.

Dr. G. Campbell Morgan tells of a man whose shop had been burned in the great Chicago fire. He arrived at the ruins the next morning carrying a table. He set it up amid the charred debris and above it placed his optimistic sign, "Everything lost except wife, children and hope. Business will be resumed as usual tomorrow morning."

Sadly, too many are like the old man in northern Maine who had turned 100. A New York reporter who went up to interview him commented, "I'll bet you have seen lots of changes in your 100 years."

The elderly fellow crossed his arms, jutted his jaw and replied with indignation, "Yes, and I've been agin' every one of them!"

I have spent much time observing why and when people start resisting change. Some strive until they are comfortable, then they settle in and don't want to grow. For most, a negative experience has made them pull back and say "never again."

At a coastal aquarium, a savage barracuda quickly tried to attack the mackerel but was stopped by the partition. After bumping his nose repeatedly, he finally quit trying. Later, the partition was removed, but the barracuda would swim only to the point where the barrier had been and stop. He thought it was still there. Many people are like that. They move forward until they reach an imaginary barrier, but then stop because of a self-imposed attitude of limitation.

If they only knew how unhealthy such an attitude is.

Change is essential for growth. A famous inventor once said, "The world hates change, yet it is the only thing that has brought progress." For the Christian, change should bring us closer to God. He has ordained change. We need to remind ourselves that not all people are born at the same time. God has ordained that there be a succession of generations: First a man is a son, then a father, then a grandfather and possibly even a great-grandfather. Each new generation is God's way of telling us that He still has a purpose for us to fulfill. In fact, each generation has three specific functions to perform: (1) conserve, (2) criticize, (3) create.

Each generation is a bank in which the previous generation deposits its valuables. The new generation examines those valuables, rejects what is no longer needed and uses what is left to create new treasures. This whole process of conserving, criticizing and creating adds up to the one thing we fear: change.

Just suppose each new generation had to discover numerals or language, or medicine or the gospel? The world would see no progress. But because each generation conserves what previous generations have discovered, we can continue to make progress in the important areas of life. This does not mean that each generation necessarily uses this conserved knowledge and skill for the best purposes, but it does mean that each new generation stands on the shoulders of the past and tries to reach higher.

When you realize that God has ordained new generations, and that new generations bring about change, you understand that one generation cannot do without the others. The older generation likes to conserve; the younger generation likes to criticize; but this interaction produces the friction that helps to generate the power for progress. The older generation is our link with the past, the younger generation is our link with the future, and we need both. The younger men need the wisdom of the older men, and the older men need the daring and the vision of the younger. To embalm the past is to turn society into a museum and destroy what future God has for us.

Even when people realize that change is inevitable, they respond differently to its challenges. Some retreat into their emotional and spiritual bombshelters and refuse to become a part of the action. One church member said to his pastor, "It's such a relief to come to a church where nothing has changed in 30 years!" My heart bleeds for that pastor.

On the other hand, there are those who go to the other extreme and change with every new gust of wind. They jump from bandwagon to bandwagon, and, like the Athenians Paul preached to, they are always looking for some new thing. The old hymns are buried, the familiar forms of worship are laid to rest, and even the traditional terminology is replaced by a jargon that may leave the poor worshipper wondering whether even God understands what is going on.

Still, the right amount of change can strengthen us. Moses uses an interesting illustration in Deuteronomy

32:11, where he describes the mother eagle forcing her young to leave the nest and fly. The eaglet wants to stay in the nest and be fed, but if he remains there, he will never use his great wings or enjoy the great heights for which he was created. So his mother has to knock him out of the nest, catch him on her wings when he falls too far and repeat the process until he learns to fly on his own.

You and I enjoy our little nests, and we have worked hard to build them. This explains why we resent it when God starts to "shake up" the nest. God wants us to grow. The timid souls pray, "Oh, that I had wings like a dove! I would fly away and be at rest" (Psalm 55:6). But the courageous should claim Isaiah 40:31 and "mount up with wings as eagles" right in the face of the wind! Not everybody who grows old grows up, and those who fail to grow up are often the ones who have run away from the challenge of change.

It is encouraging to see how many men and women God has used during what should have been their "comfortable years." Abraham and Moses were not young men when God called them, and just about the time Saul of Tarsus was settling down in his rabbinical career, God shook his nest and forced him to fly. Modern church and missionary history is filled with stories about mature people who willingly left the nest to serve God on eagles' wings.

The Night of Negativism

The fourth storm, which causes more attitude fatalities than anything else, is what I call *The Night of Negativism*.

Our thoughts govern our actions. That is a fact. In Matthew 15:19, the Lord said, "For out of the heart come evil thoughts, murders, adulteries, fornications, thefts, false witness, slander." The question is, are we governed by negative or positive thoughts? As negative thoughts produce negative actions, so positive thoughts produce positive actions. Today we are where we are and what we are because of the thoughts that dominated our minds.

Paul realized the power of our thought life and in Philippians 4 encouraged us to let our minds dwell on "Whatever is true, whatever is honorable, whatever is right, whatever is pure, whatever is lovely, whatever is of good repute," and then only if these things are excellent and worthy of praise.

Our challenge is to think right in a negative world. Every day we receive news that is less than uplifting. We all know people who can hardly wait for the future so they can look back with regret. Asked by a market research firm, R. H. Brieskin Associates, to state the best thing that had happened to them in the past five years, 12 percent of the people surveyed answered, "Nothing." These people can see only bad options in every situation. If they swallowed an egg they would be afraid to move for fear it would break and afraid to sit for fear it would hatch. Negative thinking and living does many detrimental things to our life. Let's look at a few of them.

1. Negative thinking creates clouds at critical decision times.

We become tense instead of relaxing. Taking a test is an example of this. An often-heard comment while cramming is, "I hope they don't ask me that question. I'm sure I'll miss it." We start the test and sure enough, there is the question, followed by the predicted outcome. Accident? No. It's a prophecy fulfilled. You felt negative about the question, declared your fear and responded accordingly. Next time you're studying for an exam, say to yourself, "If there ever will be a time when I remember the answer to this question, it will be when I take the test."

2. Negative talking is contagious.

A man who lived by the side of the road and sold hot dogs was hard of hearing, so he had no radio. He had trouble with his eyes, so he read no newspapers. But he sold good hot dogs. He put up signs on the highway advertising them. He stood on the side of the road and cried, "Buy a hot dog, mister?" And people bought his hot dogs. He increased his meat and bun orders. He bought a bigger stove to take care of his trade.

He finally got his son to come home from college to help out. But then something happened. "Father, haven't you been listening to the radio?" his son said. "Haven't you been reading the newspaper? There's a big recession on. The European situation is terrible. The domestic situation is worse."

Whereupon the father thought, "Well, my son's been to college, he reads the papers and he listens to the radio, and he ought to know."

So the father cut down his meat and bun orders, took down his signs and no longer bothered to stand out on the highway to sell his hot dogs. His sales fell overnight.

"You're right, son," the father said to the boy. "We certainly are in the middle of a big recession."

Has someone else's negative attitude ever changed your actions?

3. Negative thinking blows everything out of proportion.

Some people treat the drip from a leaky roof like a hurricane. Everything is a major project. They find a problem in every solution.

Murphy's Law states, "Nothing is as easy as it looks;

everything takes longer than you expect; and if anything can go wrong, it will and at the worst possible moment."

Maxwell's Law states, "Nothing is as hard as it looks; everything is more rewarding than you expect; and if anything can go right, it will and at the best possible moment."

4. Negative thinking limits God and our potential.

One of the saddest stories in the Bible is about Israel's failure to enter the promised land as told in Numbers 13 and 14. It is a classic example of how a negative report can limit God and others.

Twelve spies went into Canaan under the same orders, to the same places, at the same time and came back with different advice. For Joshua and Caleb the promised land was everything that God said it would be. They reported,

"It certainly does flow with milk and honey and this is its fruit."

The other ten men offered a negative report. In verses 28 and 29 of chapter 13, they reported facts without faith.

"Nevertheless, the people who live in the land are strong, and the cities are fortified and very large; and moreover, we saw the descendants of Anak there," they said. "Amalek is living in the land of the Negev and the Hittites and the Jebusites and the Amorites are living in the hill country, and the Canaanites are living by the sea and by the side of the Jordan."

In verse 31 we see that they had goals without God.

But the men who had gone up with him said, "We are not able to go up against the people, for they are too strong for us."

Verses 32 and 33 tell us that they continued with exaggeration without encouragement:

So they gave out to the sons of Israel a bad report of the land which they had spied out, saying, "The land through which we have gone, in spying it out, is a land that devours its inhabitants; and all the people whom we saw in it are men of great size. There also we saw Nephilim (the sons of Anak are part of the Nephilim); and we became like grasshoppers in our own sight, and so we were in their sight."

The result?

Then all the congregation lifted up their voices and cried, and the people wept that night. And all the sons of Israel grumbled against Moses and Aaron; and the whole congregation said to them, "Would that we had died in the land of Egypt! Or would that we had died in this wilderness! And why is the Lord bringing us into this land, to fall by the sword? Our wives and our little ones will become plunder; would it not be better for us to return to Egypt?" So they said to one another, "Let us appoint a leader and return to Egypt" (Numbers 14:1-4).

They settled for second best.

5. Negative thinking keeps us from enjoying life.

A negative person expects nothing off a silver platter except tarnish. If you have a negative neighbor, borrow a cup of sugar from him. He never expects to be paid back. Chisolm, a thinker and the "father of this crowd," said, "Any time things appear to be getting better you have overlooked something."

6. Negative thinking hinders others from making a positive response.

This is probably the greatest danger of a negative lifestyle. It tends to control those you influence and love the most.

Even the answer to a question depends a great deal on how you ask it. As experienced salesmen have long known, questions phrased either positively or negatively usually elicit a corresponding reply.

For example, a young psychology student drafted into the Army decided to test this theory. Drawing K.P., he was given the job of passing out apricots at the end of the chow line.

"You don't want apricots, do you?" he asked the first few men. Ninety percent said, "No."

Then he tried the positive approach: "You do want some apricots, don't you?" About half answered, "Uh, yeah, I'll take some."

Then he tried a third test, based on the fundamental either/or selling technique. "One dish of apricots, or two?" he asked. And in spite of the fact that most soldiers don't like Army apricots, 40 percent took two dishes and 50 percent took one.

The most common type of negativism that hinders others is characterized by what I call a "flat world" statement. This is a sincere statement that has been conditioned by past education and experience. It is not true yet it is accepted as fact. Therefore it directs the thinking and action of many individuals.

History abounds with tales of experts who said positively that things could not be done—and were proven wrong. The classic "flat world" illustration is about Columbus and his plans for exploration.

In 1490 Queen Isabella and King Ferdinand of Spain commissioned a royal committee to look into Christopher Columbus's scheme to find a new and shorter route to the fabled Indies.

The committee, an impressive panel of experts headed by Spain's leading geographer and scholar, examined Columbus's plans and presented its findings to the King and Queen. The scheme could not be carried out. Quite impossible, they wrote.

Columbus had trouble financing his ships and convincing a crew to sail "around" the world. Why? He was fighting a cultural trance. Most of the people believed one thing and were not open to other possibilities. For Columbus, the problem was that everyone *knew* the earth was flat.

Fortunately, Isabella, Ferdinand and, more important, Columbus himself ignored the experts. The Nina, the Pinta and the little Santa Maria set sail and a flat world was found to be round. "Impossible" new lands became thriving and very "possible" places.

During the early 1900s an impressive array of scientific wizards pooh-poohed the idea of the airplane. Stuff and nonsense, they said. An opium-induced fantasy. A crackpot idea.

One of America's influential scientific journalists hurried to say, "Time and money is being wasted on aircraft experimentation."

One week later, on a bumpy field called Kitty Hawk, North Carolina, the Wright Brothers taxied their crackpot idea down a homemade runway and launched the human race into the air.

Even after that, the experts continued to snipe at the airplane.

Marshall Foch, Supreme Commander of the Allied Forces in France in World War I, watched a display and said, "All very well for sport, but it is no use whatsoever to the Army."

Thomas Edison is on record as having said that talking pictures would never catch on. "Nobody," he said, "would pay to listen to sounds coming from a screen."

He also tried to persuade Henry Ford to abandon his

work on the fledgling idea of a motor car. "It's a worthless idea," Edison, persistent in his own endeavors, told the young Ford. "Come and work for me and do something really worthwhile."

Benjamin Franklin was told by experts to stop all that foolish experimenting with lightning. It was a waste of time, they said.

Madame Curie was urged, by experts, to forget the scientifically impossible idea of radium.

Laurence Olivier was earnestly advised by a sincere theatrical expert to give up plans for a career in the theater because he just did not have what it took to be a good actor.

No doubt, way back in the dim underside of time, a stubborn caveman kept insisting he could start the world's first man-made fire. All around him wise graybeards shook their heads and mumbled, "He's not all there. Somebody ought to tell him that it just will not work."

Today we are still having difficulty with "flat world" people. Many of our accepted assumptions have a tendency to stifle creativity and the achievement of our true potential.

To crystalize our understanding of this subtle form of negativism I have listed some "flat world" statements.

"Leaders are born, not made."
"Nice guys finish last."
"It's not what you know, but who you know."
"You can't teach an old dog new tricks."

When we become conditioned to perceived truths and closed to new positive possibilities, the following happens:

We *see* what we *expect* to see not what we *can* see.
We *hear* what we *expect* to hear, not what we *can* hear.
We *think* what we *expect* to think, not what we *can* think.

Attitude Application:

How do you make your "flat world" round?

1. Identify the reason you are a "flat world" person.

2. Identify the areas in which you think "flat world."

3. Identify people who can help you change this limiting thought process.

4. Continually check up on your progress.

5. Read and listen to positive self-help books and tapes.

6. Accept very few dogmatic, extreme statements.

7. Place all statements made into their proper context.

8. Take into account the source of the statement.

9. Remember, experience can limit your perspective rather than expand it.

10. What is possible is not always achieved quickly and endorsed enthusiastically.

Closing thought:

A "flat-world" mind-set allows us to sleep on top of it.
A "round world" mind-set keeps us moving around it.

Section IV

The Changing of Your Attitude

11

Up, Up and Away

Most people are very close to becoming the person who God wants them to be.

—John Maxwell

One of the great discoveries we make, one of our great surprises, is to find we can do what we were afraid we couldn't do. Most of the prison bars we beat against are within us; we put them there and we can take them down.

Now that statement includes some good news and some bad news. The bad news is that we bring many of our problems on ourselves. The good news is that beginning today we can break out of our prison of bad attitudes and become free for effective living.

This section is dedicated to clearly laying out a workable process to help you overcome an attitude problem. For this process to be successful, you should understand these statements.

1. The process takes a lot of dedication and work to be

effective.

2. The process of change is never complete, therefore constant review of Section IV will insure the best results.

3. All excuses for wrong attitudes must be eliminated immediately. Face changing with the sincerity and honesty of the Negro spiritual that says, "It's me, it's me, it's me, oh, Lord, standing in the need of prayer."

4. Find a friend to whom you can be accountable on a regular basis for your change of attitude.

5. Remember, as you read these next pages, you are able to change any attitude you desire.

The individual's attitude is my major emphasis in conducting leadership conferences across the country. Most people are very close to becoming the person that God wants them to be. Continually I say to them and now to you, "You're only an attitude away!" My greatest joy is in helping hundreds of people change an attitude they feel stuck with for the rest of their lives. For your encouragement, a testimonial of a changed life resulting from a changed attitude, is included in this chapter. Read this person's story and remember, this can happen to you.

"As a man thinks within himself, so he is" (Proverbs 23:7). This verse has special significance for me. I have personally experienced the influence of attitudes, for my thinking in life has produced two different men.

My conversion to Christ was the turning point for me. I changed from being a person with negative attitudes to one who lives with a positive mindset. People see me as a very positive person today, but they would not have recognized me eleven years ago. My attitudes have come through a healing, reshaping, transforming process.

Before I was a Christian, my attitude was shaped

by the world around me. My thinking was conformed to the world's values. I was reared in a broken home and was saturated with the attitude that life was a struggle, a fight for survival. I had a negative self-image because the significant people in my life (family, peers, etc.) possessed negative self-images. Criticism and negative thinking became my way of life because those attitudes were modeled by the people around me. Obstacles and problems were never seen as opportunities for growth. Problems were curses to be lived with, not blessings in disguise which could be solved.

I felt that life had dealt me a bad hand. I was doomed to have the "short end of the stick." I became self-centered and self-seeking. I wanted only to see what I could get from life. As I pursued this negative lifestyle, I found no fulfillment. Life itself seemed meaningless; it always had a dark cloud hanging over it.

The people I associated with, the literature I read, the music I listened to and my failure to know God, all shaped my attitudes in a non-positive way.

Christ came into my life at a very significant point. When I was most discouraged with living, He made me a new person. I began to see that "Christ in me" meant a transformation of my mind. I did not become a superpositive person overnight, but I began immediately to see life differently.

His Word within me, not the world around me, began to influence my attitudes. I made a willful choice to abide by God's Word. I had a battle with recurring, negative thoughts. But I desired with all my heart to be different. I wanted to be a positive person. I wanted to have the mind of Christ.

As I learned more about Christ, submitted to His will and obeyed His leading, my bitterness toward life changed. Life became a blessing, not a burden. Life was full of opportunities, not obstacles.

I purposely set out to expose myself to positive role models. I read positive-thinking books, listened to positive people, associated with positive groups. Please be aware that these changes were not always easy. I had to battle the old thinking sometimes. But the grace of God was the key factor in transforming my attitude.

I know that God can help anyone change his attitude. He changed my attitude toward life to one of positive, edifying, other-centered, Christ-directed living. I believe the key factors in my attitude transformation were faith in God, desire to change, willingness to do what was needed to be different (associate with different people, etc.) and a strong resolve to be positive each day.

I used to believe that circumstances determined my attitude. But now I know that choice, not circumstances, determines how I think. Anyone can become a positive person, if he wants to be. God will help all who desire to be different.

The process I've been through has been exciting. It's still going on. God is faithful. The work He has begun, He will finish. We don't have to remain negative people. We can be positive — if we want to submit ourselves to the process of change.

Certainly this man has undergone some tremendous changes. Every time I read his personal testimony I sense much positive growth in his life. Fortunately, he is a close friend and I have been able also to see the success of his new, positive attitude. When change is successful, we look back and call it growth.

Most people who have negative attitudes do not realize that attitudes know no barriers. The only barriers that bring our attitudes into bondage are those we place upon them. Attitudes, like faith, hope and love, can cross over any obstacle. Realizing this truth, let me encourage you to take control of your attitudes and begin the needed changes.

The pilot of an aircraft understands that he sets the attitude of the plane. He determines the direction of the attitude. The results follow. Climbing to a higher altitude takes time. Radio and television commentator Paul Harvey said, "You can tell when you are on the road to success. It's uphill all the way." It will take time to reach new heights. Be patient, knowing that anything worthwhile is worth working for. Although change itself is not progress, it is the price we pay for progress.

Before you begin the process of change, here is a prayer for you:

Dear God,

Change is never easy, yet growth demands it.

Therefore I fearfully step out of my world of defeatism and cautiously open myself to a world of winners.

It will take time, Lord.

Therefore I will be patient in letting You and others help me become "perfect and complete, lacking in nothing" (James 1:4).

I will need a lot of help.

Therefore I will accept those You send to me from various places at various times for my specific needs.

Truthfully, Father, I'm still intimidated and lack strength.

Therefore I ask that You will do something for me that I cannot do for myself.

And as my attitudes change and a "better me" becomes a reality, I will give You all the praise. Amen.

12

The Choice Within You

Take one giant step at a time. Military strategists teach their armies to fight on one front at a time. Settle on one attitude you want to tackle at this time.

—John Maxwell

We are either the masters or the victims of our attitudes. It is a matter of personal choice. Who we are today is the result of choices made yesterday. Tomorrow we will become what we choose today. To change means to choose to change.

In the Canadian northlands there are just two seasons, winter and July. When the back roads begin to thaw, they become muddy. Vehicles going into the backwood country leave deep ruts that become frozen when cold weather returns. For those entering this primitive area during the winter months, there is a sign which reads, "Driver, please choose carefully which rut you drive in, because you'll be in it for the next twenty miles."

Please follow carefully the course that you chart for your change of attitude. "Twenty miles" down the road you'll be glad you did. Only you can determine to take the steps as outlined in this chapter. They are not only the first steps that must be taken, but they are also the most important. Without taking these, it will be impossible to take the others.

Choice #1—Evaluate your present attitudes.

This will take some time. If possible, try to separate yourself from your attitudes. The goal of this exercise is not to see the "bad you" but a "bad attitude" that keeps you from being a more fulfilled person. The evaluation helps you make key changes only when you identify the problem.

When he sees a log jam, the professional logger climbs a tall tree and locates a key log, has that log blown up and lets the stream do the rest. An amateur would start at the edge of the jam and move all the logs, eventually moving the key log. Obviously, both methods will get the logs moving, but the professional does his work more quickly and effectively.

Results are the only real reason for activity. The following evaluation process is developed to help you search for the right answers in the most efficient way.

Stages of Evaluation

1. IDENTIFY PROBLEM FEELINGS—What attitudes make you feel the most negative about yourself? Usually feelings can be sensed before the problem is clarified. Write them down.

2. IDENTIFY PROBLEM BEHAVIOR—What attitudes cause you the most problems when dealing with others? Write them down.

3. IDENTIFY PROBLEM THINKING—We are the sum of our thoughts. "As a man thinks within himself, so he is." What thoughts consistently control your mind? Although this is the beginning step in correcting attitude problems, these are not as easy to identify as the first two.

4. CLARIFY BIBLICAL THINKING—What do the Scriptures teach about you as a person and about your attitudes? Later in this section I will share a scriptural view of right attitudes.

5. SECURE COMMITMENT—"What must I do to change?" now becomes "I must change." Remember, the choice to change is the one decision that must be made, and only you can make it.

6. PLAN AND CARRY OUT YOUR CHOICE—This is the process that Section IV helps you accomplish.

Suggestion: This evaluation will take time. If you have an encouraging friend who knows you well, perhaps you should enlist his or her help.

Choice #2—Realize that faith is stronger than fear.

The only thing that will guarantee the success of a doubtful undertaking is the faith from the beginning that you can do it. Jesus said, "If you have faith, and do not doubt, you shall . . . say to this mountain, 'Be taken up and cast into the sea,' and it shall happen" (Matthew 21:21).

There is a biblical way to handle fear so that an endeavor can be successful and not be limited by it. The early church in Acts was experiencing tremendous growth. However, in Acts 4, Christians came up against some stiff opposition. They were commanded to stop witnessing or suffer severe consequences. Together they withdrew to pray. Verses 29 to 31 record a process they underwent to handle their fear. As you approach changing attitudes, this formula for fear will be helpful.

Four-step Formula to Handle Fear

1. Understand that God sees your problems.

"And now, Lord, take note of their threats . . . " (verse 29).

These who encountered difficulties wanted the assurance that God had seen their persecution. When things are going well, we do not need constant assurance that God is with us. But during battle (and you will have battles), there is a strong need for security. The good news is, God Himself has said, "I will never desert you, nor will I ever forsake you" (Hebrews 13:5).

2. Ask for a filling of confidence and love that is greater than fear.

"Grant that Thy bond-servants may speak Thy word with all confidence" (verse 29).

This was a request for more positive things to fill their hearts and minds. They realized that an effective way to experience less fear was to have more courage. It is unrealistic to think that all apprehensions, questions and intimidation will flee and never haunt us again. Usually both positive and negative are at work in our lives at the same time. The secret to overcoming? Possess positive emotions and seek positive reinforcement that are stronger than the negatives.

3. Believe God is working a miracle in your life.

" . . . while Thou dost extend Thy hand to heal, and signs and wonders take place through the name of Thy holy servant Jesus" (verse 30).

Now there was a prayer for God to intercede on their behalf with miracles. They realized that what had to be done would take their effort plus God's. Notice they asked for strength first, and then they requested that God would make up the difference.

This must happen in your life. Place the changes you seek in attitude, thinking and behavior at the top of your prayer list. Ask God to help you do what is possible to bring about effective change. Then ask Him to do for you what you cannot do for yourself.

4. Be filled with the Holy Spirit.

"And when they had prayed, the place where they had gathered together was shaken, and they were all filled with the Holy Spirit, and began to speak the word of God with boldness" (verse 31).

There is a definite relationship between the filling of the Holy Spirit and boldness. Later in this section more emphasis will be given to the need for Spirit-filled living.

I know many people who use this four-step formula to handle fear on a daily basis. It guards them and imparts strength. I encourage you to continually refer to this formula when fears begin to hinder your progress.

You are now preparing to take a big step. Don't be fearful or hesitant. You can't cross a chasm in two small jumps. The future is worth the risk. Tomorrow you will look back at the changes and call them improvements.

Years ago a small town in Maine was proposed for the site of a great hydroelectric plant. Since a dam would be built across the river, the town would be submerged. When the project was announced, the people were given many months to arrange their affairs and relocate.

During the time before the dam was built, an interesting thing happened. All improvements ceased. No painting was done. No repairs were made on the buildings, roads and sidewalks. Day by day the whole town got shabbier and shabbier. A long time before the waters came, the town looked uncared for and abandoned, even though the people had not yet moved away. One citizen complained: "Where there is no faith in the future, there is no power in the present." That town was cursed with hopelessness because it had no future.

Choice #3—Write a statement of purpose.

One day Charlie Brown was in his back yard having target practice with his bow and arrows. He would pull the bow string back and let the arrow fly into a fence. Then he would go to where the arrow had landed and draw a target around it. Several arrows and targets later, Lucy said to Charlie Brown, "You don't have target practice that way. You draw the target, then shoot the arrow." Charlie's response: "I know that, but if you do it my way, you never miss!"

Sadly, many people approach their lives like Charlie Brown shoots arrows. They never draw a target so they never miss their goal. But they never really hit one either.

When I was a boy, my father decided to build a basketball court for my brother and me. He made a cement driveway, put a backboard on the garage and was just getting ready to put up the basket when he was called away on an emergency. He promised to put up the hoop as soon as he returned. *No problem,* I thought. *I have a brand new Spalding ball and a new cement driveway on which to dribble it.* For a few minutes I bounced the ball on the cement. Soon that became boring, so I took the ball and threw it up against the backboard—once. I let the ball run off the court and didn't pick it up again until Dad returned to put up the rim. Why? It's no fun playing basketball without a goal. The joy is having something to aim for.

That is the major difference between work and other enjoyable activities. Many times we find work is boring because there is no stated goal or purpose. We drag home tired, ready to sit down and relax. Then we remember, "Tonight is my bowling night." We go to the closet and pick up a sixteen-pound ball, get in the car and drive through traffic to throw that heavy ball down an alley for two hours! That doesn't make sense. We were tired and ready for rest, and now we are exercising (not working) harder than ever before. Why? All because there are ten pins at the end of the alley . . . a tangible goal. Hitting them brings immediate reinforcements. The total motivation of bowling is the ten pins, the goal. If you don't believe that, just have the operator remove the pins. See how many times you will throw a sixteen-pound ball down the alley without them.

In order to have fun and direction in changing your attitude, you must establish a clearly stated goal. This goal should be as specific as possible, written out and signed, with a time frame attached to it. The purpose statement should be placed in a visible spot where you see it several times a day to give you reinforcement. Here is an example of a statement of purpose:

"To change my attitude (specifically, negative thinking, critical remarks toward others and resentment) by following the procedure outlined in Section IV of *The Winning Attitude*. To effectively accomplish this goal I will review this process and my progress daily by being accountable to an encouraging friend. By (date)_____ I fully expect that others will be noticing my positive behavior."

You will attain this goal if each day you do three things:

1. Write specifically what you desire to accomplish each day.

The story of David's encounter with Goliath is a fine illustration of faith and how it may move out against insurmountable odds with seemingly inadequate resources. But one thing perplexed me when I first began to study David's life. Why did he pick five stones for his sling on his way to encounter Goliath? I am convinced that the Scriptures never just use words for their own sake—the number of stones had to be significant. The longer I pondered, the more perplexed I became. Why *five* stones? There was only one giant. Choosing five stones seemed to be a flaw in his faith. Did he think he was going to miss and that he would have four more chances? Some time later I was reading in 2 Samuel, and I got the answer. Goliath had four sons, so there were five giants. In David's reckoning, there was one stone per giant! Now that is what I mean about being specific in our faith.

What are the giants you must slay to make your attitude what it needs to be? What resources will you need? Don't be overcome with frustration when you see the problems. Take one giant at a time. Military strategists teach their armies to fight one front at a time. Settle which attitude you want to tackle at this time. Write it down. As you successfully begin to win battles, write them down. This will encourage you. Spend time reading about your past victories.

2. Verbalize to your encouraging friend what you want to accomplish each day.

Belief is inward conviction; faith is outward action. You will receive both encouragement and accountability by verbalizing your intentions. One of the ways people resolve a conflict is to verbalize it to themselves or someone else. This practice is also vital in reaching your desired attitudes.

I know successful salesmen who repeat this phrase out loud fifty times each morning and fifty times each evening: "I can do it." Continually saying and hearing these positive statements helps them believe in themselves and causes them to act on that belief. Start this process by changing your vocabulary. Here are some suggestions:

Eliminate These Words Completely	Make These Words a Part of Your Vocabulary
1. I can't	1. I can
2. If	2. I will
3. Doubt	3. Expect the best
4. I don't think	4. I know
5. I don't have the time	5. I will make the time
6. Maybe	6. Positively
7. I'm afraid of	7. I am confident
8. I don't believe	8. I do believe
9. (minimize) I	9. (promote) You
10. It's impossible	10. God is able

3. Take action on what you write and verbalize what you wrote each day.

Jesus teaches us that the difference between a wise man and a foolish man is his response to what he already knows. A wise man follows up on what he hears while a foolish man knows but does not act (Matthew 7:24-27).

We are told in James 1:22-25:

> But prove yourself doers of the word, and not merely hearers who delude themselves. For if anyone is a hearer of the word and not a doer, he is like a man who looks at his natural face in a mirror; for once he has looked at himself and gone away, he has immediately forgotten what kind of a person he was. But one who looks intently at the perfect law, the law of liberty, and abides by it, not having become a forgetful hearer but an

effectual doer, this man shall be blessed in what he does.

Action suggestion: For thirty days, treat every person you meet as the most important person on earth. You will find that they will begin treating you the same way. How does the world look at you? Exactly how you look at the world. Do something positive for someone else regularly. No one is useless in this world who lightens the burden of it for someone else.

Choice #4—Have the desire to change.

No choice will determine the success of your attitude change more than desiring to change. When all else fails, desire alone can keep you heading in the right direction. Many people have climbed over insurmountable obstacles to make themselves better people when they realized that change is possible if they really want it badly enough. Let me illustrate.

While hopping about one day, a frog happened to slip into a very large pothole along a country road. All his attempts at jumping out were in vain. Soon a rabbit came upon the frog trapped in the hole and offered to help him out. He, too, failed. After various animals from the forest made three or four gallant attempts to help the poor frog out, they finally gave up. "We'll go back and get you some food," they said. "It looks like you're going to be here a while." However, not long after they took off to get food, they heard the frog hopping along after them. They couldn't believe it! "We thought you couldn't get out!" they exclaimed. "Oh, I couldn't," replied the frog. "But you see, there was a big truck coming right at me, and I had to."

It is when we "have to get out of the potholes of life" that we change. As long as we have acceptable options, we will not change. The person with too many options reminds me of a story two friends told me.

They have two nieces who are sisters. One is eleven years old and is an excellent swimmer. She spends a lot of time practicing for swim meets. The younger girl is five and also swims, but she shows no willingness to pay the price to practice and win in swim meets.

Over Christmas the older sister won a 220-meter race. Her father was reading the newspaper article about Lisa's success and asked the younger daughter, "Shelley, wouldn't you like to work hard and get your name in the paper and have a good time?" "Dad," she said, "I'd rather just sit here and eat cookies and drink milk the rest of my life."

Sadly, that's where too many people live. While they drink milk and eat cookies, others pay the price and win medals. Every once in a while the cookie eaters of life stop long enough to wonder why they don't have medals. A tinge of guilt might touch them for a moment, but then they decide to go back to "cookie dunking." They lack desire.

Most people are more comfortable with old problems than new solutions. They respond to their needs for turn-around in life like the Duke of Cambridge who once said, "Any change, at any time, for any reason, is to be deplored." People who believe that nothing should ever be done for the first time never see anything done.

Cotford's Law states, "Nothing is ever done until everyone is convinced that it ought to be done and has been convinced for so long that it is now time to do something else."

But there is hope. There seems to be three times in our lives when we're most receptive to change. First, when we hurt so much that we are forced to change. Jesus tells about this type of individual in Luke 15. The parable of the prodigal son illustrates that when we are looking up from the bottom of a pigpen, it is possible to "come to ourselves" and get help by going back to father's house.

The prodigal acted similarly to the lady with an incurable disease who came to Jesus only after she had spent all that she had on other doctors and had become desperate (Luke 8:43).

For more than a year I taught Bible studies on miracles. At the end of this series I wrote down a few basic truths about the subject. My greatest discovery was that every miracle in the Bible began with a problem. Only when someone was hurting did they receive relief. Only when a person was questioning did they find answers. Now this truth has bad news and good news in it. The bad news is that usually our hurt has to be great enough to create a desire to change. We only gain after pain. The good news is that if you are desperate and need to change, you are a candidate for a miracle.

Second, receptivity to change is also heightened when we are bored and become restless. Everyone experiences this at certain times in life. Perhaps the wife senses this when the children are all in school and she finds extra time to get involved with other things. Husbands plateau on their jobs and begin to lose interest in their work. A holy dissatisfaction can be healthy when it produces positive changes.

It is a sad day for any person when he becomes so satisfied with his life, his thoughts and his deeds that he ceases to be challenged to do greater things in life.

Third, change is apt to occur when we realize we *can* change. This is the greatest motivation of all. Nothing sparks the fires of desire more than the sudden realization that you do not have to stay the same. You no longer need to feel the burden of negative attitudes. You have no valid reason to constantly feel bitter and resentful about life, others or yourself. You can change!

Because I firmly believe that people will change once they understand that it is possible, I continually share one phrase with others. When I sense bewilderment, doubt, frustration and other mental blocks, I say, "Yes you can." I have seen hundreds of faces light up with those three simple words and an encouraging smile.

One day my wife and I stopped at a fast food restaurant to buy some soft drinks. When I asked for a diet cola for Margaret, the young lady said they had no diet drinks. Then I asked her for a large cup of ice, thinking that I could stop at a market down the road to buy a can of diet soda. My request created a cloud on my waitress's face as she said, "Sir, I don't think we can do that here." "Yes you can," I replied quickly and confidently. Immediately her face lit up and she responded enthusiastically. She went off to get my cup of ice. All she needed was someone to help her believe she could do what she'd been asked.

My life is dedicated to helping others reach their potential. I suggest that you follow the advice of Mark Twain who said, "Take your mind out every now and then and dance on it. It is getting all caked up." It was his way of saying, "Get out of that rut." Too many times we settle into a set way of thinking and accept limitations that need not be placed upon us.

Life is a changing process. With all of its transitions come new opportunities for growth. What is a limiting factor yesterday may not be one today. Accept the following statement for your life: "The days ahead are filled with changes which are my challenges. I will respond to these opportunities with the confidence that my life will be better because of them. With God all things are possible."

Desire increases with love. Fall in love with the challenge of change and watch the desire to change grow. We have all known a desire that can only be expressed in the words, "Love made me do it."

Aleida Huissen, 78, of Rotterdam, Netherlands, had been smoking for fifty years. For fifty years she tried to give up the habit, but was unsuccessful. Then Leo Jensen, 79, proposed marriage and refused to go through with the wedding until Aleida gave up smoking. Aleida says, "Will power never was enough to get me off the habit. Love did it."

Be careful what you set your heart on! Luther Burbank fell in love with plants. Edison fell in love with inventions. Ford fell in love with motor cars. Kettering fell in love with research. The Wright brothers fell in love with airplanes.

Be very careful what you set your heart on, for it will surely come true!

"Delight yourself in the Lord and He will give you the desires of your heart" (Psalm 37:4).

Choice #5—Live one day at a time.

Any man can fight the battle for just one day. It is only when you and I add the burdens of those two awful eternities, yesterday and tomorrow, that we tremble. It is not the experiences of today that drive men to distraction; it is the remorse or bitterness for something that happened yesterday and the dread of what tomorrow may bring. Let us therefore live but one day at a time—today!

David, in his prayer for forgiveness (Psalm 51), asked God to "Hide Thy face from my sins." He understood that effectiveness today is determined by the healing and forgetting of yesterday. "My sin is ever before me," describes a condition in David's life that would have hindered the change he wanted to make. Therefore he used words that pointedly asked God to spiritually heal his mind and heart. "Blot out my transgressions . . . wash me thoroughly . . . cleanse me from my sin . . . purify me . . . wash me . . .

make me to hear joy and gladness . . . blot out all my iniquities . . . create in me a clean heart . . . renew a steadfast spirit within me . . . restore to me the joy of Thy salvation . . . deliver me."

Like David, you should pray these phrases and allow God to forgive you and heal your past. Only God can heal what happened yesterday and help you live effectively today. What you have not overcome in your past remains to plague you in your present.

I met an old friend at a conference. While I spoke, I noticed a new joy upon his face. During one of the breaks he came up and gave me a big hug. "John," he said, "recently during a prayer time God healed me of the scars in my past." This man had undergone severe negative experiences and now was sensing a new freedom and power to live today. Now, after you have been assured of forgiveness from God, it is important to concentrate on building a new you.

Choice #6—Change your thought patterns.

That which holds our attention determines our actions. We are where we are and what we are because of the dominating thoughts that occupy our minds. William James said, "The greatest discovery of my generation is that people can alter their lives by altering their attitudes of mind." Romans 12:1,2 says:

> I urge you therefore, brethren, by the mercies of God, to present your bodies a living and holy sacrifice, acceptable to God, which is your spiritual service of worship. And do not be conformed to this world, but be transformed by the renewing of your mind, that you may prove what the will of God is, that which is good and acceptable and perfect.

Two things must be stated to emphasize the power of

our thought life. Major premise: We can control our thoughts. Minor premise: Our feelings come from our thoughts. Conclusion? We can control our feelings by learning to change one thing: the way we think. It is that simple. Our feelings come from our thoughts. Therefore, we can change them by changing our thought patterns.

Our thought life, not our circumstances, determines our happiness. Often I see people who are convinced that they will be happy when they attain a certain goal. When they reach the goal, many times they do not find the fulfillment they anticipated.

You often can see this phenomenon among mothers. First they say, "When Johnny gets out of elementary school, I'll be happy!" And they are, for a while. Next you hear them telling their friends, "When Johnny graduates from high school, I'll be so happy!" And they are, at least for the summer. Johnny's graduation from college brings the same result, and so does Johnny's marriage. So does the birth of Johnny's first child, when Mamma becomes an ecstatic grandmother, and the feeling may continue until she becomes a babysitter.

But if Mamma has not learned how to be happy between her special blessings, she will not have a steady, enjoyable life.

The secret to staying on an even keel? Fill your mind with "whatever is true, whatever is honorable . . . whatever is of good repute, if there is any excellence and if anything worthy of praise, let your mind dwell on these things" (Philippians 4:8). Paul understood. That which holds our attention determines our action.

Choice #7 — Develop good habits.

Attitudes are nothing more than habits of thought. The cycle chart on the next page will help you form proper

habits.

This cycle can be positive or negative. The process for developing habits, good or bad, is the same. It is as easy to form a habit of succeeding as it is to succumb to the habit of failure. Observe the following two cycles and see the difference.

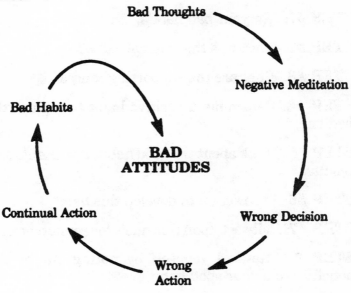

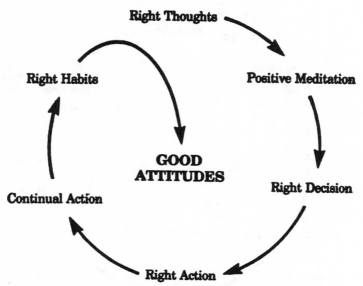

Habits aren't instincts; they're acquired actions or reactions. They don't just happen; they are caused. Once the original cause of a habit is determined, it is within your power to accept or reject it. Most people allow their habits to control them. When those habits are hurtful, they damage our attitudes. The following formula will assist you in changing bad habits into good ones.

STEP #1: List your bad habits.

STEP #2: What was the original cause?

STEP #3: What are the supporting causes?

STEP #4: Determine a positive habit to replace the bad one.

STEP #5: Think about the good habit, its benefits and results.

STEP #6: Take action to develop this habit.

STEP #7: Daily act upon this habit for reinforcement.

STEP #8: Reward yourself by noting one of the benefits from your good habit.

Choice #8—Continually choose
to have a right attitude.

Once you make the choice to possess a good attitude, the work really begins. Now comes a life of continual deciding to grow and maintaining the right outlook. Attitudes have a tendency to revert back to their original patterns if not carefully guarded and cultivated.

"The hardest thing about milking cows," observed a farmer, "is that they never stay milked." Attitudes often don't stay changed. There are three stages of change in which you must deliberately choose the right attitude.

Early Stage—The first few days are always the most difficult. Old habits are hard to break. The mental process must be on guard continually to provide right action.

Middle Stage—The moment good habits begin to take root, options open that bring on new challenges. New habits are formed that will either be good or bad. The good news is: "Like begets like." The more right choices and habits you develop, the more likely good habits will be formed.

Later Stage—Complacency can become the enemy. We all know of incidents where someone (perhaps us) successfully lost weight, only to fall back into old eating habits and gain it back.

Our decision to continually choose the right attitude will bring many benefits. A friend with whom I have worked for five years on attitude change told a large conference of leaders, "If you knew me five years ago, you would not recognize me today. My family, ministry and self-image have greatly improved. Daily I work on my attitudes. I am not what I want to be, but I'm not what I used to be either. I want to grow in the next five years like I have the last five. To do this I must continually choose the right attitude." There is no improvement except through change. To improve continually we must change continually.

You are the key to changing your attitude. When faced with the need for improvement, too many people are like the man who walked into a psychiatrist's office. He had placed half a cantaloupe on his head for a hat. Around each ear he had wrapped a piece of bacon. The psychiatrist rubbed his hands in glee, "I've got a live one this time," he thought to himself. Then the man with the cantaloupe on his head and pieces of bacon wrapped around each ear sat down. "I've come," he said to the psychiatrist, "to talk to you about my brother."

No one but you can determine what you will think and how you will act. That is good! Now, take control and begin the exciting journey of attitude improvement.

IT'S UP TO YOU!

If you think you're a winner you'll win,
If you dare to step out you'll succeed.
Believe in your heart, have a purpose to start.
Aim to help fellow man in his need.

Thoughts of faith must replace every doubt.
Use words of courage and you cannot fail.
If you stumble and fall, rise and stand ten feet tall,
You determine the course that you sail.

For in life as in death don't you see,
It's the man who has nothing to fear
Who approaches the gates, stands a moment and
        waits,
Feels the presence of God oh, so near.

You've been given the power to see
What it takes to be a real man.
Let your thinking be pure, it will make you secure.
If you want to, you know that you can.

—Author unknown

— 13 —

The Opportunities
Around You

---

*There are two keys that determine who we are:
who we conceive ourselves to be and who we associate
with.*

— Anonymous

Once you have made the choice to change your attitude,
you are ready to allow the opportunities around you
to make this decision a success.

Opportunity #1—Enlist the cooperation of a friend.

"How could one chase a thousand, and two put ten
thousand to flight, unless their Rock had sold them, and
the Lord had given them up?" (Deuteronomy 32:30).

We need each other! Few people are successful unless
a lot of people want them to be. Change has a tendency to
intimidate us. Add to that intimidation the realization that
we have a long way to go before proper attitudes are
established and we begin to feel like the two cows grazing

in a pasture who saw a milk truck pass. On the side of the truck were the words, "Pasteurized, homogenized, standardized, Vitamin A added." One cow sighed and said to the other, "Makes you feel sort of inadequate, doesn't it?"

To help you overcome this feeling of inadequacy, you need the help of a friend. Find someone who has the spirit of Tanzing, the native guide of Edmund Hillary, who made the historic climb of Mt. Everest.

Coming down from the peak, Hillary suddenly lost his footing. Tanzing held the line taut and kept them both from falling by digging his ax into the ice. Later Tanzing refused any kind of special credit for saving Hillary's life; he considered it a routine part of the job. As he put it, "Mountain climbers always help each other."

Tanzing realized that we can never do anything for others that will not have some eventual benefits for ourselves. There is a law of life which will, in time, return good for good. Therefore, enlisting someone's help will not only assist you but it will also give a friend a blessing in return.

Conditions needed for successful cooperative effort:

1. A friend you can see or talk to daily.

2. Someone who loves you and is an encourager.

3. Someone with whom you have mutual honesty and transparency.

4. A person who is successful in overcoming problems.

5. Someone who has strong faith in God and believes in miracles.

The book of Acts opens with the excitement of the early Church. In the midst of all the joy and growth we see a very significant situation—John and Peter together in ministry and fellowship. The reason? John was encouraging Peter. A few weeks previously, Peter had denied his Lord and wasn't doing particularly well. In fact, he wanted to return to fishing. John, the disciple of love, decided to make Peter his ministry. Acts 3 records the miraculous healing of the lame man, but there was another healing taking place in Peter's life, an inner healing, as John walked with him to the Temple. Could it be that Peter's greatness was at least partially a result of John's acceptance? Go find a friend like John.

Opportunity #2—Associate with the right people.

One morning I walked into my office and saw the following note on top of my desk: "Good morning, Pastor Maxwell. There are two keys to determine who we are: (1) who we perceive ourselves to be and (2) who we associate with."

How true! Yet, as I reflect on that note, I conclude that a large portion of our self-image (who we conceive ourselves to be) is determined by our friendships. Accepting attitudes are based many times on how important the attitude is in complementing or damaging the image we feel other people have of us.

Birds of a feather do flock together. From friends we acquire many of our thoughts, mannerisms and characteristics. Changing an attitude from negative to positive often requires changing friendships. It is no accident that kids with good grades run around with other kids with good grades. While counseling people facing a broken marriage, I have observed that often the couple's friends are having marriage problems.

Many times people blame circumstances for their problems. But usually it is the crowd we run with, not the circumstances we encounter, that makes the difference in our lives. Good circumstances with bad friends result in defeat. Bad circumstances with good friends result in victory.

Some time ago I was listening to commentator Paul Harvey on the radio. He opened the show with the true story of a couple who had applied to adopt a young girl. The couple was turned down by the agency, not because of debt or personality conflicts, but because, according to the agency, their "attitude was too good." They argued that the girl would not get a realistic view of today's world, a view of both the bad and the good side of life.

Can you believe that? I hope you will associate with friends who are positive and keep you from a "realistic" view of today's world. Although it is unrealistic to surround yourself with only positive people, it is possible to choose friends who have a proper outlook on life.

Opportunity #3—Select a model to follow.

Communicators say that 90 percent of what we learn is visual, 9 percent is audio and 1 percent comes through the other senses. Our dependence on the eyes to learn, no doubt, is at least partially a result of television in our culture. Visual messages last longer than those we just hear. You could select someone to follow who would give you a constant visualization of what you want to become. Making a single decision to alter an attitude is not enough. The vision of what you desire must be constantly before you. To achieve the kind of life you want, you must act, walk, talk and conduct yourself as the ideal person that you visualize yourself to be. Gradually that old self will pass away and be replaced with the new one.

The apostle Paul understood and practiced the importance of modeling. In almost every letter to the churches he encouraged the people to follow his example. He told the church at Philippi, "The things you have learned and received and heard from and seen in me, practice these things; and the God of peace shall be with you" (Philippians 4:9). He reminded Timothy, when encouraging him to be an overcomer, "You followed my teaching, conduct, purpose, faith, love, perseverance, persecutions and sufferings" (2 Timothy 3:10,11). Peter commands spiritual leaders "to be examples to the flock" (1 Peter 5:3). The greatest of motivational principles is: People do what people see. As adults we are still playing follow the leader. Nothing will more effectively inspire you to change than having a beautiful example to follow.

My attitudes came as a result of proper modeling by my parents. Usually while speaking at conferences and trying to help people with their attitudes, I give several illustrations from my home life. One couple who listened to these illustrations desperately wanted to change themselves and their children. They decided to invite my mom and dad into their home for a weekend. This time spent together was helpful. One day while my mother was gone, the hostess entered the guest room and began to pray, and she asked God to give her my mother's wisdom and positive strengths just as Elijah's mantle had fallen on the prophet Elisha.

In 1981 I visited the Santiago Methodist Pentecostal Church in Chile, South America. The congregation numbered more than 85,000 members. My heart was moved as I witnessed the wonderful work that God was doing through that congregation. Within a month I would become the senior pastor at Skyline Wesleyan Church in San Diego, California. My desire was to build a great church for God. Realizing that Pastor Vasquez had been greatly blessed by the Lord, I asked him to lay hands on me and pray for God's anointing on my ministry. I look back on that incident and rejoice that I had a model to follow, if only for a few days.

Begin looking for someone to stretch your life. If no

one seems to be available, ask God to send you a Christian with a winning attitude. Ask that individual to disciple you for a few months. Enjoy the experience of growth by example.

Opportunity #4 – Learn from your mistakes.

Pacesetters' Prayer: "Lord, give me the courage to fail; for if I have failed, at least I have tried. Amen."

The first instant an idea is conceived is a moment of decision. When an opportunity for growth is opened to you, what do you tell yourself? Will you grasp the chance with a tingle of excitement and say, "I can make it work!" or do you smother it by saying, "That's impractical . . . too difficult . . . I don't think it can be done"? In that moment, you choose between success and failure. You help to form a habit of either positive or negative thinking by what you tell yourself. So give your "better" self a chance to grow. Form the habit of positive reaction followed by positive action. We cannot cause the wind to blow the way we want, but we can adjust our sails so that they will take us where we want to go.

You cannot control all circumstances. You cannot always make right decisions which bring right results. But you can always learn from your mistakes. The following formula will assist you in making the most of your mistakes.

Formula for Overcoming Failure

1. Recognize

What is failure? Is it permanent? Is there a second chance? Complete this sentence by circling the right phrase.

A person is a failure when

(a) he makes a mistake;

(b) he quits;

(c) someone thinks he is.

2. Review

Failure should be our teacher, not our undertaker. Failure is delay, not defeat. It is a temporary detour, not a dead-end street. A winner is big enough to admit his mistakes, smart enough to profit from them and strong enough to correct them. The only difference between the unsuccessful man and the successful man is that the unsuccessful man is mistaken three times out of five.

3. Repress

Perhaps your own personal problems and hang-ups cause the failure. If so, begin to work immediately on self-discipline. If you are the problem, put yourself under control. Lord Nelson, England's famous naval hero, suffered from seasickness throughout his entire life. Yet the man who had destroyed Napoleon's fleet did not let illness interfere with his career. He not only learned to live with his personal weakness, but he also conquered it. Most of us have our own little seasickness, too. For some it may be physical, for others psychological. Usually it is a private war carried on quietly within us. No one will pin a medal on us for winning it, but nothing can dim the satisfaction of knowing that we did not surrender.

4. Readjust

An eminent plastic surgeon told of a boy who lost his hand at the wrist. When he asked the lad about his handicap, the boy replied, "I don't have a handicap. I just don't have a right hand." The surgeon went on to discover that this boy was one of the leading scorers on his high school football team. It's not what you have lost, but what you have left that counts.

5. Re-enter

Mistakes mark the road to success. He who makes no mistakes makes no progress. Make sure you generate a reasonable number of mistakes. I know that comes naturally to some people, but too many people are so afraid of error that they make their lives rigid with checks and counterchecks, discourage change and, in the end, so structure themselves that they will miss the kind of offbeat opportunity that can send their life skyrocketing. So take a look at your record, and if you come to the end of a year and see that you haven't made many mistakes, ask yourself if you have tried everything you should have.

It is a cliche to say that we learn by our mistakes, so I'll state the case more strongly than that. I'll say you can't learn without mistakes. One reason some people never grow through change is that they can't stand failure. Even the best people have a lot more failure than success. The secret is that they don't let the failures upset them. They do their very best. Let the chips fall where they may, then go on to the next attempt.

In big league baseball, anyone who gets three or more hits in ten trips to the plate is a superstar. It's a matter of percentages. And in life, it's the same way. When you strike out, forget it. If you made some mistakes, learn from them and do better the next time. Strikeouts are part of the game, nothing to be ashamed of. Just get in there and keep swinging!

Opportunity #5—Expose yourself to successful experiences.

It takes five positive experiences to overcome one negative situation. When faced with the possibility of failure, our tendency is to sit back and be anxious. Fear is nature's warning signal to get busy. We overcome it by successful action.

I once heard a speaker say, "We overcome by action." That is only partially true. Experiences that are continually unsuccessful can increase our desire to sit out the game in the arena of life. Action that produces confidence and a degree of success will encourage us to attempt new challenges.

I learned this when I played basketball in high school. One year our coach had a "brilliant" idea that would help us shoot our foul shots with greater accuracy. He replaced the regulation basketball rim with one that was smaller. He thought that if we could hit the smaller basket, it would be a cinch for us to make the larger one in the game. I watched my teammates practice foul shooting on the smaller rim They missed frequently and seemed frustrated. Since I was captain of the team and an 80 percent shot from the foul line, I decided to approach my coach cautiously. My theory was opposite his. It was my belief that continually missing foul shots on the smaller rim would create an image of failure and result in missed shots in a game. That was exactly the result! Thinking back on that incident makes me wonder what would have happened if the coach had placed larger rims upon the backboard.

Nothing intimidates us more than constant exposure to failure. Nothing motivates us more than constant exposure to success. Therefore, I have found that people change more quickly if they are continually given situations in which they can be successful. Believing this, I set out to teach my daughter Elizabeth how to hit a ball with the bat. I didn't want her to stop swinging just because she might miss, because that would have given her a sense of failure, so I gave her the following instructions. "Elizabeth, it is your responsibility to swing the bat. It is my job to hit the bat with the ball when I pitch it."

Elizabeth fearlessly began to swing the bat. She had nothing to lose! Every time she would swing the bat she was a success. The problem — I kept missing the bat with the ball I was throwing. Finally, after many swings and as many misses, Elizabeth threw down the bat, looked at me with disgust and said, "Daddy, you keep missing the bat!"

Start exposing yourself today to successful people and experiences. Read books that will make you a better person. Find something that you can do well and do it often. Help make someone who needs your spiritual gifts a better person. Feed your right attitudes, and before you know it your bad ones will starve to death. Write down your successes and review them often. Share your growth with those who are interested in you and already have excellent attitudes. Take time daily to congratulate yourself and thank others for making this change of attitude possible.

14

The God
Above You

When I am secure in Christ, I can afford to take a risk in my life. Only the insecure cannot afford to risk failure. The secure can be honest about themselves. They can admit failure. They are able to seek help and try again. They can change.
—John Maxwell

A distinguished foreigner was a big help to the American colonists during the Revolutionary War," the history teacher said. "Can you give me his name, Tommy?"

"God," Tommy answered.

E. Stanley Jones made an impressive point when he said, "Anything less than God will let you down." And he went on to explain, "Anything less than God is not rooted in eternal reality. It has a built-in failure." For every possible predicament of man, there is a corresponding grace of God. In other words: For every particular human need there is a particular supernatural resource. For every definite problem there is a definite answer. For every hurt there is a cure. For every weakness there is a strength. For every confusion there is guidance.

If you can understand that truth, your life can be different. Jeremiah understood it when he said, "Ah Lord God! Behold, Thou hast made the heavens and the earth by Thy great power and by Thine outstretched arm! Nothing is too difficult for Thee" (32:17). One of my favorite verses is 2 Chronicles 16:9: "For the eyes of the Lord move to and fro throughout the earth that He may strongly support those whose heart is completely His."

There are several ways that God supports and strengthens our lives while we change.

Strength #1—God's Word

When the truths of the Bible permeate our mind and heart, our attitude can only improve. His Word is filled with people who continually demonstrate that man's right relationship with God gives him a healthy mindset. Paul is just one example.

"I wonder why it is," an Anglican bishop once pondered, "that everywhere the apostle Paul went they had a revolution, and everywhere I go they serve a cup of tea?"

Today we live relatively easy lives. But the apostle Paul could hardly set foot in a city before a riot started. It seemed like Paul was always getting into trouble. During his first missionary journey he was stoned and left for dead. During his second missionary journey he eluded arrest on charges of turning the world upside down. Throughout his life, Paul experienced incredible hardships: imprisonment, flogging, beatings, lashings, shipwreck, destitution, exhaustion. Hardly the "victorious Christian life" we often visualize, wouldn't you say? But despite his intense hardships and sufferings, Paul consistently maintained an attitude of thankfulness and joy. They threw him in a prison. What did he do? Grumble and complain? No! He sang hymns of joy to God (Acts 16:25). They threw him into prison again. He encouraged others to "rejoice in the Lord always" (Philippians 4:4). Paul's dominant attitude—whatever his circumstance—was joy. Where did Paul's joy come from?

Perhaps we can gain insight into Paul's victorious life by reading his letter to the Romans. Chapter 8 gives us what I call "Belief Foundations for a Positive Christian Attitude."

First Foundation—"I am truly significant."

And we know that God causes all things to work together for good to those who love God, to those who are called according to His purpose. For whom He foreknew, He also predestined to become conformed to the image of His Son, that He might be the first-born among many brethren; and who He predestined, these He also called; and whom He called, these He also justified; and whom He justified, these He also glorified (verses 28-30).

My sense of significance grows upon realizing that I am "called according to His purpose" (verse 28); "predestined to become confirmed to the image of His Son" (verse 29); "called . . . justified . . . glorified" (verse 30).

Second Foundation—"I am truly secure."

What then shall we say to these things? If God is for us, who is against us? He who did not spare His own Son, but delivered Him up for us all, how will He not also with Him freely give us all things? Who will bring a charge against God's elect? God is the one who justifies; who is the one who condemns? Christ Jesus is He who died, yes, rather who was raised, who is at the right hand of God, who also intercedes for us. Who shall separate us from the love of Christ? Shall tribulation, or distress, or persecution, or famine, or nakedness, or peril, or sword? Just as it is written, "For Thy sake we are being put to death all day long; we were considered as sheep to be slaughtered." But in all these things we overwhelmingly conquer through Him who loved us. For I am convinced that neither death, nor life, nor angels, nor principalities, nor things present, nor things to come, nor powers, nor height, nor depth, nor any other created thing shall be able to separate us from the love of God, which is in Christ Jesus our Lord (verses 31-39).

When I know that I am secure in Him, I can afford to take a risk in my life. Only the insecure cannot afford to risk failure. The secure can be honest about themselves. They can admit failure. They are able to seek help and try again. They can change.

Many times people ask me to help them overcome some deep problems of their past. One person was having an especially difficult time letting go of his past. This individual's background was horrible—broken home, suicide, failure in business, mental problems and no love. Then, in desperation, there was a desire for a new life, a healing of the mind as well as the soul. That day I read to him a Scripture that will also encourage you:

> Do not call to mind the former things, or ponder things of the past. Behold, I will do something new, now it will spring forth; will you not be aware of it? I will even make a roadway in the wilderness, rivers in the desert (Isaiah 43:18,19).

Remember the words of Jeremiah, "Is anything too hard for the Lord?" The Bible, not Norman Vincent Peale, first said, "All things are possible to him who believes." God's Word, not Maxwell Maltz, author of *Psycho-Cybernetics,* first said, "All things for which you pray and ask, believe that you have received them, and they shall be granted you." The Scriptures, not Robert L. Schuller, first said, "Everything you ask in prayer, believing, you shall receive." God's Word gives us encouragement and guidance to change our lives.

Strength #2—Prayer

Many outstanding prayers in the Bible were effective yet brief. Psalm 25:1-10 is a short, simple and sincere prayer. And it is also successful. The Lord's Prayer consists of 56 words. (Compare that with the 26,911 words in a government order setting the price of cabbage.)

I read in the Colorado Legal Secretaries Association Newsletter that if an attorney had written the line of the Lord's Prayer, "Give us this day our daily bread," it might have read like this: "We respectfully petition, request and entreat that due and adequate provision be made, this date and date first above inscribed, for satisfying of petitioner's nutritional requirements and for the organizing of such methods of allocation and distribution as may be deemed necessary and proper to assure the reception by and for said petitioners of such quantity of cereal products (hereinafter called 'bread') as shall, in the judgment of the afore, and petitioners, constitute sufficient amount."

Psalm 25 describes a person who has chosen the right road yet has not found it always easy to walk. The path is lined with enemies who would like nothing better than to put the weaker to shame. The traveler is also plagued with internal doubts as he recalls previous wanderings and failures. What he must realize is that the road is too difficult to walk without the companionship and friendship of God.

The psalmist, troubled from without and within, has stopped for a moment on the way. He knows he cannot turn back, but scarcely knows how to continue. Therefore he prays that God will help him follow through on his decision to stay on the right road.

We learn five things from this man of prayer in verses 1-10.

1. He knows in which direction to look for help.

To Thee, O LORD, I lift up my soul (verse 1).

The humanist looks only to available human resources. The Christian immediately looks to God. The praying man realizes that God's blessings are not optional. They are a necessity.

2. He knows in whom to trust.

O my God, in Thee I trust, do not let me be ashamed; do not let my enemies exalt over me. Indeed, none of those who wait for Thee will be ashamed; those who deal treacherously without cause will be ashamed (verses 2,3).

An attitude of trust is the key to effective praying based on the character of God. The thrust of our trust must be God-ward.

3. He knows the purpose of prayer.

Make me know Thy ways, O LORD; teach me Thy paths. Lead me in Thy truth and teach me. For Thou art the God of my salvation; for Thee I wait all the day (verses 4,5).

The purpose of prayer is to change. Richard Foster says:

To pray is to change. Prayer is the central avenue God uses to transform us. If we are unwilling to change, we will abandon prayer as a noticeable characteristic of our lives. The more we pray, the more we come to the heartbeat of God. Prayer starts the communication process between ourselves and God. All the options of life fall before us. At that point we will either forsake our prayer life and cease to grow, or we will pursue our prayer life and let Him change us. Either option is painful. To not grow in His likeness is to not enjoy His fullness. When this happens, the priorities of the world begin to fade away.

When we pray, asking God to change a situation, He usually begins with us.

4. He knows the basis of prayer.

Remember, O LORD, Thy compassion and Thy lovingkindness, for they have been from of old. Do not remember the sins of my youth or my transgressions; according to Thy lovingkindness remember Thou me, for Thy goodness' sake, O LORD (verses 6,7).

The psalmist cannot approach God on the basis of his own greatness so he comes "according to Thy lovingkindness." David's change is based on who God is, not what He does.

5. He knows the future of prayer.

Good and upright is the LORD: therefore He instructs sinners in the way. He leads the humble in justice, and He teaches the humble His way. All the paths of the LORD are lovingkindness and truth to those who keep His covenant and His testimonies (verses 8-10).

The future is as solid as God's character. The faithfulness of God is based on His attributes, not your actions. Take those wrong attitudes to Him. Pray the prayer of verses 4 and 5.

Make me — Bring my attitudes under your control (implies trials).

Teach me — Prepare me to know Your truth (implies teachings).

Lead me — Guide and walk with me in it (implies trust).
This order keeps us from wandering off the path.

Lead me — cannot come first.
We cannot trust what we do not know.
We cannot trust what we have not tried.

Teach me—cannot come first.
> Learning without discipline (make me) cannot be
> fully effective.
> Learning without experience (lead me) cannot be
> fully appreciated.

Make me—must come first.
> Once the will is settled, the way is secure.

Once the price is paid, the pathway is plain.
> Prayer changes you. You change your attitudes.

Strength #3—The Holy Spirit

In the New Testament the Spirit is referred to nearly 300 times. The one word with which He is constantly associated is "power." Jesus in John 16:4-16 teaches clearly the need for the Helper in our lives. The disciples were insecure about their future. Jesus said:

> But these things I have spoken to you, that when their hour comes, you may remember that I told you of them. And these things I did not say to you at the beginning, because I was with you. But now I am going to Him who sent Me; and none of you asks Me, "Where are You going?" But because I have said these things to you, sorrow has filled your heart. But I tell you the truth, it is to your advantage that I go away; for if I do not go away, the Helper shall not come to you; but if I go, I will send Him to you. And He, when He comes, will convict the world concerning sin, and righteousness, and judgment; concerning sin because they do not believe in Me; and concerning righteousness, because I go to the Father, and you no longer behold Me; and concerning judgment, because the ruler of this world has been judged. I have many more things to say to you, but you cannot hear them now. But when He, the Spirit of truth, comes, He will guide you into all the truth; for He will not speak on His own initiative, but whatever He hears, He will speak; and He will disclose to you what is to come. He shall glorify Me; for He shall take of Mine, and shall disclose

it to you. All things that the Father has are Mine; therefore I said, that He takes of Mine, and will disclose it to you. A little while, and you will no longer behold Me; and again a little while, and you will see Me.

Jesus said it was "to our advantage" that He would leave so the "Helper" could be sent to us. "The Spirit of truth" will guide us and glorify Jesus. In Acts 1 we read that our Lord was ready to go back to the Father. Surrounded by a few followers, Jesus shared with them these last important words:

> He commanded them not to leave Jerusalem, but to wait for what the Father had promised, "Which," He said, "you heard of from Me; for John baptized with water, but you shall be baptized with the Holy Spirit not many days from now." And so when they had come together, they were asking Him, saying, "Lord, is it at this time You are restoring the Kingdom to Israel?" He said to them, "It is not for you to know the times or epochs which the Father has fixed by His own authority; but you shall receive power when the Holy Spirit has come upon you; and you shall be My witnesses both in Jerusalem, and in all Judea and Samaria, and even to the remotest part of the earth" (Acts 1:4-8).

Power was promised when the Holy Spirit was received. Until Pentecost, the disciples were at best a questionable crew. Of the original twelve, Judas was already gone. James and John certainly were to be questioned about their motives and political desires. Thomas, from Missouri no doubt, continually doubted. (He was probably the father of the church board member.) And there is Peter—glorious one moment, gone the next. Declaring truths, then denying them. What were his plans after the death of Christ? He had fishing on his mind.

Jesus had spent three years with the disciples. They had listened to His teaching, yet they needed something more than learning. He had performed many miracles, yet they were frustrated with their inadequate human endeavors. Upon the disciples' request, Jesus taught them to pray, yet they lacked real power in their lives. The Lord's discipline still had not given His small group of followers the effectiveness they needed to begin the early Church. Jesus knew what they needed. Therefore He encouraged them to wait for the filling of the Holy Spirit in their lives.

They waited, and they were filled. The early Church was launched! The theme of this growing group of believers was "forward through storm." Seven difficult problems confronted this New Testament Church of the book of Acts. After each obstacle, we read that the Church was enlarged and the Word of God multiplied. Setbacks became springboards. Obstacles were turned into opportunities. Barriers turned out to be blessings. Cowards became courageous. Why? Those within the Church were filled with the Holy Spirit.

That same power can be given to you. Changing an attitude is never easy. I have witnessed many attitudes make a positive turnaround through prayer. The following is a case study of a man we'll call Jim. He is thirty-three years old, had a legalistic background, experienced physical abuse as a child (spankings, constant slappings, excessive religious standards, poor father-son relationship, low self-esteem).

Jim says, "We were living in perpetual guilt. Early conversion to Christ was motivated by guilt. If something was fun, then it had to be sin. At age fifteen, I deserted God and ran away from home. When I returned, I did have a genuine experience of salvation. However, it was more than two years before I began to see a light at the end of the tunnel for my rotten attitude. It was during class at Bible college when the Holy Spirit spoke to my heart. I raised my hand and was recognized. I said, 'Professor, would you pray for me? My attitude stinks.' The entire class prayed for me, and I experienced an immediate deliverance. My attitude has slipped from time to time, but I have noticed (and so have those around me) a constant improvement since. I still need improvement, but I'm doing better. Praise the Lord."

As you desire to change and act on your plans to change, remember you're not doing this by yourself. First John 4:4 says: "You are from God, little children, and have overcome them, because greater is He who is in you than he who is in the world."

You will experience that overcoming power as you remember this:

FORMULA FOR SPIRITUAL SUCCESS
If you want to be distressed — look within.
If you want to be defeated — look back.
If you want to be distracted — look around.
If you want to be dismayed — look ahead.
If you want to be delivered — look up!

CHANNELS FOR CHANGE

Daily review this chart. It is designed to

1. encourage you in your pursuit of change;

2. direct you so you won't lose momentum; and

3. fill you with the right information.

Remember: There is no improvement except through change.

I. THE CHOICE WITHIN YOU

Choice #1—EVALUATE YOUR PRESENT ATTITUDES (Philippians 2:5). Are my attitudes today pleasing Christ and me?

Choice #2—THINK, IS YOUR FAITH STRONGER THAN FEAR (Matthew 21:21)? Am I taking faith-action on my present fears?

Choice #3—WRITE A STATEMENT OF PURPOSE (Philippians 3:13,14). Have I written, verbalized and acted on a plan to change my attitude?

Choice #4—DETERMINE IF YOU HAVE THE DESIRE TO CHANGE (Psalm 37:4). Change is possible *if* I want it bad enough. Am I willing to pay the price?

Choice #5—LIVE ONE DAY AT A TIME (Matthew 6:34). Am I allowing tomorrow's troubles to sap me of today's strength?

Choice #6—CHANGE YOUR THOUGHT PATTERNS (Philippians 4:8). That which holds our attention determines our action. Am I thinking on the right things?

Choice #7—DEVELOP GOOD HABITS (Deuteronomy 6:5-9). Am I repeatedly acting on positive habits to overcome negative ones?

Choice #8–CONTINUALLY CHOOSE THE RIGHT ATTITUDE (Proverbs 3:31). Am I continually choosing to change?

II. THE OPPORTUNITIES AROUND YOU

Opportunity #1–ENLIST THE COOPERATION OF A GOOD FRIEND (Deuteronomy 32:30). Do I meet regularly with a friend who helps me?

Opportunity #2–ASSOCIATE WITH THE RIGHT PEOPLE (James 4:4). Are my friends helping or hindering my changes?

Opportunity #3–SELECT A MODEL TO FOLLOW (Philippians 4:9). Am I spending time with a person I admire?

Opportunity #4–LEARN FROM YOUR MISTAKES (John 8:11). What recent mistakes have I made which caused me to change?

Opportunity #5–EXPOSE YOURSELF TO SUCCESSFUL EXPERIENCES (Luke 11:1). What positive event or person will I see today?

III. THE GOD ABOVE YOU

Strength #1–GOD'S WORD (2 Timothy 3:16,17). Am I receiving daily strength from God's Word?

Strength #2–PRAYER (James 5:16). Am I praying daily and specifically about my attitude?

Strength #3–THE HOLY SPIRIT (1 John 4:4). Am I continually being filled with the Holy Spirit?

Notes

Chapter Three

1. J. Sidlow Baxter, *Awake, My Heart* (Grand Rapids, Michigan: Zondervan Publishing House, 1960), p. 10.

Chapter Seven

1. Wesley Tracy, *When Adam Clarke Preached, People Listened* (Kansas City, Missouri: Beacon Hill Press, n.d.), pp. 13,14.

Chapter Eight

1. Judith Viorst, *Alexander and the Terrible, Horrible, No Good, Very Bad Day* (New York: Atheneum Publishers, 1976).

Chapter Nine

1. Source unknown.

STUDY
GUIDE

CHAPTER ONE

It's a Bird . . .
It's a Plane . . .
No, It's an Attitude!

1. Imagine you are the pilot in the cockpit of an airplane. Go ahead, you can do it! So you are flying along. . . . What would you keep your eye on to monitor the performance of the airplane? How could you control performance?

2. Now, imagine yourself seated in the cockpit of your life. What is the critical factor in determining your spiritual, mental, and physical performance, no matter what kind of "weather" you encounter?

3. Rate yourself by the standard of attitude ascribed to Jesus by the apostle Paul. Give yourself a five if you feel really good about yourself on this particular attitude.

   a. I am selfless.

   __0 __1 __2 __3 __4 __5

   b. I am secure.

   __0 __1 __2 __3 __4 __5

   c. I am submissive.

   __0 __1 __2 __3 __4 __5

   Now, if you want to know how others view you, have your spouse or close friend rate you.

4. According to Romans 12:1-2, what needs to happen if our attitude is to reflect God's will for us?

5. Tackle just one life situation that may be giving you fits, one that is clearly affecting your attitude. Apply King David's three-fold process of praise. Describe the process as it applies to your life situation.

   a. Praise begins with the will (Ps. 34:1):

   b. Praise flows to the emotion (Ps. 34:2):

   c. Praise spreads to others (Ps. 34:2–3):

6. Take the attitude indicator test:

Never been better	__Yes __No
Never been worse	__Yes __No
Nose-high	__Yes __No
Nose-down	__Yes __No

CHAPTER TWO

The Attitude—What Is It?

1. Consider a time when you had:
   - a positive attitude.
   - a problem attitude.

   Assess the impact on your family, church, work, and environment. This is not to be a judgmental exercise, but an attempt to assess the impact of attitudes.

2. "That's just my personality," you say. How does personality type affect attitudes toward others? toward life situations?

3. How do facial expressions and body language affect others in a group? How do they affect the speaker?

4. What does your predominant facial expression and body language communicate at home? on the job? in social situations?

5. What is the connection between obedience to Christ and our attitude? (Pages 22-23)

6. In what kinds of situations can we learn to trust the Lord through obedience? (Use the example of the wedding at Cana on page 23.)

7. In what way is your attitude the "librarian of your
   past"?

CHAPTER THREE
The Attitude—Why Is It Important?

1. If you have been getting negative feedback from people, what may that indicate about you?

2. Though it should be obvious, what is the primary force that will determine whether we succeed or fail?

3. Circle your response to the question, "How do you feel the world is treating you?"
   a. Terrible.
   b. Just so-so.
   c. Pretty average.
   d. Really excellent.

4. If your answer is "terrible" or "so-so," would you agree or disagree with the author's statement, "Sometimes the prison of discontent has been built by our own hands"? If you disagree, why?

5. What can we learn from the apostle Paul's statements in Philippians 3:13-14? How can we apply it in our lives?

6. Since we cannot tailor most life situations to fit our desires, what can we do about them? Over what do we have control? (Page 28)

7. What are some of the frustrating, annoying, down-right horrible experiences you are having with others that make a positive attitude appear impossible?

   a. At home:

   b. On the road:

   c. At work:

   d. At church:

8. What role does having a positive attitude in those situations play in making you a loved and successful person? (Pages 31-32)

9. Select the person with whom you are having the greatest difficulty, and for one week seek several opportunities to say positive, encouraging things to that person every day. Evaluate that person's attitude toward you after that week.

10. What gives many achievers that slight edge over their contemporaries, even though their peers may be smarter and better educated? Now, describe someone in your family or circle of acquaintances who demonstrates the qualities you've just listed.

11. Re-read the example of the wife on pages 35 and 36 who followed her husband to a training camp in the desert. In what area of your life can you turn "lemons" into "lemonade," like this woman did?

   a. Life situation:

   b. What I need to do:

12. What are you beginning right now that needs this axiom from page 36: "Our attitude at the beginning of a task will affect its outcome more than anything else"? What key idea that applies to your life situation surfaced as you read the commentary and illustrations?

13. Maxims, short truths, are like jewels that sparkle in many-faceted ways. Write down three maxims that caught your attention as you read the section under "Attitude Axiom #5."

    a.

    b.

    c.

    Now, put them on 3 x 5 cards, add the situation in your life to which each applies, and carry them with you so you can pull them out and let them inspire you anew. If you have access to a computer with graphics, make your own posters.

14. Do you know a "no-limit" person (page 42) in your family, church, community, or work? Analyze what gives that person an edge on others. It is not too late to become a "no-limit" person yourself. Identify the limitation you have placed on yourself and draw from your observation how you could be released to become a "no-limit" person.

15. Why doesn't being a Christian automatically give us a good attitude? If Christ is living in us through the Holy Spirit, who is responsible for our wrong attitudes?

16. For genuine progress, write out the five things that reflect a proper Christian attitude (page 45)—and then insert a life situation to which each attitude can be applied.

   a.

   b.

   c.

   d.

   e.

CHAPTER FOUR

**It's Hard to Soar With the Eagles When
You Have to Live With the Turkeys**

1. Give one example from your family of a behavior or mannerism that reflects the author's comment, "We easily change to fit our environment."

2. Victor Frankl asserted, "The last of the human freedoms is to choose one's attitude in *any* given set of circumstances." Do you agree or disagree? Why or why not? Can you give an example?

3. After reading the story on page 51, reflect on what attitude appears to have been passed from generation to generation in your family. What decision do you need to make?

4. Take time to fill in the **Attitude Application Chart** on page 52. Preferably retreat to your favorite "think it through" place, a special chair, a spot in the yard, a mountain park, or a beach. Pray that God will allow to surface those conditions that you need to recognize as formative, even destructive, and the choices that resulted.

CHAPTER FIVE

Foundational Truths About
the Construction of the Attitude

1. What attitude did you pick up in childhood that still threatens to derail efforts to improve your attitude? If you experienced a childhood with positive attitudes, what elements of that input are providing the "engine" for positive change?

2. What attitude growth, whether positive or negative, do you detect in yourself? in your spouse?

3. The very fact you have been reading *The Winning Attitude* and are working through this study guide provides positive reinforcement of good attitudes. But as part of that reinforcement, record which of your attitudes specifically need deepening and reinforcing. List one step you can take right now to do it.

4. Many adults struggle with experiences like that of the lady who wrote to the author. Rather than concentrating on negative input, ask God to help you find positive reinforcement from significant people in your life. And if at all possible, send at least one of those people a thank you card this week.

5. In what ways, and in what situations, have you been able with God's help to rise "triumphantly to the top" of your personal "well," generating a positive attitude toward the future?

CHAPTER SIX

Materials That Are Used in Constructing an Attitude

1. If you completed the Attitude Application review on pages 60 and 61, re-examine what you wrote in light of the answers you have given in this study guide. The lapse of time, the stirring of memories, may mean you'll want to change some answers you gave earlier.

2. Have you identified which of the four temperaments is most like yours? If so, which of the descriptive phrases used at the bottom of page 62 most accurately describes your attitude?

3. Each of us lives a part of our life in an environment that is negative. For some, home life means constantly battling a spouse's negative attitudes. For others, it may be the office, a specific customer that rubs them the wrong way. Even a long commute can generate increasingly negative attitudes. Describe the most negative environment in your life—and keep it in mind as you work through this book.

4. You've read the author's experiences of adult affirmation. What are yours? Thank God for them! Identify where and how you can provide that kind of affirmation—and write down your response as confirmation of that desire.

5. The author clearly has a positive self-image. He mentions several keys to feeling good about oneself. Highlight them in the text and write them out to fix them in your mind.

6. Notice how the author felt good about helping his daughter succeed. Whom can you help succeed? Write down a plan of action, even though it may be incomplete.

7. The author writes, "We always have a number of opportunities in our hands. We must decide whether or not to take a risk and act on them." What are the opportunities in your life that will demand taking a risk?

8. A leading pastor who experienced an emotional crisis discovered that he had only one friend who provided uplifting, growth-oriented input, more than two dozen who drained him, and several who were neutral. When he returned to active ministry, he determined to significantly increase the number of friends who were self-assured enough to provide positive input. What kind of input do your peers provide? Do you need to seek different peer relationships?

9. Our home environment, the attitudes of our spouse and children, may provide the most negative input we get. If so, what positive steps can we take to overcome that?

- See a pastor or counselor.
- Enter into a prayer pact with a close friend.
- Begin a deliberate campaign to provide positive input to that spouse.
- Lovingly, and in a neutral location (restaurant, park, beach), confront the guilty party.

CHAPTER SEVEN

The Costliest Mistake People Make in Constructing an Attitude

1. What was the label that, upon reflection, proved to be either the most limiting, or provided the greatest challenge for you when trying to break through the SAP barrier?

2. In what areas of your life are you failing to exceed the SAP strata line
   - in terms of physical exertion?
   - in terms of a spiritual discipline?
   - in terms of family experiences?
   - in terms of job risk-taking?

   Now, set a goal in one area that will help you exceed the SAP strata line.

3. Describe one experience that proved so painful that you have never ventured to repeat it. Now, analyze how you could break through the pain barrier in a similar event in the future.

CHAPTER EIGHT

Mayday! Mayday! My Attitude
Is Losing Altitude

1. What are three things the author encourages the reader to remember "when the going gets tough"?

    a.

    b.

    c.

2. Any rough weather? What key thought can keep you going, according to Galatians 6:9?

3. What is our "second wind" in serving the Lord, according to Hebrews 12:1-3?

4. Do you face a potential squall in your home life or on the job? What can you do to avoid it? Apply the following criteria:

    a. Do I lack the experience necessary to weather this storm?

    b. Do I lack the knowledge to navigate through the storm?

    c. Do I lack the time to make necessary preparations?

    d. Do I lack facts to make a proper decision?

    e. Do I lack sufficient prayer to weather the storm?

5. What is your response to the author's statement, "The key to success in decision-making is as much timing as making the right choice"?

6. How can we know if we are not in touch with the "control tower"?

7. "What really matters is what happens in us, not to us." Do you agree or disagree? Why or why not?

CHAPTER NINE

The Crash From Within

1. The author's list of major failures by men we now consider heroes reminds us that failure need not be fatal.

   a. Describe an experience of failure in your life that you thought would destroy you, but it didn't.

   b. Describe an experience of failure that proved, in retrospect, to be a stepping stone.

2. If you are truly honest with yourself, how is fear of failure in a specific area preventing you from making progress?

3. Comment on the author's statement, "Accepting failure in the positive sense becomes effective when you believe that the right to fail is as important as the right to succeed."

4. For the Christian, what are the implications of the statement, "I don't have to survive."

5. Are you facing a crucial ethical or moral issue on the job, in your church, where "survival" is at stake? If so, identify it and describe the key issue at stake.

6. What implication does the following statement have for you: "Until we accept the fact that the future of the world does not hinge on our decisions, we will be unable to forget past mistakes. Attitude is the determining factor of whether our failures make or break us."

7. How does John 12:24,25 relate to the whole issue of fear of failure?

8. What are the four things that discouragement does to us?

   a.

   b.

   c.

   d.

9. What were the factors contributing to the success of Evelyn McFarland as a bus captain?

10. Consider a discouraging situation in your life. Now, apply the four steps the author recommends, describing how they fit your situation.

    a. Positive Action:

    b. Positive Thinking:

    c. Positive Example:

    d. Positive Persistence:

11. How do you relate to the apostle Paul's struggle as described in Romans 7:15-25? Don't be afraid to be real and honest.

12. Examine the eight steps to appropriating purifying power starting on page 115. Pray your way through them, keeping your struggle with specific temptation at the forefront.

CHAPTER TEN

The Crash From Without

1. What would you consider the most traumatic, personally distressing criticism from someone close to you? If you are still smarting from this criticism, analyze whether it was justified (see number 2 at the top of page 120 for a quick test), or a case of "the best fruit is the one the birds pick."

2. Now, evaluate whether that particular criticism is, as in Jesus' case (page 119):
   - an opportunity to comfort.
   - an opportunity to heal.
   - an opportunity to overcome.
   - an opportunity to forgive.

3. What can we learn from Jesus' teaching in Matthew 5:43-48 regarding our response to criticism?

4. Name a friend who encourages you when criticism comes. Then name a person whose criticism is damaging.

5. What is the implication of Robert Louis Stevenson's comment, "I will never permit a row of medicine bottles to block my horizon"? List three or four "medicine bottles" in your life that are threatening to keep your eyes off Jesus' presence and His provisions.

6. What is the "change" that is potentially a source of discomfort
   - in your home:
   - in your church:
   - on the job:
   - in your community:

7. Examine that change and evaluate it in the light of the author's comment, "With the proper attitude, all change, whether positive or negative, will be a learning experience which results in a growing experience." What could be the learning component in that change?

   What could be the growth component?

8. The author writes, "Each generation has three specific functions to perform." Describe ways in which you might be part of this process of change (pages 125 and 126).
   a. Conserve:
   b. Criticize:
   c. Create:

9. Is there a situation in your church where friction may help to "generate the power for progress"? Consider the areas most often the focus of interaction between the older members and the younger members.
   a. Children's Ministry:
   b. Youth Ministry:
   c. Worship and Music Ministry:

10. In the U.S. today the media focuses almost exclusively on negative news. In what ways could this color your thinking about what God could do in the future? So you can bring them before the Lord in prayer and be renewed, list the typically negative thoughts that tend to dominate your life after or while watching the television news.

11. How does negative thinking limit our potential? If possible, respond in terms of a specific situation in your life at home, at church, in the community, on the job.

12. As a mother, father, or supervisor, how are you phrasing your questions in the light of the author's comments on pages 131 and 132?

13. What are some of the "Impossibles" you have achieved or seen others achieve?

14. Is someone challenging you with a "It cannot be done" attitude? What might be your response (consider the author's statements on page 135, beginning with number 3)?

CHAPTER ELEVEN

Up, Up and Away

1. What is the good news for those imprisoned by their bad attitudes?

2. What excuses have you or someone you love been giving for bad attitudes?

3. Read the personal testimony beginning on page 140. Then highlight and write down the four key factors listed on the top of page 142. Evaluate your own position in the light of those comments.

   a.

   b.

   c.

   d.

4. Identify a friend who can pray with you and hold you accountable as you work toward changing a negative attitude.

5. If you have a truly stubborn attitude problem, pray the author's prayer from page 143 or personalize the prayer by writing it out and praying it every day for a month.

CHAPTER TWELVE

The Choice Within You

Ready for real change? This is the action chapter. However, if you have been conscientiously following the suggestions in the Study Guide, you will already be well underway. In this chapter we will focus on key areas, rather than on every step suggested by the author, even though we urge you to take every step in the process he provides.

1. In keeping with the "log jam" illustration, attempt to get at the "root" attitude that spawns the negative attitudes in your life. This will probably mean backpedaling through life, exploring your feelings about events. For some this could be a painful experience, and it could actually require professional help from a Christian counselor. Write down what you at this point consider the "log" that has caused the log jam—the root attitude that tends to prevent change.

2. Now work through the **Stages of Evaluation.**
    a. Identify Problem Feelings:
    b. Identify Problem Behavior:
    c. Identify Problem Thinking:
    d. Identify Biblical Thinking:
    e. Secure Commitment:
    f. Plan and Carry Out Your Choice;

3. Identify the fear in your life. It may be fear of failure, fear of change, fear of criticism. If you are in a group, discuss the common fears that prevent change and illustrate them. After writing down these fears, initiate the **Four-Step Formula to Handle Fear.**

4. Refer back to number 1 for your "log jam" attitude. Now, express clearly what you want to do about it. You may want to use the formula suggested by the author at the bottom of page 151.

5. Though all three steps on pages 152 and 153 are vital, men will probably have the greatest difficulty with number 2, since few men have a close, encouraging friend with whom they can verbalize feelings. If in an earlier study you identified such a friend, write down his name again. Invite this friend to join you for hiking, breakfast, or a walk on the beach. Begin building a relationship that goes beyond discussing sports, job, or politics. Write down your action plan.

6. Highlight the negative words or phrases on page 153 that are most common to you. Now, copy them as part of the process of eliminating them from your vocabulary.

7. What are the three times people are most receptive to change?

   a.

   b.

c.

Look at this list and circle the condition that best describes where you are today.

8. The author writes, "Too many times we settle into a set way of thinking and accept limitations that need not be placed upon us." What are the usual kinds of limitations that prevent people from taking positive steps toward change?

9. Is there a sin, a transgression, or an abuse that is like a chain, holding you to your past? As you read Psalm 51, underline the key truths that mean the most to you. Write out what action you plan to take.

10. Compare your thought patterns with Philippians 4:8. Write out the area that most needs attention if you are to change your thought pattern.

11. Which circle of habits best describes you? If you fit the "Bad Habits" progression, work through the steps on page 162 in terms of only one bad habit at a time.

12. If earlier in this series you identified a negative attitude and began the process of change, at what stage are you? (Refer to page 163.) If at the **Later Stage**, describe how you will get back on track.

CHAPTER THIRTEEN

The Opportunities Around You

1. Review the action suggestion on page 207 (Chapter 12, number 5) to identify the friend you selected. Now, check out the "Conditions Needed for a Cooperative Effort" on page 166 to see if your friend measures up to those suggested qualifications for a friend.

2. Are the qualifications for a friend too idealistic? Can someone be a true friend without meeting every qualification suggested?

3. Why is the following observation true or false: "While counseling people facing a broken marriage, I have observed that often the couple's friends are also having marriage problems"?

4. One of the more difficult steps for a man to take is to admit he needs a model, to identify that model, and to ask for discipling by that model. Yet, amazing progress can be made by both men and women willing to submit to that discipline. If you are a young man, do not be afraid to ask an older man to meet with you regularly for discipling purposes—he will be glad to help. Write out the qualities you are looking for in a model who can assist you in changing a particular attitude.

5. Identify a recent experience of failure. Now, draw on the example of the boy who lost a hand (page 171), evaluating what you have left that is positive.

6. How can we expose ourselves to successful experiences? Do not limit yourself to your immediate circle of friends! A pastor taking on a new assignment in a large inner city church visited five pastors heading up large, successful city churches. He spent a weekend with each before beginning his new ministry and attempted to learn from each one's success. No wonder he is still pastor of a thriving church many years later. He learned and changed. So pick your "winners"; list them, and then deliberately expose yourself to their successful experiences.

CHAPTER FOURTEEN
The God Above You

1. Why do we limit God as we consider change in our lives?

2. Describe your personal feelings as you read the two "Foundation" statements. Have you been able to say them without feelings of doubt?

3. Summarize for yourself why you should be able to say the following confidently:
   a. "I am truly significant."
   b. "I am truly secure."

4. The author provides reassuring Scripture passages, but of even greater value are those you discover for yourself. Using a concordance, look up the word "power" in the letters of Paul. Highlight those verses in your Bible. Copy them on a 3 x 5 card to remind you of Christ's power available to you.

5. If prayer is so important to change, what does it do for you that is truly unique?

6. How can we appropriate the power of the Holy Spirit, since He is the true Change Agent?

7. Write down the specific steps that Jim, described on page 184, took to experience release from a bad attitude.

8. Using that experience as a springboard, what steps can you take to begin the process of change (while keeping in mind 1 John 4:4)?

About the Author

John Maxwell has over 25 years of experience in Christian leadership. Most of those years have been spent as a senior pastor, most recently at Skyline Wesleyan Church in San Diego, California. He has also served as the Executive Director of Evangelism at the Wesleyan World Headquarters. He speaks and conducts seminars throughout the United States and Canada on subjects such as leadership, relationships, church growth, and attitude. Each year he speaks to thousands of pastors and laymen from nearly every denomination.

John is the author of numerous books, including *Be All You Can Be; Be a People Person; Developing the Leader Within You; and Developing the Leaders Around You.*

ADDITIONAL LEADERSHIP AND
PERSONAL GROWTH PRODUCTS
DEVELOPED BY JOHN C. MAXWELL
ARE AVAILABLE FROM

INJOY
1-800-333-6506

Founded in 1985 by John C. Maxwell, INJOY is a leadership development institute committed to increasing the effectiveness of people in all areas of life.

Through INJOY, John Maxwell offers a wide range of training seminars, books, videos and cassette programs designed to increase an individual's ability to influence and lead others.

A unique resource is the INJOY Life Club, a one-hour teaching tape by John Maxwell, mailed monthly to thousands of subscribers. Leaders around the country have been INJOY Life Club members for over ten years.

To receive a catalogue of resources available from INJOY and additional information regarding John Maxwell's speaking itinerary, please call toll-free 1-800-333-6506 or write

INJOY
1530 Jamacha Road
Suite D
El Cajon, CA 92019

JOHN C. MAXWELL

Author of *Developing the Leader Within You*

Developing
The
Leaders
Around
You

This book is dedicated to the men who have developed me:

To Larry Maxwell, my brother, who encouraged in me the desire to grow mentally;

To Glenn Leatherwood, my junior high Sunday school teacher, who inspired me to have a heart for God;

To my high school basketball coach, Don Neff, who instilled in me the desire to win;

To Elmer Towns, pastor and friend, who strengthened my desire to reach my potential;

And above all to my father, Melvin Maxwell, my lifelong mentor. I am a leader today because of the time you spent developing me.

CONTENTS

The Leader's Key Question:

AM I RAISING UP POTENTIAL LEADERS?

One night, after working quite late, I grabbed a copy of *Sports Illustrated,* hoping its pages would lull me to sleep. It had the opposite effect. On the back cover was an advertisement that caught my eye and got my emotional juices flowing. It featured a picture of John Wooden, the coach who led the UCLA Bruins for many years. The caption beneath his picture read, "The guy who puts the ball through the hoop has ten hands."

John Wooden was a great basketball coach. Called the wizard of Westwood, he brought ten national basketball championships to UCLA in a span of twelve years. Two back-to-back championships are almost unheard of in the competitive sports world, but he led the Bruins to *seven titles in a row.* It took a consistent level of superior play; it took good coaching; and it took hard practice. But the key to the Bruins's success was Coach Wooden's unyielding dedication to his concept of teamwork.

He knew that if you oversee people and you wish to develop leaders, you are responsible to: (1) appreciate them for who they are; (2) believe that they will do their very best; (3) praise their

1

accomplishments; and (4) accept your personal responsibility to them as their leader.

Coach Bear Bryant expressed this same sentiment when he said: "I'm just a plowhand from Arkansas, but I have learned how to hold a team together—how to lift some men up, how to calm others down, until finally they've got one heartbeat together as a team. There's always just three things I say: 'If anything goes bad, I did it. If anything goes semi-good, then we did it. If anything goes real good, they did it.' That's all it takes to get people to win." Bear Bryant won people and games. Until a few years ago, he had the greatest number of wins in the history of college football.

Great leaders—the truly successful ones who are in the top 1 percent—all have one thing in common. They know that acquiring and keeping good people is a leader's most important task. An organization cannot increase its productivity—but people can! The asset that truly appreciates within any organization is people. Systems become dated. Buildings deteriorate. Machinery wears. But people can grow, develop, and become more effective if they have a leader who understands their potential value.

> **Acquiring and keeping good people is a leader's most important task.**

The bottom line—and the essential message of this book—is that you can't do it alone. If you really want to be a successful leader, you must develop other leaders around you. You must establish a team. You must find a way to get your vision seen, implemented, and contributed to by others. The leader sees the big picture, but he needs other leaders to help make his mental picture a reality.

Most leaders have followers around them. They believe the key to leadership is gaining more followers. Few leaders surround themselves with other leaders. The ones who do bring great value to their organizations. And not only is their burden lightened, but their vision is carried on and enlarged.

WHY LEADERS NEED TO REPRODUCE LEADERS

The key to surrounding yourself with other leaders is to find the best people you can, then develop them into the best leaders they can be. Great leaders produce other leaders. Let me tell you why:

THOSE CLOSEST TO THE LEADER WILL DETERMINE THE SUCCESS LEVEL OF THAT LEADER

The greatest leadership principle that I have learned in over twenty-five years of leadership is that those closest to the leader will determine the success level of that leader. A negative reading of this statement is also true: Those closest to the leader will determine the level of failure for that leader. In other words, the people close to me "make me or break me." The determination of a positive or negative outcome in my leadership depends upon my ability as a leader to develop those closest to me. It also depends upon my ability to recognize the value that others can give my organization and me. My goal is not to draw a following that results in a crowd. My goal is to develop leaders who become a movement.

Stop for a moment and think of the five or six people closest to you in your organization. Are you developing them? Do you have a game plan for them? Are they growing? Have they been able to lift your load?

Within my organizations—the leadership development institute INJOY and Skyline Wesleyan Church—leadership development is continually emphasized. In their first training session, I give new

3

leaders this principle: *As a potential leader you are either an asset or a liability to the organization.* I illustrate this truth by saying, "When there's a problem, a 'fire' in the organization, you as a leader are often the first to arrive at the scene. You have in your hands two buckets. One contains water and the other contains gasoline. The 'spark' before you will either become a greater problem because you pour the gasoline on it, or be extinguished because you use the bucket of water."

Every person within your organization also carries two buckets. The question a leader needs to ask is, "Am I training them to use the gasoline or the water?"

AN ORGANIZATION'S GROWTH POTENTIAL IS DIRECTLY RELATED TO ITS PERSONNEL POTENTIAL

When conducting leadership conferences, I often make the statement, "Grow a leader—grow the organization." A company cannot grow without until its leaders grow within.

> **Grow a leader —grow the organization.**

I am often amazed at the amount of money, energy, and marketing focus organizations spend on areas that will not produce growth. Why advertise that the customer is Number one when the personnel have not been trained in customer service? When customers arrive, they will know the difference between an employee who has been trained to give service and one who hasn't. Slick brochures and catchy slogans will never overcome incompetent leadership.

In 1981, I became Senior Pastor of Skyline Wesleyan Church in San Diego, California. This congregation averaged 1,000 in attendance from 1969 to 1981, and it was on an obvious plateau. When I assumed leadership responsibilities, the first question I asked was, "Why has the growth stopped?" I needed to find an answer, so I called my first staff meeting and gave a lecture titled *The Leadership Line*. My thesis was, "Leaders determine the level of an organization." I drew a line across a marker board and wrote the number "1,000." I shared with the staff that for thirteen years the average attendance at Skyline was 1,000. I knew the staff could lead 1,000 people effectively. What I did not know was whether they could lead 2,000 people. So I drew a dotted line and wrote the number 2,000, and I placed a question mark between the two lines. I then drew an arrow from the bottom 1,000 line to the top 2,000 line and wrote the word "change."

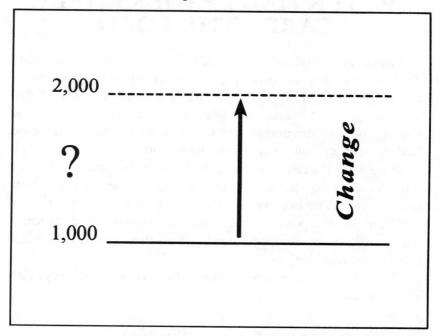

It would be my responsibility to train them and help them make the necessary changes to reach our new goal. When the leaders changed positively, I knew the growth would become automatic. Now, I had to help them change themselves, or I knew I would literally have to change them by hiring others to take their place.

Since 1981, I have given this lecture at Skyline on three occasions. The last time, the number 4,000 was placed on the top line. As I've discovered, the numbers change, but the lecture doesn't. The strength of any organization is a direct result of the strength of its leaders. Weak leaders equal weak organizations. Strong leaders equal strong organizations. Everything rises and falls on leadership.

> **Everything rises and falls on leadership.**

POTENTIAL LEADERS HELP CARRY THE LOAD

Businessman Rolland Young said, "I am a self-made man, but I think if I had it to do over again, I would call in someone else!" Usually leaders fail to develop other leaders either because they lack training or because they possess wrong attitudes about allowing and encouraging others to come alongside them. Often, leaders wrongly believe that they must compete with the people close to them instead of working with them. Great leaders have a different mind-set. In *Profiles in Courage*, President John F. Kennedy wrote, "The best way to go along is to get along with others." This kind of positive interaction can happen only if the leader has an attitude of interdependency with others and is committed to win-win relationships.

Take a look at differences between the two views leaders possess about people:

Winning by Competitiveness	*Winning by Cooperation*
Look at others as enemies	Look at others as friends
Concentrate on yourself	Concentrate on others
Become suspicious of others	Become supportive of others

Win only if you are good	Win if you or others are good
Winning determined by your skills	Winning determined by the skills of many
Small victory	Large victory
Some joy	Much joy
There are winners and losers	There are only winners

Peter Drucker was correct when he said, "No executive has ever suffered because his people were strong and effective." The leaders around me lift my load in many ways. Here are two of the most important ones:

They become a sounding board for me.

As a leader, I sometimes hear counsel that I don't want to hear but need to hear. That's the advantage of having leaders around you—having people who know how to make decisions. Followers tell you what you want to hear. Leaders tell you what you need to hear.

I have always encouraged those closest to me to give me advice on the front end. In other words, an opinion before a decision has potential value. An opinion after the decision has been made is worthless. Alex Agase, a college football coach, once said, "If you really want to give me advice, do it on Saturday afternoon between one and four o'clock, when you've got twenty-five seconds to do it, between plays. Don't give me advice on Monday. I know the right thing to do on Monday."

They possess a leadership mind-set.

Fellow leaders do more than work with the leader, they think like the leader. It gives them the power to lighten the load. This

7

becomes invaluable in areas such as decisionmaking, brainstorming, and providing security and direction to others.

National opportunities and responsibilities often take me away from my local congregation. It is essential for me to have leaders who can carry on effectively while I am gone. And they do. It happens because I have spent my life finding and developing potential leaders. The results are very gratifying.

This leadership mind-set of sharing the load is wonderfully demonstrated by, of all things, geese, as illustrated by Tom Worsham:

> When you see geese heading south for the winter flying along in a "V" formation, you might be interested in knowing that science has discovered why they fly that way. Research has revealed that as each bird flaps its wings, it creates an uplift for the bird immediately behind it. By flying in a "V" formation, the whole flock adds at least 71 percent greater flying range than if each bird flew on its own. *(People who share a common direction and sense of community get where they are going more quickly and easily because they are traveling on one another's thrust.)*
>
> Whenever a goose falls out of formation, it suddenly feels the drag and resistance of trying to go it alone. It quickly gets back into formation to take advantage of the lifting power of the bird immediately in front. *(If we as people have as much sense as a goose, we will stay in formation and so will those who are headed the same way we are.)* When the lead goose gets tired, he rotates back in the "V" and another goose flies the point. *(It pays to take turns doing hard jobs.)*
>
> The geese honk from behind to encourage those up front to keep up their speed. *(What do we say when we honk from behind?)*
>
> And finally, when a goose gets sick, or is wounded by gunfire and falls out, two other geese fall out of formation and

follow it down to help and protect it. They stay with the goose until it is either able to fly again or dead, and then they launch out on their own or with another formation to catch up with their group. *(If we have the sense of a goose, we will stand by each other like that.)*

Whoever was the first to call another person a "silly goose" didn't know enough about geese.[1]

LEADERS ATTRACT POTENTIAL LEADERS

Birds of a feather really do flock together. I really believe that it takes a leader to know a leader, grow a leader, and show a leader. I have also found that it takes a leader to attract a leader.

Attraction is the obvious first step, yet I find many people in leadership positions who are unable to accomplish this task. True leaders are able to attract potential leaders because:

- Leaders think like them.
- Leaders express feelings that other leaders sense.
- Leaders create an environment that attracts potential leaders.
- Leaders are not threatened by people with great potential.

For example, a person in a leadership position who is a "5" on a scale of 1 to 10 will not attract a leader who is a "9." Why? Because leaders naturally size up any crowd and migrate to other leaders who are at the same or higher level.

It takes a leader to know a leader, grow a leader, and show a leader.

Any leader who has only followers around him will be called upon to continually draw on his own

9

resources to get things done. Without other leaders to carry the load, he will become fatigued and burnt out. Have you asked yourself lately, "Am I tired?" If the answer is yes, you may have a good reason for it, as this humorous story illustrates:

> Somewhere in the world there is a country with a population of two hundred twenty million. Eighty-four million are over sixty years of age, which leaves 136 million to do the work. People under twenty years of age total ninety-five million, which leaves forty-one million to do the work.
>
> There are twenty-two million employed by the government, which leaves nineteen million to do the work. Four million are in the Armed Forces, which leaves fifteen million to do the work. Deduct 14,800,000, the number in state and city offices, and that leaves 200,000 to do the work. There are 188,000 in hospitals or insane asylums, so that leaves 12,000 to do the work.
>
> It is of interest to note that in this country 11,998 people are in jail, so that leaves just two people to carry the load. That's you and me—and brother, I'm getting tired of doing everything myself!

Unless you want to carry the whole load yourself, you need to be developing leaders.

LEADERS WHO MENTOR POTENTIAL LEADERS MULTIPLY THEIR EFFECTIVENESS

Not long ago, at a conference where management expert Peter Drucker was speaking, thirty of my leaders and I were continually challenged to produce and mentor other leaders. Peter asked us,

"Who will take your place?" He kept emphasizing, "There is no success without a successor."

I left that meeting with one resolve: *I was going to produce leaders who could produce other leaders.* No longer was it enough to grow by adding leaders. Now, my focus was upon *multiplying* those leaders. To accomplish this, I began to train my leaders to learn the fine art of setting parameters and priorities. I wanted them to gain a deep understanding of our goals and then go out into our organization and train others to someday replace them or help carry the load.

There is no success without a successsor.

The board of my organization has always been my focus when developing leaders. In 1989, one half of my board members were brand new, and the group faced major decisions on a $35 million relocation project. I was concerned. Could decisions of such magnitude be made by rookies? However, my fears subsided at the next board retreat when I discovered that every new board member had been mentored by former, experienced members. The old board had heard me and implemented my teachings, and the new board was now benefiting. The new members had come into their positions already running with the rest of us. It was then that I realized an important lesson: *Leaders create and inspire new leaders by instilling faith in their leadership ability and helping them develop and hone leadership skills they don't know they possess.*

My experience with the board shows what happens when people work together—side by side. When people work for a common cause, they no longer *add* to their growth potential. Their unity *multiplies* their strength. The following anecdote further illustrates my point:

At a Midwestern fair, many spectators gathered for an old-fashioned horse pull (an event where various weights are put on a horse-drawn sled and pulled along the ground). The

11

grand-champion horse pulled a sled with 4,500 pounds on it. The runner-up was close, with a 4,400-pound pull. Some of the men wondered what the two horses could pull if hitched together. Separately they totaled nearly 9,000 pounds, but when hitched and working together as a team, they pulled over 12,000 pounds.

DEVELOPED LEADERS EXPAND AND ENHANCE THE FUTURE OF THE ORGANIZATION

Recently I was asked to speak at a conference on the subject, *How to structure your organization for growth.* I politely refused. I am convinced that structure can aid growth but not give it. Pollster George Barna said, "Great organizations may have great leaders and a poor structure, but I've never seen a great organization that had a great structure and a poor leader." Structure can mean the difference between a bad organization and a good one. But the difference between a good organization and a great one is leadership.

Henry Ford knew this. He said, "You can take my factories, burn up my buildings, but give me my people, and I'll bring my business right back again." What did Henry Ford know that so many other people in leadership positions don't know? He knew that buildings and bureaucracy are not essential to growth. A company must organize around what it is trying to accomplish, not around what is being done. I have seen people in an organization do things a particular way simply because the bureaucracy states it must be done that way, even when it hinders what the organization is trying to accomplish. Organize around tasks, not functions.

Too often we are like the community that built a new bridge:

> The residents of a small town built a new bridge. Then they decided that, if they had a new bridge, they'd better hire

12

a watchman to keep an eye on it. So they did. Someone noted that the watchman needed a salary, so they hired an accountant. He in turn pointed out the need for a treasurer. With a watchman, an accountant, and a treasurer, they had to have an administrator, so residents appointed one. Congress then voted a cut in funding, and personnel had to be cut back. So, they fired the watchman!

Don't let the machinations or trappings of your organization make you lose sight of what's to be accomplished.

One of the things my father taught me was the importance of people above all other elements in an organization. He was the president of a college for sixteen years. One day, as we sat on a campus bench, he explained that the most expensive workers on campus were not the highest paid. The most expensive ones were the people who were nonproductive. He explained that developing leaders took time and cost money. You usually had to pay leaders more. But such people were an invaluable asset. They attracted a higher quality of person; they were more productive; and they continued to add value to the organization. He closed the conversation by saying, "Most people produce only when they feel like it. Leaders produce even when they don't feel like it."

THE MORE PEOPLE YOU LEAD THE MORE LEADERS YOU NEED

Moses was the greatest leader in the Old Testament. How would you like to relocate one and a half million complaining people? It was hard . . . and tiring. And as his nation grew, Moses became more tired, and the people's needs went unmet.

The problem? Moses was trying to do it all himself. His *Disorganization Chart* looked like this:

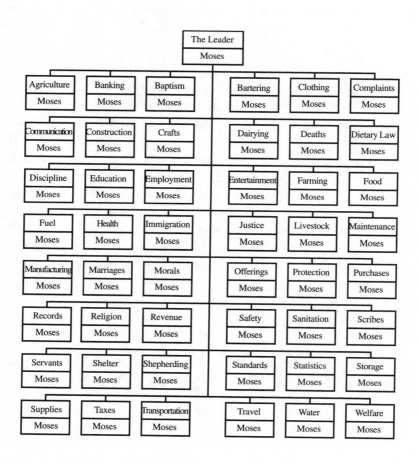

Jethro, the father-in-law of Moses, suggested that he find, recruit, and train other leaders to assist him in his leadership responsibilities. Moses followed that advice, and soon he had other leaders helping him carry the load. The result? This needed change gave added strength to Moses and enabled all the needs of the people to be met.

Zig Ziglar says, "Success is the maximum utilization of the ability that you have." I believe a leader's success can be defined as *the maximum utilization of the abilities of those under him*. Andrew Carnegie explained it like this: "I wish to have as my epitaph: 'Here lies a man who was wise enough to bring into his service men who knew more than he.' " It is my desire that the following pages help you do exactly that.

> **A leader's success can be defined as the maximum utilization of the abilities of those under him.**

The Leader's Toughest Challenge:

CREATING A CLIMATE FOR POTENTIAL LEADERS

Those who believe in our ability do more than stimulate us— they create an atmosphere in which it becomes easier for us to succeed. Creating an environment that will attract leaders is vital to any organization. Doing that is the job of leaders. They must be active; they must generate activity that is productive; and they must encourage, create, and command changes in the organization. They must create a climate in which potential leaders will thrive.

LEADERS MUST BE ENVIRONMENTAL CHANGE AGENTS

The leaders in any organization must be the environmental change agents. They must be more like thermostats than thermometers. At first glance, a person could confuse these instruments. Both are capable of measuring heat. However, they are really quite different. A thermometer is passive. It records the temperature of its environment but can do nothing to change that environment. A thermostat is an active instrument. It determines what the environment will be. It effects change in order to create a climate.

The attitude of the leader, coupled with a positive atmosphere in the organization, can encourage people to accomplish great things. And consistent accomplishment generates momentum. Many times momentum is the only difference between a winning, positive growth climate and a losing, negative growth climate.

Leaders cannot afford to overlook the importance of momentum:

With momentum,	Leaders look better than they actually are.
With momentum,	Followers increase their performance.
Without momentum,	Leaders look worse than they actually are.
Without momentum,	Followers decrease their performance.

Momentum is the greatest of all change agents. Over 90 percent of the successful changes we've instituted in our organization have been the result of creating momentum before asking people to change.

To maximize the *value* of momentum, leaders must: (1) develop an appreciation for it *early*; (2) know the key ingredients of it *immediately*; and (3) pour resources into it *always.*

The next time you find it difficult to adjust the environment in your company, keep in mind this simple fact from the laws of physics: Water boils at 212 degrees, but at 211 degrees, it is still just hot water. One extra degree, an increase of less than one half of one percent, can make the difference between a pot of languishing liquid and a bubbling caldron of power. One degree can create a full head of steam—enough power to move a train weighing tons. That one degree is usually momentum.

Leaders in some organizations don't recognize the importance of creating a climate conducive to building potential leaders. They don't understand how it works. Advertising executive William Bernbach, who understands the difference it makes, once stated, "I'm always amused when other agencies try to hire my people away. They'd have to 'hire' the whole environment. For a flower to blossom, you need the right soil as well as the right seed." Until the leaders in an organization realize this, they will not succeed, regardless of the talented individuals they bring into the firm. Right atmosphere allows potential leaders to bloom and grow. That is why the atmosphere needs to be valued and developed first.

Momentum is the greatest of all change agents.

Even when a leader from an organization with a poor climate steals away a potential leader who is beginning to bloom from the rich "greenhouse" environment of a healthy organization, the potential leader will not continue to grow and bloom. Unless, of course, the leader has already converted the environment of his own organization from "arctic" to "tropical."

To see the relationship between environment and growth, look at nature. An observation was made by a man who dives for exotic fish for aquariums. According to him, one of the most popular aquarium fish is the shark. The reason for this is that sharks adapt to their environment. If you catch a small shark and confine it, it will stay a size proportionate to the aquarium in which it lives. Sharks can be six inches long and fully mature. But turn them loose in the ocean and they grow to their normal size.

The same is true of potential leaders. Some are put into an organization when they are still small, and the confining environment ensures that they stay small and underdeveloped. Only leaders can control the environment of their organization. They can be the change agents who create a climate conducive to growth.

LEADERS MUST MODEL THE LEADERSHIP THEY DESIRE

According to noted medical missionary Albert Schweitzer, "Example is not the main thing in influencing others . . . it is the only thing." Part of creating an appealing climate is modeling leadership. People emulate what they see modeled. Positive model—positive response. Negative model—negative response. What leaders do, potential leaders around them do. What they value, their people value. The leaders' goals become their goals. Leaders set the tone. As Lee Iacocca suggests, "The speed of the boss is the speed of the team." A leader cannot demand of others what he does not demand of himself.

As you and I grow and improve as leaders, so will those we lead. We need to remember that when people follow us, they can only go as far as we go. If our growth stops, our ability to lead will stop along with it. Neither personality nor methodology can substitute for personal growth. We cannot model what we do not possess. Begin learning and growing today, and watch those around you begin to grow. As a leader, I am primarily a follower of great principles and other great leaders.

FOCUS ON THE POTENTIAL OF THE LEADER AND THE ORGANIZATION

As stated before, those who believe in our ability do more than stimulate us. They create an atmosphere in which it becomes easier to succeed. The opposite is also true. When a leader does not believe in us, success is very difficult for us to achieve. It becomes nearly impossible. As leaders, we cannot allow this to happen to those we lead if we expect our organizations to succeed.

To ensure success, identify the potential in each future leader and cultivate it in light of the needs of the organization. It produces a win-win situation. The mentoring leader wins because of the rising star working beneath him or her who can perform and produce. The organization wins because its mission is being fulfilled. The potential leader wins because he is being developed and improved. His future looks bright.

One of the best applications of this idea is expressed in what I call the 101 percent principle: *Find the one thing that you believe is the potential leader's greatest asset, and then give 100 percent encouragement in that area.* Focusing on a person's strengths promotes positive growth, confidence, and success as a potential leader.

FOCUS ON THE POTENTIAL LEADER'S NEEDS (DESIRES)

People often associate great achievement with a number of things: luck, timing, circumstance, or natural talent. The secret to a person's success often appears to be an elusive quality. Not long ago, the University of Chicago did a five-year study of leading artists, athletes, and scholars to determine what made them successful. Conducted by Dr. Benjamin Bloom, the research was based on anonymous interviews with the top twenty performers in various fields. Included were a variety of professionals such as concert pianists, Olympic swimmers, tennis players, sculptors, mathematicians, and neurologists. Bloom and his team of researchers probed for clues as to how these high achievers developed. For a more complete picture, they also interviewed their families and

21

teachers. The report stated conclusively that drive, determination, and desire, not great natural talent, led to the extraordinary success of these individuals.

Great leaders know the desires of the people they lead. As much as potential leaders respect the knowledge and ability of their leaders, these are secondary matters to them. They don't care how much their leaders *know* until they know how much their leaders *care* . . . about their needs, their dreams, their desires. Once a leader is genuinely interested in the well-being of those around him, the determination and drive of the people in that group are activated in a remarkable way. The starting point of all achievement is drive, determination, and desire.

Napoleon Bonaparte is known as one of history's greatest leaders. One of his leadership secrets was knowing the needs of his men. He first determined what his men wanted most. Then he did everything possible to help them get it. He knew this was a key to successful motivation. Most leaders do the opposite. They first decide what *they* want. Then they try to persuade others to want the same thing as much as they do.

LOOK FOR THE LEADER WITHIN THE PERSON

> **It takes a leader with vision to see the future leader within the person.**

There is no future in any job. The future lies in the person who holds the job. It takes a leader with vision to see the future leader within the person. Michelangelo, when questioned about his masterpiece *David*, answered that the sculpture had always existed within the stone. He had simply chiseled away the rock around it. Leaders must have the same kind of vision when viewing potential leaders. Some of the qualities to look for in a person include the following:

22

Positiveness: the ability to work with and see people and situations in a positive way

Servanthood: the willingness to submit, play team ball, and follow the leader

Growth potential: a hunger for personal growth and development; the ability to keep growing as the job expands

Follow-through: the determination to get the job done completely and with consistency

Loyalty: the willingness to always put the leader and the organization above personal desires

Resiliency: the ability to bounce back when problems arise

Integrity: trustworthiness and solid character; consistent words and walk

"Big picture" mind-set: the ability to see the whole organization and all of its needs

Discipline: the willingness to do what is required regardless of personal mood

Gratitude: an attitude of thankfulness that becomes a way of life

When searching for these traits within a person, the leader should emulate gold prospectors. They are always on the lookout for potential gold mines. Every mountain is a possible opportunity to strike it rich. When they find traces of ore, they assume there is a vein and begin digging. Just as I have told the pastors I lead, there's gold in "them thar pews." The same is true in every organization. If you as a leader look for and find traces of gold in your people, start digging. You will uncover the mother lode!

PLACE AN EMPHASIS ON PRODUCTION, NOT POSITION AND TITLE

Organizations that place great emphasis on titles and position are teaching their employees to do the same. Employees in that type of environment can often become preoccupied with moving up the ladder to the next position or with receiving a more important-sounding title. When it comes down to it, titles are worth little. A lofty title doesn't help a poor producer. A lowly title doesn't hinder a super producer. Position, like a title, doesn't make a leader either.

In *Developing the Leader Within You,* I describe the five levels of leadership: position, permission, production, personnel development, and personhood. *Position* is the lowest level. A person who stands on his position will never have influence beyond his or her job description.

Seniority also provides little in and of itself. A survey was recently conducted by Accountemps, a temporary personnel service and placement organization. Executives and personnel directors were asked for the most influential factors in evaluating an employee for promotion. The results: 66 percent named specific accomplishments, 47 percent named general work habits and performance, and only 4 percent cited seniority as being important. Time on the job is no substitute for production in the job.

In an organization emphasizing production, attention and energy are devoted to doing the job and doing it well. There is a team atmosphere, with accomplishing the mission of the organization as the goal. That is the kind of climate where leaders emerge. As Charles Wilson, the president of General Electric, has said, "No matter what size the bottle, the cream always came to the top."

24

PROVIDE GROWTH OPPORTUNITIES

There is a story of a tourist who paused for a rest in a small town in the mountains. He went over to an old man sitting on a bench in front of the only store in town and inquired, "Friend, can you tell me something this town is noted for?" "Well," replied the old man, "I don't rightly know except that it's the starting point to the world. You can start here and go anywhere you want."

All people do not view their current location as the starting point to wherever they want to go in the world. We as leaders must encourage those around us to see themselves in such a place. Creating an environment for personal growth is critical. However, if the people around you are unaware they are in such an environment, they may not take advantage of it. That is one reason why it is important to *create opportunities for growth.* Another reason is that established leaders are in a position to know what opportunities a potential leader needs.

In order to create the right opportunities, we must look at the potential leaders around us and ask, "What does this person need in order to grow?" A generic formula will not work. If we don't fit the opportunity to the potential leader, we may find ourselves in the position of offering things that our people don't need.

> **We must look at the potential leaders around us and ask, "What does this person need in order to grow?"**

Ernest Campbell, a faculty member at Union Theological Seminary, tells an enlightening story:

> A woman went to a pet store and purchased a parrot to keep her company. She took her new pet home but returned the next day to report, "That parrot hasn't said a word yet!"

"Does it have a mirror?" asked the storekeeper. "Parrots like to be able to look at themselves in the mirror." So she bought the mirror and returned home.

The next day she was back, announcing that the bird still wasn't speaking.

"What about a ladder?" the storekeeper said. "Parrots enjoy walking up and down a ladder." So she bought a ladder and returned home.

Sure enough, the next day she was back with the same story—still no talk.

"Does the parrot have a swing? Birds enjoy relaxing on a swing." She bought the swing and went home.

The next day she returned to the store to announce the bird had died.

"I'm terribly sorry to hear that," said the storekeeper. "Did the bird ever say anything before it died?"

"Yes," the lady replied. "It said, 'Don't they sell any food down there?'"

Many leaders are like the lady in the story. They want their people to produce. When the people don't, the leaders provide them with all the things some expert says they are supposed to like. However, the leaders themselves never look at their people to see what they really need.

As you examine potential leaders and determine what each needs, keep in mind these ideas for growth opportunities:

- Expose the potential leader to people successful in his field.
- Provide a secure environment where the potential leader is free to take risks.
- Provide the potential leader with an experienced mentor.

- Provide the potential leader with the tools and resources he needs.
- Spend the time and money to train the potential leader in his areas of need.

The idea of building potential leaders through growth opportunities can be summed up in this poem by Edwin Markham:

We are blind until we see
That in the human plan
Nothing is worth the making
If it does not make the man.

Why build these cities glorious
If man unbuilded goes?
In vain we build the world
Unless the builder also grows.[2]

LEAD (DON'T MANAGE) WITH VISION

An important part of leadership involves casting vision. Some leaders forget to cast vision because they get caught up in managing. True leaders recognize a difference between leaders and managers. Managers are maintainers, tending to rely on systems and controls. Leaders are innovators and creators who rely on people. Creative ideas become reality when people who are in a position to act catch the vision of their innovative leader.

An effective vision provides guidance. It gives direction for an organization . . . direction that cannot effectively result from rules and regulations, policy manuals, or organizational charts. True direction for an organization is born with a vision. It begins

27

when the leader accepts it. It gains acceptance when the leader models it. And it becomes reality when the people respond to it.

DO BIG THINGS

Nearly everything a leader does hinges on the type of vision he has. If his vision is small, so will be his results and his followers. A high-ranking French official who understood this concept once expressed it thus when addressing Winston Churchill: "If you are doing big things, you attract big men. If you are doing little things, you attract little men. Little men usually cause trouble." An effective vision attracts winners.

Too often people limit their own potential. They think small. They are afraid of risk. People no longer willing to stretch are no longer able to grow. As author Henry Drummond says, "Unless a man undertakes more than he possibly can do, he will never do all he can do."

SPEND MORE EFFORT ON THE "FARM TEAM" THAN ON THE FREE AGENTS

Once a leader has a vision, he needs to build a team to carry it out. Where does he find winners? It's not easy. In fact, most winners are made, not found. In major league baseball, teams generally recruit players in one of two ways. They either bring players up from their own minor league farm teams or go outside the organization in search of free agents. Time after time, baseball fans have seen their teams bring in expensive free agents with the expectation of winning a World Series. Time after time they are disappointed.

The "farm team" method involves bringing in the best undeveloped players who can be found and allowing them to start with the organization at their own level. They are coached and developed. Their managers and coaches discover their strengths and weaknesses and find the right positions for them. The players gain experience and have an opportunity to bring up their level of play. If their performance is good enough, they get promoted to the major league team.

The vast majority of the leadership in our organization is recruited and promoted from within. It has not always been easy, but there are tremendous advantages in using the farm team method. The first is that you already know the individual's character and attitude. When you interview somebody on the outside, you take a risk. You have to base a hiring decision on what the potential employee and the recommendations tell you. Job descriptions on a resume address skills, not character. Most employers agree that character and attitude are the most important factors in hiring a new employee. Skills can be taught.

The second advantage is that a person promoted from within already knows the organization and its people. A successful employee who is considered for promotion has already caught the leader's vision. He shares the philosophy of the organization. He has spent time building relationships with the people. A person brought in from outside must spend time learning these things. Once hired, he may even be unwilling or unable to assimilate. When you hire people from within, they hit the ground running.

The third advantage is that a person brought up from the farm team is a proven performer. You have already seen his gifts and impact. You know he can hit the ball in your park. As a result, the risk is relatively small. With a free agent, you have had limited opportunity to observe him firsthand. It is possible that he may not be able to hit the ball in your park, because the conditions are different. Developing the talent on your farm team will require strategic action and a particular attitude from the team's leader. The leader must:

- Invest time and money in his potential leaders.
- Commit to promoting from within.

- Show his people that personal and professional growth within the organization are not only possible but also actual.

MAKE DIFFICULT DECISIONS

Willard C. Butch, chairman of the Chase Manhattan Corporation, was once given some advice by Marion Folsom, then a top Eastman Kodak Company executive: "Bill, you're going to find that 95 percent of all the decisions you'll ever make in your career could be made as well by a reasonably intelligent high school sophomore. But they'll pay you for the other five percent."

Some of the toughest decisions a leader faces concern poor performers. Great leaders make smart choices concerning them. A leader who does not effectively handle them will hurt:

- the organization's ability to achieve its purpose
- the morale of top performers
- his own credibility
- the low performers' self-image and potential effectiveness

To discover the proper course concerning a poor performer, a leader needs to ask himself, "Should this person be trained, transferred, or terminated?" The answer will determine the appropriate course of action.

If low performance is due to poor or undeveloped skills, it calls for training. Likewise, training can often benefit an employee needing to be taught the organization's philosophy or vision. Training is often the most positive of solutions, because it invests in the employee. It is also more economical to improve a current employee than start a new person from scratch.

Sometimes an employee is a low performer because he is expected to perform a job that does not match his gifts and abilities.

If the employee has a good attitude and a desire to succeed, he can be transferred to a position matching his gifts. There he may flourish.

Terminating an employee is by far the most difficult of the tough decisions a leader faces. It is also one of the most important decisions he may make. In fact, removing poor performers from an organization is as important as finding good ones. Terminating a poor performer benefits the organization and everyone in it. It also gives the former employee the opportunity to reevaluate his potential and find the place and position where he or she can be a winner.

PAY THE PRICE
THAT ATTRACTS LEADERS

Success always comes at a price. That is a lesson I learned a long time ago. My father taught me that a person can pay now and play later, or he can play now and pay later. Either way, he is going to pay.

Creating a climate for potential leaders also requires a leader to pay a price. It begins with personal growth. The leader must examine himself, ask himself the hard questions, and then determine to do the right thing regardless of atmosphere or mood. There are few ideal and

> **A person can pay now and play later, or he can play now and pay later.**

leisurely settings for the disciplines of growth. Most of the significant things done in the world were done by persons who were either too busy or too sick to do them. Emotion-based companies allow the atmosphere to determine the action. Character-based companies allow the action to determine the atmosphere.

Successful leaders recognize that personal growth and the development of leadership skills are lifetime pursuits. Warren Bennis and Burt Nanus, in *Leaders: The Strategies for Taking Charge,* did a

31

study of ninety top leaders in all fields. They found that "it is the capacity to develop and improve their skills that distinguishes leaders from their followers." They came to the conclusion that "leaders are perpetual learners."

Commitment to provide a climate where potential leaders may grow must start with the leader's commitment to personal growth. Answer the following questions to determine your current commitment level.

QUESTIONS ON COMMITMENT TO PERSONAL GROWTH

1. Do I have a game plan for personal growth?   Yes No

2. Am I the leader of that plan?   Yes No

3. Am I willing to change to keep growing, even if it means giving up my current position if I am not experiencing growth?   Yes No

4. Is my life an example for others to follow?   Yes No

5. Am I willing to pay the price to become a great leader?   Yes No

A no on any of these questions should cause a leader to examine his plan and commitment to personal growth. A lack of commitment on the part of a leader makes it difficult for potential leaders around him to be developed. If you as a leader have not made this commitment, your future is limited, and you will never become a great leader. Now is the time to change.

The environment in which you work will influence you and those you lead. Answer the following questions to help determine your organization's dedication to developing leaders and providing a climate that promotes organizational and personal growth.

QUESTIONS TO ASK CONCERNING ORGANIZATIONAL GROWTH

1. Has the organization made a specific commitment to grow and develop people?
    Seldom   Sometimes   Usually

2. Is the organization willing to spend money to develop employees' growth?
    Seldom   Sometimes   Usually

3. Is the organization willing to make changes to keep itself and its people growing?
    Seldom   Sometimes   Usually

4. Does the organization support leaders willing to make the difficult decisions necessary for people's personal growth and the growth of the organization?
    Seldom   Sometimes   Usually

5. Does the organization place an emphasis on production rather than position or title?
    Seldom   Sometimes   Usually

6. Does the organization provide growth opportunities for its people?
    Seldom   Sometimes   Usually

7. Do organizational leaders have vision and share it with their people?
    Seldom   Sometimes   Usually

8. Does the organization think big?
    Seldom   Sometimes   Usually

9. Does the organization promote from within?
    Seldom   Sometimes   Usually

10. Are there other leaders in the organization willing to pay
    the price of personal sacrifice to insure their growth and the
    growth of others?
    Seldom   Sometimes   Usually

If the majority of the answers to these questions is Seldom or
Sometimes, a change is in order. If the organization is controlled
by you, begin changing now. If you head a department in the
organization, then you are in a position to make positive changes.
Do as many things as your organization will allow to create a positive climate for potential leaders. If you are in a position only to
make changes for yourself, try to find someone in the organization
who will develop you—or change your job. Great leaders share
themselves and what they have learned with the learners who will
become tomorrow's leaders. A person can impress potential leaders from a distance, but only from up close can he impact them.

> **Great leaders share themselves and what they have learned.**

Here are a few closing thoughts on
creating a climate for potential leaders.
Sports records provide tangible evidence
of the positive changes that can occur
when the right climate has been established. One Olympic athlete, Pat
O'Brien, won a gold medal by throwing
a 16-pound shot 57 feet to set a new world record. Experts at the
time said O'Brien, the best in the world, might beat his record by a
few inches if he practiced. They were certain that no one would
ever be able to break the 60-foot barrier.

Pat O'Brien was determined to continue improving himself. He

34

began experimenting with different styles. Four years later he won the Olympics again—not by a few inches, but by a few *feet*. He broke the unbreakable barrier by tossing the shot 60 feet 11 inches. From that time on, every shot-putter worth his salt has tossed the shot beyond that length. Today, the record is over 70 feet.

The same is true of the four-minute mile. No one, the experts said, would ever be able to run the mile in less than four minutes. Then, in 1954, a young medical student named Roger Bannister did the impossible by breaking that barrier. Today, every world-class runner can run the mile in less than four minutes. Why? Because one man decided to keep improving. One man decided to pay the price of personal growth. He was willing to lead. As a result, he created a climate for those achievers who followed him. Are you the type of leader who is willing to pay the price and create a climate in which your people can follow you and emerge as the leaders of tomorrow?

The Leader's Primary Responsibility:

IDENTIFYING POTENTIAL LEADERS

There is something much more important and scarce than ability: It is the ability to recognize ability. One of the primary responsibilities of a successful leader is to identify potential leaders. It's not always an easy job, but it is critical.

Dale Carnegie was a master at identifying potential leaders. Once asked by a reporter how he had managed to hire forty-three millionaires, Carnegie responded that the men had not been millionaires when they started working for him. They had become millionaires as a result. The reporter next wanted to know how he had developed these men to become such valuable

> **To develop positive, successful people, look for the gold, not the dirt.**

leaders. Carnegie replied, "Men are developed the same way gold is mined. Several tons of dirt must be moved to get an ounce of gold. But you don't go into the mine looking for dirt," he added. "You go in looking for the gold." That's exactly the way to develop positive, successful people. Look for the gold, not the dirt;

the good, not the bad. The more positive qualities you look for, the more you are going to find.

SELECTING THE RIGHT PLAYERS

Professional sports organizations recognize the importance of selecting the right players. Every year, coaches and owners of professional baseball, basketball, and football teams look forward to the draft. To prepare for it, sports franchises spend much time and energy scouting new prospects. For instance, scouts from pro football organizations travel to regular-season college games, bowl games, senior-only bowl games, and camps to gain knowledge about prospective players. All of this enables the scouts to bring plenty of information back to the owners and head coaches so that when draft day arrives, the teams can pick the most promising players. Team owners and coaches know that the future success of their teams depends largely on their ability to draft effectively.

It's no different in business. You must select the right players in your organization. If you select well, the benefits are multiplied and seem nearly endless. If you select poorly, the problems are multiplied and seem endless.

Too often, leaders hire employees haphazardly. Because of desperation, lack of time, or just plain ignorance, they quickly grab any candidate who comes along. Then they hold their breath and hope everything works out. But hiring needs to be done strategically. Before you hire a new employee, your options are nearly limitless. Once you have made the hiring decision, your options are few. Hiring an employee is like skydiving: once you've jumped out of the plane, you're committed.

The key to making the right choice depends on two things: (1) your ability to see the big picture, and (2) your ability to judge potential employees during the selection process.

It is a good idea to start with an inventory. I use this one because I always want to look inside as well as outside the organization to find candidates. I call this list the Five A's:

Assessment of needs:	What is needed?
Assets on hand:	Who are the people already in the organization who are available?
Ability of candidates:	Who is able?
Attitude of candidates:	Who is willing?
Accomplishments of candidates:	Who gets things done?

Notice that the inventory begins with an assessment of needs. The leader of the organization must base that assessment on the big picture. While he was manager of the Chicago Cubs, Charlie Grimm reportedly received a phone call from one of his scouts. The man was excited and began to shout over the telephone, "Charlie, I've landed the greatest young pitcher in the land! He struck out every man who came to bat. Twenty-seven in a row. Nobody even hit a foul until the ninth inning. The pitcher is right here with me. What shall I do?" Charlie replied, "Sign up the guy who got the foul. We're looking for hitters." Charlie knew what the team needed.

There is one situation that supersedes a needs analysis: when a truly exceptional person is available but doesn't necessarily match the current need, do whatever you can to hire him or her anyway. In the long run, that person will positively impact the organization. You see this kind of decision-making in sports. Football coaches generally draft players to fill specific needs. If they lack a strong running back, they draft the best running back available. But sometimes they get an opportunity to draft an "impact player," a superstar who can instantly change the whole complexion of the team. Incidentally, impact players usually possess not only athletic ability but also leadership skills. Even as rookies, they have all the qualities to be team captains. When I have an opportunity to hire someone who is exceptional—a superstar—I do it. Then I find a place for him. Good people are hard to find, and there is always room for one more productive person in an organization.

> **Hiring an employee is like skydiving: once you've jumped out of the plane, you're committed.**

Usually we are not judging superstars, and the decisions are harder to make. How do pro sports teams evaluate potential players? Many use a grid that yields a score for each player based on his abilities. In the same way, we need to have a tool to help evaluate people's potential as leaders. Here is a list of twenty-five characteristics to help you rate and identify a potential leader.

ASSESSMENT OF CURRENT LEADERSHIP QUALITIES (FOR POTENTIAL LEADERS)

Scale
0 = Never   1 = Seldom   2 = Sometimes   3 = Usually   4 = Always

1. The person has influence.   0   1   2   3   4

2. The person has self-discipline.   0   1   2   3   4

3. The person has a good track
    record.   0   1   2   3   4

4. The person has strong people
    skills.   0   1   2   3   4

5. The person has the ability
    to solve problems.   0   1   2   3   4

6. The person does not accept the
    status quo.   0   1   2   3   4

7. The person sees the big picture.   0   1   2   3   4

8. The person has the ability to
    handle stress.   0   1   2   3   4

9. The person displays a positive
    spirit.   0   1   2   3   4

10. The person understands people.   0   1   2   3   4

11. The person is free of personal
    problems.   0   1   2   3   4

41

12. The person is willing to take responsibility. 0 1 2 3 4

13. The person is free from anger. 0 1 2 3 4

14. The person is willing to make changes. 0 1 2 3 4

15. The person has integrity. 0 1 2 3 4

16. The person is growing closer to God. 0 1 2 3 4

17. The person has the ability to see what has to be done next. 0 1 2 3 4

18. The person is accepted as a leader by others. 0 1 2 3 4

19. The person has the ability and desire to keep learning. 0 1 2 3 4

20. The person has a manner that draws people. 0 1 2 3 4

21. The person has a good self-image. 0 1 2 3 4

22. The person has a willingness to serve others. 0 1 2 3 4

23. The person has the ability to bounce back when problems arise. 0 1 2 3 4

24. The person has the ability to develop other leaders. 0 1 2 3 4

25. The person takes initiative. 0 1 2 3 4

Total Points _____

When assessing a potential leader, pay more attention to the quality of the person as addressed by the characteristics than to the specific score. Since leaders grade differently, scores vary. Here is my grading scale:

90–100	Great leader (should be mentoring other good and great leaders)
80–89	Good leader (must keep growing and keep mentoring others)
70–79	Emerging leader (focus on growth and begin mentoring others)
60–69	Bursting with potential (excellent person to be developed)
Below 60	Needs growth (may not be ready to be mentored as a leader)

The "Below 60" category is often the most difficult to judge. Some people in this group will never become leaders. Others are capable of becoming great leaders. The better leader the evaluator is, the better will be his judgment of a person's leadership potential. Thus, it is important that a successful leader do the interviewing and hiring of potential leaders.

In *Inc.* magazine, marketing expert I. Martin Jacknis identifies a trend he has seen in hiring. He terms it the *Law of Diminishing Expertise.* Simply stated, leaders tend to hire people whose ability and expertise are beneath their own. As a result, when organizations grow and more people are hired, the number of people with low expertise far exceeds the leaders who have great expertise.

Here's how this works. Let's say, for example, you are an outstanding leader with great vision, self-discipline, right priorities, and super problem-solving skills. You score a 95 on the Assessment of Current Leadership Qualities. So you decide to start your own business, called *Leader to Leader, Inc.* Your business does so well that you soon need four new employees. You would like to hire four 95s, but, chances are, 95s want to work for themselves (just as you do) and are not available. You need help, so you hire four 85s, not as skilled as you, but each a leader in his or her own right.

I must mention at this crucial stage in the company's development, you may have been tempted to hire less than 85s for your staff. You may be thinking to yourself, "The four people I hire just have to follow me and my direction, and the company will do fine. I can settle for a couple of followers who are 65s." That is the critical error many leaders make. By selecting followers rather than potential leaders, the leader of an organization limits its potential for growth. But for the moment, let's say that you don't make that mistake, and you hire four leaders with scores of 85.

You and your team of leaders are doing great. The business can hardly keep up with demand. Then you land a national account. Your hard work has paid off, but you now estimate that you will need about one hundred employees working around the clock to carry the load. You now need to build a whole organization.

You begin with your faithful four employees. They're good leaders, they helped you make it, and you're dedicated to promoting from within. They are going to be your four managers. You decide the best way to structure the new organization is to have one manager overseeing sales, and each of the other three managers overseeing an eight-hour shift to keep production going twenty-four hours a day. Each manager will supervise two assistant managers and about twenty other employees.

The four managers hire their assistants who, consistent with the law of diminishing expertise, rate as 75s. The managers give the assistants the job of hiring the twenty employees. You guessed it. They hire 65s. As a result, almost overnight, the company whose staff leadership score averaged 87 and looked like this

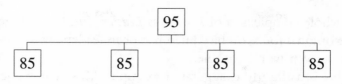

Leader to Leader, Inc. with five employees

now has a leadership score averaging 67 and looks like this:

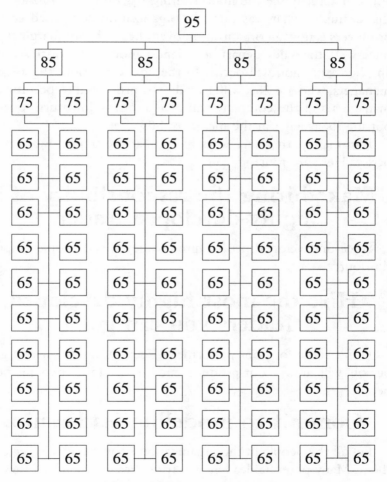

Leader to Leader, Inc. with nearly one hundred employees

The whole complexion of *Leader to Leader, Inc.* has changed. And if the original four you hired had not been leaders, you would have been in even worse trouble.

This is a slightly exaggerated example. Most companies don't go from five to one hundred employees overnight. But the organizations of great leaders expand quickly. What's important is that you can actually see the impact hiring has on an organization. In this example, what was once an organization comprised of high producers is now an organization overwhelmed with marginal producers. If the sales department lands another national account, another expansion will occur. In the next expansion, the assistant managers, who are 75s, will probably be promoted to become new managers and the company will take another downturn, possibly putting its average in the mediocre 50s.

Fortunately, there are ways to combat the trend toward mediocrity. Here are four:

Make hiring the responsibility of a highly-developed leader.

Since undeveloped people hire less developed people, improve the source.

Hire the most highly developed leaders you can get.

Don't settle for poor performers. Keep in mind that one great person will always out-produce and out-perform two mediocre people.

Commit to modeling leadership.

Let all the people in the organization know what is expected of them. Many potential leaders will try to reach a standard they can see.

Commit to developing those around you.

If you develop the potential leaders around you, by the next expansion, the dedicated assistant managers who were 75s will be 85s and ready to lead.

I would say that David Ogilvy, founder of the giant advertising agency Ogilvy and Mather, understood the law of diminishing expertise, based on the information Dennis Waitley gives about him in *The New Dynamics of Winning*. He states that Ogilvy used to give each new manager in his organization a Russian doll. The doll contained five progressively smaller dolls. A message inside the smallest one read: "If each of us hires people who are smaller than we are, we shall become a company of dwarfs. But if each of us hires people who are bigger then we are, Ogilvy and Mather will become a company of giants." Commit to finding, hiring, and developing giants.

QUALITIES TO LOOK FOR IN A LEADER

To hunt for leaders, you first need to know what they look like. Here are ten leadership qualities to seek in anyone you hire:

CHARACTER

The first thing to look for in any kind of leader or potential leader is strength of character. I have found nothing more important than this quality. Serious character flaws cannot be ignored. They will eventually make a leader ineffective—every time.

Character flaws should not be confused with weaknesses. We all have weaknesses. They can be overcome through training or experience. Character flaws cannot be changed overnight. Change usually takes a long period of time and involves significant relational investment and dedication on the part of the leader. Any person that you hire who has character flaws will be the weak link in your organization. Depending on the nature of the character flaw, the person has the potential to destroy the organization.

Character flaws cannot be ignored. They will eventually make a leader ineffective.

Some of the qualities that make up good character include: honesty, integrity, self-discipline, teachability, dependability, perseverance, conscientiousness, and a strong work ethic. The words of a person with right character match the deeds. His reputation is solid. His manner is straightforward.

The assessment of character can be difficult. Warning signs to watch for include:

- a person's failure to take responsibility for his actions or circumstances
- unfulfilled promises or obligations
- failure to meet deadlines

You can tell much about a person's ability to lead others from how well he manages his own life.

Finally, look at his interaction with others. You can also tell much about a person's character from his relationships. Examine his relationships with superiors, colleagues, and subordinates. Talk to your employees to find out how the potential leader treats them. This will give you additional insight.

INFLUENCE

Leadership is influence. Every leader has these two characteristics: (A) he is going somewhere and (B) he is able to persuade others to go with him. Influence by itself is not enough. That influence must be measured to determine its *quality*. When looking at a potential employee's influence, examine the following:

What is the leader's level of influence?

Does that person have followers due to position (he uses the power of his job title), permission (he has developed relationships which motivate), production (he and his followers consistently produce results), personnel development (he has developed others around him), or personhood (he transcends the organization and develops people on a world-class scale)?[3]

Who influences the leader?

Who is he following? People become like their models. Is his model ethical? Does his model have the right priorities? Whom does he influence?

Whom does he influence?

Likewise, the quality of the follower will indicate the quality of the leader. Are his followers positive producers or a bunch of mediocre yes-men?

Stuart Briscoe, in *Discipleship for Ordinary People,* tells the story of a young clergyman who officiated at the funeral of a war veteran. The veteran's military friends wanted to participate in the service to honor their comrade, so they requested that the young pastor lead them down to the casket for a moment of remembrance and then out through a side door. The occasion failed to have the desired effect when the clergyman led them through the wrong door. In full view of the other mourners, the men marched with military precision into a broom closet and had to beat a hasty and confused retreat. Every leader must know where he is going. And every follower had better be sure he's behind a leader who knows what he's doing.

POSITIVE ATTITUDE

A positive attitude is one of the most valuable assets a person can have in life. My belief in this is so strong that I wrote an entire book on the subject, *The Winning Attitude: Your Key to Personal Success*. So often, what people say their problem is really isn't their problem. Their problem is the attitude which causes them to handle life's obstacles poorly.

The individual whose attitude causes him to approach life from an entirely positive perspective is someone who can be called a no-limit person. In other words, the person doesn't accept the normal limitations of life as most people do. He or she is determined to walk to the very edge of his potential, or his product's potential, before he accepts defeat. People with positive attitudes are able to go places where others can't. They do things that others can't. They are not restricted by self-imposed limitations.

A person with a positive attitude is like a bumblebee. The bumblebee should not be able to fly because the size, weight, and shape of its body in relationship to its wingspread makes flying aerodynamically impossible. But the bumblebee, being ignorant of scientific theory, flies anyway and makes honey every day.

This no-limit mind-set allows a person to start each day with a positive disposition, as did an elevator operator I once read about. One Monday morning, in a full elevator, the man began humming

50

a tune. One passenger, irritated by the man's mood, snapped, "What are you so happy about?" "Well sir," replied the operator happily, "I ain't never lived this day before." Not only does the future look bright when the attitude is right, but the present is much more enjoyable too. The positive person understands that the journey is as enjoyable as the destination.

Think of the attitude like this:

It is the advance man of our true selves.
Its roots are inward but its fruit is outward.
It is our best friend or our worst enemy
It is more honest and more consistent than our words.
It is an outward look based on past experiences.
It is a thing which draws people to us or repels them.
It is never content until it is expressed.
It is the librarian of our past.
It is the speaker of our present.
It is the prophet of our future.[4]

Attitude sets the tone, not only for the leader with the attitude, but for the people following him.

EXCELLENT PEOPLE SKILLS

A leader without people skills soon has no followers. Andrew Carnegie, a fantastic leader, is reported to have paid Charles Schwab a salary of $1 million a year simply because of his excellent people skills. Carnegie had other leaders who understood the job better and whose experience and training were better suited to the work. But they lacked the essential human quality of being able to get others to help them, and Schwab could get the best out of his fellow workers. People may admire a person who has only talent and ability, but they will not follow him—not for long.

Excellent people skills involve a genuine concern for others, the

51

ability to understand people, and the decision to make positive interaction with others a primary concern. Our behavior toward others determines their behavior toward us. A successful leader knows this.

EVIDENT GIFTS

Every person God creates has gifts. One of our jobs as leaders is to make an assessment of those gifts when considering a person for employment. I think of every job candidate as a "wanna be" leader. My observation is that there are four types of wanna bes:

Never be

Some people simply lack the ability to do a particular job. As I mentioned before, all people are gifted. However, not all are gifted for the particular task at hand. A *never be* who is directed into an area where he is not gifted becomes frustrated, often blames others for his lack of success, and eventually burns out. Redirected, he has a chance of reaching his potential.

Could be

A *could be* is a person with the right gifts and abilities but lacking self-discipline. He may even be a person with superstar abilities who just can't get himself to perform. This person needs to develop the self-discipline to "just do it."

Should be

A *should be* is someone with raw talent (gifts) but few skills for harnessing that ability. He needs training. Once he is given help in

52

developing those skills, he will begin to become the person he was created to be.

Must be

The only thing a *must be* lacks is opportunity. He has the right gifts, the right skills, and the right attitude. He has the drive to be the person he was created to be. It is up to you to be the leader who gives him that opportunity. If you don't, he will find someone else who will.

God creates all people with natural gifts. But he also makes them with two ends, one to sit on and one to think with. Success in life is dependent on which one of these ends is used the most, and it's a toss up: Heads you win, and tails you lose!

PROVEN TRACK RECORD

Poet Archibald MacLeish once said, "There is only one thing more painful than learning from experience, and that is not learning from experience." Leaders who learn this truth develop successful track records over time. Everyone who breaks new ground, who strives to do something, makes mistakes. People without proven track records either haven't learned from their mistakes or haven't tried.

I have many people working for me who are talented and have established tremendous track records. Two in particular are first-rate leaders capable of the highest quality of leadership (they score in the top category on the Assessment of Current Leadership Qualities). Dick Peterson, who worked with IBM for years, quickly demonstrated that experience had not been wasted on him. Dick already had a proven track record when I asked him to team with me in starting the INJOY leadership institute. In the beginning, we were long on potential and short on resources. Dick's hard work, planning, and insight have turned a shoestring business operating out of his garage into an enterprise producing materials and influencing thousands of leaders nationally and internationally every year. I am privileged to have Dick as the president of INJOY.

Dan Reiland, executive pastor of Skyline Wesleyan Church, has quite a different story. Dan is totally a product of the farm team. He started at Skyline as a church member. After attending seminary, he returned to the church as an intern.

> **A proven leader always has a proven track record.**

He was not the best intern we ever had. In fact, at one point I thought he wasn't going to make it. But through his hard work and mentoring on my part, he soon became one of the finest pastors on staff and developed an outstanding track record. Because of that record I asked him to become the executive pastor of the church and continued to train him. Today he is one of the finest executive pastors in the country, and he carries a tremendous load. Now one of the things I enjoy most about watching him lead is his ability to develop other leaders.

Management expert Robert Townsend notes, "Leaders come in all sizes, ages, shapes, and conditions. Some are poor administrators, some not overly bright. But there is one clue for spotting them. Since most people *per se* are mediocre, the true leader can be recognized because somehow or other, his people consistently turn in superior performances." Always check a candidate's past performance. A proven leader always has a proven track record.

CONFIDENCE

People will not follow a leader who does not have confidence in himself. In fact, people are naturally attracted to people who convey confidence. An excellent example can be seen in an incident in Russia during an attempted coup. Army tanks had surrounded the government building housing President Boris Yeltsin and his pro-democracy supporters. High-level military leaders had ordered the tank commander to open fire and kill Yeltsin. As the army rolled into position, Yeltsin strode from the building, climbed up on a tank, looked the commander in the eye, and thanked him for coming over to the side of democracy. Later the commander admitted that they had not intended to go over to his side. Yeltsin had appeared so confident and commanding that the soldiers talked after he left and decided to join him.

Confidence is characteristic of a positive attitude. The greatest achievers and leaders remain confident regardless of circumstances. There's a wonderful story about baseball great Ty Cobb's confidence: When Cobb was seventy years old, a reporter asked, "What do you think you'd hit if you were playing these days?" Cobb, a lifetime .367 hitter, said, "About .290, maybe .300." The reporter said, "That's because of the travel, the night games, the artificial turf, and all the new pitches like the slider, right?" "No," said Cobb, "it's because I'm seventy." Strong confident leaders recognize and appreciate confidence in others.

Reprinted with special permission of King Features Syndicate

Confidence is not simply for show. Confidence empowers. A good leader has the ability to instill within his people confidence in himself. A great leader has the ability to instill within his people confidence in themselves.

SELF-DISCIPLINE

Great leaders always have self-discipline—without exception. Unfortunately, our society seeks instant gratification rather than self-discipline. We want instant breakfast, fast food, movies on demand, and quick cash from ATMs. But success doesn't come instantly. Neither does the ability to lead. As General Dwight D. Eisenhower said, "There are no victories at bargain prices."

Because we live in a society of instant gratification, we cannot take for granted that the potential leaders we interview will have self-discipline—that they will be willing to pay the price of great leadership. When it comes to self-discipline, people choose one of two things: the pain of discipline which comes from sacrifice and growth or the pain of regret which comes from the easy road and missed opportunities. Each person in life chooses. In *Adventures in Achievement*, E. James Rohn says that the pain of discipline weighs ounces. Regret weighs tons.

There are two areas of self-discipline we must look for in potential leaders. The first is in the emotions. Effective leaders recognize that their emotional reactions are their own responsibility. A leader who decides not to allow other people's actions to dictate his reactions experiences an empowering freedom. As the Greek philosopher Epictetus said, "No person is free who is not master of himself."

> **A great leader has the ability to instill within his people confidence in themselves.**

The second area concerns time. Every person on the planet is given the same allotment of minutes in a day. But each person's level of self-discipline dictates how effectively those minutes are used. Disciplined people are always growing, always striving for improvement, and they maximize the use of their time. I have found three things that characterize disciplined leaders:

- They have identified specific long- and short-term goals for themselves.
- They have a plan for achieving those goals.
- They have a desire that motivates them to continue working to accomplish those goals.

Progress comes at a price. When you interview a potential leader, determine whether he or she is willing to pay the price. The author of the popular cartoon comic strip *Ziggy* recognized this when he drew the following scene:

As our friend Ziggy, in his little automobile, drove down a road, he saw two signs. The first stated in bold letters, THE ROAD TO SUCCESS. Farther down the road stood the second sign. It read, PREPARE TO STOP FOR TOLLS.

EFFECTIVE COMMUNICATION SKILLS

Never underestimate the importance of communication. It consumes enormous amounts of our time. One study, reported by D.K. Burlow in *The Process of Communication,* states that the average American spends 70 percent of his active hours each day communicating verbally. Without the ability to communicate, a leader cannot effectively cast his vision and call his people to act on that vision. President Gerald Ford once said, "Nothing in life is more important than the ability to communicate effectively." A leader is not capable of reaching his potential without effective communication skills.

A leader's ability to convey confidence and his ability to communicate effectively are similar. Both require action on his part and a response from the follower. Communication is positive *inter-*

Liking people is the beginning of the ability to communicate.

action. When communication is one-sided, it can be comical. You may have heard the story of the frustrated judge preparing to hear a divorce case:

> "Why do you want a divorce?" the judge asked. "On what grounds?"
>
> "All over. We have an acre and a half," responded the woman.
>
> "No, no," said the judge. "Do you have a grudge?"
>
> "Yes, sir. Fits two cars."
>
> "I need a reason for the divorce," said the judge impatiently. "Does he beat you up?"
>
> "Oh, no. I'm up at six every day to do my exercises. He gets up later."
>
> "Please," said the exasperated judge. "What is the reason you want a divorce?"
>
> "Oh," she replied. "We can't seem to communicate with each other."

When I look at a potential leader's communication skills, I look for the following:

A genuine concern for the person he's talking to

When people sense that you have a concern for them, they are willing to listen to what you have to say. Liking people is the beginning of the ability to communicate.

The ability to focus on the responder

Poor communicators are focused on themselves and their own opinions. Good communicators focus on the response of the person they're talking to. Good communicators also read body language. When I interview a potential employee, and he can't read in my body language that I'm ready to move on to another subject, it sends up a red flag.

The ability to communicate with all kinds of people

A good communicator has the ability to set a person at ease. He can find a way to relate to nearly anyone of any background.

Eye contact with the person he's speaking to

Most people who are being straight with you are willing to look you in the eye. Personal integrity and conviction make communication credible.

A warm smile

The fastest way to open the lines of communication is to smile. A smile overcomes innumerable communication barriers, crossing the boundaries of culture, race, age, class, gender, education, and economic status.

If I expect a person to lead, I must also expect him to be able to communicate.

DISCONTENT WITH THE STATUS QUO

I've told my staff before that *status quo* is Latin for "the mess we're in." Leaders see what is, but more important, they have a vision for what could be. They are never content with things as they are. To be leading, by definition, is to be in front, breaking new ground, conquering new worlds, moving away from the status quo. Donna Harrison states, "Great leaders are never satisfied with current levels of performance. They constantly strive for higher and higher levels of achievement." They move beyond the status quo themselves, and they ask the same of those around them.

Dissatisfaction with the status quo does not mean a negative attitude or grumbling. It has to do with willingness to be different and take risks. A person who refuses to risk change fails to grow. A leader who loves the status quo soon becomes a follower. Raymond Smith of the Bell Atlantic Corporation once remarked, "Taking the safe road, doing your job, and not making any waves may not get you fired (right away, at least), but it sure won't do much for your career or your company over the long haul. We're not dumb. We know that administrators are easy to find and cheap to keep. Leaders—risk takers—are in very short supply. And ones with vision are pure gold."

> A leader who loves the status quo soon becomes a follower.

Risk seems dangerous to people more comfortable with old problems than new solutions. The difference between the energy and time that it takes to put up with the old problems and the energy and time it takes to come up with new solutions is surprisingly small. The difference is attitude. When seeking potential leaders, seek people who seek solutions.

> Seek people who seek solutions.

Good leaders deliberately seek out and find potential leaders. Great leaders not only find them, but transform them into other great leaders. An ability to recognize ability and a strategy for finding leaders make it happen. What is your plan for locating and identifying potential leaders?

60

CHAPTER FOUR

The Leader's Crucial Task:

NURTURING POTENTIAL LEADERS

Many organizations today fail to tap into their potential. Why? Because the only reward they give their employees is a paycheck. The relationship between employer and employee never develops beyond that point. Successful organizations take a different approach. In exchange for the work a person gives, he receives not only his paycheck, but also nurturing from the people for whom he works. And nurturing has the ability to transform people's lives.

Once you have identified potential leaders, you need to begin the work of building them into the leaders they can become. To do this you need a strategy. I use the *BEST* acronym as a reminder of what people need when they get started with my organization. They need me to:

B *elieve in them.*
E *ncourage them.*
S *hare with them.*
T *rust them.*

The *BEST* technique is the beginning of the next element of developing the leaders around you: nurturing potential leaders.

Nurturing has the ability to transform people's lives.

Nurturing benefits everyone. Who wouldn't be more secure and motivated when his leader *believes* in him, *encourages* him, *shares* with him, and *trusts* him? People are more productive when nurtured. Even more important, nurturing creates a strong emotional and professional foundation within workers who have leadership potential. Later, using training and development, a leader can be built on that foundation.

The nurturing process involves more than just encouragement. It also includes modeling. In fact, the leader's major responsibility in the nurturing process is modeling . . . leadership, a strong work ethic, responsibility, character, openness, consistency, communication, and a belief in people. Even when he is in the process of giving to the people around him, he is also modeling. The modeling process is at its best when a leader chooses a model of his own to emulate and then becomes a model to his team members. As eighteenth-century writer Oliver Goldsmith once said, "People seldom improve when they have no other model but themselves to copy." We leaders must provide ourselves as models to copy.

Mark Twain once joked, "To do right is wonderful. To teach others to do right is even more wonderful—and much easier." I have a corollary to Twain's idea: "To lead others to do right is wonderful. To do right and then lead them is more wonderful—and harder." Like Twain, I recognize that the self-disciplines of doing right and then teaching others to do right are made difficult by human nature. Everyone can find excuses for not giving to those around them. Great leaders know the difficulties and nurture their people anyway. They know that there are people who will respond positively to what they give, and they focus on those positive results.

Here are the things I have found a leader must do to nurture the potential leaders around him.

CHOOSE A LEADERSHIP MODEL FOR YOURSELF.

As leaders, you and I are first responsible for finding good models for ourselves. Give careful thought to which leaders you will follow because they will determine your course. I have developed six questions to ask myself before picking a model to follow:

Does my model's life deserve a following?

This question relates to quality of character. If the answer is not a clear yes, I have to be very careful. I will become like the people I follow, and I don't want models with flawed character.

Does my model's life have a following?

This question looks at credibility. It is possible to be the very first person to discover a leader worth following, but it doesn't happen very often. If the person has no following, he or she may not be worth following.

If my answer to either of the first two questions is no, I don't have to bother with the other four. I need to look for another model.

What is the main strength that influences others to follow my model?

What does the model have to offer me? What is his best? Also note that strong leaders have weaknesses as well as strengths. I don't want to inadvertently emulate the weaknesses.

Does my model produce other leaders?

The answer to this question will tell me whether the model's leadership priorities match mine in regard to developing new leaders.

Is my model's strength reproducible in my life?

If I can't reproduce his strength in my life, his modeling will not benefit me. For instance, if you admire Shaquille O'Neil's ability as a basketball center, but you're only 5 feet 9 inches tall and weigh 170 pounds, you are not going to be able to reproduce his strengths. Find appropriate models . . . but strive for improvement. Don't be too quick to say that a strength is not reproducible. Most are. Don't limit your potential.

If my model's strength is reproducible in my life, what steps must I take to develop and demonstrate that strength?

You must develop a plan of action. If you only answer the questions and never implement a plan to develop those strengths in yourself, you are only performing an intellectual exercise.

The models we choose may or may not be accessible to us in a personal way. Some may be national figures, such as a president. Or they may be people from history. They can certainly benefit you, but not the way a personal mentor can.

GUIDELINES FOR MENTORING RELATIONSHIPS

When you find someone who can personally mentor you, use these guidelines to help develop a positive mentoring relationship with that person:

Ask the right questions.

Give thought to questions you will ask before you meet with your mentor. Make them strategic for your own growth.

Clarify your level of expectations.

Generally, the goal of mentoring is improvement, not perfection. Perhaps only a few people can be truly excellent—but all of us can become better.

Accept a subordinate, learning position.

Don't let ego get in the way of learning. Trying to impress the mentor with your knowledge or ability will set up a mental barrier between you. It will prevent you from receiving what he is giving.

Respect the mentor but don't idolize him.

Respect allows us to accept what the mentor is teaching. But making the mentor an idol removes the ability to be objective and critical—faculties we need for adapting a mentor's knowledge and experience to ourselves.

Immediately put into effect what you are learning.

In the best mentoring relationships, what is learned comes quickly into focus. Learn, practice, and assimilate.

Be disciplined in relating to the mentor.

Arrange for ample and consistent time, select the subject matter in advance, and do your homework to make the sessions profitable.

Reward your mentor with your own progress.

If you show appreciation but make no progress, the mentor experiences failure. Your progress is his highest reward. Strive for growth, then communicate your progress.

Don't threaten to give up.

Let your mentor know you have made a decision for progress and that you are a persistent person—a determined winner. Then he will know he is not wasting his time.

There is no substitute for your own personal growth. If you are not receiving and growing, you will not be able to give to the people you nurture and develop.

BUILD TRUST

I have learned that trust is the single most important factor in building personal and professional relationships. Warren Bennis and Burt Nanus call trust "the glue that binds followers and leaders together." Trust implies accountability, predictability, and reliability. More than anything else, followers want to believe in and trust their leaders. They want to be able to say, "Someday I want to be like him or her." If they don't trust you, they cannot say it. People first must believe in you before they will follow your leadership.

Trust must be built day by day. It calls for consistency. Some of the ways a leader can betray trust include: breaking promises, gossiping, withholding information, and being two-faced. These actions destroy the environment of trust necessary for the growth of potential leaders. And when a leader breaks trust, he must work twice as hard to regain it. As Christian leader Cheryl Biehl once said, "One of the realities of life is that if you can't trust a person at all points, you can't truly trust him or her at any point."

Every fall I look forward to seeing poor Charlie Brown try to placekick a football. He always ends up on his face or back because Lucy, his holder, jerks the ball away at the last moment. After she pulls the ball away, Lucy often tells Charlie she is trying to teach him not to be so trusting. But he keeps on trying to kick the football anyway, year after year. Why? Charlie really does want to trust people. Lucy is not a leader, and she never will be. Leadership can only function on the basis of trust; Lucy is untrustworthy.

People will not follow a leader they do not trust. It is the leader's responsibility to actively develop that trust in him from the people around him. Trust is built on many things:

> **Leadership can only function on the basis of trust.**

T *ime.*   Take time to listen and give feedback on performance.

R *espect.*   Give the potential leader respect and he will return it with trust.

U *nconditional Positive Regard.*   Show acceptance of the person.

S *ensitivity.*   Anticipate the feelings and needs of the potential leader.

T *ouch.*   Give encouragement—a handshake, high five, or pat on the back.

Once people trust their leader as a person, they become able to trust his leadership.

SHOW TRANSPARENCY

All leaders make mistakes. They are a part of life. Successful leaders recognize their errors, learn from them, and work to correct their faults. A study of 105 executives determined many of the characteristics shared by successful executives. One particular trait was identified as the most valuable: They admitted their mistakes and accepted the consequences rather than trying to blame others.

We live among people who try to make someone else responsible for their actions or circumstances. People don't want to reap the consequences of their actions. You can see this attitude everywhere. Television advertisements invite us daily to sue "even if you were at fault in an accident" or "declare bankruptcy" to avoid creditors. A leader who is willing to take responsibility for his actions and be honest and transparent with his people is someone they will admire, respect, and trust. That leader is also someone they can learn from.

OFFER TIME

People cannot be nurtured from a distance or by infrequent, short spurts of attention. They need you to spend time with them —planned time, not just a few words on the way to a meeting. I make it a priority to stay in touch with the leaders in my organization. I plan and perform training sessions for my staff, I schedule one-on-one time for mentoring, and I schedule meetings where team members can share information. Often I'll take a potential leader to lunch. I frequently check with my people to see how their area of responsibility is progressing and give assistance if needed.

Time spent with a potential leader is an investment.

We live in a fast-paced, demanding world, and time is a difficult thing to give. It is a leader's most valuable commodity. Peter Drucker wrote, "Nothing else, perhaps, distinguishes effective executives as much as their tender loving care of time." Time is valuable, but time spent with a potential leader is an investment. When you give of yourself, it benefits you, the organization, and the receiver. Nurturing leaders must maintain a giving attitude. Norman Vincent Peale expressed it well when he said that the man who lives for himself is a failure; the man who lives for others has achieved true success.

BELIEVE IN PEOPLE

When you believe in people, you motivate them and release their potential. And people can sense intuitively when a person really believes in them. Anyone can see people as they are. It takes a leader to see what they can become, encourage them to grow in that direction, and believe that they will do it. People

When you believe in people, you motivate them and release their potential.

always grow toward a leader's expectations, not his criticism and examinations. Examinations merely *gauge* progress. Expectations *promote* progress. You can hire people to work for you, but you must win their hearts by believing in them in order to have them work with you.

GIVE ENCOURAGEMENT

Too many leaders expect their people to encourage themselves. But most people require outside encouragement to propel them forward. It is vital to their growth. Physician George Adams found encouragement to be so vital to a person's existence that he called it "oxygen to the soul."

New leaders need to be encouraged. When they arrive in a new situation, they encounter many changes and undergo many changes themselves. Encouragement helps them reach their potential; it empowers them by giving them energy to continue when they make mistakes.

> **People always grow toward a leader's expectations.**

Use lots of positive reinforcement with your people. Don't take acceptable work for granted; thank people for it. Praise a person every time you see improvement. And personalize your encouragement any time you can. Remember, what motivates one person may leave another cold or even irritated. Find out what works with each of your people and use it.

UCLA basketball coach John Wooden told players who scored to give a smile, wink, or nod to the player who gave them a good pass. "What if he's not looking?" asked a team member. Wooden replied, "I guarantee he'll look." Everyone values encouragement and looks for it—especially when his leader is a consistent encourager.

EXHIBIT CONSISTENCY

Consistency is a crucial part of nurturing potential leaders, just as it is in any other kind of nurturing. When we are consistent, our people learn to trust us. They are able to grow and develop because they know what to expect from us. They can answer the question, "What would my leader do in this situation?" when they face difficult decisions. They become secure because they know what our response to them will be, regardless of circumstances.

Perhaps you've heard the story about the farmer who had experienced several bad years. He went to see the manager of his bank:

"I've got some good news and some bad news to tell you. Which would you like to hear first?" the farmer asked.

"Why don't you tell me the bad news first and get it over with?" the banker replied.

"Okay. With the bad drought and inflation and all, I won't be able to pay anything on my mortgage this year, either on the principal or the interest."

"Well, that is pretty bad."

"It gets worse. I also won't be able to pay anything on the loan for all that machinery I bought, not on the principal or interest."

"Wow, is that ever bad!"

"It's worse than that. You remember I also borrowed to buy seed and fertilizer and other supplies. Well, I can't pay anything on that either—principal or interest."

"That's awful and that's enough! Tell me what the good news is."

"The good news," replied the farmer with a smile, "is that I intend to keep on doing business with you."[5]

Fortunately, most of our potential leaders do better than our friend the farmer. Unlike him, they won't need consistent support for quite so long before they are able to turn things around. When we believe in our potential leaders, and we consistently support and encourage them, we give them the added strength they need to hang in there and perform well for us.

HOLD HOPE HIGH

Hope is one of the greatest gifts leaders can give to those around them. Its power should never be underestimated. It takes a great leader to give hope to people when they can't find it within themselves. Winston Churchill recognized the value of hope. He was prime minister of England during some of the darkest hours of World War II. He was once asked by a reporter what his country's greatest weapon had been against Hitler's Nazi regime. Without pausing for a moment he said: "It was what England's greatest weapon has always been—hope."

It is the leader's job to hold hope high.

People will continue working, struggling, and trying if they have hope. Hope lifts morale. It improves self-image. It reenergizes people. It raises their expectations. It is the leader's job to hold hope high, to instill it in the people he leads. Our people will have hope only if we give it to them. And we will have hope to give if we maintain the right attitude. Clare Boothe Luce, in *Europe in the Spring*, quotes Battle of Verdun hero Marshal Foch as saying, "There are no hopeless situations: there are only men who have grown hopeless about them."

Maintaining hope comes from seeing the potential in every situation and staying positive despite circumstances. Dr. G. Campbell Morgan tells the story of a man whose shop burned to the ground in the great Chicago fire. He arrived at the ruins the next morning carrying a table and set it up amid the charred debris. Above the table he placed this optimistic sign: "Everything lost except wife, children, and hope. Business will resume as usual tomorrow morning."

ADD SIGNIFICANCE

No one wants to spend his time doing work that is unimportant. People want to do work that matters. Workers often say things like, "I want to feel that I've achieved, that I've accomplished, that I've made a difference. I want excellence. I want what I do to be important work. I want to make an impact." People want significance.

It is the leader's job to add significance to the lives of the people he leads: One of the ways we can do this is to make them a part of something worthwhile. Too many people simply fall into a comfortable niche in life and stay there rather than pursue goals of significance. Leaders can't afford to do that. Every leader must ask himself, "Do I want survival, success, or significance?" The best leaders desire significance and expend their time and energy in pursuit of their dreams. As former *Washington Post* CEO Katharine Graham said, "To love what you do and feel that it matters—how could anything be more fun?"

Moishe Rosen teaches a one-sentence mental exercise that is an effective tool in helping a person identify his dream. He asks a person to fill in the blanks:

*If I had*_____,

*I would*_____.

The idea is that if you had anything you wanted—unlimited time, unlimited money, unlimited information, unlimited staff (all the resources you could ask for)—what would you do? Your answer to that question is your dream.

Acting on your dream adds significance to your life. There is a classic example of this from history. Everyone has heard the story of Isaac Newton's discovery of the law of gravity after observing the fall of an apple. What few people know is that Edmund Halley, the astromoner who discovered Halley's Comet, is almost single-handedly responsible for Newton's theories becoming known. Halley challenged Newton to think through his original notions. He corrected Newton's mathematical errors and prepared geometrical figures to support his work. Not only did he encourage Newton to write his great work, *Mathematical Principles of Natural Philosophy,* but he edited the work, supervised its publication, and financed its printing, even though Newton was wealthier and could easily afford the printing costs.

Halley encouraged Newton to act on his dream, and it added immeasurable significance to his life. Newton began to reap the rewards of prominence almost immediately. Halley received little credit, but he must have gained great satisfaction in knowing he had inspired revolutionary ideas in the advancement of scientific thought.

Identify and pursue your dream. Make it personal, attainable, measurable, visible, and expandable. The desire for significance can stretch us to our very best. And being a part of the achievement of our dream can enrich the lives of those around us.

Another way to add significance to the lives of the people you lead is to show them the big picture and let them know how they contribute to it. Many people get so caught up in the task of the moment that they cannot see the importance of what they do.

A member of my staff who was once dean of a vocational college told me of a day on which he was showing around a new employee. As he introduced each person and described each person's position, the receptionist overheard him say that hers was a very important position. The receptionist commented, "I'm not important. The most important thing I do each day is fill out a report."

74

"Without you," the dean replied, "this school wouldn't exist. Every new student who comes here talks to you first. If they don't like you, they won't like the school. If they don't like the school, they won't come to school here, and we would soon run out of students. We would have to close our doors."

"Wow! I never thought of it that way," she replied. The dean immediately saw her appear more confident, and she sat up taller behind her desk as she answered the phone. The leader of her department had never explained to her the significance of her job. He had never explained her value to the organization. By seeing the big picture, she had significance added to her life.

PROVIDE SECURITY

Norman Cousins said, "People are never more insecure than when they become obsessed with their fears at the expense of their dreams." People who focus on their fears don't grow. They become paralyzed. Leaders are in a position to provide followers with an environment of security in which they can grow and develop. A potential leader who feels secure is more likely to take risks, try to excel, break new ground, and succeed. Great leaders make their followers feel bigger than they are. Soon the followers begin to think, act, and produce bigger than they are. Finally, they become what they think they are.

Henry Ford once said, "One of the great discoveries a man makes, one of his great surprises, is to find he can do what he was afraid he couldn't do." A nurturing leader provides the security a potential leader needs to make that discovery.

REWARD PRODUCTION

People rise to our level of expectations. They try to give us what we reward. If you want your people to produce, then you must reward production.

Thomas J. Watson, Sr., the founder of IBM, was famous for

carrying a checkbook as he walked through offices and plants. Whenever he saw somebody doing an exceptional job, he wrote out a check to that person. It may have been for $5, $10, or $25. The amounts were small, but the impact of his action was tremendous. In many cases, people never cashed the checks. They framed them and put them on their walls. They found their reward not in the money, but in the personal recognition of their production. That's what gives significance and leads a person to give his personal best.

Even a person who is industrious and hardworking will finally get demoralized if production is discouraged rather than rewarded. You probably remember the children's story of the little red hen, the one who wanted help baking bread. Here is a modern version:

> Once upon a time there was a little red hen who scratched about the barnyard until she uncovered some grains of wheat. She called her neighbors and said, "If we plant this wheat, we shall have bread to eat. Who will help me plant it?"
>
> "Not I," said the cow.
>
> "Not I," said the duck.
>
> "Not I," said the pig.
>
> "Not I," said the goose.
>
> "Then I will," said the little red hen, and she did. The wheat grew tall and ripened into golden grain. "Who will help me reap my wheat?" asked the little red hen.
>
> "Not I," said the duck.
>
> "That's out of my classification," said the pig.
>
> "I'd lose my seniority," said the cow.
>
> "I'd lose my unemployment compensation," said the goose.
>
> "Then I will," said the little red hen, and she did.
>
> At last, it came time to bake the bread. "Who will help me bake the bread?" asked the little red hen.
>
> "That would be overtime for me," said the cow.

"I'd lose my welfare benefits," said the duck.

"If I'm to be the only helper, that would be discrimination," said the goose.

"Then I will," said the little red hen. She baked five loaves and held them up for her neighbors to see. They all wanted some. In fact, they demanded a share. But the little red hen said, "No, I can eat the five loaves myself."

"Excess profits," yelled the cow.

"Capitalist leech," cried the duck.

"I demand equal rights," shouted the goose.

The pig just grunted. Then the others hurriedly painted picket signs and marched around, shouting obscenities.

The government agent came and said to the little red hen, "You must not be greedy."

"But I earned the bread," said the little red hen.

"Exactly," said the agent. "That is the wonderful free enterprise system. Anyone in the barnyard can earn as much as he wants. But, under government regulations, the productive workers must divide their product with the idle."

They all lived happily ever after. But the little red hen's neighbors wondered why she never again baked bread.[6]

We leaders must be certain that our people don't feel like the little red hen. We must never be like the government agent. We must give positive acknowledgement and encouragement to the producers, and we must be careful not to reward the idle. Take a hard look at your organization. What are you rewarding?

ESTABLISH A SUPPORT SYSTEM

Develop a support system for employees. Nothing hurts morale more than asking people to do something and not giving them resources to accomplish it. I believe every potential leader needs support in five areas:

Emotional support

Provide a "yes you can" atmosphere. Even when support is lacking in other areas, a person can forge ahead when given emotional support. This support costs the least and yields an incredible return.

Skills training

One of the fastest ways to build people up is to train them. People receiving training perceive that the organization believes in them. And they are more productive because they are more highly skilled.

Money

Invest money in people; it always yields the highest return on your investment.

Stingy leaders produce stingy workers. It is difficult for people to give of themselves when their leader does not give of himself. If you pay peanuts, expect to get monkeys. Invest money in people; it always yields the highest return on your investment.

Equipment

To do the job right, you need the right tools. Too often a poor leader looks at things from a short-term perspective. Investing in the right equipment will give your people the time to be more productive, and it will keep up their morale.

Personnel

Provide the people needed to get the job done. And provide good people. Personnel problems can eat up the time and energy of a potential leader, leaving little time for production.

Create a support system for all the people around you. But increase it for any individual only as he grows and is successful. I have found the familiar 80/20 principle that I discussed at length in *Developing the Leader Within You* holds especially true here. The top 20 percent of the people in the organization will perform 80 percent of the organization's production. So when structuring your support system, provide the top 20 percent producers with 80 percent of the total support.

People who have a support system have the environment and the tools to succeed. They are a part of a cooperative environment. A business training exercise, described in a speech by Tom Geddie of Central and South West Services, is a wonderful illustration of what can happen in a cooperative environment:

> Draw an imaginary line on the floor, and put one person on each side. The purpose is to get one person to convince the other, without force, to cross the line. U.S. players almost never convince one another, but their Japanese counterparts simply say, "If you'll cross the line, so will I." They exchange places and they both win.

The Japanese recognize the importance of cooperation and mutual support. It has been a key to their success in the last fifty years. It can be a key to your success and to that of the leaders around you.

DISCERN AND PERSONALIZE THE POTENTIAL LEADER'S JOURNEY

Teddy Roosevelt once had a little dog that was always getting in fights and always getting licked. Somebody said, "Colonel, he's not much of a fighter." Teddy replied, "Oh, he's a good fighter. He's just a poor judge of dogs."

Leaders must be good at judging others. Leadership expert Peter Drucker has often said, "It is important to disciple a life, not teach a lesson." Discipleship of another person involves discerning where that person is, knowing where he is supposed to go, and giving him what he needs to get there. The person and the assignments he is given must match. As Drucker says, people are much like flowers. One, like a rose, needs fertilizer. Another, more like a rhododendron, doesn't. If you don't give flowers the care they need, they'll never bloom. The leader must be able to tell which is which.

> **Spend 80 percent of your time on the most promising 20 percent of the potential leaders around you.**

In the previous chapter, we discussed the identification of potential leaders. Everyone you recruit for your organization should be a potential leader, but you should not try to personally mentor everyone in your organization. Lead and nurture everyone within your influence, but spend 80 percent of your time on the most promising 20 percent of the potential leaders around you. Here are some guidelines for selecting the right people to mentor and develop:

Select people whose philosophy of life is similar to yours.

It will be difficult to develop someone whose values are too different from yours.

Choose people with potential you genuinely believe in.

If you don't believe in them, you won't give them the time they need. And they will discern your lack of confidence in them. Belief in their potential, on the other hand, will empower them. Some of the nation's greatest professional athletes have come from tiny colleges that receive no publicity. All those ball players needed was for pro scouts to recognize the potential that the right opportunity could bring out. The secret of mentoring in any field is to help a person get where he or she is willing to go.

Determine what they need.

Determining what potential leaders need involves looking at their strengths and weaknesses objectively. Their strengths indicate the directions they need to go, what they can become. Their weaknesses show us what we need to help them improve. Encouraging them in their strengths and helping them overcome their weaknesses will move them closer to reaching their potential.

Evaluate their progress constantly.

People need feedback, especially early in their development. Ben Franklin said, "The eye of the master will do more work than both his hands." He knew that a leader's ability to evaluate was his greatest strength. An honest mentor will be objective. If necessary, he or she will encourage the person to stay on course, to seek another direction, or even to enter into a relationship with another mentor.

Be committed, serious, and available to the people you mentor.

The development of the potential leaders will be a reflection of your commitment to them: poor commitment equals poor development; great commitment equals great development.

Danny Thomas said, "All of us are born for a reason, but all of us don't discover why. Success in life has nothing to do with what you gain in life or accomplish for yourself. It's what you do for others." By personalizing each person's journey, you are helping him to maximize his potential. You are giving him a chance to discover his purpose. You also maximize his contribution to you and your organization.

Most people agree that nurturing is important to the development of children. However, they often fail to see its importance in the workplace. They assume that potential leaders will nurture themselves. If we as leaders do not nurture the potential leaders around us, they will never develop into the types of leaders we desire. As Ralph Waldo Emerson said, "It is one of the most beautiful compensations of this life that no man can sincerely try to help another without helping himself." When you nurture the people around you, everyone wins.

The Leader's Daily Requirement:

EQUIPPING POTENTIAL LEADERS

A t this point you know how to identify potential leaders, how to create a climate in which they can be nurtured, and how to nurture them in some basic ways. It is time to look more specifically at how to prepare them for leadership within the organization. That preparation process is called equipping.

Equipping is similar to training. But I prefer the term "equipping" because it more accurately describes the process potential leaders must go through. Training is generally focused on specific job tasks; for instance, you train a person to use a copy machine or to answer a phone in a particular way. Training is only a part of the equipping process that prepares a person for leadership.

When I think of equipping a potential leader, I think of preparing an unskilled person to scale a tall mountain peak. His preparation is a process. Certainly he needs to be outfitted with equipment, such as cold-weather clothing, ropes, picks, and spikes. He also needs to be trained how to use that equipment.

A mountain climber's preparation, though, involves much more than simply having the correct equipment and knowing how to use it. The person must be conditioned physically to prepare him for the difficult climb. He must be trained to be a part of a team. Most important, he must be taught to *think* like a mountain climber. He needs to be able to look at a peak and *see* how it is to be conquered. Without going through the complete equipping process, he not only won't make it to the top of the mountain, but he also might find himself stranded on the side of the mountain, freezing to death.

> **Equipping is an ongoing process.**

Equipping, like nurturing, is an ongoing process. You don't equip a person in a few hours or a day. And it can't be done using a formula or a video tape. Equipping must be tailored to each potential leader.

The ideal equipper is a person who can impart the vision of the work, evaluate the potential leader, give him the tools he needs, and then help him along the way at the beginning of his journey.

The equipper is a *model*—a leader who does the job, does it well, does it right, and does it with consistency.

The equipper is a *mentor*—an advisor who has the vision of the organization and can communicate it to others. He or she has experience to draw upon.

The equipper is an *empowerer*—one who can instill in the potential leader the desire and ability to do the work. He or she is able to lead, teach, and assess the progress of the person being equipped.

> **Equipping must be tailored to each potential leader.**

To see how your discernment skills measure up, take a look at this chart of potential leader characteristics adapted from author and leadership consultant Bobb Biehl[7]:

PERFORMANCE FACTORS	FAR EXCEEDS JOB REQUIREMENTS	EXCEEDS JOB REQUIREMENTS	MEETS JOB REQUIREMENTS	NEEDS SOME IMPROVEMENT	DOES NOT MEET MINIMUM REQUIREMENTS
Quality	Leaps tall buildings with a single bound	Must take running start to leap over tall buildings	Can only leap over a short building or medium with no spires	Crashes into buildings when attempting to jump over them	Cannot recognize building at all, what's more jump
Timeliness	Is faster than a speeding bullet	Is as fast as a speeding bullet	Not quite as fast as a speeding bullet	Would you believe a slow bullet?	Wounds self with bullet when attempting to shoot gun
Initiative	Is stronger than a locomotive	Is stronger than an elephant	Is stronger than a bull	Shoots the bull	Smells like a bull
Adaptability	Walks on water consistently	Walks on water in emergencies	Washes with water	Drinks water	Passes water in emergencies
Communication	Talks with God	Talks with the angels	Talks to self	Argues with self	Loses those arguments

EQUIPPING QUESTIONS

Effective equipping begins with asking questions. We ask them to determine the direction our equipping efforts must take. If we don't, we may find ourselves teaching the wrong people the wrong things for the wrong purpose. I begin the process with analysis of the organization, myself, and the potential leaders. To get the information I need, I ask three sets of questions:

QUESTIONS ABOUT THE ORGANIZATION

These questions will determine what equipping needs to be done and the direction it should take to best serve the organization:

What is the statement of purpose for the organization?

The development of leaders in an organization must begin with a review of the organization's purpose. (Presumably, the purpose of your organization is already in writing. If not, write it down. Or ask someone in authority to provide you with a statement of purpose.) Don't even consider performing equipping or training that does not contribute to the fulfillment of the organization's purpose.

What is the primary need of the organization?

If you know what the organization needs most in order to fulfill its purpose, then you know its primary equipping need. Define that need as specifically as possible.

Is there a training program in place to meet that need?

If there isn't, you know where to start. If there is, then use the ideas in this chapter to improve it.

What areas within the organization have the greatest growth potential?

When you train and equip to prepare for growth, you play to your strengths. You are being proactive rather than reactive. You are putting yourself in a position to meet the future totally prepared.

Do those potential growth areas have the needed leaders to accomplish the task?

Without leaders ready to make things happen, the area of growth potential will never move from "potential" to reality. If the leaders don't already exist, they will have to be equipped and developed.

QUESTIONS ABOUT MYSELF

The questions concerning the organization indicate the direction the equipping must take. This next set of questions will make clear how the equipping will be done. As the leader, I set the tone for the equipping process.

Am I willing to pour my life into others?

Giving to potential leaders is a way of life for the best leaders. They do it daily. The development of their people is more important than the development of their own status. They are willing to share the credit when things go right. Equipping involves sacrifice.

Am I committed to an equipping organization?

Equipping requires commitment. It takes time and effort on the part of an organization's leadership. Everyone knows it's quicker and easier for a leader to do a job himself than it is for him to teach other people to do it. But doing it yourself is a short-term solution. The longer, harder road of equipping others pays in the long run, but it requires commitment from everyone in the organization.

87

Am I effective in the areas I need to equip?

This is a tough question that requires an honest answer. If the answer is "no," the leader must locate a person, inside or outside the organization, effective in those areas who can do some of the training. Either that, or he had better go out and get himself equipped.

Have I developed a prospect list of potential leaders?

As I mentioned in chapter three, a good leader is always looking for potential leaders. You always begin with the best people you can. As you nurture them, a group of people with the most potential will emerge. From that group, draw up a prospect list of potential leaders to be considered for equipping and development.

What assumptions have I made that need to be changed?

People often get a false first impression of other people. Many times leaders build their expectations of the people they will develop on assumptions from those false first impressions. When you are aware that you have made some assumptions, you can go beyond the superficial and move to a new level in your relationships with your potential leaders. It allows you to better understand where they are, what they need, and what you can provide them.

QUESTIONS ABOUT THE POTENTIAL LEADER

Once you have identified the organization's equipping needs, examined yourself, and developed a prospect list, you are ready to select the people to be equipped. The goal now is to narrow the field of prospective leaders down to the few people with the most potential. Ask yourself these questions about each person to find the ones with the highest potential:

Is this person compatible philosophically with the organization and my leadership?

If the answer is no, don't even consider equipping or mentoring this person. There must be compatibility first; otherwise, no amount of training in the world will make this person the type of leader you want and need.

Does this person show a potential for growth?

Potential for growth does not guarantee growth, but a lack of growth potential guarantees no growth will occur. If the person does not appear to have the desire and the ability to grow, look for another candidate.

Are there lingering questions I have about this person?

The time to have lingering questions answered is before the person is selected for equipping. Take time to interview, then do follow-up interviews to answer other questions that occur to you later. You may want to have someone you respect in your organization do an interview as well. He or she will sometimes see things you missed. If you can positively answer 95 percent of your questions about this person, then the person is probably a good candidate. The one exception is character. If you have any lingering questions concerning his character, don't choose him for development.

Am I selecting this person because of obvious strengths or because I don't see any glaring weaknesses?

When you look at a potential leader and don't see even one great strength, don't choose him for equipping and development —even if you see no great weaknesses. As tempting as it may be to select that person, don't do it. Why? Because if you do, you are asking for mediocrity.

Management expert Peter Drucker, in *The Effective Executive,* explains that Abraham Lincoln made this mistake early in his presidency when selecting generals. He sought men without glaring weaknesses. As a result, the well-equipped Union army fared poorly against the Confederates. Lincoln once remarked irritably that if General McClellen didn't plan to use the Army, he would like to borrow it for a while.

The Confederate army was staffed with generals who, although they had obvious weaknesses, were picked for their great and obvious strengths. These strengths, properly developed and applied, gave them victory after victory. Lincoln finally learned this lesson and selected as leader of the Union army Ulysses Grant, a great general but also an alcoholic. When you look for potential leaders, select people with obvious strengths even if you see weaknesses.

What is the potential leader's fit?

There are two kinds of "fit" to consider. First, a person's gifts and abilities must fit the job he is to perform. Consider such gifts and abilities as temperament, background, job experience, skills, personality, and passion. People need to be trained and developed primarily in their areas of strength. And most of the work they are asked to do should be in those areas. I often talk about the 80/20 principle, and it applies here as well. A person should be spending 80 percent of his time doing things that require his greatest gifts and abilities. This will help keep him fulfilled.

> **People need to be trained and developed primarily in their areas of strength.**

> **A person should be spending 80 percent of his time doing things that require his greatest gifts and abilities.**

The second has to do with how well he will fit into the team. No matter how great the player, if he can't play with the team, he won't help the organization. The addition of a new team member always changes the chemistry of the team.

It's obvious in sports: A good team is made up of people with different talents playing different positions to accomplish one goal. (Can you imagine a whole basketball team of seven-foot centers who specialize in blocking shots —no shooting guards, no shooting or rebounding forwards, and no playmakers—just centers? What a disaster.)

Teams outside of sports need to be created strategically too. They must have the right chemistry. When each player brings his particular style and talents to the team, and they come together with respect and appreciation for one another, it can create a wonderful and powerful team.

91

* * *

If you haven't already stopped to answer these questions, I want to encourage you to do so right now. Write down your answers. If you have your own organization, you cannot afford to let any more time go by without preparing for your organization's future. Even if you are not the CEO of the organization, you can still apply these principles. Do it now!

HOW TO EQUIP FOR EXCELLENCE

Now that you know who you are going to equip and for what you are going to equip them, you are ready to get started. The steps that follow will take you through the whole process. They begin with building a relationship with your potential leaders. From that foundation, you can build a program for their development, supervise their progress, empower them to do the job, and finally get them to pass on the legacy.

DEVELOP A PERSONAL RELATIONSHIP WITH THE PEOPLE YOU EQUIP

All good mentoring relationships begin with a personal relationship. As your people get to know and like you, their desire to follow your direction and learn from you will increase. If they don't like you, they will not want to learn from you, and the equipping process slows down or even stops.

92

> **All good mentoring relationships begin with a personal relationship.**

To build relationships, begin by listening to people's life story, their journey so far. Your genuine interest in them will mean a lot to them. It will also help you to know their personal strengths and weaknesses. Ask them about their goals and what motivates them. Find out what kind of temperament they have. You certainly don't want to equip and develop a person whose greatest love is numbers and financial statements for a position where he would be spending 80 percent of his time dealing with disgruntled customers.

One of the best ways to get to know people is to see them outside of the business world. People are usually on their guard at work. They try to be what others want them to be. By getting to know them in other settings, you can get to know who they really are. Try to learn as much as you can about the people and do your best to win their hearts. If you first find their hearts, they'll be glad to give you their hands.

SHARE YOUR DREAM

While getting to know your people, share your dream. It helps them to know you and where you're going. There's no act that will better show them your heart and your motivation.

Woodrow Wilson once said, "We grow by dreams. All big individuals are dreamers. They see things in the soft haze of a spring day, or in the red fire on a long winter's evening. Some of us let those great dreams die, but others nourish and protect them; nourish them through bad days until they bring them to the sunshine and light which comes always to those who sincerely hope that their dreams will come true." I have often wondered, "Does the person make the dream, or does the dream make the person?" My conclusion is both are equally true.

All good leaders have a dream. All great leaders share their dream with others who can help them make it a reality. As Florence Littauer suggests, we must

Dare to dream:	Have the desire to do something bigger than yourself.
Prepare the dream:	Do your homework; be ready when the opportunity comes.
Wear the dream:	Do it.
Share the dream:	Make others a part of the dream, and it will become even greater than you had hoped.

ASK FOR COMMITMENT

In his book *The One Minute Manager,* Ken Blanchard says, "There's a difference between interest and commitment. When you are interested in doing something, you do it only when it is convenient. When you are committed to something, you accept no excuses." Don't equip people who are merely interested. Equip the ones who are committed.

Commitment is the one quality above all others that enables a potential leader to become a successful leader. Without commitment, there can be no success. Football coach Lou Holtz recognized the difference between being merely involved and being truly committed. He pointed out, "The kamikaze pilot that was able to fly 50 missions was involved—but never committed."

To determine whether your people are committed, first you must make sure they know what it will cost them to become leaders. That means that you must be sure not to undersell the job—let them know what it's going to take. Only then will they know what they are committing to. If they won't commit, don't go any further in the equipping process. Don't waste your time.

SET GOALS FOR GROWTH

People need clear objectives set before them if they are to achieve anything of value. Success never comes instantaneously. It comes from taking many small steps. A set of goals becomes a map a potential leader can follow in order to grow. As Shad Helmsetter states in *You Can Excel in Times of Change,* "It is the goal that shapes the plan; it is the plan that sets the action; it is the action that achieves the result; and it is the result that brings the success. And it all begins with the simple word *goal.*" We, as equipping leaders, must introduce our people to the practice of setting and achieving goals.

Lily Tomlin once said, "I always wanted to be somebody, but I should have been more specific." Many people today find themselves in the same situation. They have some vague idea of what success is, and they know they want to achieve it. But they haven't worked out any kind of plan to get there. I have found that the greatest achievers in life are people who set goals for themselves and then work hard to reach them. What they get by reaching the goals is not nearly as important as what they become by reaching them.

When you help your people set goals, use the following guidelines:

Make the goals appropriate.

Always keep in mind the job you want the people to do and the desired result: the development of your people into effective leaders. Identify goals that will contribute to that larger goal.

Make the goals attainable.

Nothing will make people want to quit faster than facing unachievable goals. I like the comment made by Ian MacGregor, former AMAX Corporation chairman of the board: "I work on the same principle as people who train horses. You start with low fences, easily achieved goals, and work up. It's important in management never to ask people to try to accomplish goals they can't accept."

Make the goals measurable.

Your potential leaders will never know when they have achieved their goals if they aren't measurable. When they are measureable, the knowledge that they have been attained will give them a sense of accomplishment. It will also free them to set new goals in place of the old ones.

Clearly state the goals.

When goals have no clear focus, neither will the actions of the people trying to achieve them.

Make the goals require a "stretch."

The leader must know his people well enough to identify attainable goals that require a stretch.

As I mentioned before, goals have to be achievable. On the other hand, when goals don't require a stretch, the people achieving them won't grow. The leader must know his people well enough to identify attainable goals that require a stretch.

Put the goals in writing.

When people write down their goals, it makes them more accountable for those goals. A study of a Yale University graduating class showed that the small percentage of graduates who had written down their goals accomplished more than all of the other graduates combined. Putting goals in writing works.

It is also important to encourage your potential leaders to review their goals and progress frequently. Ben Franklin set aside time every day to review two questions. In the morning he asked himself, "What good shall I do today?" In the evening he asked, "What good have I done today?"

COMMUNICATE THE FUNDAMENTALS

For people to be productive and satisfied professionally, they have to know what their fundamental responsibilities are. It sounds so simple, but Peter Drucker says one of the critical problems in the workplace today is that there is a lack of understanding between the employer and employee as to what the employee is to do. Often employees are made to feel they are vaguely responsible for everything. It paralyzes them. Instead, we need to make clear to them what they *are* and *are not* responsible for. Then they will be able to focus their efforts on what we want, and they will succeed.

Look again at how a basketball team works. Each of the five players has a particular job. There is a shooting guard whose job is to score points. The other guard is a point guard. His job is to pass the ball to people who can score. Another player is a power forward who is expected to get rebounds. The small forward's job is to score. The center is supposed to rebound, block shots, and score. Each person on the team knows what his job is, what his unique contribution to the team must be. When each concentrates on his particular responsibilities, the team can win.

One of the best ways to clarify expectations is to provide your people with job descriptions. In the description, identify the four to six primary functions you want the person to perform. Avoid long laundry lists of responsibilities. If the job description can't be summarized, the job is probably too broad. Also try to make clear what authority they have, the working parameters for each function they are to perform, and what the chain of authority is within the organization.

Another essential that has to be communicated to new leaders is how they are to prioritize. I tell people that everything they do is either an "A" or a "B" priority. The concept helps them understand what is most important.

"A" priorities are ones that move the organization, department, or job function forward. They break ground, open doors to new opportunities, or develop new markets. They prompt growth within people or the organization. "B" priorities are concerned with maintenance. They are required for things to continue running smoothly, such as answering letters or phone calls, and taking care of details. They are things that cannot be neglected, but they don't add value to the organization. I have found that people often expend their best on "B" priorities because they seem urgent, and they give "A" priorities what's left over. I always encourage my people to give 80 percent of their time and energy to the "A" priorities and the remaining 20 percent to the "B" group.

Finally, a leader must communicate to his or her people that their work has value to the organization and to the individual leader. To the employee, this often is the most important fundamental of all.

PERFORM THE FIVE-STEP PROCESS OF TRAINING PEOPLE

Part of the equipping process includes training people to perform the specific tasks of the jobs they are to do. The approach the leader takes to training will largely determine his people's success or failure. If he takes a dry, academic approach, the potential leaders will remember little of what's taught. If he simply throws the people into the job without any direction, they may feel like this employee of Hagar the Horrible:

Reprinted with special permission of King Features Syndicate

The best type of training takes advantage of the way people learn. Researchers tell us that we remember 10 percent of what we hear, 50 percent of what we see, 70 percent of what we say, and 90 percent of what we hear, see, say, and do. Knowing that, we have to develop an approach to how we will train. I have found the best training method to be a five-step process:

Step 1: I model.

The process begins with my doing the tasks while the people being trained watch. When I do this, I try to give them an opportunity to see me go through the whole process. Too often when leaders train, they begin in the middle of the task and confuse the

99

people they're trying to teach. When people see the task performed correctly and completely, it gives them something to try to duplicate.

Step 2: I mentor.

During this next step, I continue to perform the task, but this time the person I'm training comes alongside me and assists in the process. I also take time to explain not only the *how* but also the *why* of each step.

Step 3: I monitor.

We exchange places this time. The trainee performs the task and I assist and correct. It's especially important during this phase to be positive and encouraging to the trainee. It keeps him trying and it makes him want to improve rather than give up. Work with him until he develops consistency. Once he's gotten down the process, ask him to explain it to you. It will help him to understand and remember.

Step 4: I motivate.

I take myself out of the task at this point and let the trainee go. My task is to make sure he knows how to do it without help and to keep encouraging him so he will continue to improve. It is important for me to stay with him until he senses success. It's a great motivator. At this time the trainee may want to make improvements to the process. Encourage him to do it, and at the same time learn from him.

Step 5: I multiply.

This is my favorite part of the whole process. Once the new leaders do the job well, it becomes their turn to teach others how to do it. As teachers know, the best way to learn something is to teach it. And the beauty of this is it frees me to do other important developmental tasks while others carry on the training.

GIVE THE "BIG THREE"

All the training in the world will provide limited success if you don't turn your people loose to do the job. I believe that if I get the best people, give them my vision, train them in the basics, and then let go, I will get a high return from them. As General George S. Patton once remarked, "Never tell people how to do things. Tell them what to do and they will surprise you with their ingenuity."

You can't turn people loose with no structure, but you also want to give them enough freedom to be creative. The way to do that is to give them the big three: *responsibility, authority,* and *accountability.*

For some people, responsibility is the easiest of the three to give. We all want the people around us to be responsible. We know how important it is. As author/editor Michael Korda said, "Success on any major scale requires you to accept responsibility. . . . In the final analysis, the one quality that all successful people have . . . is the ability to take on responsibility."

What is more difficult for some leaders is allowing their people to keep the responsibility after it's been given. Poor managers want to control every detail of their people's work. When that happens, the potential leaders who work for them become frustrated and don't develop. Rather than desiring more responsibility, they become indifferent or avoid responsibility altogether. If you want your people to take responsibility, truly give it to them.

With responsibility must go authority. Progress does not come unless they are given together. Winston Churchill, while addressing the House of Commons during the Second World War, said, "I am your servant. You have the right to dismiss me when you please. What you have no right to do is ask me to bear responsibility without the power of action." When responsibility and authority come together, people become genuinely empowered.

There's an important aspect of authority that needs to be noted. When we first give authority to new leaders, we are actually *giving them permission* to have authority rather than *giving them authority* itself. True authority has to be earned. George Davis, in *Magic Shortcuts to Executive Success,* notes:

> Authority is not something we buy, are born with, or even have delegated to us by our superiors. It is something we earn —and we earn it from our subordinates. No manager has any real authority over his people until he has proved himself worthy of it—in the eyes of his people—not his own, nor those of his superiors.

We must give our people permission to develop authority. That is our responsibility. They, in turn, must take responsibility for earning it.

I have found there are different levels of authority:

Levels of Authority

Position

The most basic kind of authority comes from a person's position on the organizational chart. This type of authority does not extend beyond the parameters of the job description. This is where all new leaders start. From here they may either earn greater authority, or they can minimize what little authority they have been given. It's up to them.

Competence

This type of authority is based on a person's professional capabilities, the ability to do a job. Followers give competent leaders authority within their area of expertise.

Personality

Followers will also give authority to people based on their personal characteristics, such as personality, appearance, and charisma. Authority based on personality is a little broader than competence-based authority, but it is not really more advanced because it tends to be superficial.

Integrity

Authority based on integrity comes from a person's core. It is based on character. When new leaders gain authority based on their integrity, they have crossed into a new stage of their development.

Spirituality

In secular circles, people rarely consider the power of spiritually-based authority. It comes from people's individual experiences with God and from His power working through them. It is the highest form of authority.

* * *

Leaders must earn authority with each new group of people. However, I have found that once leaders have gained authority on a particular level, it takes very little time for them to establish that level of authority with another group of people. The higher the level of authority, the more quickly it happens.

Once responsibility and authority have been given to people, they are empowered to make things happen. But we also have to be sure they are making the right things happen. That's where accountability comes into the picture. True responsibility on the part of new leaders includes a willingness to be held accountable. If we are providing them the right climate (as described in chapter two), our people will not fear accountability. They will admit mistakes and see them as a part of the learning process.

The leader's part of accountability involves taking the time to review the new leader's work and give honest, constructive criticism. It is crucial that the leader be supportive but honest. It's been said that when Harry Truman was thrust into the presidency upon the death of President Franklin D. Roosevelt, Speaker of the House Sam Rayburn gave him some fatherly advice: "From here on out you're going to have lots of people around you. They'll try to put a wall around you and cut you off from any ideas but theirs. They'll tell you what a great man you are, Harry. But you and I both know you ain't." Rayburn was holding President Truman accountable.

GIVE THEM THE TOOLS THEY NEED

Giving responsibility without resources is ridiculous; it is incredibly limiting. Abraham Maslow said, "If the only tool you have is a hammer, you tend to see every problem as a nail." If we want our people to be creative and resourceful, we need to provide resources.

Obviously, the most basic tools are pieces of equipment, such as copying machines, computers, and whatever else simplifies some-one's work. We must be sure not only to provide everything necessary for a job to be done, but also equipment that will allow jobs, especially "B" priorities, to be done more quickly and efficiently. Always work toward freeing people's time for important things.

Tools, however, include much more than equipment. It is important to provide developmental tools. Spend time mentoring people in specific areas of need. Be willing to spend money on things like books, tapes, seminars, and professional conferences. There is a wealth of good information out there, and fresh ideas from outside an organization can stimulate growth. Be creative in providing tools. It will keep your people growing and equip them to do the job well.

CHECK ON THEM SYSTEMATICALLY

I believe in touching base with people frequently. I like to give mini-evaluations all the time. Leaders who wait to give feedback only during annual formal evaluations are asking for trouble. People need the encouragement of being told they're doing well on a regular basis. They also need to hear as soon as possible when they are not doing well. It prevents a lot of problems within the organization, and it improves the leader.

Factors Determining Follow-Up

How often I check on people is determined by a number of factors:

The importance of the task

When something is critical to the success of the organization, I touch base often.

105

The demands of the work

I find that if the work is very demanding, the person performing it needs encouragement more often. He may also need questions answered or need help solving difficult problems. Occasionally, when the job is really tough, I tell the person to take a break —demanding work can lead a person to burn-out.

The newness of the work

Some leaders have no problem tackling a new task, no matter how different it is from previous work. Others have great difficulty adapting. I check often on the people who are less flexible or creative.

The newness of the worker

I want to give new leaders every possible chance to succeed. So I check on newer people more often. That way I can help them anticipate problems and make sure that they have a series of successes. By that they gain confidence.

The responsibility of the worker

When I know I can give a person a task and it will always get done, I may not check on that person until the task is complete. With less responsible people, I can't afford to do that.

Included in follow-up

My approach to checking on people also varies from person to person. For instance, rookies and veterans should be treated differently. But no matter how long people have been with me, there are some things I always do:

Discuss feelings.

I always give my people an opportunity to tell me how they feel. I also tell them how I'm feeling. It clears the air and makes it possible for us to get down to business.

Measure progress.

Together, we try to determine their progress. I often ask questions to find out what I need to know. If people are hitting obstacles, I remove the ones I can.

Give feedback.

This is a critical part of the process. I always give them some kind of evaluation. I'm honest, and I do my homework to make sure I'm accurate. I give constructive criticism. This lets them know how they're doing, corrects problems, encourages improvement, and speeds the work.

Give encouragement.

Whether the person is doing well or poorly, I always give encouragement. I encourage poor performers to do better. I encourage peak performers. I praise milestones. I try to give hope and encouragement when people are experiencing personal issues. Encouragement keeps people going.

*   *   *

Though it doesn't happen very often, I occasionally have a person whose progress is repeatedly poor. When that happens, I try to determine what's gone wrong. Usually poor performance is a result of one of three things: (1) a mismatch between the job and the person; (2) inadequate training or leadership; or (3) deficiencies in the person performing the work. Before I take any action, I always try to determine what the issues are. I line up my facts to be sure there really is a deficiency in performance and not just a problem with my perception. Next I define as precisely as possible what the deficiency is. Finally, I check with the person who is not performing to get the other side of the story.

Once I've done my homework, I try to determine where the deficiency is. If it's a mismatch, I explain the problem to the person, move him to a place that fits, and reassure him of my confidence in him. If the problem involves training or leadership issues, I back up and redo whatever step hasn't been performed properly. Once again, I let the person know what the problem was and give him plenty of encouragement. If the problem is with the person, I sit down with him and let him know about it. I make it clear where his failures are and what he must do to overcome them. Then I give him another chance. But I also begin the documentation process in case I have to fire him. I want him to succeed, but I will waste no time letting him go if he doesn't do what it takes to improve.

CONDUCT PERIODIC EQUIPPING MEETINGS

Even after you've completed most of your people's training and are preparing to take them into their next growth phase—development—continue to conduct periodic equipping meetings. It helps your people stay on track, helps them keep growing, and encourages them to begin taking responsibility for equipping themselves.

When I prepare an equipping meeting, I include the following:

Good news

I always start on a positive note. I review the good things that are happening in the organization and pay particular attention to their areas of interest and responsibility.

Vision

People can get so caught up in their day-to-day responsibilities that they lose sight of the vision that drives the organization. Use the opportunity of an equipping meeting to recast that vision. It will also give them the appropriate context for the training you are about to give.

Content

Content will depend on their needs. Try to focus training on areas that will help them in the "A" priority areas, and orient the training on the people, not the lesson.

Administration

Cover any organizational items that give the people a sense of security and encourage their leadership.

Empowerment

Take time to connect with the people you equip. Encourage them personally. And show them how the equipping session empowers them to perform their jobs better. They will leave the meeting feeling positive and ready to work.

* * *

The entire equipping process takes a lot of time and attention. It requires more time and dedication from the equipping leader than mere training. But its focus is long term, not short term. Rather than creating followers or even adding new leaders, it multiplies leaders. As I explained in the section on the five-step process of equipping, it is not complete until the equipper and the new leader select someone for the new leader to train. It is only then that the equipping process has come full circle. Without a successor, there can be no success.

Leaders who are equipping others have the greatest possibility of success, no matter what type of organization they're in. When a leader is dedicated to the equipping process, the whole level of performance within the organization rises dramatically. Everyone is better prepared to get the work done. More important, the best-equipped people will be ready for the final growth stage that creates the very best leaders—development. As Fred A. Manske, Jr. said, "The greatest leader is willing to train people and develop them to the point that they eventually surpass him or her in knowledge and ability." The following chapter will show you how to take that step.

The Leader's Lifelong Commitment:

DEVELOPING POTENTIAL LEADERS

If you have done all the things I've discussed so far in this book—created a great environment, nurtured your people, and equipped the best people around you—your achievements have already surpassed those of the majority of managers in the work force today. You can consider yourself a better-than-average leader. If you go no further, though, you will never become a *great* leader. No matter how hard or how smart you work, you will never become one of the best of the best. Why? Because the very best leaders, the top 1 percent, take their people the next step and develop them so they can reach their potential. The growth and development of people is the highest calling of leadership.

You're probably wondering why most leaders don't take this final step. They don't because it's hard work. I once heard the story of a preacher who quit the ministry after twenty years and became a funeral director. When asked why he made the change, he replied, "Well, I

> **The growth and development of people is the highest calling of leadership.**

spent three years trying to straighten out Fred, and Fred is still an alcoholic. And I spent six months trying to straighten out Susan's marriage, and she filed for divorce. Then I spent over two and a half years trying to straighten out Bob's drug problem, and he's still an addict. Now at the funeral home, when I straighten them out—they stay straight."

Living, breathing human beings require continual attention. And development is demanding work. It takes more attention and commitment than either nurturing or equipping. To see the differences in emphases in nurturing, equipping, and developing, look at the following table:

Nurturing	Equipping	Developing
Care	Training for Work	Training for Personal Growth
Focus is on Need	Focus is on Task	Focus is on Person
Relational	Transactional	Transformational
Service	Management	Leadership
Maintains Leadership	Adds Leadership	Multiplies Leadership
Establishing	Releasing	Empowering
Helping	Teaching	Mentoring
Need Oriented	Skill Oriented	Character Oriented
What They Want	What the Organization Needs	What They Need
A Desire	A Science	An Art
Little or No Growth	Short-Term Growth	Long-Term Growth
All	Many	Few

Take a look at the qualities associated with developing leaders. They are based on what the potential leaders need, on their growth. The process is designed to build into them, to bring out their best qualities, to develop their character, and to help them discover and reach their potential.

Because the development of leaders requires time, attention, and commitment, a developer can only work with a few people at a time, as the last entry in the table indicates. Nurture all of your people, and equip many. But develop only a few—the few who are ready and willing.

There is another important difference between equipping and developing people. Equipping is essentially a step-by-step process. You can take people through specific steps to equip them. That is the *science* of equipping as noted in the table on page 114. Leadership development is more of an *art*. It is not a series of specific steps that you take people through. Instead, there are aspects that must be addressed throughout the whole process.

Here are the twelve actions a leader must take to develop potential leaders into the best they can be.

ASK THE THREE MOTIVATION QUESTIONS

All growth begins with motivation. You as the developer must find your potential leaders' motivation and harness it. Begin by asking these questions:

What do they want?

Everyone wants something. Even the person who appears not to be motivated has desires. You need to find out what your people want. Sometimes they will tell you. Other times you need to use discernment. Since you will have already built relationships with them, use information that you've learned during your personal interaction with them. No matter how, you need to find out what your people want because then you will know what will motivate them to develop.

Do they have a way of getting what they want?

Whenever people want something but see no way to get it, they will not be motivated. One of your jobs as the leader is to determine how your potential leaders can achieve what they desire and show them a way to do it. Because you have already traveled the road of achievement, you may be able to see the way more clearly and can help point the way. Sometimes you may even have the power to create a way for them to achieve what they want on a personal level.

Will they be rewarded if successful?

Sometimes even people who have goals and see a way of achieving them lack motivation. Why? Because they don't believe the rewards will outweigh the work required to achieve them. As their leader, you can share from your own experience that the rewards are worth the effort. You are also in a position to show them how their personal goals and desires coincide with those of the organization. When both have the same goals, the rewards are multiplied.

For example, if the goal of one of your people is to become an outstanding salesman, that goal also benefits the organization, and the organization will reward it (in commission or salary). As a result, if that person achieves that goal, he will receive the personal

114

benefits to himself as well as the monetary rewards from the organization. The rewards are multiplied.

Ask the questions to find your people's motivation, and then harness that motivation to help them develop.

BE A GOOD LISTENER

Good leaders are good listeners. Listening to your people will add to your success and to their development. When you listen to their ideas and opinions, especially before you make decisions, you

> **Good leaders are good listeners.**

give them a chance to increase their contribution. Each time you use their ideas and give them credit, they will feel valued, and they will be encouraged to keep contributing. This is one of the best ways to get them to start thinking creatively. They will also develop judgment and begin to understand the reasons why you use some of their ideas and choose not to use others. They will learn to see things more clearly and more in terms of the big picture.

> **Every idea is a good idea until you've settled on the best idea.**

The critical aspect of this process is that you genuinely seek their advice and then listen to their views actively and positively. If you are simply going through the motions, your people will know it. Likewise, never criticize the person making a suggestion, even if it's a poor one. People who feel belittled will soon stop making suggestions, and you may miss out on their next great idea because you've discouraged them from contributing. Try to adopt this attitude: Every idea is a good idea until you've settled on the best idea.

DEVELOP A PLAN
FOR PERSONAL GROWTH

One of the things I enjoy most is doing conferences around the country. I especially love the five or six leadership conferences sponsored each year through our organization INJOY. One of the most important things I talk about at those conferences is personal growth. I often invite anyone in the audience who has already created a personal plan for growth to come up during the break to tell me about it. Do you know that in all the years I have been doing that, not once has anyone come up to me. Why? Because not one had created a personal growth plan for himself.

People think personal growth is a natural result of being alive. Well it's not. Growth is not automatic; it does not necessarily come with experience, nor simply as a result of gathering information. Personal growth must be deliberate, planned, and consistent.

One of the best things you can do for the people you are developing, besides modeling personal growth yourself, is to help them develop their own personal plans for growth. I want to emphasize that growth requires a *plan*. As my friend Zig Ziglar says, "You were born to be a winner, but to be a winner you must plan to win and prepare to win." Growing is the same. You have to create a plan and follow it.

I have devoted the greater part of my life to my own personal development and the creation of materials for the personal development of others. I have created leadership development tapes every month for the last nine years and sent them out to people across the country through INJOY, because my greatest desire is to help others reach their potential. That is why I hold leadership conferences. Let me outline for you a plan for growth that I give people at these conferences. Help your people adapt it to their needs. And use it yourself if you aren't already using another plan that works for you.

116

PRACTICAL STEPS FOR PERSONAL GROWTH

Set aside time daily for growth.

There are two important concepts in this step. First, time for growth must be *planned*. Getting sidetracked is one of the easiest things in the world to do. Growth time that is not strategically planned into the day soon disappears because our lives are busy. People must find a time that works for them and schedule it into their calendar. Then they must guard that time as they would any other appointment. Second, the time set aside must be set aside daily—for no fewer than five days a week. Educators report that people learn more effectively in shorter regular sessions than long infrequent blocks of time. A daily discipline pays dividends.

Here is the weekly plan that I recommend at my conferences:

Monday:	One hour with God
Tuesday:	One hour listening to a leadership tape
Wednesday:	Another hour with the same tape (including time filing notes on highlights and reflecting on what has been learned)
Thursday:	One hour reading a leadership book
Friday:	Another hour with the same book (including time filing notes on highlights and reflecting on what has been learned)

Besides the daily plan, I also recommend going through materials during times that other people normally consider wasted time. For instance, whenever I travel, I take along books and magazines that may not be as meaty as my daily reading but that have good material. If I'm waiting in an airport or flying on a plane, I'm also reviewing material and clipping out useful articles and quotes.

File quickly what you learn.

Every good piece of information a person finds needs to be processed and filed. I have used this system for over thirty years. As I find good articles or quotes, I clip and file them. This has two advantages. First, whenever I need materials for a talk or seminar, I have thirty years of collected resources to draw upon. Second, each time I reduce an article down to its one most relevant sentence or paragraph, I have processed through all the information, digested it, summarized it, and learned it.

Apply quickly what you learn.

Simply knowing a thing will not make it a part of you. To do that, you must apply it. Each time you learn something new, it's good to ask yourself, "Where, when, and how can I use this?" I prefer to do more than simply make a mental connection with the things I learn, so I use this system:

- Select one thing each week that I've learned.
- Put it on a 3 x 5 card. (I keep it in front of me for a week.)
- Share it with my wife.
- Share it with someone else within twenty-four hours.
- Teach it to someone else. (I put it in a lesson.)

Grow with someone.

I have a number of people around me who share things with me and whom I deliberately share things with. When you share what

118

you are learning with others, it increases your insight, builds your relationship with them, gives you a common vision, and holds you accountable. It also creates worthwhile conversation.

Plan your growth and follow it for a year.

The five-day plan outlined above was designed to be followed yearly. Using that plan, you can easily read twelve books and listen to fifty-two tapes per year. At the end of a year, you will have tremendous resources to draw on and will have grown tremendously. If you want to become an expert in a subject, according to Earl Nightengale, spend an hour a day for five years focusing on that subject.

There's one more thing I must say about developing a plan for your people's growth: Start them today! People may tell you that they are too old to start now, that they're too busy to start now, or that the timing isn't right. Personal growth is like investing. It's not your *timing*. It's your *time in*. Get them going now.

> **Personal growth is like investing. It's not your timing. It's your time in.**

KEEP THE GROWTH GOING

We live in a competitive society that focuses on making it. Baseball players live for the day they make it to the big leagues. Business people climb the corporate ladder with the hope of someday being the CEO or chairman of the board. A few of the businesses that use network marketing techniques propose the idea that if a person builds a big enough organization, he or she can sit back and let others do the work. The individual will have made it; he will have arrived. But the idea of arriving is an illusion. Our society is filled with people who arrive somewhere only to find themselves as discontented as they were before they succeeded. The point of the journey is not arriving. The point is what you learn and whom you become along the way. Having goals is positive. Thinking that our journey is over once we achieve some of them is a danger we all face.

John Wooden, one of the most successful basketball coaches of all time, focused on the growing process. In *Six Timeless Marketing Blunders,* William L. Shanklin writes about Wooden's approach to coaching. Shanklin tells that while Wooden coached UCLA, he did not stress winning. He emphasized preparation, teamwork, a willingness to change, and the desire for each person to perform at peak potential. His focus was on the process, not the end product.

The same thing is true in industry. From a quality control expert I heard, "In quality control, we are not concerned about the product. We are concerned about the process. If the process is right, the product is guaranteed." The same is true when it comes to personal growth.

As the developers of leaders, we must keep our people growing. We must model growth, encourage it, and reward it. We must show our people how to keep growing for the long haul. They are to be like trees which grow their entire lives. There is no such thing as a full-grown tree. The day a tree stops growing is the day it dies.

USE THE FOUR-STAGE PROCESS OF ADAPTATION

It takes most people time to adopt new ideas and adapt to new situations. They usually have to go through four stages before new concepts become their own. I have found that they usually accept things in this order:

Visually

Most people are visual. They usually have to see something new in order to understand it.

Emotionally

After people see something new, then they respond to it emotionally. Give them time to work through their emotions before going on to the next phase.

Experientially

Once people understand something and have accepted it emotionally, they are ready to give it a try. Experience enables them to reach the final phase.

Convictionally

After people see something, accept it emotionally, and experience it positively, it becomes truly a part of their thinking, their belief system.

If you are aware of these phases, you will be able to bring people along in their development without as many obstacles.

FOLLOW THE IDEA GRID

Even though you will be helping your people create a personal growth plan and encouraging them to do as much growing as possible on their own, you will also need to teach them yourself.

121

Ideally, you will share with them what you are learning in your own development. I continue to do this with the people in my organization. The best method I have found is represented in the following acronym:

I *nstruction*
D *emonstration*
E *xposure*
A *ccountability*

First I instruct my people in a life-related context. Any idea or theory that cannot be applied to real life is useless. Besides, if it can't be applied to real life, I won't be able to demonstrate it, which is the next step. By actually living and demonstrating any idea before I present it to others, I am able to test it, better able to learn it, and better qualified to teach it. Next I expose my people to actual experience. Once they have heard and seen it, they are ready to try it themselves. Finally, I make sure there is accountability for them, either with me or with each other. If you don't set some kind of accountability, your people may think the ideas are great, but they may forget to use them. And when people are held accountable for using them, the ideas become a part of them.

GIVE THEM VARIED EXPERIENCES

People resist change. If given a chance to do something comfortable and easy that they've done before versus the chance to do something difficult and new, most people will take the safe, easy route. As leaders, we can't let our people become complacent.

Varied experiences add incredibly to people's development. It keeps them growing, stretching, and learning. The broader people's base of experience, the better they will be at handling new challenges, solving problems, and overcoming difficult situations. In my organization, we have a three-year rule. Our leaders must change a significant number of their major duties and responsibilities every three years. It forces them to gain new skills. It gives newer leaders the opportunity to develop by having them step into new areas of responsibility. It allows older leaders to tackle new challenges. And it enhances everyone's creativity.

It is often tempting for us to leave successful people where they are—to keep them in the same jobs. But we must keep in mind that we are doing more than just getting the job done well. We are building leaders, and that takes extra effort and time. Angus J. MacQueen tells a story about James Garfield that illustrates this point. He says that prior to becoming President of the United States, Garfield was principal of Hiram College in Ohio. When a father asked if the course of study couldn't be simplified so his son might finish school sooner, Garfield replied, "Certainly. But it all depends upon what you want to make of your boy. When God wants to make an oak tree, He takes a hundred years. When He wants to make a squash, He requires only two months." Give your leaders deep, broad roots by growing them slowly and varying their experiences.

STRIVE FOR EXCELLENCE

Vince Lombardi, a great leader and one of the best ever to coach professional football, once said, "The quality of a person's life is in direct proportion to their commitment to excellence, regardless of their chosen field of endeavor." Lombardi recognized the importance of striving for excellence. And he was able to instill that desire in the people he coached.

When you strive for excellence, you prompt your people to shoot for the top. When a leader's goal is acceptability rather than excellence, then even the best people in the organization will produce what is merely acceptable. The rest may not even produce that minimum. When excellence is the standard, the best will hit the mark, and the others will at least hit the board.

> **Excellence breeds character, and character breeds excellence.**

Another advantage of focusing on excellence is that it shows your people's character. The success of any organization will not reach beyond the character of its leaders. Excellence breeds character, and character breeds excellence. Demand excellence from your people, and they will develop into people who also demand excellence of themselves and the people they lead.

IMPLEMENT THE LAW OF EFFECT

Educational psychologist E. L. Thorndyke did work in behavior modification around the turn of the century. It led him to discover what he called the Law of Effect. Simply stated, it is this: "Behaviors immediately rewarded increase in frequency; behaviors immediately punished decrease in frequency."

We must ask ourselves what is being rewarded in our organizations. Do we reward personal growth and development? If so, our people will be growing.

Several years ago I developed a list of behaviors and qualities that I expect from the people in my organization, and I determined to reward those behaviors. I call it the RISE program:

R *ewards*
I *ndicating*
S *taff*
E *xpectations*

In other words, I decided I would give rewards to staff members to indicate they were meeting or exceeding expectations. The qualities I value most highly and reward are a positive attitude, loyalty, personal growth, leadership reproduction, and creativity. Notice that personal growth is on the list. I want to encourage you to decide what you value and determine to reward it in your people, and put personal growth on your list. You will find that once you set up a positive reward system for achieving the right goals, your people will become their own best managers, and they will develop as leaders.

CARE ENOUGH TO CONFRONT

Rewarding the positive takes effort, but it is pretty easy to do. Confronting negative behavior is tougher. Many people avoid confrontation. Some fear being disliked and rejected. Others are afraid confrontation will make things worse by creating anger and resentment in the person they confront. But when a person's behavior is inappropriate, *avoiding confrontation always worsens the situation.* First, the organization suffers because the person is not acting in its best interest. Second, you suffer because the person's deficiencies reduce your effectiveness. And finally, when a person is acting inappropriately and isn't told, you have robbed him of an important opportunity to learn and grow in his development process. Any time a leader avoids a confrontation, he should ask himself whether he is holding back for his own good or for the good of the organization. If it is for himself, he is acting under selfish motives.

Confrontation, in its best form, is a win-win situation. In this country we have been conditioned to believe that conflict always produces a winner and a loser. But that does not have to be true. To produce a win-win, we must approach confrontation with the right attitude. Think of confrontation as a chance to help and develop your people. And never confront in anger or out of a desire to show power. Do it with respect and the other person's best interest at heart. Here are ten guidelines I use to make sure I'm doing just that:

Confront ASAP.

The longer I wait, the less likely I am to do what must be done. Another benefit to confronting immediately is that I am not likely to have to argue with the person over details.

Separate the person from the wrong action.

I am to address myself to the action and confront it, not the person. I must continue to support and encourage the person.

Confront only what the person can change.

If I ask a person to change something he can't, he will become frustrated and it will strain our relationship.

Give the person the benefit of the doubt.

I always try to start from the assumption that people's motives are right and work from there. If I can give them the benefit of the doubt, I do—especially in areas that are open to interpretation or unclear.

Be specific.

The person I'm confronting can only address and change what is specifically identified. If you can't identify specifics, you may be making some false assumptions.

Avoid sarcasm.

Sarcasm indicates anger with people, not their actions. When confronting, I avoid sarcasm.

Avoid words like *always* and *never*.

When I tell a person never to do a certain behavior, I am asking him to cling blindly to a rule, even in situations when it's not the best thing to do. I'd rather encourage him to use his head and take the right course of action in any given situation, based on right principles.

Tell the person how you feel about what was done wrong.

If the person's actions have offended me, I tell him right then and there. I don't want to be going back over old ground later in order to vent emotions.

Give the person a game plan to fix the problem.

I always want to help the person succeed, not fail. If I can help him fix the problem, everybody wins.

Affirm him or her as a person and a friend.

I prepare to confront in the same way that I fix a sandwich. I put the confrontation in the middle like meat. On both sides I put affirmation and encouragement.

> **Positive confrontation is a sure sign that you care for a person.**

Positive confrontation is a sure sign that you care for a person and have his best interests at heart. Each time you build up your people and identify their problems, you give them an opportunity to grow.

MAKE THE HARD DECISIONS

In chapter two I pointed out that leaders must be willing to make difficult decisions in order to create a climate that encourages development. Some of those difficult decisions concerned letting employees go. But there are hard decisions to be made during your leaders' development process too.

People respond differently to development, and I have found from personal experience that each person who does grow will plateau at one of six levels of development:

128

Level 1. Some growth

Some people experience growth at a very slow rate and their growth lacks direction. These people improve almost imperceptibly. They may be competent, but they will never shine in their jobs.

Level 2. Growth that makes them capable in their job

Many people mistakenly believe that simply doing their job well is the final goal in their development. It's not. Many people without a good developer or a strong desire for personal growth stop here in the growth process.

Level 3. Growth that makes them able to reproduce themselves in their job

At this level of growth, people are beginning to add to their value because they are able to train others in their area of expertise. Some people who are technically strong but have marginal leadership skills are able to do this. Others with strong leadership skills can do it despite marginal technical abilities. People who are strong in both areas often move up to the next level.

Level 4. Growth that takes them to a higher level job

The jump from Level 3 to Level 4 is difficult. It requires that people be willing to dedicate themselves to growing both personally and professionally. As they are able to broaden their thinking and experience, they become more capable and valuable to their organization and leaders.

Level 5. Growth that allows them to take others higher

It is at this level that great leaders begin to emerge. These people are true developers of people, and they no longer add value to their leaders and organization—they *multiply* it.

Level 6. Growth that allows them to handle any job

People who develop to this level are rare. If you have the privilege of helping people to this level, treat them with the greatest love and respect. These people are leaders who could make it anywhere. And they have skills and abilities that transcend any particular field or industry. In your lifetime if God blesses you with one or more of these people, together you will have the ability to make an impact far beyond your own individual capabilities.

Take a look at the figure below. As you can see, the pool of people at each level is represented by a circle. The higher the level, the fewer people at that level. You will also notice that each successive jump gets more difficult as the levels get higher. Each takes more commitment, dedication, and tenacity than the one before.

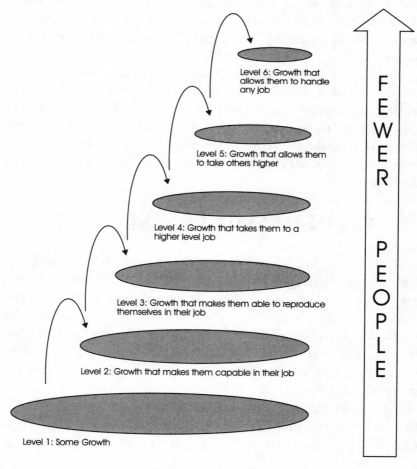

Pools of people at each level of growth

The reason I write about hard decisions is that you will have to make hard decisions concerning every person you develop other than the person who makes it to Level 6. When you are a developer of people, you meet each person on the level where you find him, usually on Level 1, then you begin a journey. Your job is to walk alongside that person and help him for as long as he is willing to keep going and growing. When that person stops growing, that's when you have to do something difficult: You have to leave that person behind. Your relationship can continue, but your development of that person won't.

That is one of the difficult things about being a developer of people. We give people so much time, attention, and love that leaving one behind can be like letting go of one of our children. But you can't force a person to keep growing to the highest level. You have to make the hard decision of leaving that person on his own plateau. It's difficult, but it's a price worth paying in order to develop people.

BE PERSONALLY SECURE

To be a great developer of people, you must be personally secure, because taking your people to the height of their potential may mean they will pass you by. As I mentioned in chapter one, Andrew Carnegie wanted to be remembered as "a man who was wise enough to bring into his service men who knew more than he." It takes a very secure person to face that possibility, but without such a mind-set, you may be competing with your people instead of developing them.

As you prepare to lead and develop the people around you, I'd like you to keep in mind something Harvey Firestone said: "It is only as we develop others that we permanently succeed." All of the certificates of recognition we receive in life will fade. The monuments we build will crumble. The trophies will corrode. But what we do for others will make a lasting impact on our world.

The Leader's Highest Return:
FORMING A DREAM TEAM OF LEADERS

Anyone who has ever experienced being on a team—from playing on a professional sports team to being a member of the junior high band—knows that being a part of a successful team can be one of the most rewarding experiences in life. And on the right team, it can also be one of the most powerful.

First, just what is a team? We know it's more than simply a group of people. If that's all it were, then people waiting at a trolley stop would make up a team. But they don't. I need to add that to be a team, a group must have a *common goal,* although that's not enough. Our people at the trolley stop have the common goal of waiting for the trolley car that will take them somewhere. Even if they had the same destination, it would help, but it would not be enough to make them a team. There must be *cooperation,* but once again, that doesn't complete the whole picture. Add *communication*—there is no team without communication. But teams also must have *commitment.* It ensures that the group will work together no matter what adverse circumstances arise.

Let's look again at our people waiting for the trolley to see how an ordinary group may act compared to a team. It's a hot, humid summer day. The group at the stop includes business people in suits, mothers with toddlers and infants in strollers, construction workers, and homeless people. Finally, a crowded trolley pulls up to the stop. When everyone sees that the cars are packed, they all scramble. Each person runs to get a spot. A woman with a stroller does her best to herd her four children to the door of one of the cars, but she can't find a place with enough room to fit her whole family. By the time she tries another car, the doors close and the trolley moves away. She will have to wait thirty minutes for the next trolley.

The same trolley pulls into the next stop. Waiting is a team of twelve high school baseball players on a field trip with their coach. When they see how crowded the trolley cars are, they prepare to scramble, too. One player shouts, "I'll check the first car to see if there's room." Another says, "I'll take the last one." The coach holds open the door to the full middle car because he knows that the trolley can't leave while a door is open. The player at the last car shouts, "There's room back here" as he holds that door open. Yet another player goes to find the teammate who went forward. As they reassemble in the last car, the coach counts to make sure everyone has made it.

As important as teamwork is, and as powerful as it can be to the success of an organization, many leaders don't teach their people how to work in teams. Management consultant Kenneth Blanchard observed:

> As I work in companies around the country, I often ask people what percent of their time do they spend in groups. Although managers report 60 to 90 percent of their time is usually spent in group activities, they also say they get little or no training in skills needed to work efficiently in groups. I know of few companies that focus training on this important skill.

Many leaders think that building a team and developing team-work is only for sports. They don't realize that they can build a team within their organization. Nor do they have any idea how to approach the task.

Developing leaders is wonderful: It's fulfilling and rewarding. But developing a team of leaders—that's incredible. A good team is always greater than the sum of its parts, but teams of *leaders* increase their effectiveness exponentially. With the right leaders teamed together, there is nothing they can't accomplish. Anyone who is developing leaders can also develop them into a team. It is the last development task that will yield the highest return.

THE QUALITIES OF A DREAM TEAM

In all my years of people development and team building, I have found that all successful teams share some common charac-teristics. If you as the team leader, or coach, can cultivate these qualities in your group of leaders, they will become a cohesive team capable of leaping tall buildings or performing any other re-quired task. Here are those characteristics:

THE TEAM MEMBERS CARE FOR ONE ANOTHER

All great teams begin with this quality. It is the foundation upon which everything else is built. Teams that don't bond can't build. Why? Because they never become a cohesive unit.

One of the best descriptions of this quality that I've ever come across was given by Notre Dame football coach Lou Holtz. He said that he had once watched a television program that examined why men died for their country. In the program, which looked at United States Marines, the French Foreign Legion, and the British Commandos, it was noted that men died for their country because of the love they had for their fellow man. In the show, they interviewed a soldier who had been wounded in combat and was recovering in a hospital when he heard his unit was going back out on a dangerous mission. The soldier escaped from the hospital and went with them, only to be wounded again. When asked why he did it, he said that after you work and live with people, you soon realize your survival depends on one another.

> **Teams that don't bond can't build.**

For a team to be successful, the teammates have to know they will look out for one another. When a team member cares about no one but himself, the whole team suffers. Uncaring people on a team remind me of a couple of guys in a story I once read: Two shipwrecked men sat together at one end of a lifeboat, doing nothing. As they watched intently, the people at the other end of the boat were bailing furiously. One man then said to the other, "Thank God that hole isn't in *our* end of the boat!"

I have found that one of the best ways to get members of a team to care about one another is to get them together outside of a work context in order to build relationships. Every year in our organization we plan retreats and other events that put our people together in social settings. And during those times, we also make sure they spend part of their time with staff members they don't know very well. That way they're not only building relationships, they're being prevented from developing cliques.

THE TEAM MEMBERS KNOW WHAT IS IMPORTANT

One of the things I enjoy most about a team experience is how the team functions as a single unit. All of its parts have a common goal and purpose. This quality is developed by making sure each team member knows what is important to the team. This quality, like the previous one, is foundational to team building. Without it team members cannot truly work together.

In a sport such as basketball, the players on a team recognize that scoring is what is important. When a team is more effective at scoring than the opponent, it wins. Because the team members know that, they spend their time improving and perfecting their ability to score. That is their focus. In contrast, in many organizational settings, the team members don't know what it means to "score." They may have a list of duties, but they don't know how those duties go together to make a score. It would be the equivalent of a basketball player who knew how to set a pick, dribble, pass, or toss up a ball, but who never knew all these skills were used together to score baskets. Without that knowledge, every time a player who was a good ball handler got the ball, he might dribble it until the shot clock ran out. That player could be the finest dribbler in all the world, and his ball handling could give spectators great joy. But the team would fail to score every time he touched the ball, and they would never win a game. On the other hand, if he knew dribbling was merely a tool used by a player so the team could score, then his attitude, actions, and effectiveness would change dramatically. And the whole team's success would follow in the wake of those changes.

You can see what happens if just one player on a basketball team doesn't know what is important to the team. It makes him ineffective. And when he is in the game, it is impossible for the team to succeed. The same is true in any organization. Anyone who doesn't know what's important to the team not only fails to contribute to the team, but actually *prevents the team from achieving success*. That is why it is so important for the leader of the team to identify what is important to the team and to communicate that information to his team members.

THE TEAM MEMBERS COMMUNICATE WITH ONE ANOTHER

The third foundational quality of an effective team is communication. Just as it is important for the team leader to communicate what is important to the team, the individual members of the team must communicate with one another. Without it, the players are likely to work against each other. Important tasks can be left undone, and team members can find themselves duplicating work.

Anyone who has played basketball is familiar with the situation in which two players go up for a rebound and fight one another for the ball, only to find that they are on the same team. On teams where players communicate with one another, a third player will shout, "Same team!" to make sure they don't lose the ball while trying to take it away from one another. That is what communication on the team is all about: letting each other know what's going on so the team's best interest is protected.

The same is true in nonsporting organizations. Clear and formal lines of communication must be established. But even more important, an atmosphere of positive communication must be established and encouraged on a daily basis. People on the team must be made to feel that they are in an environment where it is safe to offer suggestions or criticism without feeling threatened, freely trade information in the spirit of cooperation, and discuss ideas without being negatively criticized. Open communication among teammates increases productivity.

THE TEAM MEMBERS GROW TOGETHER

Once the members of the team care for one another, have a common goal, and communicate with one another, they are ready to start growing. Growth within a team is much like growth within a marriage. It is important and necessary. Without it, the team and its individual members do not improve. But like marriage, the growth should include shared experiences and periods of communication so team members stay connected to one another. In a marriage, when growth is not continuously interactive, eventually the two people's lives develop parallel but very separate courses. They cease to function together as a team. If much time passes, their two courses move further and further apart until each doesn't know what the other is doing. Finally they won't care for each other, their goals will be different, and they will stop communicating. Their team is likely to fall apart.

In an organization, it is the team leader's responsibility to orchestrate the team's growth. He must make sure his people grow both personally and professionally. And he must ensure that their growth happens together—as a team.

When I work on growing my team members, I take several different approaches. First, we all learn together on a regular basis, at least once a month. In this way, I *know* there are some things everyone in the organization knows, and they share the common experience of learning these things together, regardless of their position or responsibilities.

Second, I regularly build small teams of learners. I periodically have groups of three or four work together on a project that requires them to learn. It builds strong relational bonds between those people. It's a good idea, by the way, to vary the members of these teams so that different people are learning to work together. It also gives you an idea about the particular chemistry of different groups as they work together.

141

Finally, I frequently send different people to conferences, workshops, and seminars. When they return, I ask them to teach others in the organization what they've learned. It gets everyone used to teaching and learning from each other. Shared experiences and the give-and-take of communication are the greatest ways to promote team growth.

THERE IS A TEAM FIT

As people who care about each other grow together and work toward a common goal, they get to know each other better. They start to appreciate each other's strengths and become aware of each other's weaknesses. They begin to recognize and appreciate each player's unique qualities. And that leads to the development of a team "fit."

The type of fit a team has depends on many things. It is more than just the way a group of people with particular talents come together. We have probably all seen teams made up of talented players at each position who should have been able to play well together but couldn't. Despite their talents, they didn't have the right chemistry.

A good team fit requires an attitude of partnership.

A good team fit requires an attitude of partnership. Every team member must respect the other players. They must desire to contribute to the team, and they must come to expect a contribution from every other person. Above all, they must learn to trust each other. It is trust that makes it possible for them to rely on one another. It allows them to make up for each other's weaknesses instead of trying to exploit them. It enables one team member to say to the other, "You go ahead and do this task because you are

Trust allows team members to begin working as a single unit.

better at it than I am," without shame or manipulation. Trust allows team members to begin working as a single unit, to begin accomplishing the things that together they recognize as important. Once the players know and trust one another, and develop a fit, the team's personality will begin to emerge.

THE TEAM MEMBERS PLACE THEIR INDIVIDUAL RIGHTS BENEATH THE BEST INTEREST OF THE TEAM

Once team members believe in the goals of their team and begin to develop genuine trust in one another, they will be in a position to demonstrate true teamwork. Their mutual trust will make it possible for them to place their own rights and privileges beneath the best interest of the team.

Notice that I mention the team members will be in a *position* to demonstrate true teamwork. That does not necessarily mean that they will. For there to be teamwork, several things must happen. First, they must genuinely believe that the value of the team's success is greater than the value of their own individual interests. They will be able to believe it only if they care about one another and if their leader has effectively cast the vision of what is important. Then they will recognize that their success will come with the team's success.

Second, for team members to place their individual rights beneath the team's best interest, personal sacrifice must be encouraged and then rewarded—by the team leader and the other members of the team. As this happens, the people

> **Individualism wins trophies, but teamwork wins pennants.**

will come to identify themselves more and more with the team. At that point they will recognize that individualism wins trophies, but teamwork wins pennants.

EACH TEAM MEMBER PLAYS A SPECIAL ROLE

As the team fit becomes stronger and each person is willing to put the team first, people begin to recognize their different roles on the team. They can do this because they know what must be accomplished to win, and they know their teammates' capabilities. With that knowledge and some encouragement from the team leader, people will gladly assume appropriate roles. Philip Van Auken, in *The Well-Managed Ministry,* recognizes this as the *Niche Principle.* He says, "People who occupy a special place on the team feel special and perform in a special way. Team niches humanize teamwork."

In an ideal situation, each person's role is built on his or her greatest strengths. That way each person's talents can be maximized. But it doesn't always work exactly that way. Because the team's success is what is most important, sometimes the team members must be flexible. For example, anyone who follows professional basketball has heard of Magic Johnson. He played for the Los Angeles Lakers during the 1980s when they were one of the best teams. His greatest talent was his ability for making plays happen, especially assists using incredible look-away passes. But Johnson was a player who was always willing to fill whatever role the team needed. Over several seasons, he started in NBA championship games as a guard, forward, and center. He may be the only professional basketball player who has ever done that.

The important thing is that all the team members take a role that fits the goals and needs of the organization as well as their own personal talents and abilities. When any role is not filled, the whole team suffers. The situation can be like the one in a story that management consultant James Lukaszewski told in one of his speeches:

[One day a farmer] was sitting on his porch noticing a highway department truck pulling over on the shoulder of the road. A man got out, dug a sizeable hole in the ditch, and got back into the vehicle. A few minutes later, the other occupant of the truck got out, filled up the hole, tamped the dirt, and got back in the truck. Then they drove forward on the shoulder about fifty yards and repeated the process—digging, waiting, refilling. After a half-dozen repetitions, the farmer sauntered over to them. "What are you doing?" he asked.

"We're on a highway beautification project," the driver said. "And the guy who plants the trees is home sick today."

As team leaders, we must recognize what roles need to be filled by our team members for the team to accomplish its goal. And when we see a role not being filled, we must make adjustments to the team to make sure the job gets done.

AN EFFECTIVE TEAM HAS A GOOD BENCH

In sports, the bench may be the most misunderstood resource of the team. Many "starting" players believe that they are important while the people on the bench are not. They believe they could do without them. Others who spend much of their time on the bench don't recognize their own contribution. Some mistakenly believe they don't have to bother preparing the way the starters do, that they don't have to be ready to play. But the truth is that a good bench is indispensable. Without a good bench, a team will never succeed.

The first thing a good bench gives is depth. In sports, many teams can produce a winning season. But when the level of competition goes up, such as in a play-off or a national tournament, a team without depth just can't make it. If the team does not have

145

good reserve players, it will not be able to go the distance. I have yet to see a championship team that did not have a good bench. In fact, developing a good bench is what much of this book is about: selecting, equipping, and developing people to do their best and get the job done when they are needed.

Having a pool of good players able to play different roles gives the team leader great flexibility in any situation. In basketball, for instance, a coach will start a game with one group of people when playing against an opponent whose players are particularly tall. He may have another lineup when playing a particularly quick opponent. Some combinations of players will be great defensively. Others may be great at executing a run-and-gun offense. Which players he puts in the game will often depend on who his opponent is. Team leaders in other organizations will have the same kinds of options when they have a strong bench. With depth, the team can handle a variety of situations and demands with grace and effectiveness.

Another property of a team's bench is that it sets the tone for the whole team's level of play. This is true because the team's preparation depends on the bench. In sports, teams practice against their own players. If the starters practice only against weak players, their performance will not improve. But a good bench causes them to do their best all the time, to constantly improve. The same is true in any organization. If the level of play in the organization is high every day, then the team's performance will be top-notch when it really counts.

Finally, a good bench is a requirement for a successful team because it provides a place for a weary player to rest. On successful teams, when one of the players cannot make it any further due to fatigue or injury, his teammates carry the load and give him a rest. This is possibly the finest quality of teamwork—the willingness of one player to step up his level of play and go the extra mile for his teammate in a time of need. It is the ultimate indication of a player's desire to put the team and its goals first.

THE TEAM MEMBERS KNOW EXACTLY WHERE THE TEAM STANDS

In sports, the ability to know where their team stands at every moment during a game separates the great players from adequate players. That quality as much as talent enables a player to move from one level of play up to the next, such as college to the pros. Coaches have different terms for this quality. A football coach, for instance, might call it *football sense*. A basketball coach might call it *court sense* or *vision*. It is the ability to know how many seconds are left on the clock, how many points they are down, and which players are hot or hurt on each team. It is a quality that makes players, and therefore teams, great.

> **Knowing where the team stands at every moment separates the great players from the adequate players.**

Outside of sports, the quality could be called *organizational sense*. It is the ability to know what is happening within the organization, how the organization stands in reference to its goals, how it stacks up against the competition, how the different players are doing, and how much more they can give in order to get the team where it needs to go. Not all team members are equally gifted with this sense. It is the job of the team leader to keep all of the players informed. He must get them to check on the team's progress and listen to the other players to know where the team stands. If all the team members are informed of where the team stands, they are in a better position to know what it is going to take for the team to succeed.

147

THE TEAM MEMBERS ARE WILLING TO PAY THE PRICE

Time after time, success comes down to sacrifice—willingness to pay the price. The same is true of a winning team. Each member of the team must be willing to sacrifice time and energy to practice and preparation. He must be willing to be held accountable. He must be willing to sacrifice his own desires. He must be willing to give up part of himself for the team's success.

> **Success comes down to sacrifice— willingness to pay the price.**

It all comes down to the desire and dedication of the individuals on the team. It's as true in business as it is in sports. It's even true in war. In an interview with David Frost, General Norman Schwarzkopf, commander of the Allied forces in the Gulf War, was asked, "What's the greatest lesson you've learned out of all this?" He replied:

> I think that there is one really fundamental military truth. And that's that you can add up the correlation of forces, you can look at the number of tanks, you can look at the number of airplanes, you can look at all these factors of military might and put them together. But unless the soldier on the ground, or the airman in the air, has the will to win, has the strength of character to go into battle, believes that his cause is just, and has the support of his country . . . all the rest of that stuff is irrelevant.

Without each person's conviction that the cause is worth the price, the battle will never be won, and the team will not succeed. There must be commitment.

When you build a team within your organization, you will be

capable of a level of success you never thought possible. Teamwork for a worthwhile vision makes it possible for common people to attain uncommon results. And when the team members are not common people, but leaders, their accomplishments can multiply. All the team needs is the right coach. And becoming that coach is the subject of the next chapter.

The Leader's Greatest Joy:

COACHING A DREAM TEAM OF LEADERS

A few years ago, American sports journalists could talk about nothing but the Dream Team—the United States Olympic basketball team composed of Michael Jordan, Larry Bird, Magic Johnson, Charles Barkley, and other basketball greats. Some players on that team have been called the best ever to play the game of basketball. When people watched them play, the question was not whether they would win or lose. The question was, "What magnificent plays will I see, and how big a margin will the team win by?" The team was such an assembly of stars that even the players on the opposing teams were asking them for their autographs.

All coaches dream of having a team like that—players who know the game inside and out, who have the talent, the desire, and the discipline to compete and succeed on the highest level. Most leaders dream of the same thing, but most of them think it will never happen to them. And for many that's true—it won't. Why? Because they don't know what it means to be a winning coach.

Banker Walter Wriston, in *Harvard Business Review,* says, "The person who figures out how to harness the collective genius of the people in his or her organization is going to blow the competition away!" That is what a great leader does: He harnesses the collective genius of his team members. He knows how to select, motivate, and empower his people.

In over twenty-five years of leadership, I have been privileged to lead some wonderful teams of people. Through those years, I have discovered that in order to become a dream team coach, a leader must develop ten qualities.

THE QUALITIES OF A DREAM TEAM COACH

As Charles Frances once said, "You can buy a man's time, you can even buy his physical presence at a given place, but you cannot buy enthusiasm . . . you cannot buy loyalty . . . you cannot buy the devotion of hearts, minds, or souls. You must earn these." The following ten characteristics of a dream team coach are qualities which will earn a team's respect and loyalty, and they will motivate and empower the people to play like a dream team.

A DREAM TEAM COACH CHOOSES PLAYERS WELL

Throughout the book, I've given a lot of attention to identifying and selecting potential leaders. And you already know how to go about developing people into effective individual players. Choosing the right people is vital. Red Auerbach, longtime Boston Celtics president, said, "How you select people is more important than how you manage them once they're on the job. If you start with the right people, you won't have problems later on. If you hire the wrong people, for whatever reason, you're in serious trouble and all the revolutionary management techniques in the world won't bail you out." Another great sports leader, Lou Holtz, put it this way: "You've got to have great athletes to win. . . . You can't win without good athletes, but you can lose with them. This is where coaching makes the difference." Both men recognized that you have to begin with the right raw materials to create a winning team.

As Bobb Biehl says in *Increasing Your Leadership Confidence,* along with clear direction and sound finances, having the right players determines 60 to 80 percent of the success of any company or organization. If you want to give yourself a chance to win, start by picking winners.

> **Having the right players determines 60 to 80 percent of the success of any organization.**

I can identify what a winner looks like for my organization. I can tell whether a person has the potential to be an all-star contributor. I want the people close to me to:

Know my heart:	This takes time for both of us and desire on their part.
Be loyal to me:	They are an extension of me and my work.
Be trustworthy:	They must not abuse authority, power, or confidences.
Be discerning:	They make decisions for me.
Have a servant's heart:	They carry a heavy load because of my high demands.

153

Be a good thinker:	Our two heads are better than my one.
Be a finisher:	They take authority and carry out the vision.
Have a heart for God:	My heart for God is my driving force in life.

When a person displays those qualities, I know he or she has the potential to play on my dream team.

A DREAM TEAM COACH CONSTANTLY COMMUNICATES THE GAME PLAN

Every good coach I've ever seen has worked from a game plan. He's got one not only for each individual game, but a plan for the development of the whole team over the course of the current and upcoming seasons. Once the game plan has been drawn up, he then communicates it to his team on an almost continual basis.

Bear Bryant, the late University of Alabama football coach, effectively communicated his game plan to his players. He recognized there were specific things his players needed to know. Five points explain what he believed a coach should do:

Tell them what you expect of them. [This tells them how they are to fit into the game plan so they know what they should try to do.]

Give them an opportunity to perform. [This gives them a chance to be a part of the game plan, to carry out the vision.]

Let them know how they're getting along. [This lets them have an opportunity to learn, improve, and increase their contribution.]

Instruct and empower them when they need it. [This gives them the means to learn, improve, and increase their contribution.]

Reward them according to their contribution. [This gives them incentive for their effort.]

The process must begin with communicating the game plan. That is the key to productivity. But it must continue with the exchange of information. Or as Sydney J. Harris said, information is giving out while communication is getting through. When there is interactive communication between the team leader and his people, it empowers them to succeed.

A DREAM TEAM COACH TAKES THE TIME TO HUDDLE

Another important part of the communication process is huddling. When a team huddles, it recalls the game plan and how it is to be implemented. When players don't take time to huddle, the results can be disastrous—or even comical.

The story is told of a gentleman who was walking down a residential street when he noticed a man struggling with a washing machine at the doorway of his house. When he volunteered to help, the homeowner was overjoyed, and the two men together began to work and struggle with the bulky appliance. After several minutes of fruitless effort, the two stopped and just looked at each other. They were on the verge of total exhaustion. Finally, when they caught their breath, the first man said to the homeowner: "We'll never get this washing machine in there!" To which the homeowner replied: "In? I'm trying to move it out!"

I find that things are never too busy or urgent to take the time to huddle. Here are five things that a huddle provides:

Focus

No matter how often or well a coach communicates the game plan, it never hurts to use huddle time to get people to refocus on what's important. In basketball, successful coaches take time-outs to huddle the players, especially when the opposing team is causing them to get out of their game plan. When they huddle, they go over the fundamentals to get back on track.

Even in politics focus is important. In 1992, following what analysts called flat campaigning by all the candidates, Bill Clinton was elected president. One reason was he was able to keep his campaign agenda focused on the areas where the American people most wanted change.

An opportunity to listen

When the team gets together, all the players and coaches have a chance to exchange information. Communication must flow both ways. When the coach is receiving the right information, it helps him send out the right information. New information can also prompt a coach to make adjustments.

An opportunity to make personnel changes

Sometimes the adjustments coaches need to make are changes in personnel or their responsibilities. Often the best way to solve a problem is to allow a different player to tackle it. A good coach can see that and is willing to make a change.

An opportunity to make play changes

Other times, the players are fine. What needs to be changed are the plays being run. Flexibility is a valuable quality in a coach. The best coaches are good at making necessary adjustments.

An opportunity to rest

Sometimes players just need an opportunity to stop and take a breather and regroup. A well-timed huddle can help the team revitalize so they can carry on and succeed.

A DREAM TEAM COACH KNOWS WHAT HIS OR HER PLAYERS PREFER

Bringing out the best in team members requires that their coach know them and what is important to them. Padgett Thompson, a Kansas-based training organization, recently asked employees to rank their workplace wants in order of importance. They published those findings in *Training and Development Journal*. Of the many items they listed, the three things employees most valued were:

157

- Appreciation for a job well done
- A feeling that they're "in" on things
- Management understanding of their personal problems

Padgett Thompson then compared these results with the things supervisors *thought* employees would value. By comparison, the supervisors ranked these three items eighth, tenth, and ninth.

The supervisors' lack of knowledge concerning their employees may account for another survey statistic reported by John D. Hatfield and Richard C. Huseman in *Managing the Equity Factor*. It states that 85 percent of the workers across the United States said they could work harder on the job. More than half claimed they could double their effectiveness "if they wanted to."

The truth of the matter is that people don't produce because they aren't motivated or appreciated. Their leaders don't know what they want. People often change jobs for personal reasons, not for professional ones. And their emotions play the greatest part in their motivation. Good coaches know what their people prefer, and they use that knowledge to attain the team's and the individual player's goals.

A DREAM TEAM COACH EXCELS IN PROBLEM SOLVING

"A great leader doesn't treat problems as special," said Al Davis, successful owner of the Los Angeles Raiders. "He treats them as normal." Successful coaches never have "perfection" as their goal. If they did, they would fail every time. We live in an imperfect world where problems always occur. Certainly, a leader should strive for excellence, but he should expect problems to occur. And believe it or not, he should welcome them. Problems almost always create opportunities—to learn, grow, and improve.

> **Problems almost always create opportunities— to learn, grow, and improve.**

All leaders can become good problem solvers. To do so, they must do four things: They must anticipate problems *before they occur*. They must maintain a positive attitude *while they occur*. They must use all their resources to solve them as quickly as possible so they *cease to occur*. And finally, they must learn from them so the same problems *do not occur again*.

Most issues requiring a coach's problem-solving skills fall into one of three categories. They are either player, preparation, or game issues:

Problem-solving issues with players

Issues with players require good communication skills as well as good problem-solving skills. One common problem is that the players don't work together as a team. (See chapter seven for ways to resolve this problem.) Another problem may involve players who are facing personal issues that require a coach's assistance and patient understanding. Possibly the most frustrating problem occurs when a player is not reaching his potential. A good coach must work with the player to help him identify his goals and then motivate him so that he begins to grow again.

Problem-solving issues with preparation

Probably the most common problem associated with preparation is the boredom factor. Many of the basics that must be taken care of in the preparation process can be boring. Good coaches provide a climate that minimizes boredom and reminds players of the positive results that preparation brings.

Related to the problem of boredom is morale. When morale is low, so is production. Good coaches keep their players' attitudes positive.

> **Good coaches approach each challenge from a fresh perspective.**

The last problem is a failure to prepare differently for different opponents (or projects). Good coaches approach each opponent from a fresh perspective and with creativity. If each new opponent is regarded as unique, success is more likely to come to the team.

Problem-solving issues with the game

As I discussed before, good coaches always approach the game with a game plan. That is a proactive approach. However, because problems do occur, good coaches also recognize that they may need to make reactionary decisions—decisions that should be made quickly then communicated clearly and immediately.

I once read that General Ulysses S. Grant kept a rather simpleminded soldier close to him at all times. When he prepared to give an order to one of his generals, he first gave the command to the common soldier to be sure he could understand it. In that way, he was sure all of his communication was clear and understandable.

Finally, all coaches recognize that their decisions will be criticized. No matter how the problem is solved, someone will say it was the wrong decision. A coach must learn to follow his convictions despite the roar of the crowd.

As you prepare for problems, keep in mind these words by Tom Landry, former head coach of the Dallas Cowboys. He said, "A successful leader has to be innovative. If you're not one step ahead of the crowd, you'll soon be a step behind everyone else." Approach problem solving creatively. And use all your people as resources. That's one of the reasons you've worked so hard to select and develop them.

A DREAM TEAM COACH PROVIDES THE SUPPORT NEEDED FOR SUCCESS

The greatest environment of support is created when coaches decide to be facilitators rather than dictators. The more the players and other coaches are involved, the more successful the team. Total control by the coach, even if he is somehow able to achieve it, is never as effective as a group effort. Look at the difference between how dictators and facilitators operate:

Dictators:

1. Hoard decisions.

2. Make decisions alone or restrict them to an elite group.

3. View truth and wisdom as their domain since they are the leaders.

4. Surprise their workers with edicts from above.

5. Guard their own interests.

6. Take for themselves.

Facilitators:

1. Push decisions down line.

2. Involve others as much as possible in key decisions and give people space to make those decisions.

3. View truth and wisdom as being accessible to everyone throughout the organization.

4. Let those responsible decide how the jobs will be done.

5. Serve everyone's interest by developing people.

6. Give to the organization.

161

In addition to providing an atmosphere of support in which everyone's participation is encouraged, great coaches also give their people plenty of affirmation. There isn't a player in the world who doesn't respond to it.

Another way the best coaches support their players is by simplifying their lives. Can you think of anyone who responds positively to bureaucratic red tape? I believe that Forms, Forms, Forms + Rules, Rules, Rules = Frustration, Frustration, Frustration. If I can simplify, I do. I want to give my most creative and innovative people an open field to run in, not hoops to jump through.

Finally, one of the best ways to provide lasting support is by creating a winning tradition for the organization. Rookie professional players drafted by teams such as the Boston Celtics or Dallas Cowboys often speak admiringly of the team's tradition of winning. That tradition creates a positive atmosphere. It creates an invaluable momentum.

When a team gets a few wins under its belt, it creates a positive attitude and momentum. When it gets a few seasons of wins under its belt, it has a tradition. Then instead of the coach having to go out and find winners, winners come looking for him.

A DREAM TEAM COACH COMMANDS THE RESPECT OF THE PLAYERS

Without respect, a coach will never be able to get his players to do what he asks. In *The Seven Habits of Highly Effective People*, Stephen Covey states it this way:

If I try to use human influence strategies and tactics of how to get other people to do what I want, to work better, to be more motivated, to like me and each other—while my character is fundamentally flawed, marked by duplicity or insincerity —then, in the long run, I cannot be successful. My duplicity will breed distrust, and everything I do—even using so-called good human relations techniques—will be perceived as manipulative.

It simply makes no difference how good the rhetoric is or even how good the intentions are; if there is little or no trust, there is no foundation for permanent success. Only basic goodness gives life to technique.

Respect must be earned over time. There are no shortcuts. It is earned through the consistent embodiment of three attributes:

> **Respect must be earned over time. There are no shortcuts.**

Trustworthiness

People never respect a person they cannot trust. Never. The best coaches know this and work immediately on letting their players know they can be trusted. Mike Krzyzewski, head basketball coach of Duke University, put it this way: "If you set up an atmosphere of communication and trust, it becomes a tradition. Older team members will establish your credibility with newer ones. Even if they don't like everything about you, they'll still say, 'He's trustworthy, committed to us as a team.' "

A caring attitude

In all my years of leading people, I must have said this more than a thousand times: "People don't care how much you know until they know how much you care." It's true. If players sense

163

that you really care about them, that you have their interests at heart, they will listen to you and respect you. As former University of Michigan head football coach Bo Schembechler said, "Deep down, your players must know you care about them. This is the most important thing. I could never get away with what I do if the players felt I didn't care. They know, in the long run, I'm in their corner."

The ability to make hard decisions

Players cannot respect a coach who cannot make the hard decisions necessary for a team to succeed. When a coach is willing to make those decisions, the players know he is acting in the team's best interest. They feel secure, and they in turn are more likely to act in the team's best interest themselves. Tom Landry said, "Perhaps the toughest call for a coach is weighing what is best for an individual against what is best for the team. Keeping a player on the roster just because I liked him personally, or even because of his great contributions to the team in the past, when I felt someone else could do more for the team would be a disservice to the team's goals." He would also lose his players' respect.

A DREAM TEAM COACH DOES NOT TREAT EVERYONE THE SAME

One of the biggest mistakes a coach can make is to believe he must treat all of his players the same. Coaches are hired to win—not to make everyone happy or give everyone equal time, money, or resources. Every player must be given support and encouragement. But to believe that everyone must receive the same treatment is not only unrealistic but destructive. When all players are treated and compensated the same, poor or mediocre performance is being rewarded the same as outstanding contributions by the best players.

Great coaches give opportunities, resources, and playing time according to players' past performance. The greater the performer, the greater the opportunity. When you have a player like Michael Jordan, former Chicago Bulls great, you want to put the ball in his hands as often as possible.

> **Give opportunites, resources, and playing time according to players' past performance.**

There will be times you aren't sure about a player's performance level because you haven't had time to observe him. This is especially true when you have a rookie player. When that happens, give him frequent but small opportunities, and try to vary the opportunities as much as possible. If you do, you will soon be able to determine his caliber of play. And that will show you how to respond.

A DREAM TEAM COACH CONTINUES TO WIN

There is only one challenge more difficult than winning that a successful coach faces: continuing to win. As tennis pro, golf pro, and former Olympic champion Althea Gibson said, "In sports, you simply aren't considered a real champion until you have defended your title successfully. Winning it once can be a fluke; winning it twice proves you are the best." Nearly anyone can point to a single victory they've had. But it takes more than one win to make a great coach. It takes continued positive performance.

Putting together successive winning seasons is so difficult in sports that teams bring in consultants such as psychologist Bruce Ogilvie to help them learn how to do it. In the July/August, 1988 issue of *Success* magazine, journalist Dan Gutman writes that Ogilvie suggests the following major points to ensure success:

Work on specific skills. [No matter how many successes a team has had, there is room for improvement. There are people on the team who have not yet come close to fulfilling their potential. Work with each team member to foster improvement and growth. Focus each player on a new goal for the season.]

Make a change. [Every winner's temptation is to continue doing things exactly as before. But that is a flawed approach to success. You and your team will end up standing still, and another team will blow right past you. Use the momentum you've gained from past successes to continue to change and grow.]

Reward the unrewarded. [Every team has unsung heroes—people who were underappreciated for their contribution to the team's success. Find those people and reward them with praise, money, and further opportunities.]

Transfer the burden. [As I've said before, success always comes at a price. If your team has succeeded, it is because some members of the team have carried the burden by making sacrifices. They have given up time with their families, worked long hours, put their primary goals after the team's. Some people will have made such extensive sacrifices that they cannot continue to make them. Give them a break and transfer the burden to others who are willing and able.]

Above all, don't dwell on yesterday's victory. [If your focus is on what's behind you rather than what's ahead, you will crash. It's like the story I heard about a salesman who broke the all-time one-month sales record for his company during the month of June. In the sales meeting held on July 1, the manager said, "I want to congratulate Kent on a job well done.

He has sold more cars in a month than any other salesman." Everyone applauded. "But that was last month. Now let's focus on July." Celebrate victories, enjoy them briefly, and then look forward.]

Another way to help players continue to win is to help them avoid burnout. The best way to do that is to see it coming and avoid it. Workplace psychologist Beverly Potter believes burnout can be prevented when it is caught in time. She suggests that a person look for lack of energy, sleeplessness, lack of creativity, inability to make decisions, chronic anger, bitter or sarcastic language, or physical symptoms such as exhaustion, tension headaches, body aches, and nausea.

John Madden, sports analyst and former championship coach of the Oakland Raiders, was a victim of burnout. He was once asked what the first signs of his burnout were. He said, "You won't have the energy because you won't have the interest. Suddenly, you don't care about the draft. You're not interested in minicamp. You don't care who the best college linebacker is. You don't care if they've signed any of your veteran players to contracts. When you don't care, it's time to go . . . you're history . . . you're done." Because he burned out, he was not able to continue coaching. The same can happen to you or your players. To continue winning, you've got to avoid burnout.

A DREAM TEAM COACH UNDERSTANDS THE LEVELS OF THE PLAYERS

One of the most common mistakes a coach can make is to misjudge the level of one of his players. If the leader doesn't work with each player according to where he is in his development, the player won't produce, succeed, and develop. According to management consultant Ken Blanchard, all team members fit into one of four categories with regard to the type of leadership they need:

Players who need direction: [Players who need direction don't really know what to do or how to do it. At this stage in their development, you need to instruct them every step of the way. Anything these rookie players produce will be essentially what you do through them because they aren't capable of working independently.]

Players who need coaching: [At some point, a rookie starts being able to do more of the job on his own. He becomes more independent but still relies on you for direction and feedback. The two of you will be working in partnership.]

Players who need support: [At this level, the player is able to work without your direction. But he will still require your support and encouragement.]

Players to whom you delegate: [At this stage the player can be given a task, and you can be confident that it will be done. This player only needs you to lead. Provide vision on the front end and accountability on the back end, and the person will multiply your efforts toward success.]

DELEGATION: THE DREAM TEAM COACH'S MOST POWERFUL TOOL

A leader may possess all ten of the previously mentioned characteristics, but if he does not learn the art of delegation, then he will never find himself coaching a dream team. Delegation is the most powerful tool leaders have; it increases their individual productivity as well as the productivity of their department or organization. Leaders who can't or won't delegate create a bottleneck to productivity.

The other benefit of delegation is that it increases the initiative of the people within the organization because it gives them a chance to grow and accustom themselves to succeeding.

> **Delegation is the most powerful tool leaders have.**

If delegation is so important to a leader's success, why do some leaders fail to delegate effectively? Why do they prevent themselves from becoming great coaches? There are many reasons:

INSECURITY

Some leaders are afraid that if they're not in control of everything, it means they're not doing their job. They fear that others will criticize them for shirking their responsibility. The bottom line is they are afraid that they will lose their job.

LACK OF CONFIDENCE IN OTHERS

Some leaders believe their employees are not competent enough to do the job, so they never delegate anything. They fail to realize that people grow into delegation by being given a chance to perform, make mistakes, and learn from them. To be successful, all leaders must eventually take the crucial step of allowing others to take part of the load. Leaders will make mistakes in delegation, and the people to whom they delegate will make mistakes. But that is when learning takes place.

LACK OF ABILITY TO TRAIN OTHERS

Successful delegators cannot simply dump tasks on their people without preparing them for the tasks. If they do, their people will fail and resent them. Instead, they must train their people both before delegating and afterward when mistakes have been made. When leaders learn to train others, they are better equipped to delegate.

PERSONAL ENJOYMENT OF THE TASK

It is difficult for people to give up tasks they love to perform. But sometimes giving up an enjoyable task is the best thing leaders can do. The question leaders must ask themselves is whether the task can be done by someone else. If so, it should probably be delegated. The leader should focus on performing tasks no one else can do, not simply on doing tasks he or she enjoys.

170

HABIT

Similar to enjoyment of a task is habit. Just because people master a task doesn't necessarily mean they should continue doing it. When a task becomes simple and straightforward, the leaders doing it should delegate it and move on to something more complex.

INABILITY TO FIND SOMEONE ELSE TO DO IT

Mark Twain once said, "Never learn to do anything. If you don't learn, you will always find someone else to do it for you." Although he wasn't serious, there is a kernel of truth in his statement. That truth is you must always be looking for people to whom you can give tasks. The times that people will track you down to ask you for something to do will be rare. A leader who can't find people to delegate to may not be looking hard enough.

RELUCTANCE CAUSED BY PAST FAILURES

As I mentioned, when leaders' early efforts to delegate fail, they sometimes become reluctant to delegate. As Ken Allen states in *The Effective Executive*, we should not try to rely solely on ourselves as a result of delegation failure, nor should we blame the people to whom we have given the task. "Rarely is delegation failure the subordinate's fault," he notes. "Maybe you picked the wrong person for the job, didn't train, develop or motivate sufficiently." If you have had trouble with delegation in the past, don't give up. Try to determine why the problem occurred, learn from it, and give delegation another try.

171

LACK OF TIME

Not having enough time to teach another person to do a job is probably the most common reason people give for not delegating. And not delegating is probably the most common reason people don't have enough time. Inability to delegate due to lack of time is short-term thinking. Time lost in delegating on the front end is recovered at the back end.

For example, let's say a leader takes an hour to perform a certain weekly task. He determines that to teach someone else to do that task, it will take him five hours initially, then an hour a week for the following three weeks. That totals eight hours of his time— *one whole day that he will lose* out of his busy schedule. He could continue to do the task himself for the next two months by devoting the same amount of time.

However, if he thinks long term, he realizes that by the end of the year, the eight-hour investment he makes will give him an additional forty-four hours of time to do other tasks. *That's one whole week of time he has gained!* And there is also the added advantage that the employee he has delegated to is better equipped to take on other tasks for him in the future. To break the vicious lack-of-time cycle, a leader needs the right person to delegate to and a willingness to put in the initial training time.

AN "I DO IT BEST" MIND-SET

Leaders who believe that to have something done right they have to do it themselves will end up accomplishing very little. The greatest problem new leaders have is their reluctance to move from *doing* the job to *managing* the job. Edgar Speer, chairman of U. S. Steel, said, "You don't even try to control how people do their jobs. There's no way to do that, furthermore, no purpose. Everyone does the job a different way, and they all want to show how well they can do it their way. The function of a supervisor is to

172

analyze results rather than try to control how the job is done." If you want to do a few small things right, do them yourself. If you want to do great things and make a big impact, learn to delegate.

If you recognize yourself in any of the descriptions above, you probably aren't doing enough delegating. If you begin to miss deadlines, and crises become increasingly frequent, these may also be indications that you need to delegate tasks. And be on the lookout for employees under you who are ready to conquer new worlds—this is a prime time to delegate jobs to them.

STEPS TOWARD DELEGATION

Easing people into delegation is important. As I mentioned earlier, you can't simply dump tasks on people if you want them to succeed. I delegate according to the following steps:

Ask them to be fact finders only.

It gives them a chance to get their feet wet and to become acquainted with the issues and objectives.

Ask them to make suggestions.

This gets them thinking, and it gives you a chance to understand their thought processes.

Ask them to implement one of their recommendations, but only after you give your approval.

This is a critical time. Set them up for success, not failure. And give lots of encouragement.

173

Ask them to take action on their own, but to report the results immediately.

This will give them confidence, and you will still be in a position to perform damage control if necessary.

Give complete authority.

This is the final step—what you've been working toward.

It is the job of a coach to make team members do what they don't want to do so they can become what they've always wanted to be. It can be done with the right tools and the right attitude. The more you work on your skills, the more you work on your own development; and the more you give of yourself to your players, the more successful you can become as a coach. If you truly give it all you've got, you, too, can someday coach a dream team. It will be one of the greatest joys of your life.

Here are two quizzes to help you gauge some of your coaching skills. The first one concerns delegation.

MISCONCEPTIONS ABOUT DELEGATION

Questions:

Answer each question as either True (T) or False (F).

1. Always delegate to the subordinate who
    has experience with similar tasks.   T   F

174

2. The person you delegate to should have as much information about the task as possible.   T   F

3. Controls should be built into a delegated task from the beginning.   T   F

4. In delegated tasks, monitoring the method is as important as getting the desired results.   T   F

5. The crucial decisions involved in a delegated task are still considered the territory of the delegator.   T   F

6. Always make the delegated task seem like a challenge even if it's drudgery.   T   F

7. Delegating means assigning work.   T   F

8. Don't offer advice when delegating.   T   F

9. Use the same procedures and systems of accountability with every subordinate when delegating to avoid favoritism.   T   F

10. If a subordinate fails in a delegated task, do not delegate to him or her again.   T   F

Answers:

1. FALSE: If you repeatedly delegate similar tasks to the same people, they won't get additional opportunities to grow. It also shortchanges less experienced subordinates who need a chance to develop.

2. TRUE: The more background information you give the person who is about to do the task, the faster and easier the delegating process works. For more experienced

subordinates, you may be able to provide some information and then give them ideas on how to obtain additional information on their own.

3. TRUE: Controls not only help prevent disaster, they also give you the confidence to delegate.

4. FALSE: This is one of the most common pitfalls of an inexperienced delegator. Results are everything. Demanding that other people use your method can stifle initiative and creativity needed for successful delegation.

5. FALSE: This is another common mistake poor delegators make. With true delegation comes the right and responsibility to make decisions.

6. FALSE: Deceptive characterization of delegated tasks insults subordinates. And it erodes trust.

7. FALSE: True delegation includes handing over the right and responsibility to determine what work must be done, how it will be approached, and who will do it.

8. FALSE: Let people handle tasks their own way, but give them as much advice (and vision) as you think they need before they get started. Make yourself available to answer questions, but don't constantly peer over their shoulders or solve their problems for them. Learning to solve problems is part of the development process.

9. FALSE: Tasks are different, and so are people. The difficulty of the task as well as the experience and skill of the person must always be taken into account. When you delegate, tailor the system of accountability to fit the delegatee.

10. FALSE: Don't give up on a subordinate because of a single failure. It might be due to circumstances beyond the person's control. The failure could even be a result

of your method of delegation. Examine what went wrong and why.

Scoring:

Give yourself one point for each correct answer.

9–10   You're a top-notch delegator.
6–8   You know the fundamentals, but keep learning.
5 or less   You've uncovered a serious weakness in your leadership skills.

If you are currently responsible for leading or supervising people, you are responsible for their interaction as a team. This second test will help you determine how well you are doing as a coach:

HOW WELL ARE YOU COACHING YOUR TEAM?

Answer the questions using the following key; then total your score.

1	Haven't thought about it yet
2	Just in the early stages
3	Solidly in progress
4	Nearly accomplished
5	Fully accomplished

1. I have chosen my players well. 1 2 3 4 5

2. I have proven to my players I care about them. 1 2 3 4 5

3. I have encouraged them to care about one another. 1 2 3 4 5

4. I know what my players prefer. 1 2 3 4 5

5. I actively encourage team growth. 1 2 3 4 5

6. I have developed a team that "fits." 1 2 3 4 5

7. I support my players. 1 2 3 4 5

8. I have taught them what is important. 1 2 3 4 5

9. I frequently show them the game plan. 1 2 3 4 5

10. I have modeled paying the price to them. 1 2 3 4 5

11. My players are willing to put the team before themselves. 1 2 3 4 5

12. I have developed a good bench. 1 2 3 4 5

13. I have encouraged each player to find and play his role. 1 2 3 4 5

14. I have my players' respect. 1 2 3 4 5

15. I reward my players according to their performance. 1 2 3 4 5

16. I have built a winning tradition. 1 2 3 4 5

17. I expect and prepare for problems. 1 2 3 4 5

18. I know the level of all my players. 1 2 3 4 5

19. I take the time to teach and delegate. 1 2 3 4 5

20. I do only the tasks that
cannot be delegated.   1 2 3 4 5

Scoring:

90–100   You are a great coach with a dream team;
you're ready for the championship.

80–89   You are an excellent coach; keep fine tuning
your team and your skills.

70–79   You are a solid coach; don't stop now; keep up
the good work, and strive for the excellence
that is within your reach.

60–69   Your players are beginning to look like a team;
keep learning and building.

Below 60 You have a lot of work before you, but don't
despair; use the principles in this chapter to begin team building and improving your coaching skills today.

The Leader's Finest Hour:

REALIZING VALUE TO AND FROM LEADERS

A lex Haley, the author of *Roots,* used to keep a picture in his office of a turtle sitting atop a fence. He kept it there to remind him of a lesson he had learned years before: "If you see a turtle on a fence post, you know he had some help." Haley remarked, "Anytime I start thinking, 'Wow, isn't this marvelous what I've done!' I look at that picture and remember how this turtle—me—got up on that post."

Both developed leaders and the people who developed them are like that turtle. They've gotten a lot of help. Their view from the fence post is made possible by others. Through the development process, the new leaders and the developers have value added to their lives.

Adding value to a person is much more than personal promotion or organizational improvement. It is true that people who have been developed get promoted. And it is equally true that organizations improve and expand when they have leaders devoted to the devel-

> **People development is life-changing for everyone involved.**

opment of others. But adding value is much more than that. It is the enrichment of people's quality of life. It is the expansion of their life purpose and capabilities. People development is life-changing for everyone involved. In *Bringing Out the Best in People,* Alan McGinnis said, "There is no more noble occupation in the world than to assist another human being." And as I noted in chapter four, Emerson said that we always benefit ourselves as well when we assist others.

VALUE ADDED TO NEW LEADERS

To illustrate the concept of adding and receiving value, I have done some analysis of my own organizations. I chose them not necessarily because they offer the best examples, but because I know them well. To examine what value I have added to leaders, I asked about ten of mine to give me some feedback. They knew I was working on this book, and I asked them, "Tell me about the value I add to you and the value I receive from you." What follows is a summary of their responses. People said many kind things, but that is not the reason I am sharing their responses. I share them because I want to offer concrete examples showing that the development of people yields tangible results which can be recognized and later passed on to others. (In chapter ten I will share how some of these people are carrying on the development process with others around them.) After you spend time developing your people, you will find that they will respond in the same way that mine do.

182

MODELING

Most of the leaders in my organization identified modeling as something important that I do for them. One person said, "You set the pace for the organization. You never ask for more than you are willing to give yourself. This 'water mark' provides continual motivation for me to give my best." Modeling is an important motivator because it shows people not only what you expect, but what can be accomplished.

One of the most important things that my people said I model is a dedication to continue growing personally. When they see it in me, they recognize its importance. And they soon adopt that belief as their own. Even if they leave me tomorrow, they will continue to grow because they now recognize that belief as their own.

VISION AND DIRECTION

The leader of every successful organization casts vision for his people. I have always made sure that the people around me know my vision, because without that focus we cannot accomplish our goals. A staff member observed, "His ability to keep focused on the big picture . . . keeps me from having tunnel vision." Said another, "He provides vision and direction. By keeping in touch with him, I know that I am staying on target with my professional focus." Burt Nanus, in *Visionary Leadership,* wrote, "There is no more powerful engine driving an organization toward excellence and long-range success than an attractive, worthwhile, and achievable vision of the future, widely shared."

Having and sharing a vision does even more than drive an organization. It also gives people vision and direction for their individual lives. As they contribute to the larger goals of the organization, they begin to identify more clearly a vision for themselves. As that vision becomes clearer and that sense of direction stronger, their lives become more meaningful.

183

ENCOURAGEMENT AND AFFIRMATION

Everyone I surveyed said that they felt encouraged by me. That delights me because I want more than anything else to let my people know that I love them and want the best for them. One person said, "He gives me personal encouragement and affirmation. He's the best I have ever seen at this in my life. Almost to a fault. . . . Sometimes I run into people who are not doing something real well [but] their opinion is that John loves them." Another said, "He cares about me personally, and I believe he has my best interests at heart. He wants me to win. His positive attitude and encouragement let me know that he is happy when I succeed. He cares about what is most important to me—my family."

People in our society are underencouraged. They desire encouragement desperately but get it infrequently. There are two main reasons why the people in my organization feel very encouraged. First, I have spent time getting to know them and developing relationships with them. I know who they are, where they've come from, who their spouse is, who their children are. I know their gifts and their goals. I really know them. Second, I love them, and I express that love to them on a regular basis. I'm not talking about simply praising them for the work they do. I let them know that I care about them and love them as people first. There is no substitute for a relational foundation with people. You must have that to build upon if you are going to develop people. Even if you do nothing more than get to know your people and love and accept them, you will have added value to their lives.

BELIEF IN THEMSELVES

Most of the people I have spent my time developing are not shrinking violets. Even before they met me, they were not timid.

Yet even people who already have confidence can be encouraged to believe more strongly in themselves. One staff member wrote, "John will often drop by my office to see how I am doing, to affirm me, to tell me once again how much he appreciates the load I carry. From the beginning, he encouraged me to do anything I dreamed. He encouraged me . . . to take on projects that I've never tackled before, and to always keep growing."

One of the ideas I examine in detail in my book *The Winning Attitude* is that it is impossible for people to perform consistently in a manner inconsistent with the way they see themselves. This is true no matter what positive or negative circumstances people face. People who believe that they can succeed do so even when repeatedly dealt adversity. Others can be given the best of everything in life and still fail because they see themselves as failures.

> **Believe in people and they will rise to fulfill that belief.**

When I know the leaders in my organization, believe in them, encourage them, and help them to succeed, it helps to strengthen their belief in themselves. I try to help them win increasingly larger victories. People almost always rise to meet your level of expectations. Believe in them, and they will rise to fulfill that belief.

WILLINGNESS TO TRY NEW THINGS

"He gives me confidence to risk and thereby reach new heights. And all the while he has a sincere positive belief in me," one of my leaders said. One of the most important results of people's belief in themselves is their willingness to try new things. When people do only what is comfortable for them, they get into a rut. They stop growing. But by being willing to take risks, people perform tasks they thought were impossible. They achieve more than they

185

thought they could and become more than they thought they were. The kind of growth that comes with risk adds incredible value to people's lives.

PERSONAL DEVELOPMENT

I have made it a practice to set aside time to develop those around me. One leader said, "You have purposefully mentored and coached me now for more than a decade." I give my leaders time for counsel and advice. I help them wrestle with difficult situations. I also schedule time for equipping them on a regular basis. Several leaders cited the monthly leadership instruction that I give as being valuable. Another reminded me of the experiences I've shared. She said, "He always wants the people around him to be able to experience with him the privileges and opportunities he has been given."

Look for opportunities to share yourself with people.

I try to give my people what I can. Sometimes it is time with them. At other times I am able to give guidance. If I can share a valuable experience, I do. As an example, that same staff member mentioned how with my help she was able to have breakfast in Korea with Dr. Cho, pastor of the largest church in the world. Another one of my staff members had always dreamed of meeting Billy Graham in person. When I had an opportunity to meet with the great evangelist, I shared that experience with that staff member by taking him with me. These two incidents were exciting to them, but they were no more valuable than the more common growing experiences that I try to share with them day to day. I look for opportunities to share myself with my people, and you should too.

COMMITMENT TO PERSONAL GROWTH

By now you know how important personal growth is to a person's success. It is what adds the greatest value to a person's life. Here is what one leader in my organization said about it:

> John is committed to growth, both personally and corporately, no matter what the cost. Because he lives on the edge, always desiring growth and challenge in his life, he gives me energy, motivation, and courage to make the tough decisions and never to become satisfied. John has had to fire people, say no to people, and prioritize his life in order to keep growing. He is willing to pay the price of loneliness as a leader!

As she indicated, I'm not the only one in my organization paying the price of personal growth. All of the top leaders around me are dedicated to it, day in and day out. If I were to leave the organization tomorrow, they would continue to pay the price necessary to keep growing. And as Walter Lippman said, "The final test of a leader is that he leaves behind in other people the convictions and will to carry on."

EMPOWERMENT

I have found that people become empowered when you provide them with three things: opportunity, freedom, and security. I give my leaders opportunities to do new things for the organization, the freedom to accomplish those things using creativity and initiative, and the security of knowing I will back them up, even when everything doesn't go as planned. Said one staff member, "You

People become empowered when you provide them with three things: opportunity, freedom, and security.

187

have assured me that you will do anything in your power to help me, which provides me a sense of security and trust." I love to see the people in my organization succeed, and empowering them makes that possible.

Empowerment can be a tricky thing to give. You have to balance your own needs with the empowered leader's development while always keeping in mind the best interests of the organization. One of the leaders in my organization identified this as the "rope principle":

> John is constantly giving me enough rope to allow me to get the job done myself, but not so much that I hang myself. . . . He also balances the development of the person with the good of the organization using the "rope principle." He will wait a little longer than he prefers to get something accomplished if the staff member will be developed in the process, but he will never let the rope go so long as to hurt the organization as a whole.

One of the leaders I surveyed identified empowerment as the characteristic that adds the greatest value to leaders. He said:

> Motivation, believing in, mentoring, and all the other traits tap into what is inside the person. Empowerment adds a new dimension to the person that did not and often cannot exist or come into existence on its own. . . . There is a great responsibility with the gift of empowerment. With the wrong motives a leader can empower for his/her own good rather than for the good of the people and the organization. John has always put the organization and individual people before himself.

Adding that new dimension to a person in your organization will not only make him a more powerful leader, it will also enable him to receive the value of the next item on the list.

BEING A PART OF SOMETHING GREATER THAN THEMSELVES

> **To live a worthwhile, meaningful life, a person must be a part of something greater than himself.**

To live a worthwhile, meaningful life, a person must be a part of something greater than himself. I challenge the people around me to live a life that has not temporal but eternal impact. I want each member of my staff to become the person he was created to be—to reach his potential. One of my staff members, for instance, began as an administrative assistant. Now she is one of the pastors. She said, "You motivate me to dream big dreams and trust God for the impossible."

One of the most encouraging comments came from one of the people closest to me at INJOY. He said, "He allows me to accomplish greater things with him than I could alone." That is true. Equally true is that this man allows me to accomplish greater things than I could alone. That is one of the greatest rewards of adding value to people's lives. It comes back to you multiplied.

> **One of the greatest rewards of adding value to people is that it comes back to you multiplied.**

VALUE ADDED TO ME BY THE PEOPLE I HAVE DEVELOPED

If I were only able to add value to my people and receive nothing in return, I would still do it. But that's not how it works. No

189

matter how much I give, I always receive more in return. It's absolutely incredible.

In my years as an organizational leader, I have found that all employees are one of two types: salary takers or salary makers. The takers give as little as possible and take their salary. The makers give everything they've got and make a contribution beyond the salary they earn. I have found that people who are willing to be developed are always salary makers. You can see the difference between the two types of people by the things they say:

Salary Takers	*Salary Makers*
What will I receive?	What can I give?
What will it take to get by?	I'll do whatever it takes to get it right.
It's not my job.	Whatever the job, I can help you.
Someone else is responsible.	I'm responsible.
How can I look good?	How can the team look good?
Will it pass?	Is it my best?
The paycheck is the reason I work.	The paycheck is a by-product of my work.
Am I better off because I work here?	Is the team better off because I work here?
Pay me now. I'll produce later.	I'll produce now. You can pay me later.

Here are the specific ways the leaders in my organization add value to me. This list consists of the items of value they identified in response to a memo I sent them. I added "Balance of gifts." It

190

is an added value important to me that they did not specifically identify.

LOYALTY

Many of the leaders in my organization identified loyalty—to me and to the organization—as a characteristic of the esteem they feel for me. One person joked, "I might not walk off a cliff for him, but I would certainly consider it!" Others mentioned their desire to protect the interests of the organization because they believe in it, or to protect me from minor pressures that I don't need to handle myself. I am grateful for all of these things.

I also recognize the loyalty of my leaders as a belief in what the organization is doing and a sense of commitment to the team. The people around me work beautifully together. They always seem ready to jump in and do whatever they can. They put their own personal interests beneath the best interests of the team.

ENCOURAGEMENT

Encouraging others makes them want to encourage you too. One of my leaders wrote, "I make it a point to continually encourage John. I believe we all need encouragement from time to time. He is a great model in this area, and I take great joy in reciprocity."

I am naturally a very positive person, so I don't get down in the dumps. But my schedule is often very demanding, and I do get tired. When that happens, my staff is always there for me. Not only do they encourage me, they also offer to help carry the load in any way they can.

PERSONAL COUNSEL AND SUPPORT

A valuable result of developing leaders is the advice and counsel you can receive from them. I benefit from the knowledge and wisdom of the leaders in my organization. One of them said, "I am able to confront and share with John what I think or feel, even when I know he may disagree. I'm not a yes-person." I enjoy hearing the perspective of another leader. And I respect honesty. In fact, the opinion of a person who doesn't agree with me often teaches me more than the perspective of someone who agrees. Another leader said, "I believe that John knows that I am always prepared to provide input to him in any area he requests and desires. He also hopefully knows that he can count on me for 100 percent support." I appreciate the support and advice I get from my people. It adds incredibly to my life.

FOLLOW-THROUGH

I have a great group of people around me that I call "door closers." I call them that because I can hand off a task or project to them and know that they will follow through with it to the very end and close the door behind them. They implement ideas, complete projects, handle details, and perform problem solving for me. They also create and implement their own ideas within the context of the vision I cast. They are constantly furthering the goals of the organization. As one of them said, "I free you up for more important work. I carry part of the load."

The work these leaders do is very important to me and the organization. It must be done, and it is something they can do effectively. Each time I am faced with a new task, project, or activity, I always ask myself, "Is there someone else in the organization who can do this effectively?" If there is, I delegate it. I allow someone else to do the follow through. That, in turn, leads to the next valuable thing that the people around me give to me.

TIME

I have many highly skilled, effective leaders working in my organization. Partly due to the time I have spent developing them, there are few things that they can't do for me and the organization. That allows me more time to do the things that only I can do or that others cannot do as well. As one person in my organization said, "I free him up to do what he does best: teach, lead, preach, motivate, etc." Time is an incredible gift to receive. The people around me free me from being a slave to the urgent so that I can accomplish the important.

BALANCE OF GIFTS

Like all people, I have strengths and weaknesses. Some of my areas of weakness I have been able to improve through personal growth and development. There are other areas where I have much room for improvement, especially in areas that go against my temperament. The people around me add value to me by balancing out my deficiencies with their gifts.

I was born with a sanguine choleric temperament—emphasis on choleric.[8] I enjoy making things happen. And I'm always moving forward. Stopping to reflect on what I've done in the past is not one of my strengths. For example, each Sunday I preach sermons at Skyline Wesleyan Church where I am the senior pastor. There are times when I teach principles in a sermon that I could teach to others outside our church or I could include them in one of the lesson tapes that I send out to leaders each month through IN-JOY. But once I finish the last Sunday service, I file the sermon and move on to my next responsibility. I don't think about it again. That is a weakness.

Fortunately, the people I've developed help me to round out

193

those areas of weakness. In the case of my sermons, for over ten years I had an assistant who would ask me questions each Monday to make me reflect on what I'd taught. Then she made notes on my comments and filed them away for my future use in other lessons.

ATTRACTION OF OTHERS

For an organization to continue building and growing, it must continually attract new people of high quality. In chapter three I shared with you that it is important to have leaders identify and recruit potential leaders. As important as that is, I can't give it as much time as I'd like. But the leaders in my organization do. They are constantly raising up new leaders. Unlike many people who head organizations, I have been fortunate never to find myself in a place where I had positions in leadership to be filled with no people to fill them.

PEOPLE DEVELOPMENT

Every leader I surveyed listed the development of other people as one of their top priorities and a way they add value to me. They know that the development of leaders adds more value than anything else they do. Of people development, one leader wrote, "This is my passion. To select, equip, and develop people to love God, and to love and lead people." Another leader said, "I give depth to his leadership organization through discipling others and passing on to others what he has done for me, i.e., providing an environment for growth." And their development of people is focused not just on others around them, but also on themselves. They continue to be committed to their own personal growth. As one leader commented, "I work on maintaining personal integrity and the development of my character for the sake of the organization and its influence." And what he does in his own development

194

continues to make a positive impact on everyone in his sphere of influence, including me.

INCREASED INFLUENCE

Truly the bottom line on developing the leaders around you is that it increases your influence. In an earlier book I wrote, *Developing the Leader Within You,* I give what I consider to be the greatest definition of leadership: *Leadership is influence.* One of the leaders I surveyed said, "I represent you to the masses that you cannot touch on a regular basis due to sheer time and numbers." He recognized my personal limitations, which are intensified because I lead two organizations: INJOY and Skyline Wesleyan Church. At Skyline, attendance on a busy Sunday is close to 4,000 people. If I wanted to touch each of those people personally by meeting with them for just thirty minutes, in addition to all of my other responsibilities, I would have to meet with more than ten people every day for about six hours, seven days a week, for fifty-two weeks without missing a single person or taking a single day off. At the end of a year, I would have met with everyone who had attended Skyline on *one* Sunday. No one could keep up that kind of pace.

But even though I can't personally meet with every one of those people, I can still influence them—through my team of leaders. Each of them reaches out and touches hundreds of lives. And each of them develops a team of leaders who, in turn, reach out and touch others' lives. As I continue to grow personally and develop others, my influence continues to grow. By the end of my life, if God grants me the productive life I anticipate, I will have positively influenced over ten million people—not just by myself alone, but through the leaders I have developed around me. As one of the top leaders in INJOY said, "I afford him the opportunity to increase his influence way beyond what he could do by himself single-handedly."

When you develop leaders rather than followers, they will do the same for you. And they will carry on the tradition just as some of my leaders have. The final chapter of this book describes how four of the leaders I developed have become first-rate developers of leaders in their own right.

The Leader's Lasting Contribution:
REPRODUCING GENERATIONS OF LEADERS

It is time for a new generation of leadership," John F. Kennedy said in a television address during his 1960 campaign for the White House. Perhaps no president realized the need for successive generations of leaders more than Kennedy, the first commander-in-chief born in the twentieth century. He emerged as the nation's leader on the brink of a decade filled with radical changes.

As I explain in *Developing the Leader Within You,* most people believe that each new generation of leaders is born rather than developed. They think that new leaders come out of the womb as leaders and simply wait until they are old enough to take their rightful place in society. As a result, many leaders are willing simply to produce followers, expecting new leaders to show up on the scene when their time comes. Those types of leaders have no idea how much they are limiting their own potential and the potential of the people around them.

As I have said before, a leader who produces followers limits his success to what his direct, personal influence touches. His success ends when he can no longer lead. On the other hand, a leader who produces other leaders multiplies his influence, and he and his people have a future. His organization continues to build and grow even if he is personally unable to carry on his leadership role.

> **A leader who produces other leaders multiplies his influence.**

As a leader you may have followed all the guidelines in this book. You've created the right climate and identified potential leaders. You've nurtured, equipped, and developed them. You've built a great team and learned to coach them. At this point, you may think your job is done. It's not. There is one more crucial element, and it is the true test of success for a leader who develops other leaders. The leaders you've developed must carry on the tradition of development and produce a third generation of leaders. If they don't, the building process stops with them. True success comes only when every generation continues to develop the next generation, teaching them the value and the method of developing the next group of leaders.

I have spent the greater part of my life developing leaders who are in turn producing another generation of leaders. And by the way, the new generation of leaders they are developing includes many people chronologically older than they. In fact, the majority of people I've spent my time developing have been older than I; I was called to begin dedicating myself to the process of developing leaders around me when I was still in my twenties.

> **True success comes only when every generation continues to develop the next generation.**

Many leaders make the mistake of believing that they can only develop people like themselves—in personality, temperament, natural abilities, and socioeconomic background. But that is not true. Leaders can develop many kinds of people. In my life, there are four people I consider to be my greatest successes in leadership development, and what was required for their development was very different in each case. Yet they have been developed, and they have added incredible value to my life—more than anyone else outside of my family. Each person has not only lightened my load and extended my influence, but they have been especially successful at carrying on the tradition of developing leaders around them.

Each of the four people presented a different challenge to me as a developer of leaders. They had very different levels of experience. Their temperaments were different from mine and from each others'. Some had well-developed relational skills, while others didn't. But despite their differences, they all were capable of becoming leaders and of developing other leaders. I have found that there are three things that are required for a person to become a leader:

DESIRE

The ability to become a leader begins with desire. It is the only thing that the developer cannot supply. The amount of desire will largely determine the potential leader's progress. Great desire can overcome a multitude of natural deficiencies in a leader.

RELATIONAL SKILLS

In all my life, I have never met a great leader who did not possess good relational skills. They are the most important abilities in leadership. Without them, a person cannot lead effectively. Many people believe that relational skills are determined at birth and cannot be learned. But that's not true. People's temperaments incline them to relate to others in a particular way, but they do not dictate their relational abilities. Even the most introspective, melancholic person can learn to develop good relational skills. For nearly everyone, relational skills can be learned and improved.

> **Relational skills are the most important abilities in leadership.**

199

PRACTICAL LEADERSHIP SKILLS

These are the "how tos" of leadership which a person acquires through your modeling, equipping, and developing. These, too, are learned.

When I came into contact with each of the four leaders I will introduce to you, they all had different skills, but they had in common great desire.

A FOLLOWER BECOMES A LEADER

Barbara Brumagin, who was my personal assistant for eleven years, came to me as a highly competent secretary. She worked hard, and she had a wonderful servant's heart, but she did not lead others. It wasn't a natural part of her personality, nor was she well equipped to lead. She had always been a follower, but I could see that she had great potential. And even more important, she had great desire.

When I first came to Skyline Church, I began looking for an assistant, and Barbara was recommended to me by one of the pastors on staff. When we met to discuss the position and I began asking her questions, she was uncommunicative almost to the point of being rude. I quickly changed tacks and began doing the talking: showing her my goals and vision for the church, myself, and her. After listening for a few minutes, she began communicating with me. I immediately saw that she would be perfect for the

200

position, and I hired her. I found out later that she had come to the interview against her will because she had envisioned being a secretary in a church as boring and devoid of growth opportunities. She was more interested in learning and growing, and grow she did. Barbara was like a sponge.

With Barbara's development, I went slowly. It took her about two years before she felt really confident in her position and began showing signs of leadership. I modeled leadership, exposed her to teaching, and worked interactively with her. I was always careful to spend time explaining not only what things I wanted her to do but why I wanted her to do those things. She told me recently that she felt like she was getting personally developed every day. After we had worked together for a few years, she knew me so well that she could answer any question for me or make nearly any decision in the same way I would. In fact, she and I once took a personality test. I answered each question, and then she took the same test and answered the questions as *she thought I would*. When we compared answers, she had only missed two questions. She was quick to point out that she had missed one of those because I had answered it wrong—and she was right!

You may have people you are preparing to develop who are nonleaders like Barbara was. If you do, there are four things to keep in mind as you develop them:

MAINTAIN A POSITIVE ENVIRONMENT

People who do not already possess leadership skills must have an environment that is positive and conducive to their growth. Without that environment, they will be afraid of growth. With it, they will be willing to learn and try new things. Provide the environment; then keep them close to you so that they can begin learning how you think.

EXPRESS HIGH BELIEF IN THEM

People who are not naturally inclined toward leadership and who have no leadership experience often get discouraged easily. Because they have not been leaders before, they will make mistakes. They may make a lot of them, especially in the beginning. Their development is likely to be a long process. By expressing a high belief in them, you encourage them to persevere, even when things get tough.

EMPOWER THEM

In the beginning, followers are reluctant to assume leadership roles, so they must be empowered by their leaders. Start by walking alongside of them and giving them authority in your name. As they gain experience using your authority, begin giving them authority of their own—first in smaller things and then in larger ones. It is important that you also affirm them publicly. It will reinforce their authority and competency. As time goes by, others will begin to reframe their view of the new leaders, and their view of themselves as leaders will also change. Eventually, people will begin recognizing them for their own authority.

PLAY TO THEIR STRENGTHS

It is critical that you begin the development process by playing to their strengths. Because they have experienced few successes in leadership before, they need a few wins under their belts. It really accelerates the development process, and the new leader begins building momentum.

When you begin developing a follower into a leader, the time and energy required will slow down your progress. You may be tempted to stop developing the person, but don't. It could be a terrible mistake. In the case of Barbara, developing her took a little bit of time in the beginning, but not only did she more than make up for it by giving me eleven wonderful years of service, she is now passing on what she has learned to others.

Not too long ago Barbara moved to Seattle and began working for a church in that area. When I spoke to her recently, I asked her what she valued most of all the things she learned while we worked together. Without hesitation, she said she most valued learning people development. She told me that it first helped her in her own personal growth and then in her development of others. Currently, she is developing leaders in that church using the principles she learned during her own development. She's excited about passing that along and told me that developing people gives her great joy.

A MANAGER BECOMES A LEADER

When I first met Dan Reiland and his wife Patti at a leadership conference I was holding in Indiana, he was still a seminary student. Dan had been a member of Skyline, felt the call to ministry, and gone to seminary before I became the senior pastor there. He then returned as an intern during my first year at the church.

Dan's development was very interesting. Dan's smart, he's a good scholar, and he was a good student in seminary. He had often been put in charge of the activities he was involved in, and he had even been the president of his class. But despite his good qualities, he wasn't a leader. He was really more of a manager.

Managers think differently from leaders. Managers tend to focus on tasks and systems. They have narrow vision, and they sometimes tend to be dogmatic. And most of all, their focus is not relational. Dan tended to focus on tasks and the work at hand. He was a hard worker, but he put tasks ahead of people. I remember one day several of us were talking in an office hallway, and Dan walked right through us without saying a word. It was at that point that I knew he and I needed to have a serious conversation, or he wasn't going to make it on my team.

I was able to sit down with Dan and confront him about his relational skills, because he knew that I believed in him and genuinely cared about him. Ironically, I found out that Dan really loved people, and in his heart, he wanted to relate to them. But his internal desire wasn't made clear by his actions. People working with him had no idea how much they mattered to him. It was then that I began spending extra time with him developing his skills to relate to others as a leader does. I taught him to walk slowly through a crowd, interacting with people rather than going past them in order to accomplish tasks. Now, as I mentioned in chapter three, he is the executive pastor of Skyline, and he is invaluable to me. His ability to relate to others has become one of his strongest qualities, and he considers it foundational to his ability to lead.

How big we think determines the size of our accomplishments.

If you have potential leaders who think like managers, your goal is to help them develop better relational skills and help them change their pattern of thinking. While you have to *slow down* to teach a follower how to lead, you may have to come to a *complete stop* in order to help a manager become a leader. The reason is that you will sometimes need to stop what you're doing, walk the person through your thought process, and then explain why you're doing what you're doing. You must constantly show them the big picture until they begin to see it for themselves.

I have found that all true leaders share some common characteristics in their thinking:

LEADERS THINK BIG

They always look at the big picture, and they know that their success is only as great as their goals. As David Schwartz said, "Where success is concerned, people are not measured in inches, or pounds, or college degrees, or family background; they are measured by the size of their thinking. How big we think determines the size of our accomplishments." If you consistently show the people you are developing the big picture and keep stressing possibilities rather than problems, they will start thinking big.

LEADERS THINK IN TERMS OF OTHER PEOPLE

Leaders don't focus on themselves and their own individual success. They think about the success of the organization and other people. They have an other-people mind-set. To develop others, you must teach them to think in terms of how they can promote others, develop others, take along others.

LEADERS THINK CONTINUALLY

People who are not leaders are content to sit back and allow others to do the thinking. Leaders are constantly entertaining new ideas, considering new resources, thinking about improving, contemplating finances, managing their time. Thinking continually enables leaders to keep stretching themselves and growing their organizations. As you develop leaders, model this kind of thinking, and promote it by asking questions.

205

LEADERS THINK BOTTOM LINE

While others get bogged down in the details, leaders look for the bottom line. If you often ask the people you are developing to give you the bottom line, they will soon begin determining what it is before you ask for it. Eventually they will begin thinking in those terms unprompted.

LEADERS THINK WITHOUT LINES

People who are not leaders automatically gravitate toward lines —limitations set by others. Maybe people are taught this in kindergarten when they are instructed to stay within the lines while coloring. But leaders are more creative than that. They look for options and opportunities. They try to take things in a new direction, or beyond the limit. Progress and innovation are made by people who think without lines.

> **Progress and innovation are made by people who think without lines.**

LEADERS THINK IN TERMS OF INTANGIBLES

Leaders are abstract thinkers. They think in terms of intangibles like timing, morale, attitude, momentum, and atmosphere. They read between the lines. They anticipate the unexpected.

LEADERS THINK QUICKLY

Leaders size up a situation quickly and then seize it immediately. Two reasons leaders are able to do this are that they think in terms of the big picture, and they do their homework so that they have information to use to help them make decisions quickly.

As Dan has developed as a leader, he has taken up a tremendous amount of the load for me. He runs Skyline for me, directly leads thirteen pastors, and oversees a staff of over forty. But Dan does more than that. Where he most excels is in the development of other men. Since 1987, Dan has selected a handful of men each year to personally develop. Already he has worked with and developed over fifty of them.

Dan's development of leaders is systematic and strategic. He constantly looks for potential leaders to develop, and he sees himself as a lightning rod, able to capture and focus the energy required to make men grow. For his part, he says he is effective because he always keeps in mind the *vision* of developing leaders, he maintains people development as a *lifestyle,* and he renews his *commitment* to it regularly. The key to the whole process, though, is relationships. He says that the men he develops grow as leaders due to their relationships with one another, the equipping that they receive, and the synergy of their interaction with him and one another. What sustains the whole process, though, is the relational part of it—the area in which he himself has grown the most.

A LEADER CHANGES
LEADERSHIP STYLE

When I hired Sheryl Fleisher on my staff, I knew she was a strong leader. She had vision, was able to make decisions, thought big, and had a bottom-line mentality. But she also tended to be autocratic and a bit dogmatic. She was a leader, but she did not lead relationally. She describes herself as having been "mission-minded" rather than "people-minded."

The turning point in Sheryl's development came when she handled a difficult situation with a person less effectively than she could have. She describes the way she did things as "politically naive and relationally stupid." Soon after it happened, I sat down with her and told her that I supported her and believed in her but that she would have to grow and change her leadership style if she wanted to make it on the team. Now, more than ten years later, not only is she on the team—she is one of its best leaders.

With Sheryl, my goal was not to change her personality. It was to change her mode of operation, her style of leadership. She relied on structure and position to establish her leadership. I wanted her to become a relational/empowering leader. There were times that I had to stop what I was doing and do some backtracking to re-train her, but it was definitely worth the effort. Any time you want to change a leader's style, you must do the following:

MODEL A BETTER LEADERSHIP STYLE

The very first thing you must do is show them your better leadership style. If they don't see that there is a better way to lead, they will never change.

IDENTIFY WHERE THEY ERR

Observe them to determine where they make their mistakes. You won't be able to help them change if you don't know what must be changed.

GET THEIR PERMISSION TO HELP THEM CHANGE

If they are not committed to the process of change and to allowing you to help them, all your effort will be wasted. People will give you their permission when they hurt enough to need change, learn enough to want change, or receive enough to make them able to change.

SHOW THEM HOW TO GET FROM HERE TO THERE

Even when they have the knowledge that they need to change and the desire to make a change, they may not be capable of making a change. Show them the way, step by step.

GIVE IMMEDIATE FEEDBACK

Because you will be helping them break bad habits, you must respond to their actions immediately. Learning something for the first time is always easier than unlearning something that was learned wrong. I learned that lesson when I had to unlearn my golf swing. When you retrain people to lead relationally, give them immediate feedback for both the good things and the bad.

As Sheryl grew and began to lead from the heart, she became a wonderful developer of leaders. She identifies people development as her passion in life. As pastor of personal growth ministries at Skyline, she, like Dan, is always searching for people to develop. She looks for the following qualities in the women she is to develop:

209

F *aithful*   They must be consistent in their actions, reliable, and committed.

A *vailable*   They must be accessible to her personally and willing to grow.

I *nitiating*   They must be inquisitive and hungry to grow.

T *eachable*   They must be receptive to her style of mentoring and teaching.

H *onest*   They must be transparent and honestly willing to develop others.

Recently Sheryl and I sat and talked about the way she develops people. I think she has lost track of how many women she has worked with, but she is very aware of the positive effect her mentoring has on Skyline. She told me that her joy is to recognize where people are, meet them there, love and accept them, and then mentor them. Her goal is to get them to develop into the people they were created by God to be. And she wants to get them to carry on the tradition of leadership development. She succeeds too. She mentioned that one of the women she developed pointed out *six generations of leaders* in one room who had been mentored starting with Sheryl. That's quite an accomplishment.

A GOOD LEADER BECOMES A GREAT LEADER

Dick Peterson was already a first-class leader before he met me. When I came to Skyline, he was a manager in what was America's premier corporation at the time—IBM. In fact, Dick was one of the top three managers in the country in IBM's administrative area. Had he stayed with IBM, his next step would have been to regional management, then on to a vice presidency. And I'm sure he would have made it. As a leader, he was probably in the top 5 percent in the country.

When I had been at Skyline for about a year, I asked him to become a member of the church board. I wanted him on the team. I knew he would be a great contributor to the church and me, and I believed he would also benefit from the experience. You see, I give more thought, time, and attention to the development of the people on my board than to anyone else, with the exception of my family. Board members are the top leaders and influencers I have contact with.

I spent three years developing Dick while he was on the board. I built a good personal relationship with him, I spent time equipping him, and I constantly challenged him to grow. Once when I was preparing to fly to Dallas to talk to some people about ways to begin equipping leaders on a larger scale, I took Dick with me. He was a part of the discussion that gave birth to INJOY. As a leader, he jumped right in and helped get it off the ground. He started as a volunteer. He later resigned at IBM to run INJOY full time. Now he's the president of the organization, and I wouldn't want to be without him.

One of the beauties of developing a person who is already a strong leader is that it gives you momentum. Where a leader must *slow down* to develop followers, *stop* to develop managers, and *backtrack* to change the style of misguided leaders, he can actually *speed up* as he strengthens good leaders. They practically teach themselves. They pick things up just by being around you, often with little to no effort on your part.

If you are fortunate enough to have strong leaders in your influence, begin developing them by doing the following:

211

PUT THEM ON A PERSONAL PLAN FOR GROWTH

Most good leaders are growing, but they frequently do not have a personal plan for growth. After you have gotten to know them—their strengths, weakness, desires, goals, etc.—sit down with them and prepare a personal growth plan tailored to them. Then follow up periodically to encourage them, check their progress, and help them make adjustments.

CREATE OPPORTUNITIES TO STRETCH THEM

It is while doing activities that we thought were beyond our capabilities that our greatest growth occurs. It actually accelerates our development. It also gives us additional opportunities to apply the principles we are learning. As you further develop leaders, plan to put them in situations that will stretch them.

LEARN FROM THEM

Whenever I spend time developing someone who is already a good leader, I learn too. You will also learn much from leaders as long as you maintain a teachable attitude. Plan shared projects with them. It's a great way to learn and to get tremendous things accomplished at the same time.

Dick and I do many things together, and we continue to learn from one another. Dick, like Barbara, Dan, and Sheryl, is wonderful at continuing the development process. In the time I've known him, he has personally developed about twenty men at Skyline one-on-one. He brings the same mind-set to INJOY, not only with the employees, but with the customers. He never loses sight of the fact that ours is an organization whose purpose is to equip and develop leaders. All of his decisions are based on his thinking in those terms. He is probably most proud of the way he is developing his children. He has good relationships with them, and he does everything he can to teach them the right kind of attitude. As he tells them, "It's not what happens *to* you; it's what happens *in* you that counts."

Dick's development has transformed him. He was already a strong leader, but now he is a strong builder of leaders. Developing people is now like breathing to him. Without it, he wouldn't be who he is. That is the key to developing the lead-

> **It's not what happens to you; it's what happens in you.**

ers around you. As a leader, you must make the development of others a lifestyle. When you live it, your success in life is multiplied exponentially. Your influence is expanded incredibly beyond your personal reach. A positive future is assured for you. Leaders who do not develop people will one day find themselves hitting a wall in their success. No matter how efficient and strategic they are, eventually they run out of time.

I found that to be true in my life. I cannot personally create more material than I am currently creating. I cannot mentor more people than I am presently mentoring. I cannot travel and do more conferences than I do now. I am a very energetic person, but I have reached my own physical limits. The only way I can now do more is by doing it through other people. Any leader who learns that lesson and makes it a lifestyle will never hit the wall again.

So I ask you, are you developing the leaders around you?

NOTES

Chapter One

1. Tom Worsham, "Are You a Goose?" *The Arizona Surveyor,* 1992.

Chapter Two

2. Edwin Markham, "Human Worth . . ."

Chapter Three

3. John C. Maxwell, *Developing the Leader Within You* (Nashville, Tennessee: Thomas Nelson, 1993).

4. John C. Maxwell, *The Winning Attitude: Your Key to Personal Success* (Nashville, Tennessee: Thomas Nelson, 1993).

Chapter Four

5. David A. Seamands, *Healing Grace* (Wheaton, Illinois: Victor Books, 1988).

6. *Success Unlimited* (Magazine no longer in print).

Chapter Five

7. Bobb Biehl, *Increasing Your Leadership Confidence* (Sisters, Oregon: Questar, 1989).

Chapter Nine

8. Florence Littauer, *Personality Plus* (Grand Rapids, Michigan: Revel, 1994).

OTHER BOOKS FROM SPEAKER AND BEST-SELLING AUTHOR JOHN C. MAXWELL

Developing the Leader Within You
Develop the vision, values, influence, and motivation needed to become a successful leader. Detailing the five characteristics of outstanding leaders, this book will help you discover how to lead others effectively and help them reach their highest potential. Arranged with the busiest of readers in mind.

Becoming a Person of Influence
Power is the ability to influence the thoughts and actions of others. In this book you will learn the principles of effective leadership, ways to positively impact others, and the pitfalls of negative and ineffective leadership.

The 21 Irrefutable Laws of Leadership
After more than thirty years of serving in leadership positions and speaking on leadership, John Maxwell is often asked, "If you were to take everything you've learned about leadership over the years and boil it down into a short list, what would it be?" This book is his answer. In it John outlines the essentials of leadership that transcend time, place, culture, and situation.

See your local bookstore or call: 1-800-333-6506

BECOMING A PERSON OF INFLUENCE

HOW TO POSITIVELY IMPACT THE LIVES OF OTHERS

JOHN C. MAXWELL
JIM DORNAN

THOMAS NELSON PUBLISHERS
Nashville • Atlanta • London • Vancouver

To all those who have been people of influence in
our lives,
and especially to Eric Dornan,
whose life, experiences, and attitude
have contributed more significantly
than anything else
to Jim and Nancy's ability to positively influence
people.

Contents

Preface

When the two of us met a few years ago, we sensed instantly that there was great chemistry between us, almost like that of brothers. We had so much in common—despite having very different backgrounds. Jim has spent the last thirty years in the business environment teaching people how to become successful. In the process, he built a worldwide business organization. On the other hand, John has spent the last twenty-eight years working in a nonprofit environment as a pastor, denominational executive, and motivational speaker. He is recognized as one of the top equippers in the United States in leadership and personal growth development.

What we have in common is an understanding of people and of the positive impact that one person's life can have on others. And it all boils down to one idea: influence. We know the power of influence, and we want to share it with you.

So please join us and continue reading. We're going to give you many of our insights, tell some entertaining and informative stories, and share dynamite principles that have the power to change your life—and the lives of all the people you can influence.

Acknowledgments

There are special people in our lives whose encouragement and assistance have made this book possible:

To Margaret Maxwell, whose positive support has made it possible for her husband to become a person of influence.

To Nancy Dornan, an incredible influencer to her husband, her family, and hundreds of thousands of people around the world.

To Mea Brink, for her ideas and assistance on this project.

To Stephanie Wetzel, for her proofing and editing.

To Linda Eggers, the greatest assistant any person could ever have.

To Charlie Wetzel, our writer, for his partnership on this book.

Introduction

When you were a child, what did you want to be when you grew up? Did you dream about being a famous actor or singer? How about president of the United States? Maybe you wanted to become an Olympic athlete or one of the wealthiest people in the world. We all have dreams and ambitions. Undoubtedly, you've accomplished some of yours. But no matter how successful you are now, you still have dreams and goals that are waiting to be fulfilled. And our desire is to help you realize the dreams, to help you realize your potential.

Let's start by doing a little experiment. Take a look at the following list of people. It's quite a diverse group, but they all have one thing in common. See if you can figure out what it is.

JOHN GRISHAM

GEORGE GALLUP

ROBERT E. LEE

DENNIS RODMAN

JAMES DOBSON

DAN RATHER

MADONNA

HIDEO NOMO

JERRY AND PATTY BEAUMONT

RICH DEVOS

MOTHER TERESA

BETH MEYERS

PABLO PICASSO

ADOLF HITLER

TIGER WOODS

ANTHONY BONACOURSI

ALANIS MORRISETTE

GLENN LEATHERWOOD

BILL CLINTON

JOHN WESLEY

ARNOLD SCHWARZENEGGER

Influence doesn't come to us instantaneously. It grows by stages.

Have you figured it out? What do they have in common? It certainly isn't their professions. The names have been drawn from lists of writers and statesmen, sports figures and artists, evangelists and dictators, actors and business professionals. Both men and women are included. Some are single and others are married. They are of various ages. And many ethnic groups and nationalities are represented. Some of the people are famous, and you probably recognize their names. But you have undoubtedly never heard of others. So what's the key? What do they all have in common? The answer is that *every one of them is a person of influence.*

EVERYONE HAS INFLUENCE

We created this list almost at random, selecting well-known people as well as ones from our lives. You could just as easily do the same thing. We did it to make a point: Everyone is an influencer of other people. It doesn't matter who you are or what your occupation is. A politician, such as the president of the United States, has tremendous influence on hundreds of millions of people, not only in his own country but around the globe. And entertainers, such as Madonna and Arnold Schwarzenegger, often influence an entire generation of people in one or more cultures. A teacher, such as Glenn Leatherwood, who instructed John and hundreds of others boys in Sunday school, touches the lives of his own students and also indirectly influences all the people those boys grow up to influence.

But you don't have to be in a high-profile occupation to be a person of influence. In fact, if your life in any way connects with other people, you are an influencer. Everything you do at home, at church, in your job, or on the ball field has an impact on the lives of other people. American poet-philosopher Ralph Waldo Emerson said, "Every man is a hero and an oracle to somebody, and to that person, whatever he says has an enhanced value."

If your desire is to be successful or to make a positive impact on your world, you need to become a person of influence. Without influence, there is no success. For example, if you're a salesperson wanting to sell more of your product, you need to be able to influence your customers. If you're a manager, your success depends on your ability to influence your employees. If you're a coach, you can build a winning team only by influencing your players. If you're a pastor, your ability to reach people and grow your church depends on your influence with your congregation. If you want to raise a strong, healthy family, you have to be able to influence your children positively. No matter what your goals are in life or what you want to accomplish, you can achieve them faster, you can be more effective, and the contribution you make can be longer lasting if you learn how to become a person of influence.

> ## *If your life in any way connects with other people, you are an influencer.*

An amusing story about the impact of influence comes from the administration of President Calvin Coolidge. An overnight guest at the White House was having breakfast with Coolidge one morning, and he wanted to make a good impression on the president. He noticed that Coolidge, having been served his coffee, took the coffee cup, poured some of its contents into a deep saucer, and leisurely added a little bit of sugar and cream. Not wanting to breach any rules of etiquette, the visitor followed the commander in chief's lead, and he poured some of his coffee into his saucer and added sugar and cream. Then he waited for the president's next move. He was horrified to see him place the saucer on the floor for the cat. No one reported what the visitor did next.

YOUR INFLUENCE IS NOT
EQUAL WITH ALL PEOPLE

Influence is a curious thing. Even though we have an impact on nearly everyone around us, our level of influence is not the same with everyone. To see this principle in action, try ordering around your best friend's dog the next time you visit him.

You may not have thought much about it, but you probably know instinctively which people you have great influence with and which ones you don't. For example, think of four or five people you work with. When you present an idea to them or make a suggestion, do they all respond in the same way? Of course not. One person may think all your ideas are inspired. Another may view everything you say with skepticism. (No doubt you can identify which one you have the influence with.) Yet that same skeptical person may love every single idea presented by your boss or one of your colleagues. That just shows your influence with her may not be as strong as that of someone else.

Once you start paying closer attention to people's responses to yourself and others, you'll see that people respond to one another according to their level of influence. And you'll quickly recognize how much influence you have with various people in your life. You may even notice that your influence is on many different levels in your household. If you're married and have two or more children, think about how they interact with you. One child may respond especially well to you, while another does better with your spouse. It's a matter of which parent has the greater influence with the child.

Stages of Influence
and Their Impact

If you've read John's *Developing the Leader Within You,* then you probably remember the description of the five levels of leadership contained in chapter 1. Visually, it looks like this:

PERSONHOOD

PEOPLE DEVELOPMENT

PRODUCTION

PERMISSION

POSITION

Leadership (which is a specific application of influence) is at its lowest level when it is based on position only. It grows and goes to a higher level as you develop relationships with others. That's when they give you permission to lead beyond the limits of your job description. As you and your followers become more productive together in your work, then your leadership can go to level 3. And when you begin to develop people and help them reach their potential, your leadership moves up to level 4. Only a few people reach level 5 because it requires a person to spend a lifetime developing others to their highest potential.[1]

Influence functions in a similar way. It doesn't come to us instantaneously. Instead, it grows by stages. Visually, it looks something like this:

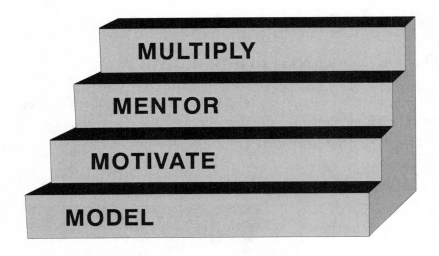

Let's consider each level:

Level 1: Modeling

People are first influenced by what they see. If you have children, then you've probably observed this. No matter what you *tell* your children to do, their natural inclination is to follow what they *see you doing*. For most people, if they perceive that you are positive and trustworthy and have admirable qualities, then they will seek you as an influencer in their lives. And the better they get to know you, the greater your credibility will be and the higher your influence can become—if they like what they see.

When you meet people who don't know you, at first you have no influence with them at all. If someone they trust introduces you to them and gives you an endorsement, then you can temporarily "borrow" some of that person's influence. They will assume that you are credible until they get to know you. But as soon as they have some time to observe you, you either build or bust that influence by your actions.

One interesting exception to this modeling process occurs in the case of celebrities. Because of their preoccupation with television, movies, and the media, many people are strongly influenced by others that they have never met. More often than not, they are influenced not by the actual individual, but by the image of that person. And that image may not be an accurate representation of that actress, politician, sports figure, or entertainer. Nonetheless, they admire that person and are influenced by the actions and attitudes they believe that person represents.

You can be a model to the masses, but to go to the higher levels of influence, you have to work with individuals.

Level 2: Motivating

Modeling can be a powerful influence—either positively or negatively. And it's something that can be done even from a distance. But if you want to make a really significant impact on the lives of other people, you have to do it up close. And that brings you to the second level of influence: motivating.

You become a motivational influencer when you encourage people and communicate with them on an emotional level. The process does two things: (1) It creates a bridge between you and them, and (2) it builds up their confidence and sense of self-worth. When people feel good about you and themselves during the times they're with you, then your level of influence increases significantly.

Level 3: Mentoring

When you reach the motivational level of influence with others, you can start to see a positive impact in their lives. To increase that impact and make it long-lasting, you have to move up to the next level of influence, which is mentoring.

Mentoring is pouring your life into other people and helping them reach their potential. The power of mentoring is so strong that you can actually see the lives of the persons you are influencing change before your eyes. As you give of yourself, helping them overcome obstacles in their lives and showing them how to grow personally and professionally, you help them achieve a whole new level of living. You can truly make a difference in their lives.

Level 4: Multiplying

The highest level of influence you can have in others' lives is the multiplication level. As a multiplying influencer, you help people you're influencing to become positive influencers in the lives of others and pass on not only what they have received from you, but also what they have learned and gleaned on their own. Few people ever make it to the fourth level of influence, but everyone has the potential to do so. It takes unselfishness, generosity, and commitment. It also takes time. In order to move up a level in influence with people, you have to give them more individual attention. You can be a model to the masses, but to go to the higher levels of influence, you have to work with individuals.

Bill Westafer, a friend of John's, who formerly worked at Skyline Church in San Diego, observed, "There are people whose feelings and well-being are within my influence. I will never escape that fact." That's a good concept for all of us to remember. If you lead many people or have a high-profile position, you have a greater responsibility because of your increased influence. What you say—and, more important, what you do—is a model for those who follow you. Their actions will reflect your influence.

YOUR INFLUENCE IS EITHER POSITIVE OR NEGATIVE

Now that you recognize your influence with others, you must think about how you are going to use it. You probably noticed that professional basketball player Dennis Rodman was on the list of influencers at the beginning of this introduction. Many times we've heard Dennis Rodman say that he doesn't want to be a role model. He just wants to be himself. Dennis doesn't understand (or refuses to acknowledge) that he already is a role model. It's not something he can decline. He is an example to everyone in his family, his neighbors, and the people at the neighborhood store where he shops. And because of the profession he has chosen, he is a role model to millions of others— to more people than he would be if he had chosen to be, for example, an auto mechanic. He is influencing others, and he has made a choice concerning the kind of influence he is having.

Even if you've had a negative effect on others in the past, you can turn that around and make your impact a positive one.

Baseball legend Jackie Robinson noted, "A life isn't significant except for its impact on other lives." Robinson's impact on people in the United States has been incredible. In the mid-1940s, he became the first African-American athlete to play major-league baseball despite prejudice, racial taunts, abuse, and death threats. And he did it with character and dignity. Brad Herzog, author of *The Sports 100,* has identified Robinson as the most influential person in American sports history:

First, there are those who changed the way the games were played. . . . Then there are the men and women whose presence and performance forever altered the sporting scene in a fundamental manner. . . . And, finally, there are the handful of sports figures whose influence transcended the playing fields and impacted American culture. . . . Robinson, to a greater extent than anyone else, was all three types in one.[2]

Martin Luther King, Jr., one of the most influential Americans of the twentieth century, acknowledged the positive impact Jackie Robinson made on his life and the cause for which he fought. To African-American baseball pioneer Don Newcombe, King said, "You'll never know what you and Jackie and Roy [Campanella] did to make it possible to do my job."

Most of the time we recognize the influence we have on those who are closest to us in our lives—for good or ill. But sometimes we overlook the impact we can have on other people around us. The anonymous author of this poem probably had that in mind when he wrote,

> *My life shall touch a dozen lives before this day is done,*
> *Leave countless marks for good or ill ere sets the*
> *evening sun,*
> *This is the wish I always wish, the prayer I always pray;*
> *Lord, may my life help other lives it touches by the way.*

As you interact with your family, your coworkers, and the clerk at the store today, recognize that your life touches many others' lives. Certainly, your influence on your family members is greater than that on the strangers you meet. And if you have a high-profile occupation, you influence people you don't know. But even in your ordinary day-to-day interactions with people, you make an impact. You can make the few moments that you interact with a store clerk and a bank teller a miserable experience, or you can get them to smile and make their day. The choice is yours.

POSITIVE INFLUENCERS ADD VALUE TO OTHER PEOPLE

As you move up to the higher levels of influence and become an active influencer, you can begin to have a positive influence on people and add value to their lives. That's true for any positive influencer. The baby-sitter who reads to a child encourages him to love books and helps him become a lifelong learner. The teacher who puts his faith, confidence, and love in a little girl helps her to feel valued and good about herself. The boss who delegates to her employees and gives them authority as well as responsibility enlarges their horizons and empowers them to become better workers and people. The parents who know how and when to give their children grace help them to stay open and communicative, even during their teenage years. All of these people add lasting value to the lives of other people.

We don't know what kind of influence you have on others today as you read this book. Your actions may touch the lives of thousands of people. Or you may influence two or three coworkers and family members. The number of people is not what's most important. The crucial thing to remember is that your level of influence is not static. Even if you've had a negative effect on others in the past, you can turn that around and make your impact a positive one. And if your level of influence has been relatively low up to now, you can increase it and become a person of influence who helps others.

In fact, that's what this book is all about. We want to help you become a person of high influence, no matter what stage of life you're in or what you do for a living. You can have an incredibly positive impact on the lives of others. You can add tremendous value to their lives.

WHO IS ON THE INFLUENCE LIST?

Everyone could sit down and make a list of people who have added value to his or her life. We mentioned that the list at the beginning of this introduction contains the names of some people who have influenced us. Some of the names are big. For example, John considers eighteenth-century evangelist John Wesley to be a significant influence on his life and career. Wesley was a dynamic leader, preacher, and social critic. During his lifetime, he turned the Christian church in England and America upside down, and his thoughts and teachings continue to influence the way churches function and Christians believe even today. John considers Wesley to be the greatest person to have lived since the apostle Paul.

Other people named on that list are not well known, but that in no way lessens their level of influence. For example, Jerry and Patty Beaumont had a profound impact on the lives of Jim and his wife, Nancy. Here's their story:

Nancy and I first met Jerry and Patty almost twenty-five years ago when Nancy and Patty were both pregnant. The Beaumonts were a classy couple—really sharp and confident. We were attracted to them immediately because it seemed that they really had their lives together, and we observed that they were living out their strong spiritual convictions with integrity and consistency.

Nancy met Patty one day while they were in the obstetrician's waiting room. They hit it off instantly and began to build a relationship. We had no idea how much their friendship was going to mean to us just a few months later when our lives got turned upside down.

Nancy and I think back on those days now as a good time in our lives. Our daughter, Heather, was five years old, and we were really enjoying her. We were also just beginning to build our business. It was taking a lot of time and energy to get it going, but it was fun. We were beginning to see that all our work was going to pay off in the future.

When Nancy told me that she was pregnant, I was ecstatic. It meant our little family was about to grow, and we hoped our second child would be a boy.

After nine months of routine pregnancy, Nancy gave birth to our first son, Eric. At first everything appeared to be normal. But a few hours later, the doctors discovered that Eric had been born with some very serious physical problems. His back was open and his spinal cord had not formed properly. They told us he had a condition called spina bifida. To make things worse, his spinal fluid had gotten infected during the delivery, so he was suffering from severe systemic meningitis.

Our whole life seemed to be thrown into chaos. After Nancy's hours of labor, we were exhausted and confused. They told us Eric needed brain surgery, and we had to make a decision right then. Without it, he didn't stand a chance. Even with it, things didn't look good. We cried as they prepared to take our little boy—only a few hours old—and transport him to Children's Hospital for emergency brain surgery. All we could do was pray that he would make it.

We waited for hours, but the doctors finally came out and told us Eric was going to live. We were shaken when we saw him after the surgery. We wondered how someone so small could have so many wires attached to him. The opening in his back was closed, but we could see that they had surgically implanted a shunt tube in his brain to drain off excess spinal fluid and relieve the pressure.

The first year of Eric's life was a blur for us as he repeatedly entered Children's Hospital. In the first nine months, he underwent eleven more surgeries—three of those operations came in one weekend. Things were happening so fast that we were overwhelmed, and we couldn't even comprehend what we might have to face in the future.

While we were trying to survive the midnight trips to the hospital and hold up under the pain and fear we had for Eric, guess who came alongside us and helped us survive each day as it came? Jerry and Patty Beaumont. They had come to the hospital that first day of Eric's life and given us comfort and encouragement while he was in the operating room. They brought food for us and sat with Nancy and me in hospital waiting rooms. And all the while they shared their incredible faith with us.

Most important, they helped us to believe that God had a special plan for Eric and us. "You know," Patty told Nancy one day, "you and Jim can make Eric's problems the center of everything you do, or you can use them as a launching pad for a whole new way of looking at life."

It was then that we turned a corner in our lives. We began looking beyond our circumstances and saw that there was a bigger picture. We realized God had a plan for us as well as Eric, and our faith gave us strength and peace. The Beaumonts had helped us consider and answer some of life's most important questions. From that day on, our entire attitudes changed and we had great hope.

That was more than two decades ago. Jim and Nancy lost touch with the Beaumonts, though they have since tried to find them. Now Eric has grown up and gets around pretty well in his electric wheelchair despite having experienced a stroke during one of his surgeries. He is a constant source of joy, inspiration, and humor for the Dornan family. And though their contact with Jerry and Patty Beaumont lasted only about a year, Jim and Nancy recognize the tremendous value they added to them and still consider them to be two of the greatest influencers in their lives.

Today, Jim and Nancy are people of influence. Their business has expanded into more than twenty-six countries around the world: from Eastern Europe to the Pacific, from Brazil and Argentina to mainland China. Through seminars, tapes, and videos, they impact hundreds of thousands of individuals and families each year. And their business continues to grow. But more important to them, they are sharing their strong values and faith with the people they influence. They are doing all they can to add value to the life of everyone they touch.

Recently, John was talking to Larry Dobbs. He is the president and publisher of the Dobbs Publishing Group, which produces magazines such as *Mustang Monthly, Corvette Fever,* and *Muscle-car Review.* They talked about the subject of influence, and Larry shared a little bit of his story: "John, my daddy was a sharecropper, so he never had much. When he died, the only money he left me was a dollar. But he gave me so much more than that. He passed on his values to me." Then Larry said something very insightful: "The only inheritance that a man will leave that has eternal value is his influence."

We don't know exactly what your dream is in life or what kind of legacy you want to leave. But if you want to make an impact, you will have to become a man or woman capable of influencing others. There is no other way of effectively touching people's lives. And if you become a person of influence, then maybe someday when other people write down the names of those who made a difference in their lives, your name just might be on the list.

A Person of Influence Has . . .

INTEGRITY WITH PEOPLE

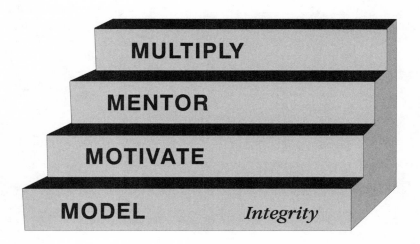

A few years ago, while my wife, Nancy, and I were on a business trip to Europe, we celebrated her birthday in London. As her gift, I decided to take her to the Escada boutique to buy her an outfit or two.

She tried on a number of things and liked all of them. And while she was in the dressing room trying to decide which one to pick, I told the salesperson to wrap up the whole lot of it. Nancy tried to protest; she was embarrassed to buy so many things at one time, but I insisted. We both knew she'd get good use out of the clothes. Besides, she looked fabulous in everything.

A couple of days later, we took the long flight out of Heathrow Airport in London to San Francisco International Airport. After we landed, we got in line for the inevitable customs check. When they asked what we had to declare, we told them about the clothes Nancy had bought and the amount we had spent.

"What?" the agent said. "You're declaring clothes?" He read the figure that we'd written and said, "You've got to be kidding!" It's true that we had spent a little bit of money on them, but we didn't think it was *that* big a deal. "What are the clothes made of?" he asked.

That seemed like an odd question. "A bunch of different things," answered Nancy. "Wool, cotton, silk. Everything's different. There are dresses, coats, blouses, shoes, belts, accessories. Why?"

"Each kind of fabric has a different duty," he said. "I'll have to get my supervisor. I don't even know what all the different rates are. Nobody declares clothes." He looked frustrated. "Go ahead and pull everything out and sort it according to what it's made of." As we opened up our bags, he walked away and we could hear him saying to a coworker, "Bobby, you'll never believe this. . . ."

It must have taken us a good forty-five minutes to sort everything out and tally up how much we'd spent on each type of item. The duty turned out to be quite a bit—about two thousand dollars. As we were putting everything back into our suitcase, the agent said, "You know what? I think I know you. Aren't you Jim Dornan?"

"Yes," I answered. "I'm sorry, have we met before?" I didn't recognize him.

"No," he said. "But I've got a friend who's in your organization. Network 21, right?"

"That's right," I said.

"I've seen your picture before. You know," the agent said, "my friend has been telling me that I'd really benefit from hooking up with your organization. But I haven't really listened. Now I'm thinking I should reconsider. He might be right after all. See, most people I see every day try to get all kinds of things through customs without paying duty, even stuff they should know better about. But you guys, you're declaring stuff you could have gotten through with no problem. That's sure a lot of money you could've saved!"

"That may be true," answered Nancy, "but I can spare the money for customs a lot more than I can spare not having a clear conscience."

As we stood in line that day, it didn't even occur to Nancy or me that anyone there might know us. If our intention had been to cheat our way through, we never would have suspected that we'd be recognized. We thought we were anonymous. And I think that is what a lot of people think as they cut corners in life. "Who will ever know?" they say to themselves. But the truth is that other people know. Your spouse, children, friends, and business associates all know. And more important, even if you cover your tracks really well, and they don't know what you are up to, *you do!* And you don't want to give away or sell your integrity for *any* price.

Jim's experience with the customs agent is just one small example of how people today think when it comes to integrity. Sad to say, it no longer appears to be the norm, and when confronted by an example of honest character in action, many people seem shocked. Common decency is no longer common.

Genuine Integrity Is Not for Sale

You can see character issues coming up in every aspect of life. A few years ago, for example, financier Ivan Boesky openly described *greed* as "a good thing" while speaking at UCLA's business school. That flawed thinking soon got him into trouble. When his unethical practices on Wall Street came to light, he was fined $100 million and sent to prison for three years. Recently, he was reported to be ruined financially and living on alimony from his former wife.

> *The need for integrity today is perhaps as great as it has ever been. And it is absolutely essential for anyone who desires to become a person of influence.*

Government hasn't been immune to integrity issues either. The Department of Justice is prosecuting public officials as never before, and it recently boasted that it had convicted more than 1,100 in one year—a dubious record.

Just about everywhere you look, you see examples of moral breakdowns. TV preachers fall morally; mothers drown their children; professional athletes are found with drugs and prostitutes in hotel rooms. The list keeps growing. It seems that many people view integrity as an outdated idea, something expendable or no longer applicable to them in our fast-paced world. But the need for integrity today is perhaps as great as it has ever been. And it is absolutely essential for anyone who desires to become a person of influence.

In his best-selling book *The Seven Habits of Highly Effective People,* Stephen Covey wrote about the importance of integrity to a person's success:

> If I try to use human influence strategies and tactics of how to get other people to do what I want, to work better, to be more motivated, to like me and each other—while my character is fundamentally flawed, marked by duplicity or insincerity— then, in the long run, I cannot be successful. My duplicity will breed distrust, and everything I do—even using so-called good human relations techniques—will be perceived as manipulative.
>
> It simply makes no difference how good the rhetoric is or even how good the intentions are; if there is little or no trust, there is no foundation for permanent success. Only basic goodness gives life to technique.[1]

Integrity is crucial for business and personal success. A joint study conducted by the UCLA Graduate School of Management and Korn/Ferry International of New York City surveyed 1,300 senior executives. Seventy-one percent of them said that integrity was the quality most needed to succeed in business. And a study by the Center for Creative Research discovered that though many errors and obstacles can be overcome by a person who wants to rise to the top of an organization, that person is almost never able to move up in the organization if he compromises his integrity by betraying a trust.

INTEGRITY IS ABOUT THE
SMALL THINGS

As important as integrity is to your business success, it's even more critical if you want to become an influencer. It is the foundation upon which many other qualities are built, such as respect, dignity, and trust. If the foundation of integrity is weak or fundamentally flawed, then being a person of influence becomes impossible. As Cheryl Biehl points out, "One of the realities of life is that if you can't trust a person at all points, you can't truly trust him or her at any point." Even people who are able to hide their lack of integrity for a period of time will eventually experience failure, and whatever influence they have temporarily gained will disappear.

Think of integrity as having benefits similar to that of a house's foundation during a huge storm. If the foundation is sound, then it will hold up against the raging waters. But when there are cracks in the foundation, the stress of the storm deepens the cracks until eventually the foundation—and then the whole house—crumbles under the pressure.

Integrity is the quality most needed to succeed in business.

That's why it's crucial to maintain integrity by taking care of the little things. Many people misunderstand that. They think they can do whatever they want when it comes to the small things because they believe that as long as they don't have any major lapses, they're doing well. But that's not the way it works. *Webster's New Universal Unabridged Dictionary* describes *integrity* as "adherence to moral and ethical principles; soundness of moral character; honesty." Ethical principles are not flexible. A little white lie is still a lie. Theft is theft—whether it's $1, $1,000, or $1 million. Integrity commits itself to character over personal gain, to people over things, to service over power, to principle over convenience, to the long view over the immediate.

Nineteenth-century clergyman Phillips Brooks maintained, "Character is made in the small moments of our lives." Anytime you break a moral principle, you create a small crack in the foundation of your integrity. And when times get tough, it becomes harder to act with integrity, not easier. Character isn't created in a crisis; it only comes to light. Everything you have done in the past—and the things you have neglected to do—come to a head when you're under pressure.

Developing and maintaining integrity require constant attention. Josh Weston, chairman and CEO of Automatic Data Processing, Inc., says, "I've always tried to live with the following simple rule: 'Don't do what you wouldn't feel comfortable reading about in the newspapers the next day.'" That's a good standard all of us should keep.

Integrity Is an Inside Job

One of the reasons many people struggle with integrity issues is that they tend to look outside themselves to explain any deficiencies in character. But the development of integrity is an inside job. Take a look at the following three truths about integrity that go against common thinking:

1. Integrity Is Not Determined by Circumstances

Some psychologists and sociologists today tell us that many people of poor character would not be the way they are if only they had grown up in a different environment. Now, it's true that our upbringing and circumstances affect who we are, especially when we are young. But the older we are, the greater the number of choices we make—for good or bad. Two people can grow up in the same environment, even in the same household, and one will have integrity and the other won't. Ultimately, you are responsible for your choices. Your circumstances are as responsible for your character as a mirror is for your looks. What you see only reflects what you are.

2. Integrity Is Not Based on Credentials

In ancient times, brick makers, engravers, and other artisans used a symbol to mark the things they created to show that they were the makers. The symbol that each one used was his "character." The value of the work was in proportion to the skill with which the object was made. And only if the quality of the work was high was the character esteemed. In other words, the quality of the person and his work gave value to his credentials. If the work was good, so was the character. If it was bad, then the character was viewed as poor.

The same is true for us today. Character comes from who we are. But some people would like to be judged not by who they are, but by the titles they have earned or the position they hold, regardless of the nature of their character. Their desire is to influence others by the weight of their credentials rather than the strength of their character. But credentials can never accomplish what character can. Look at some differences between the two:

Credentials	**Character**
Are transient	Is permanent
Turn the focus to rights	Keeps the focus on responsibilities
Add value to only one person	Adds value to many people
Look to past accomplishments	Builds a legacy for the future
Often evoke jealousy in others	Generates respect and integrity
Can only get you in the door	Keeps you there

No number of titles, degrees, offices, designations, awards, licenses, or other credentials can substitute for basic, honest integrity when it comes to the power of influencing others.

3. Integrity Is Not to Be Confused with Reputation

Some people mistakenly emphasize image or reputation. Listen to what William Hersey Davis has to say about the difference between character and its shadow, reputation:

> The circumstances amid which you live determine your reputation . . .
> the truth you believe determines your character. . . .
> Reputation is what you are supposed to be;
> character is what you are. . . .
> Reputation is the photograph;
> character is the face. . . .
> Reputation comes over one from without;

character grows up from within. . . .

Reputation is what you have when you come to a new community;

character is what you have when you go away.

Your reputation is made in a moment;

your character is built in a lifetime. . . .

Your reputation is learned in an hour;

your character does not come to light for a year. . . .

Reputation grows like a mushroom;

character lasts like eternity. . . .

Reputation makes you rich or makes you poor;

character makes you happy or makes you miserable. . . .

Reputation is what men say about you on your tombstone;

character is what the angels say about you before the
throne of God.

Certainly, a good reputation is valuable. King Solomon of ancient Israel stated, "A good name is more desirable than great riches."[2] But a good reputation exists because it is a reflection of a person's character. If a good reputation is like gold, then having integrity is like owning the mine. Worry less about what others think, and give your attention to your inner character. D. L. Moody wrote, "If I take care of my character, my reputation will take care of itself."

If you struggle with maintaining your integrity, and you're doing all the right things on the *outside*—but you're still getting the wrong results—something is wrong and still needs to be changed on the *inside*. Look at the following questions. They may help you nail down areas that need attention.

QUESTIONS TO HELP YOU MEASURE
YOUR INTEGRITY

1. How well do I treat people from whom I can gain nothing?
2. Am I transparent with others?
3. Do I role-play based on the person(s) I'm with?
4. Am I the same person when I'm in the spotlight as I am when I'm alone?

5. Do I quickly admit wrongdoing without being pressed to do so?
6. Do I put other people ahead of my personal agenda?
7. Do I have an unchanging standard for moral decisions, or do circumstances determine my choices?
8. Do I make difficult decisions, even when they have a personal cost attached to them?
9. When I have something to say about people, do I talk *to* them or *about* them?
10. Am I accountable to at least one other person for what I think, say, and do?

Don't be too quick to respond to the questions. If character development is a serious area of need in your life, your tendency may be to skim through the questions, giving answers that describe how you wish you were rather than who you actually are. Take some time to reflect on each question, honestly considering it before answering. Then work on the areas where you're having the most trouble. And remember this:

> *Many succeed momentarily by what they know;*
> *Some succeed temporarily by what they do; but*
> *Few succeed permanently by what they are.*

The road of integrity may not be the easiest one, but it's the only one that will get you where you ultimately want to go.

INTEGRITY IS YOUR BEST FRIEND

The esteemed nineteenth-century American writer Nathaniel Hawthorne offered this insight: "No man can for any considerable time wear one face to himself and another to the multitude without finally getting bewildered as to which is the true one." Anytime you compromise your integrity, you do yourself an incredible amount of damage. That's because integrity really is your best friend. It will never betray you or put you in a compromising position. It keeps your priorities right. When you're tempted to take shortcuts, it helps you stay the right course.

When others criticize you unfairly, it helps you keep going and take the high road of not striking back. And when others' criticism is valid, integrity helps you to accept what they say, learn from it, and keep growing.

Abraham Lincoln once stated, "When I lay down the reins of this administration, I want to have one friend left. And that friend is inside myself." You could almost say that Lincoln's integrity was his best friend while he was in office because he was criticized so viciously. Here is a description of what he faced as explained by Donald T. Phillips:

> Abraham Lincoln was slandered, libeled and hated perhaps more intensely than any man ever to run for the nation's highest office. . . . He was publicly called just about every name imaginable by the press of the day, including a grotesque baboon, a third-rate country lawyer who once split rails and now splits the Union, a coarse vulgar joker, a dictator, an ape, a buffoon, and others. The *Illinois State Register* labeled him "the craftiest and most dishonest politician that ever disgraced an office in America. . . ." Severe and unjust criticism did not subside after Lincoln took the oath of office, nor did it come only from Southern sympathizers. It came from within the Union itself, from Congress, from some factions within the Republican party, and, initially, from within his own cabinet. As president, Lincoln learned that, no matter what he did, there were going to be people who would not be pleased.[3]

Through it all, Lincoln was a man of principle. And as Thomas Jefferson wisely said, "God grant that men of principle shall be our principal men."

INTEGRITY IS YOUR FRIENDS' BEST FRIEND

Integrity is your best friend. And it's also one of the best friends that your friends will ever have. When the people around you know that you're a person of integrity, they know that you want to influence them because of the opportunity to add value to their lives. They don't have to worry about your motives.

Recently, we saw a cartoon in the *New Yorker* that showed how difficult it can be to sort out another person's motives. Some hogs were assembled for a feeding, and a farmer was filling their trough to the brim. One hog turned to the others and asked, "Have you ever wondered *why* he's being so good to us?" A person of integrity influences others because he wants to *bring* something to the table that will benefit them—not *put* them on the table to benefit himself.

If you're a basketball fan, you probably remember Red Auerbach. He was the president and general manager of the Boston Celtics from 1967 to 1987. He truly understood how integrity adds value to others, especially when people are working together on a team. And he had a method of recruiting that was different from that of most NBA team leaders. When he reviewed a prospective player for the Celtics, his primary concern was the young man's character. While others focused almost entirely on statistics and individual performance, Auerbach wanted to know about a player's attitude. He figured that the way to win was to find players who would give their best and work for the benefit of the team. Players who had outstanding ability but whose character was weak or whose desire was to promote only themselves were not really assets.

THE BENEFIT OF INTEGRITY: TRUST

The bottom line when it comes to integrity is that it allows others to trust you. And without trust, you have nothing. Trust is the single most important factor in personal and professional relationships. It is the glue that holds people together. And it is the key to becoming a person of influence.

Trust is an increasingly rare commodity these days. People have become increasingly suspicious and skeptical. Bill Kynes expressed the feelings of a whole generation when he wrote,

We thought we could trust the *military,*
  but then came *Vietnam;*
We thought we could trust the *politicians,*

but then came *Watergate;*
We thought we could trust the *engineers,*
    but then came the *Challenger disaster;*
We thought we could trust our *broker,*
    but then came *Black Monday;*
We thought we could trust the *preachers,*
    but then came *PTL and Jimmy Swaggart.*
So who can I trust?[4]

At one time you could assume that others would trust you until you gave them a reason not to. But today with most people, you must prove your trustworthiness first. That's what makes integrity so important if you want to become a person of influence. Trust comes from others only when you exemplify solid character.

Character is made in the small moments of our lives.
—Phillips Brooks

People today are desperate for leaders, but they want to be influenced only by individuals they can trust, persons of good character. If you want to become someone who can positively influence other people, you need to develop the following qualities of integrity and live them out every day:

- **Model consistency of character.** Solid trust can develop only when people can trust you *all the time.* If they never know from moment to moment what you're going to do, the relationship will never deepen to a confident level of trust.
- **Employ honest communication.** To be trustworthy, you have to be like a good musical composition; your words and music must match.
- **Value transparency.** People eventually find out about your flaws, even if you try to hide them. But if you're honest with people and admit your weaknesses, they will appreciate

your honesty and integrity. And they will be able to relate to you better.

- **Exemplify humility.** People won't trust you if they see that you are driven by ego, jealousy, or the belief that you are better than they are.

- **Demonstrate your support of others.** Nothing develops or displays your character better than your desire to put others first. As our friend Zig Ziglar says, help enough other people to succeed, and you will succeed also.

- **Fulfill your promises.** Never promise anything you can't deliver. And when you say you'll do something, follow through on it. A sure way to break trust with others is to fail to fulfill your commitments.

- **Embrace an attitude of service.** We have been put on this earth not to be served, but to serve. Giving of yourself and your time to others shows that you care about them. Missionary-physician Sir Wilfred T. Grenfell held that "the service we render to others is really the rent we pay for our room on this earth." People of integrity are givers, not takers.

- **Encourage two-way participation with the people you influence.** When you live a life of integrity, people listen to you and follow you. Always remember that the goal of influence is not manipulation; it's participation. Only as you include others in your life and success do you permanently succeed.

It has been said that you don't really know people until you have observed them when they interact with a child, when the car has a flat tire, when the boss is away, and when they think no one will ever know. But people with integrity never have to worry about that. No matter where they are, who they are with, or what kind of situation they find themselves in, they are consistent and live by their principles.

THE BENEFIT OF TRUST: INFLUENCE

When you earn people's trust, you begin to earn their confidence, and that is one of the keys to influence. President Dwight D. Eisenhower expressed his opinion on the subject this way:

In order to be a leader, a man must have followers. And to have followers, a man must have their confidence. Hence, the supreme quality for a leader is unquestionably integrity. Without it, no real success is possible, no matter whether it is on a section gang, a football field, in the army, or in an office. If a man's associates find that he lacks forthright integrity, he will fail. His teachings and actions must square with each other. The first great need, therefore, is integrity and high purpose.

When people begin to trust you, your level of influence increases. And that's when you will be able to start impacting their lives. But it's also the time to be careful because power can be a dangerous thing. In most cases, those who want power probably shouldn't have it, those who enjoy it probably do so for the wrong reasons, and those who want most to hold on to it don't understand that it's only temporary. As Abraham Lincoln said, "Nearly all men can stand adversity, but if you want to test a man's character, give him power."

Few people in the world today have greater power and influence than the president of the United States. George Bush, the nation's forty-first president, had strong beliefs about power and advised, "Use power to help people. For we are given power not to advance our own purposes nor to make a great show in the world, nor a name. There is but one just use of power and it is to serve people." To keep your ambition in check and the focus of your influence on helping and serving others, periodically ask yourself this question: If the whole world followed me, would it be a better world?

BECOME A PERSON OF INTEGRITY

In the end, you can bend your actions to conform to your principles, or you can bend your principles to conform to your actions. It's a choice you have to make. If you want to become a person of influence, then you better choose the path of integrity because all other roads ultimately lead to ruin.

To become a person of integrity, you need to go back to the fundamentals. You may have to make some tough choices, but they'll be worth it.

Commit Yourself to Honesty, Reliability, and Confidentiality

Integrity begins with a specific, conscious decision. If you wait until a moment of crisis before settling your integrity issues, you set yourself up to fail. Choose today to live by a strict moral code, and determine to stick with it no matter what happens.

Decide Ahead of Time That You Don't Have a Price

President George Washington perceived that "few men have the virtue to withstand the highest bidder." Some people can be bought because they haven't settled the money issue before the moment of temptation. The best way to guard yourself against a breach in integrity is to make a decision today that you won't sell your integrity: not for power, revenge, pride, or money—any amount of money.

Major in the Minor Things

The little things make or break us. If you cross the line of your values—whether it's by an inch or by a mile—you're still out of bounds. Honesty is a habit you ingrain by doing the right thing all the time, day after day, week after week, year after year. If you consistently do what's right in the little things, you're less likely to wander off course morally or ethically.

Each Day, Do What You Should Do Before What You Want to Do

A big part of integrity is following through consistently on your responsibilities. Our friend Zig Ziglar says, "When you do the things you have to do when you have to do them, the day will come when you can do the things you want to do when you want to do them." Psychologist-philosopher William James stated the idea more strongly: "Everybody ought to do at least two things each day that he hates to do, just for the practice."

Swiss philosopher and writer Henri Frédéric Amiel maintained, "The man who has no inner life is the slave of his surroundings." *Slaves* is the right term to describe people who lack integrity because they often find themselves at the whim of their own and others' changing desires. But with integrity, you can experience freedom. Not only are you less likely to be enslaved by the stress that comes from bad choices, debt, deceptiveness, and other negative character issues, but you are free to influence others and add value to them in an incredible way. And your integrity opens the door for you to experience continued success.

It's almost impossible to overestimate the impact of integrity in the lives of people. You probably remember the Tylenol scare from years ago. Several people were poisoned to death, and investigators traced the cause to contaminated Tylenol capsules. John's friend Don Meyer sent him a commentary on the incident. Here's what it said:

> Some years earlier in their mission statement, they had a line saying they would "operate with honesty and integrity." Several weeks before the Tylenol incident, the president of Johnson and Johnson sent a memo to all presidents of divisions of the company asking if they were abiding by and if they believed in the mission statement. All of the presidents came back with an affirmative answer.
>
> Reportedly, within an hour of the Tylenol crisis, the president of the company ordered all capsules off the shelf knowing it was a $100 million decision.
>
> When reporters asked how he could decide so easily and rapidly on such a major decision, his reply was, "I was practicing what we agreed on in our mission statement."

At the bottom of the commentary, Don Meyer wrote this note: "John, it is always easy to do right when you know ahead of time what you stand for."

What's true for Johnson and Johnson is true for you and us. If you know what you stand for and act accordingly, people can trust you. You are a model of the character and consistency that other people admire and want to emulate. And you've laid a good foundation, one that makes it possible for you to become a person of positive influence in their lives.

Influence Checklist
HAVING INTEGRITY WITH PEOPLE

❑ **Commit yourself to developing strong character.** In the past, have you made it a practice to take full responsibility for your character? It's something that you need to do in order to become a person of influence. Set aside the negative experiences you have had, including difficult circumstances and people who have hurt you. Forget about your credentials or the reputation you've built over the years. Strip all that away, and look at what's left. If you don't see solid integrity in yourself, make the commitment to change today.

Read the following statement, and then sign the line below:

I commit myself to being a person of character. Truth, reliability, honesty, and confidentiality will be the pillars of my life. I will treat others as I expect to be treated. I will live according to the highest standards of integrity amid all of life's circumstances.

Signature: _____ Date: _____

❑ **Do the little things**. Spend the next week carefully monitoring your character habits. Make a note to yourself each time you do any of the following:

- Don't tell the whole truth.
- Neglect to fulfill a commitment, whether it's promised or implied.
- Leave an assignment uncompleted.
- Talk about something that you might have been expected to keep in confidence.

❑ **Do what you *should* do before you do what you *want* to do**. Every day this week, find two items on your to-do list that you should do but that you have been putting off. Complete those tasks before doing anything on the list that you enjoy.

A Person of Influence . . .

NURTURES
OTHER PEOPLE

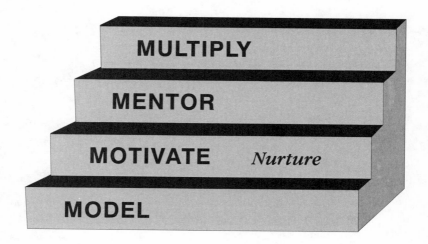

Several years ago Nancy and I decided that we wanted to help our son Eric become a little more independent. In general he does really well. In fact, he participates in many activities that someone who does not use a wheelchair never gets to. But we thought he'd enjoy taking another step in his personal development, so we looked into something we'd heard about called Canine Companions for Independence (CCI), an organization that matches specially trained dogs to people with disabilities.

CCI has been around for about twenty years and has offices all around the country, including in Oceanside, California. That's just a short drive from San Diego, so one Saturday morning we piled into the car and went up the coast to check it out.

Eric was very excited as we got up there and toured the training facility. We met with a few staff members, and we saw a lot of great dogs. We found out that these animals spend the first year of their lives in the homes of volunteers who raise them and teach them basic obedience and socialization skills. Then the dogs are moved to a CCI center where they live and are given specialized training by staff members for the next eight months. They learn how to become working companions to just about every kind of person with disabilities other than blindness. The dogs learn how to open doors, carry objects, and do things like that. Some are trained to help people who are hearing impaired, and they learn to signal their owners when a phone or doorbell rings, a baby cries, a smoke alarm goes off, and so forth. Once a dog is fully trained, it's matched to a new owner, and the two of them go through a kind of "boot camp" to learn how to work together.

Eric loved the idea of getting a dog, and we applied to receive one that would match his needs. For the next several weeks, we waited. And not a day went by that Eric didn't talk about it. Finally, one afternoon we received a call from CCI telling us that they had a dog for Eric, and the next morning, we took off again to Oceanside.

Eric fell in love with Sable immediately. She was an energetic golden retriever who was a little over a year and a half old. The two of them went through boot camp and learned how to work together. Sable could turn lights off and on for Eric, accompany him to the store with money and carry his purchases back for him, and do a bunch of other things.

As boot camp was coming to a close, one of the trainers sat down with Eric and talked with him. He said, "Eric, no matter what else you do or don't do with Sable, be sure of one thing. You have to be the one who feeds her. That's very important. It's the only way to be sure that she will bond with you and look to you as her master."

For Eric, giving the dog love and affection was easy. He enjoyed petting and grooming her, but it was harder for him to learn how to take charge. He has a pretty docile personality. But in time, he learned to feed her, and it eventually became his favorite part of their routine.

Feeding a dog is the best way to create a relationship with her. It not only provides what the dog needs, giving her life and strength, but it also teaches her to trust and follow you. And in most cases, when you do the feeding, the care you give is returned with loyalty, obedience, and affection.

THE NATURE OF NURTURE

In some regards, people respond similarly to the way some animals do. And like animals, people need to be cared for, not just physically, but emotionally. If you look around, you'll discover that there are people in your life who want to be fed—with encouragement, recognition, security, and hope. That process is called nurturing, and it's a need of every human being.

If you desire to become an influencer in others' lives, start by nurturing them. Many people mistakenly believe that the way to become an influencer is to become an authority figure—correct others' errors, reveal the weak areas they can't easily see in themselves, and give so-called constructive criticism. But what clergyman

John Knox said more than four hundred years ago is still true: "You cannot antagonize and influence at the same time."

At the heart of the nurturing process is genuine concern for others. When you hear the word *nurture,* what do you first think of? If you're like most people, you probably envision a mother cradling a baby. She takes care of her child, protecting him, feeding him, encouraging him, making sure that his needs are met. She doesn't give him attention only when she has spare time or when it's convenient. She loves him and wants him to thrive. Similarly, as you try to help and influence the people around you, you must have positive feelings and concern for them. If you want to make a positive impact on them, you cannot dislike, despise, or disparage them. You must give them love and respect. Or as human relations expert Les Giblin put it, "You can't make the other fellow feel important in your presence if you secretly feel that he is a nobody."

If you nurture others but allow them to become dependent on you, you're really hurting them, not helping them.

You may be wondering why you should take on a nurturing role with the people you want to influence, especially if they are employees, colleagues, or friends—not family members. You may be saying to yourself, Isn't that something they can get somewhere else, for example, at home? The unfortunate truth is that most people are desperate for encouragement. And even if a few people in their lives build them up, you still need to become a nurturer to them because people are influenced most by those who make them feel the best about themselves. If you become a major nurturer in the lives of others, then you have an opportunity to make a major impact on them.

Check and recheck your motives as you help and encourage others. Don't be like a little girl named Emily. Her father, Guy Belleranti, was driving the family home from church one Sunday when the five-year-old girl said, "When I grow up, I want to be like the man who stood in front."

"You want to be a minister?" asked Emily's mother.

"No," said Emily, "I want to tell people what to do."

Your goal is others' growth and independence. If you nurture others but allow them to become dependent on you, you're really hurting them, not helping them. And if you help them because of your desire to meet your needs or to heal the hurts of your past, your relationship with them can become codependent. It's not healthy to try to correct your personal history by reliving it vicariously through others. Besides, codependent people never become positive influencers in the lives of others.

A Nurturing Influencer Is a Giver

Now that you have a better idea about what it means to nurture others, you're probably ready to learn how to do it with the people in your life: employees, family members, friends, fellow church workers, and colleagues. You do it by focusing on *giving* rather than *getting*. Start by giving to others in these areas:

Love

Before you can do anything else in the lives of others, you must show them love. Without it, there can be no connection, no future, and no success together. Think back to some key people who have had an impact on your life: an incredible teacher, a fantastic boss, a special aunt or uncle. Undoubtedly, when you spent time with those people, you could sense that they cared about you. And in return, you responded positively to them.

We discovered this example of how love can make a difference in the lives of students. Here is something written by a thoughtful teacher:

I had a great feeling of relief when I began to understand that a youngster needs more than just subject matter. I know mathematics well, and I teach it well. I used to think that was all I needed to do. Now I teach children, not math. I accept the fact that I can only succeed partially with some of them. When I don't have to know all the answers, I seem to have more answers than when I tried to be the expert. The youngster who really made me understand this was Eddie. I asked him one day why he thought he was doing so much better than last year. He gave meaning to my whole new orientation. "It's because I like myself now when I'm with you," he said.[1]

Eddie responded to love in a way that he never would have to knowledge, psychology, technique, or educational theory. When he knew his teacher cared about him, he blossomed.

Without love, there can be no connection, no future, and no success together.

The length and breadth of our influence on others are directly related to the depth of our concern for them. When it comes to helping people grow and feel good about themselves, there is no substitute for love. Even a tough guy like Vince Lombardi, the legendary coach of the Green Bay Packers, understood the power of love to bring out people's best and make an impact on their lives. He said, "There are a lot of coaches with good ball clubs who know the fundamentals and have plenty of discipline but still don't win the game. Then you come to the third ingredient: If you're going to play together as a team, you've got to care for one another. You've got to *love* each other. Each player has to be thinking about the next guy."

You can positively impact people by nurturing them. It doesn't matter what profession you're in. And it doesn't matter how successful the people around you are or what they have accomplished in the past. Everyone needs to feel valued. Even someone who was once the leader of the free world needs love. In his book *In the Arena,* former president Richard Nixon described his depression following his resignation from the White House and his undergoing surgery. At one point when he was in the hospital, he told his wife, Pat, that he wanted to die.

When he was at the absolute lowest point in his life, a nurse in the hospital came into his room, opened the drapes, and pointed out a small plane that was flying back and forth overhead. It was pulling this sign: GOD LOVES YOU, AND SO DO WE. Ruth Graham, evangelist Billy Graham's wife, had arranged for the plane to fly by the hospital. That's when Nixon experienced a turning point. Seeing that expression of love gave him the courage and desire to keep going and recover.

Take time to express your love and appreciation for the people close to you. Tell them how much they mean to you. Write them notes telling how much you care. Give them a pat on the back and, when appropriate, a hug. Don't ever assume that people know how you feel about them. Tell them. Nobody can be told too often that he or she is loved.

Respect

We read a story about a woman who moved to a small town. After being there a short time, she complained to her neighbor about the poor service she received at the local drugstore. She was hoping her new acquaintance would repeat her criticism to the store's owner.

The next time the newcomer went to the drugstore, the druggist greeted her with a big smile, told her how happy he was to see her again, and said he hoped she liked their town. He also offered himself as a resource to the woman and her husband as they got settled. Then he took care of her order quickly and efficiently.

Later the woman reported the incredible change to her friend. "I suppose you told him how poor I thought the service was?" she declared.

"Well, no," the neighbor said. "In fact—and I hope you don't mind—I told him you were amazed at the way he had built up this small town drugstore, and that you thought it was one of the best-run drugstores you'd ever seen."[2]

That woman's neighbor understood that people respond to respect. In fact, most people will do nearly anything for you if you treat them respectfully. And that means making it clear to them that their feelings are important, their preferences are respected, and their opinions are valuable. It means giving them the benefit of the doubt. Or as poet-philosopher Ralph Waldo Emerson put it, "Every man is entitled to be valued by his best moments."

Where love focuses on giving to others, respect shows a willingness to receive from them. Respect acknowledges another person's ability or potential to contribute. Listening to other people and putting their agenda ahead of your own reflect your respect for them and have the potential to make you and them more successful. According to a recent study by Teleometrics International reported in the *Wall Street Journal,* executives understand the power of respect. Among the sixteen thousand executives surveyed, the researchers concentrated on a group of high achievers. Within that group, all had positive attitudes about their subordinates, frequently sought their advice, regularly listened to their concerns, and treated them with respect.

If you have had the opportunity to work in many environments, and you have worked for both types of people—those who *have* and those who *have not* shown you respect—you understand how motivational respect can be. And you also know that you are more easily influenced by people who treat you well.

Sense of Security

Another important part of nurturing is giving people a sense of security. People are reluctant to trust you and reach their potential when they are worried about whether they're safe with you. But when they feel secure, they are in a position to respond positively and do their best. Virginia Arcastle remarked, "When people are made to feel secure and important and appreciated, it will no longer be necessary for them to whittle down others in order to seem bigger in comparison."

Part of making people feel secure comes from integrity, which we talked about in the previous chapter. People feel secure with you when your actions and words are consistent and conform to a high moral code that includes respect. Former Notre Dame head football coach Lou Holtz addressed that issue when he said, "Do what's right! Do the best you can and treat others the way you want to be treated because they will ask three questions: (1) Can I trust you? (2) Are you committed? . . . (3) Do you care about me as a person?"

People desire security not only from you but also from their environment. Good leaders recognize this and create an environment where people can flourish. Mike Krzyzewski, successful head basketball coach of Duke University, understands the impact a leader can make when he provides security to the people who follow him: "If you set up an atmosphere of communication and trust, it becomes a tradition. Older team members will establish your credibility with newer ones. Even if they don't like everything about you, they'll still say, 'He's trustworthy, committed to us as a team.'"

Not until people can completely trust you will you be able to positively influence them and have an impact on their lives.

Recognition

A too common mistake, especially among leaders in the marketplace, is failure to share recognition and show appreciation to others. For example, J. C. Staehle did an analysis of workers in America and found that the number one cause of dissatisfaction among employees was their superiors' failure to give them credit. It's difficult for people to follow someone who doesn't appreciate them for who they are and what they do. As former secretary of defense and World Bank president Robert McNamara said, "Brains are like hearts—they go where they are appreciated."

Recognition is greatly appreciated by everyone, not just people in business and industry. Even a little bit of recognition can go an incredibly long way in a person's life. For example, we recently read a story written by Helen P. Mrosla, a teaching nun. She told about her experience with Mark Eklund, a student she had taught in third grade and then again in junior high math. Here's her story:

> One Friday [in the classroom] things just didn't feel right. We had worked hard on a new concept all week, and I sensed that the students were growing frustrated with themselves—and

edgy with one another. I had to stop this crankiness before it got out of hand. So I asked them to list the names of the other students in the room on two sheets of paper, leaving a space between each name. Then I told them to think of the nicest thing they could say about each of their classmates and write it down.

It took the remainder of the class period to finish the assignment, but as the students left the room, each one handed me their paper. . . .

That Saturday, I wrote down the name of each student on a separate sheet of paper, and I listed what everyone else had said about that individual. On Monday I gave each student his or her list. Some of them ran two pages. Before long, the entire class was smiling. "Really?" I heard whispered. "I never knew that meant anything to anyone!" "I didn't know others liked me so much!"

No one ever mentioned those papers in class again. I never knew if they discussed them after class or with their parents, but it didn't matter. The exercise had accomplished its purpose. The students were happy with themselves and one another again.

That group of students moved on. Several years later, after I had returned from a vacation, my parents met me at the airport. As we were driving home, Mother asked the usual questions about the trip: How the weather was, my experiences in general. There was a slight lull in the conversation. Mother gave Dad a sideways glance and simply said, "Dad?" My father cleared his throat. "The Eklunds called last night," he began.

"Really?" I said. "I haven't heard from them for several years. I wonder how Mark is."

Dad responded quietly. "Mark was killed in Vietnam," he said. "The funeral is tomorrow, and his parents would like it if you could attend." To this day I can still point to the exact spot on I-494 where Dad told me about Mark.

I had never seen a serviceman in a military coffin before. . . . The church was packed with Mark's friends. [His old classmate] Chuck's sister sang "The Battle Hymn of the Republic." Why did it have to rain on the day of the funeral? It was difficult enough at the grave side. The pastor said the usual prayers and the bugler played taps. One by one those who loved Mark took a last walk by the coffin and sprinkled it with holy water.

I was the last one to bless the coffin. As I stood there, one of the soldiers who had acted as a pallbearer came up to me. "Were you Mark's math teacher?" he asked. I nodded as I continued to stare at the coffin. "Mark talked about you a lot," he said.

After the funeral most of Mark's former classmates headed to Chuck's farmhouse for lunch. Mark's mother and father were there, obviously waiting for me. "We want to show you something," his father said, taking a wallet out of his pocket. "They found this on Mark when he was killed. We thought you might recognize it."

Opening the billfold, he carefully removed two worn pieces of notebook paper that had obviously been taped, folded and refolded many times. I knew without looking that the papers were the ones on which I had listed all the good things each of Mark's classmates had said about him. "Thank you so much for doing that," Mark's mother said. "As you can see, Mark treasured it."

Mark's classmates started to gather around us. Chuck smiled rather sheepishly and said, "I still have my list. It's in the top drawer of my desk at home." John's wife said, "John asked me to put his in our wedding album." "I have mine too," Marilyn said. "It's in my diary." Then Vicki, another classmate, reached into her pocketbook, took out her wallet and showed her worn and frazzled list to the group. "I carry this with me at all times," Vicky said without batting an eyelash. "I think we all saved our lists."

That's when I finally sat down and cried.[3]

What would make so many adults hold on to pieces of paper they had received years before as kids, some of them carrying those pages with them everywhere they went—even into battle in a rice paddy halfway around the world? The answer is appreciation. Everyone is incredibly hungry for appreciation and recognition. As you interact with people, walk slowly through the crowd. Remember people's names and take time to show them you care. Make other people a priority in your life over every other thing, including your agenda and schedule. And give others recognition at every opportunity. It will build them up and motivate them. And it will make you a person of significant influence in their lives.

Encouragement

An experiment was conducted years ago to measure people's capacity to endure pain. Psychologists measured how long a barefooted person could stand in a bucket of ice water. They found that one factor made it possible for some people to stand in the ice water twice as long as others. Can you guess what that factor was? It was encouragement. When another person was present, giving support and encouragement, the sufferers were able to endure the pain much longer than their unencouraged counterparts.

> *When a person feels encouraged, he can face the impossible and overcome incredible adversity.*

Few things help a person the way encouragement does. George M. Adams called it "oxygen to the soul." German philosopher-poet Johann Wolfgang von Goethe wrote, "Correction does much, but encouragement after censure is as the sun after a shower." And William A. Ward revealed his feelings when he said: "Flatter me, and I may not believe you. Criticize me, and I may not like you. Ignore me, and I may not forgive you. Encourage me, and I will not forget you."

The ability to influence is a natural by-product of encouragement. Benjamin Franklin wrote in a letter to naval commander John Paul Jones, "Hereafter, if you should observe an occasion to give your officers and friends a little more praise than is their due, and confess more fault than you can justly be charged with, you will only become the sooner for it, a great captain." Jones evidently learned the lesson. He eventually became a hero of the American Revolution and later achieved the rank of rear admiral in the Russian navy.

Just as encouragement makes others want to follow you, withholding praise and encouragement has the opposite effect. We read an account by Dr. Maxwell Maltz that shows the incredible negative impact a person can have when he doesn't encourage persons close to him. Maltz described a woman who came to his office seeking his help. Evidently, her son had moved from her home in the Midwest to New York where Maltz had his practice. When their son was only a boy, the woman's husband died, and she ran his business, hoping to do so only until the son became old enough to take it over. But when the son became old enough, he didn't want to be involved with it. Instead, he wanted to go to New York and study. She came to Maltz because she wanted him to find out why her son had behaved that way.

A few days later the son came to Maltz's office, explaining that his mother had insisted on the visit. "I love my mother," he explained, "but I've never told her why I had to leave home. I've just never had the courage. And I don't want her to be unhappy. But you see, Doctor, I don't want to take over what my father started. I want to make it on my own."

"That's very admirable," Maltz said to him, "but what do you have against your father?"

"My father was a good man and worked hard, but I suppose I resented him," he said. "My father came up the hard way. And he thought he should be tough on me. I guess he wanted to build self-reliance in me or something. When I was a boy, he never encouraged me. I can remember playing catch with him out in the yard. He'd pitch and I'd catch. We had a game to see if I could catch ten balls in a row. And, Doctor, he'd never let me catch the tenth ball! He'd throw eight or nine to me, but he always threw the tenth ball into the air, or into the ground, or where I couldn't catch it." The young man paused for a moment and then said, "He would never let me catch the tenth ball—never! And I guess I had to leave home and the business he started because I wanted somehow to catch that tenth ball!"

Lack of encouragement can hinder a person from living a healthy, productive life. But when a person feels encouraged, he can face the impossible and overcome incredible adversity. And the person who gives the gift of encouragement becomes an influencer in his life.

WHAT THEY RECEIVE

To become a nurturer, learn to be other-minded. Instead of thinking of yourself, put others first. Instead of putting others in their place, try to put *yourself* in their place. That's not always easy. Only when you have a sense of peace about yourself and who you are will you be able to be other-minded and give yourself away to others. But the rewards of nurturing are many. When you nurture people, they receive several things:

Positive Self-Worth

Nathaniel Branden, a psychiatrist and expert on the subject of self-esteem, states that no factor is more decisive in people's psychological development and motivation than the value judgments they make about themselves. He says that the nature of self-evaluation has a profound effect on a person's values, beliefs, thinking processes, feelings, needs, and goals. In his view, self-esteem is the most significant key to a person's behavior.

A poor self-concept can have all kinds of negative effects on a person's life. Poet T. S. Eliot asserted, "Half of the harm that is done in this world is due to people who want to feel important. . . . They do not mean to do harm. . . . They are absorbed in the endless struggle to think well of themselves." Poor self-worth creates an invisible ceiling that can stop a person from attempting to rise above self-imposed limitations.

If you are confident and have a healthy self-image, then you may be saying, "Hey, I can see trying to boost a child's self-worth, but when it comes to my employees or colleagues, let them take care of themselves. They're adults. They need to get over it." The reality is that most people, whether they're seven or fifty-seven, could use help with their feelings about themselves. They would love to have their sense of identity boosted. If you question that, try this experiment. Ask a couple of people you know to write down on a piece of paper all their personality strengths. Each person usually comes up with about half a dozen. Then ask them to write down all their weaknesses. Most of the time, the lists of weaknesses are at least twice as long!

Eighteenth-century writer-critic Samuel Johnson expressed this thought: "Self-confidence is the first great requisite to great undertakings." Self-esteem impacts every aspect of a person's life: employment, education, relationships, and more. For example, the National Institute for Student Motivation conducted a study showing that the impact of self-confidence on academic achievement is greater than that of IQ. And Martin Seligman, a professor of psychology at the University of Pennsylvania, discovered that people with high self-esteem get better-paying jobs and are more successful in their careers than people with low self-esteem. When he surveyed representatives of a major life insurance company, he found that those who expected to succeed sold 37 percent more insurance than those who did not.

If you want to help people improve their quality of life, become more productive at work, and develop more positive relationships, then build their self-worth. Make them feel good about themselves, and the positive benefits will spill over into every aspect of their lives. And when they begin to experience those benefits, they will be grateful to you.

Sense of Belonging

Belonging is one of the most basic human needs. When people feel isolated and excluded from a sense of communion with others, they suffer. Albert LaLonde pointed out the dangers of this isolation: "Many young people today have never experienced a deep emotional attachment to anyone. They do not know how to love and be loved. The need to be loved translates itself into the need to belong to someone or something. Driven by their need . . . they will do anything to belong."

Positive influencers understand this need for a sense of belonging and do things that make people feel included. Parents make sure their children feel like important members of the family. Spouses make the person to whom they are married feel like a cherished equal partner. And bosses let their employees know that they are valued members of the team.

Great leaders are particularly talented at making their followers feel they belong. Napoleon Bonaparte, for example, was a master at making people feel important and included. He was known for wandering through his camp and greeting every officer by name. As he talked to each man, he asked about his hometown, wife, and family. And the general talked about a battle or maneuver in which he knew the man had taken part. The interest and time he took with his followers made them feel a sense of camaraderie and belonging. It's no wonder that his men were devoted to him.

If you desire to become a better nurturer of people, develop an other-person mind-set. Look for ways to include others. Become like the farmer who used to hitch up his old mule to a two-horse plow every day and say, "Get up, Beauregard. Get up, Satchel. Get up, Robert. Get up, Betty Lou."

One day his neighbor, hearing the farmer, asked, "How many names does that mule have?"

"Oh, he has only one," answered the farmer. "His name is Pete. But I put blinders on him and call out all the other names so he will think other mules are working with him. He has a better attitude when he's a part of a team."

Perspective

Another thing that people gain when they are nurtured is a better perspective on themselves. Most people receive more than their share of negative comments and criticism from others—so much that they sometimes begin to lose sight of their value. There is a telling example of this in *A Touch of Wonder* by Arthur Gordon. He relates the story of a friend who belonged to a club at the University of Wisconsin. It was comprised of several bright young men who had genuine talent for writing. Each time they met, one of the men would read a story or essay he had written, and the rest of the group would dissect and criticize it. The viciousness of their comments prompted them to call themselves the Stranglers.

On the same campus, some women formed a group, and they called themselves the Wranglers. They also read their manuscripts

to one another, but instead of showering criticism on one
another, they tried to find positive things to say. Every member
was given encouragement, no matter how weak or undeveloped
her writing was.

For most people,
it's not
what they are that
holds them back. It's what
they think they're not.

The results of the two groups' activities came to light twenty
years later when the careers of the classmates were examined. Of
the talented young men in the Stranglers, not one of them had
made a name for himself as a writer. But half a dozen successful
writers emerged from the Wranglers, even though they had not
necessarily shown greater promise. And some of the women had
gained national prominence, such as Pulitzer prize–winner Mar-
jorie Kinnan Rawlings.[4]

For most people, it's not what they are that holds them back.
It's what they think they're not. The Stranglers undoubtedly made
one another suspect that they were unqualified to write, and in
time they became convinced of it. Who knows what kind of talent was squashed by their negativism? But if someone in the
group had taken the initiative to be nurturing instead of negative,
maybe another Hemingway, Faulkner, or Fitzgerald would have
emerged and given the world another library of masterpieces.

Everyone appreciates being nurtured, even great men and
women. A small exhibit at the Smithsonian Institution bears this
out. It contains the personal effects found on Abraham Lincoln the
night he was shot: a small handkerchief embroidered "A. Lincoln,"
a country boy's penknife, a spectacle case repaired with cotton
string, a Confederate five-dollar bill, and a worn-out newspaper

clipping extolling his accomplishments as president. It begins, "Abe Lincoln is one of the greatest statesmen of all time. . . ."[5]

As we mentioned in the previous chapter, Lincoln faced fierce criticism while in office, and it would have been easy for him to become totally discouraged. That article, worn with repeated reading, undoubtedly helped him during some very difficult times. It nurtured him and helped him retain his perspective.

Feeling of Significance

Woody Allen once quipped, "My only regret in life is that I'm not someone else." And while he probably said that to get a laugh, with the relationship problems he has had over the years, we can't help wondering how much truth there is to his comment. In life, the price tag that the world puts on us is almost identical to the one we put on ourselves. People who have a great deal of self-respect and who believe that they have significance are usually respected and made to feel valued by others.

When you nurture people and add value to them without expecting anything in return, they feel significant. They realize that they are valued, that they matter to others. And once they consistently feel positive about themselves, they're free to live more positively for themselves and others.

Hope

Writer Mark Twain warned, "Keep away from people who try to belittle your ambitions. Small people always do that, but the really great make you feel that you, too, can become great." How do most people feel when they're around you? Do they feel small and insignificant, or do they believe in themselves and have hope about what they can become?

The key to how you *treat* people lies in how you *think* about them. It's a matter of attitude. How you act reveals what you believe. Johann Wolfgang von Goethe emphasized, "Treat a man as he appears to be and you make him worse. But treat a man as if he already were what he potentially could be, and you make him what he should be."

Hope is perhaps the greatest gift you can give others as the result of nurturing because even if their sense of self is weak and they fail to see their own significance, they still have a reason to keep trying and striving to reach their potential in the future.

In *Building Your Mate's Self-Esteem,* Dennis Rainey tells a wonderful story about nurturing hope that can lead to the development of tremendous potential. He says that there was a boy named Tommy who had a particularly hard time in school. He continually asked questions, and he never could quite keep up. It seemed that he failed every time he tried something. His teacher finally gave up on him and told his mother that he could not learn and would never amount to much. But Tommy's mother was a nurturer. She believed in him. She taught him at home, and each time he failed, she gave him hope and encouraged him to keep trying.

What ever happened to Tommy? He became an inventor, eventually holding more than one thousand patents, including those of the phonograph and the first commercially practical incandescent electric lightbulb. His name was Thomas Edison.[6] When people have hope, there is no telling how far they can go.

How to Become a Natural Nurturer

Maybe you weren't born a nurturing person. Many people find it hard to be loving and positive to others, especially if the environment they grew up in wasn't particularly uplifting. But anyone can become a nurturer and add value to others. If you cultivate a positive attitude of other-mindedness, you, too, can become a natural at nurturing and enjoy the added privilege of influence in the lives of others. Here's how to do it:

- **Commit to them.** Make a commitment to become a nurturer. Making a commitment to help people changes your priorities and your actions. Love for others always finds a way to help; indifference to others finds nothing but excuses.

- **Believe in them.** People rise or fall to meet the expectations of those closest to them. Give people your trust and hope, and they will do everything they can to keep from letting you down.

- **Be accessible to them.** You can't nurture anyone from a distance. You can only do it up close. When you first start the process with people, you may need to spend a lot of time with them. But as they gain confidence in themselves and the relationship, they will require less personal contact. Until they reach that point, make sure they have access to you.

- **Give with no strings attached.** If you need people, you cannot lead them. And nurturing is an aspect of leadership. Instead of trying to make a transaction out of it, give freely without expecting anything in return. Nineteenth-century economist Henry Drummond wisely observed, "You will find as you look back upon your life that the moments when you have really lived are the moments when you have done things in a spirit of love."

- **Give them opportunities.** As the people you nurture gain strength, give them additional opportunities to succeed and grow. You will continue to nurture them, but as time goes by, their actions and accomplishments will help them remain secure, respected, and encouraged.

- **Lift them to a higher level.** Your ultimate goal should always be to help people go to a higher level, to reach their potential. Nurturing is the foundation upon which they can begin the building process.

Walt Disney is reported to have said that there are three kinds of people in the world. There are well-poisoners who discourage others, stomp on their creativity, and tell them what they can't do. There are lawn-mowers, people who have good intentions but are self-absorbed, who mow their own lawns but never help others. And there are life-enhancers. This last category contains people who reach out to enrich the lives of others, who lift them up and inspire them. Each of us needs to do everything in our power to become a life-enhancer, to nurture people so that they are motivated to grow and reach their potential. It is a process that takes time. (And in coming chapters, we'll share insights that will show you how to help people take additional steps in that process.)

One of the most inspiring stories of encouragement and nurturing we've ever heard concerns John Wesley—an influencer we mentioned in this book's introduction. In 1791, Wesley wrote a letter to William Wilberforce, a member of England's Parliament who was in the midst of fighting for the abolition of the British slave trade. The letter, which has since become famous, said this:

London, February 26, 1791
Dear Sir:

Unless the divine power has raised you up . . . I see not how you can go through your glorious enterprise, in opposing that execrable villainy, which is the scandal of religion, of England, and of human nature. Unless God has raised you up for this very thing, you will be worn out by the opposition of men and devils. But "if God be for you, who can be against you?" Are all of them stronger than God? O "be not weary in well doing!" Go on, in the name of God and in the power of His might, till even American slavery (the vilest that ever saw the sun) shall vanish away before it. . . .

That He who has guided you from your youth up, may continue to strengthen you in this and all things, is the prayer of,

Your affectionate ser-
vant,
J. Wesley

Four days later, Wesley was dead at age eighty-eight, yet his influence in Wilberforce's life continued for years. Wilberforce did not succeed in convincing Parliament to abolish slavery at that time, but he didn't give up the fight. He kept at it for decades despite slander, vilification, and threats. And when he thought he couldn't go on, he looked to Wesley's letter for encouragement. Finally, in 1807, the slave trade was abolished. And in 1833, several months after Wilberforce's death, slavery was outlawed in all of the British Empire.

Though condemned by many during his career, Wilberforce was buried with honor in Westminster Abbey, one of the most esteemed men of his day. Part of his epitaph reads:

Eminent as he was in every department of public labour,
*   And a leader in every work of charity,*
Whether to relieve the temporal or the spiritual wants
*   of his fellow men*
His name will ever be specially identified
*   With those exertions*
Which, by the blessing of God, removed from England
*   The guilt of the African slave trade,*
And prepared the way for the abolition of slavery

in every colony of the Empire.

Maybe there is a William Wilberforce in your life, just waiting to be nurtured to greatness. The only way you'll ever know is to become a nurturer who is other-minded and adds value to the people you meet.

Influence Checklist
NURTURING OTHER PEOPLE

❑ **Develop a nurturing environment in your home, place of business, or church**. Make it your goal to make the people around you feel loved, respected, and secure. To do that, commit to eliminating all negative criticism from your speech for one month and searching for only positive things to say to others.

❑ **Give special encouragement.** Pick two or three people to encourage this month. Send each person a short handwritten note every week. Make yourself accessible to these people. And give of your time without expecting something in return. At the end of the month, examine your relationships with them for positive change.

❑ **Rebuild bridges.** Think of one person with whom you have tended to be negative in the past. (It can be anyone: a colleague, a family member, or an employee, for instance.) Go to that person and apologize for your past actions or remarks. Then find the quality you most admire about the person and tell him or her about it. During the following weeks, look for ways to build and strengthen the relationship.

A Person of Influence Has . . .

FAITH IN PEOPLE

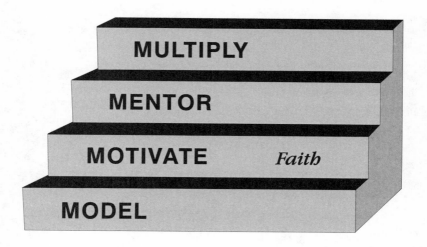

Jim grew up in Niagara Falls, New York. Today the population is about 60,000, but when Jim lived there, it had closer to 100,000 people. It was a thriving industrial center, with companies such as DuPont Chemical. It also had cultural offerings, a strong one-hundred-year-old university, and other attractions, but the main focus of the town then was the incredible natural wonder of the falls, as it still is today.

The Iroquois called it *Niagara*, meaning "thunder of waters." It's an awesome sight. Every minute more than 12 million cubic feet of water drop a distance of about 180 feet over the edge of the falls. And its total width, including both the Canadian and the American portions, measures more than 3,100 feet. It is rightly called one of the natural wonders of the world. Jim says,

Back when we were growing up, we heard a lot of stories about the falls and the daredevil stunts people used to pull—like Annie Edson Taylor's going over the falls in a barrel and things like that. One of the great legends of the town was a French acrobat named Charles Blondin who lived from 1824 to 1897. He crossed over the entire width of the falls on a tightrope back in 1859. That must have taken nerves of steel since a fall certainly would have killed him. In fact, he crossed the falls several times. He did it once with a wheelbarrow, another time blindfolded, and yet another time on stilts. They say he was quite remarkable. He continued performing even into his seventies.

One of the most incredible feats he performed was crossing the falls on a tightrope while carrying a man on his back. Can you imagine that? I guess just crossing over by himself wasn't tough enough for him! But as difficult as that feat must have been on Blondin, I can't help wondering how he got someone to go with him. That's what you call trust: to climb onto the back of a man who is going to walk more than half a mile on *a rope* suspended over one of the most powerful waterfalls in the world.

I used to think about that as a kid. What would it be like to see the falls from up on a rope above them? And more important, what person would trust me to carry him across the falls the way that man trusted Blondin?

FACTS ABOUT FAITH IN PEOPLE

We can't tell you the identity of the man Blondin carried across the falls, but there is no question that he had great faith in the French acrobat. After all, he put his life in the man's hands. You don't see that kind of trust in others every day. But the times you do, it is a very special thing.

Faith in people is an essential quality of an influencer when working with others, yet it's a scarce commodity today. Take a look at the following four facts about faith:

1. Most People Don't Have Faith in Themselves

Not long ago we saw a *Shoe* comic strip by Jeff MacNelly that showed Shoe, the crusty newspaper editor, standing on the mound in a baseball game. His catcher said to him, "You've got to have faith in your curve ball." In the next frame Shoe remarked, "It's easy for him to say. When it comes to believing in myself, I'm an agnostic."

> *When you believe in people,*
> *they do the impossible.*
> *—Nancy Dornan*

That's the way too many people feel today. They have trouble believing in themselves. They believe they will fail. Even when they see a light at the end of the tunnel, they're convinced it's a train. They see a difficulty in every possibility. But the reality is that difficulties seldom defeat people; lack of faith in themselves usually does it. With a little faith in themselves, people can do miraculous things. But without it, they have a really tough time.

2. Most People Don't Have Someone Who Has Faith in Them

In *Just for Today,* James Keller tells this story: "A sidewalk flower vendor was not doing any business. Suddenly a happy thought struck him and he put up this sign: 'This gardenia will make you feel important all day long for 10 cents.' All at once his sales began to increase."

In our society today, most people feel isolated. The strong sense of community that was once enjoyed by most Americans has become rare. And many people don't have the family support that was more common thirty or forty years ago. For example, evangelist Bill Glass noted, "Over 90 percent of prison inmates were told by parents while growing up, 'They're going to put you in jail.'" Instead of teaching their children to believe in themselves, some parents are tearing them down. For many people, even those who are closest to them don't believe in them. They have no one on their side. No wonder even a little thing like a flower can make a difference in how a person approaches the day.

3. Most People Can Tell When Someone Has Faith in Them

People's instincts are pretty good at knowing when others have faith in them. They can sense if your belief is genuine or phony. And truly having faith in someone can change her life. Jim's wife, Nancy, often says, "When you believe in people, they do the impossible."

In his book *Move Ahead with Possibility Thinking,* John's friend Robert Schuller, pastor of the Crystal Cathedral in Garden Grove, California, tells a wonderful story about an incident that changed his life as a boy. It occurred when his uncle had faith in him and showed it in his words and actions:

His car drove past the unpainted barn and stopped in a cloud of summer dust at our front gate. I ran barefooted across the splintery porch and saw my uncle Henry bound out of the car. He was tall, very handsome, and terribly alive with energy. After many years overseas as a missionary in China, he was visiting our Iowa farm. He ran up to the old gate and put both of his big hands on my four-year-old shoulders. He smiled widely, ruffled my uncombed hair, and said, "Well! I guess you're Robert! I think you are going to be a preacher someday." That night I prayed secretly, "And dear God, make me a preacher when I grow up!" I believe that God made me a POS-SIBILITY THINKER then and there.

As you work to become a person of influence, always remember that your goal is not to get people to think more highly of you. It's to get them to think more highly of themselves. Have faith in them, and they will begin to do exactly that.

> ## *Difficulties seldom defeat people; lack of faith in themselves usually does it.*

4. Most People Will Do Anything to Live Up to Your Faith in Them

People rise or fall to meet your level of expectations for them. If you express skepticism and doubt in others, they will return your lack of confidence with mediocrity. But if you believe in them and expect them to do well, they will go the extra mile trying to do their best. And in the process, they and you benefit. John H. Spalding expressed the thought this way: "Those who believe in our ability do more than stimulate us. They create for us an atmosphere in which it becomes easier to succeed."

If you've never been one to trust people and put your faith in them, change your way of thinking and begin believing in others. Your life will quickly improve. When you have faith in others, you give them an incredible gift. Give others money, and it's soon spent. Give resources, and they may not be used to their best advantage. Give help, and people will often find themselves back where they started in a short period of time. But give them your faith, and they become confident, energized, and self-reliant. They become motivated to acquire what they need to succeed on their own. And then later if you share money, resources, and help, they're better able to use them to build a better future.

FAITH IS BELIEF IN ACTION

In the late 1800s, a salesman from back east arrived at a frontier town somewhere on the Great Plains. As he was talking to the owner of a general store, a rancher came in, and the owner excused himself to take care of his customer. As they talked, the salesman couldn't help overhearing their conversation. It seemed the rancher wanted credit for some things he needed.

"Are you doing any fencing this spring, Jake?" asked the storekeeper.

"Sure am, Bill," said the rancher.

"Fencing in or fencing out?"

"Fencing in. Taking in another 360 acres across the creek."

"Good to hear it, Jake. You got the credit. Just tell Steve out back what you need."

The salesman was dumbfounded. "I've seen all kinds of credit systems," he said, "but never one like that. How does it work?"

"Well," said the storekeeper, "let me tell you. If a man's fencing out, that means he's scared, trying to just hold on to what he's got. But if he's fencing in, he's growing and trying to improve. I always give credit to a man who's fencing in because that means he believes in himself."

Having faith in people requires more than just words or positive feelings about them. We have to back it up with what we do. As W. T. Purkiser, professor emeritus of religion at Point Loma College, clearly saw: "Faith is more than thinking something is true. Faith is thinking something is true to the extent that we act on it."

If you want to help other people and make a positive impact on their lives, you have to treat them with that kind of confidence. Ralph Waldo Emerson said, "Trust men and they will be true to

you; treat them greatly and they will show themselves great."
Become a believer in people, and even the most tentative and
inexperienced people can bloom right before your eyes.

How to Become a
Believer in People

We're fortunate because we grew up in positive, affirming
environments. As a result, we have an easy time believing in people and expressing that belief. But we realize that not everyone
had the benefit of a positive upbringing. Most people need to
learn how to have faith in others. To build your belief in others,
try using these suggestions, created using the initial letters of the
word *BELIEVE*.

Believe in Them Before They Succeed

Have you ever noticed how many people support a sports
team as soon as it starts winning? That happened here in San
Diego a couple of years ago when the Chargers won their division, then won all their play-off games leading into the Super
Bowl. The whole town went crazy. You could see the team's
lightning bolt symbol everywhere: on people's houses, on the
back windows of cars, on lapel pins, and so forth.

During the height of the Chargers' success, a couple of local
radio personalities named Jeff and Jer rallied the people of San
Diego by sponsoring a big event at the stadium one morning.
Their plan was to give the people who showed up T-shirts in the
team colors and have them line up in the parking lot in the shape
of a giant lightning bolt. Then they would take a picture of it from
a helicopter and put it in the newspaper the next morning. A couple of thousand people were required to pull it off, but they
hoped enough would show to make it happen. Imagine their surprise when so many people showed up that they ran out of T-
shirts, and ended up surrounding the "human bolt" with a border
of extras. It was such a big deal that some of the news services
picked it up and televised it on the national news.

Everyone loves a winner. It's easy to have faith in people who have already proved themselves. It's much tougher to believe in people *before* they have proved themselves. But that is the key to motivating people to reach their potential. You have to believe in them first, before they become successful, and sometimes before they even believe in themselves. French writer and moralist Joseph Joubert said, "No one can give faith unless he has faith. It is the persuaded who persuade." You need faith in others before you can persuade them to believe in themselves.

Some people in your life desperately want to believe in themselves but have little hope. As you interact with them, remember the motto of French World War I hero Marshal Ferdinand Foch: "There are no hopeless situations; there are only men and women who have grown hopeless about them." Every person has seeds of greatness within, even though they may currently be dormant. But when you believe in people, you water the seeds and give them the chance to grow. Every time you put your faith in them, you're giving life-sustaining water, warmth, food, and light. And if you continue to give encouragement through your belief in them, these people will bloom in time.

Emphasize Their Strengths

We mentioned previously that many people mistakenly think that to be influential in other people's lives, they have to be an "authority" and point out others' deficiencies. People who try that approach become like Lucy from the comic strip *Peanuts* by Charles Schulz. In one strip Lucy told poor Charlie Brown, "You, Charlie Brown, are a foul ball in the line drive of life! You're in the shadow of your own goal posts! You are a miscue! You are three putts on the eighteenth green! You are a seven-ten split in the tenth frame. . . . You are a missed free throw, a shanked nine iron and a called third strike! Do you understand? Have I made myself clear?" That's hardly a way to positively impact the life of another person!

The road to becoming a positive influence on others lies in exactly the opposite direction. The best way to show people your faith in them and motivate them is to focus your attention on their strengths. According to author and advertising executive Bruce Barton, "Nothing splendid has ever been achieved except by those who dared believe that something inside them was superior to circumstances." By emphasizing people's strengths, you're helping them believe that they possess what they need to succeed.

> ***B**elieving in people* **before** *they have proved themselves is the key to motivating people to reach their potential.*

Praise them for what they do well, both privately and publicly. Tell them how much you appreciate their positive qualities and their skills. And anytime you have the opportunity to compliment and praise them in the presence of their family and close friends, do it.

List Their Past Successes

Even when you emphasize people's strengths, they may need further encouragement to show them you believe in them and to get them motivated. Entrepreneur Mary Kay Ash advised, "Everyone has an invisible sign hanging from his neck saying, 'Make me feel important!' Never forget this message when working with people." One of the best ways to do that is to help people remember their past successes.

The account of David and Goliath presents a classic example of how past successes can help a person have faith in himself. You may remember the story from the Bible. A nine-foot-tall Philistine champion named Goliath stood before the army of Israel and taunted them every day for forty days, daring them to send out a warrior to face him. On the fortieth day a young shepherd named David came to the front lines to deliver food to his brothers, who were in Israel's army. While he was there, he witnessed the giant's contemptuous display of taunts and challenges. David was so infuriated that he told King Saul of Israel that he wanted to face the giant in battle. Here's what happened:

> David said to Saul, "Let no one lose heart on account of this Philistine; your servant will go and fight him." Saul replied, "You are not able to go out against this Philistine and fight him; you are only a boy, and he has been a fighting man from his youth." But David said to Saul, "Your servant has been keeping his father's sheep. When a lion or a bear came and carried off a sheep from the flock, I went after it, struck it and rescued the sheep from its mouth. When it turned on me, I seized it by its hair, struck it and killed it. Your servant has killed both the lion and the bear. . . . The LORD who delivered me from the paw of the lion and the paw of the bear will deliver me from the hand of this Philistine."[1]

David looked back on his past successes, and he had confidence in his future actions. And of course, when he faced the giant, he felled him like a tree, using nothing but a rock and sling. And when he cut off Goliath's head, his success inspired his fellow countrymen; they routed the Philistine army.

Not everyone has the natural ability to recognize past successes and draw confidence from them. Some people need help. If you can show others that they have done well in the past and help them see that their past victories have paved the way for future success, they'll be better able to move into action. Listing past successes helps others believe in themselves.

Instill Confidence When They Fail

When you have encouraged people and put your faith in them, and they begin to believe they can succeed in life, they soon reach a critical crossroads. The first time or two that they fail—and they will fail because it's a part of life—they have two choices. They can give in or go on.

Some people are resilient and willing to keep trying in order to succeed, even when they don't see immediate progress. But others aren't that determined. Some will collapse at the first sign of trouble. To give them a push and inspire them, you need to keep showing your confidence in them, even when they're making mistakes or doing poorly.

One of the ways to do that is to tell them about your past troubles and traumas. Sometimes people think that if you're currently successful, you have always been that way. They don't realize that you have had your share of flops, failures, and fumbles. Show them that success is a journey, a process, not a destination. When they realize that you have failed and yet still managed to succeed, they'll realize that it's okay to fail. And their confidence will remain intact. They will learn to think the way baseball legend Babe Ruth did when he said, "Never let the fear of striking out get in the way."

Experience Some Wins Together

It's not enough just knowing that failure is a part of moving forward in life. To really become motivated to succeed, people need to believe they can win. John, like many of us, got a taste for winning when he was just a kid. He says,

> Growing up, I idolized my brother Larry, who is two and a half years older than I am. After my parents, he was probably the greatest influencer in my life when I was a kid. Larry has always been a great leader and an excellent athlete. And whenever we played basketball, football, or baseball with the kids in the neighborhood, Larry was a captain.
>
> A lot of times when they picked teams, I would be one of the last picked, because I was younger and smaller than most of the kids. But as I got older, Larry began picking me more, and that always made me feel good, not only because it meant my brother cared about me, but because I knew that when Larry picked me, I was going to be on the winning team. You see, Larry was a fierce competitor, and he didn't like losing. He always played to win, and he usually did. Together we put quite a few wins under our belts, and I came to expect victory when I played with my brother.

Winning is motivating. Novelist David Ambrose acknowledged this truth: "If you have the will to win, you have achieved half your success; if you don't, you have achieved half your failure." Coming alongside others to help them experience some wins with you gives them reasons to believe they will succeed. And in the process, they sense victory. That's when incredible things begin to happen in their lives. Take a look at this comparison between what happens when people sense victory versus when they expect defeat:

When People Sense Victory	When People Sense Defeat
They sacrifice to succeed.	They give as little as possible.
They look for ways to win.	They look for excuses.
They become energized.	They become tired.
They follow the game plan.	They forsake the game plan.
They help other team members.	They hurt others.

To help people believe they can achieve victory, put them in a position to experience small successes. Encourage them to perform tasks or take on responsibilities you know they can handle and do well. And give them the assistance they need to succeed. As Greek orator Demosthenes said, "Small opportunities are often the beginning of great enterprises." In time as their confidence grows, they will take on more difficult challenges, but they will be able to face them with confidence and competence because of the positive track record they're developing.

Visualize Their Future Success

We heard about an experiment performed with laboratory rats to measure their motivation to live under different circumstances. Scientists dropped a rat into a jar of water that had been placed in total darkness, and they timed how long the animal would continue swimming before it gave up and allowed itself to drown. They found that the rat usually lasted little more than three minutes.

Then they dropped another rat into the same kind of jar, but instead of placing it in total darkness, they allowed a ray of light to shine into it. Under those circumstances, the rat kept swimming for thirty-six hours. That's more than seven hundred times longer than the one in the dark! Because the rat could see, it continued to have hope.

If that is true of laboratory animals, think of how strong the effect of visualization can be on people, who are capable of higher reasoning. It's been said that a person can live forty days without food, four days without water, four minutes without air, but only four seconds without hope. Each time you cast a vision for others and paint a picture of their future success, you build them up, motivate them, and give them reasons to keep going.

Expect a New Level of Living

German statesman Konrad Adenauer observed: "We all live under the same sky, but we don't all have the same horizon." As an influencer, you have the goal of helping others see beyond today and their current circumstances and dream big dreams. When you put your faith in people, you help them to expand their horizons and motivate them to move to a whole new level of living.

> *To help people believe they can achieve victory, put them in a position to experience small successes.*

Integral to that new way of living is a change in attitude. According to Denis Waitley, "The winner's edge is not in a gifted birth, a high IQ, or in talent. The winner's edge is all in the attitude, not aptitude. Attitude is the criterion for success." As people's attitudes change from doubt to confidence—in themselves and their ability to succeed and reach their potential—everything in their lives changes for the better.

Jim and Nancy gained incredible insights about the power of putting their faith into others several years ago when they decided to take a chance with their son Eric on a mountain in Utah. Here's Jim's account of it:

> When you have a disabled child, you constantly fight a battle of emotions between providing him new experiences and protecting him from injury or failure. Our life with Eric has been no exception. Despite his limitations, which include having to use a wheelchair and having very little use in his right hand, Eric has a great positive spirit. And often if there is hesitation to try new things, it comes from Nancy and me rather than him.
>
> About five years ago Nancy got the idea that we should take Eric skiing. She had heard from a friend about a place in Park City, Utah, called the National Ability Center. There they offer people with disabilities instruction and assistance in snow skiing, swimming, tennis, waterskiing, horseback riding, rafting, and other activities. She thought the experience would be great for his self-esteem.
>
> I have to admit, I was skeptical about it from the very beginning. Knowing how difficult the sport is for me, I had trouble imagining Eric racing down a 10,000-foot mountain. And that wasn't helped by the knowledge that a blow to Eric's head could cause him to have a seizure that would put him in the hospital for more brain surgery. But Nancy had faith that Eric could do it, and when she believes, so does he. And off we went to give it a try.
>
> When we got up to Deer Valley and met some of the people who work at the National Ability Center, I started to feel a little bit better about it. They were professional and extremely positive, and they showed us the equipment that Eric would be using, a type of bi-ski with a molded seat. Eric would be put in the chair and steer using a bar attached to outrigger skis.
>
> When we started to fill out paperwork, we were momentarily paralyzed when we read the waiver that said that Eric would be "engaging in activities that involve risk of serious injury, including permanent disability and death." It made the risk seem very real, but by this time Eric was very excited and we didn't want him to see any hesitation from us.

After Velcro-fastening Eric into his bi-ski and giving him some pointers, Stephanie, his young instructor, took him up the bunny slope. About ten minutes later, we got excited as we saw Eric coming down the hill with the biggest smile on his face. We were so proud of him that we were giving him high fives and patting him on the back. I thought to myself, *That wasn't so bad.*

Then off they went again. What we didn't know was that this time they were going to the top of the mountain. At the bottom of the hill we waited. And waited. We weren't sure whether we'd see Eric come down the mountain on his skis or on a stretcher with the ski patrol. Finally after about thirty minutes, we saw him and Stephanie come around a bend and ski to the bottom of the slope. His cheeks were flushed, and he was grinning like the Cheshire cat. He loved it.

"Move over, Dad," he said as he blew past us. "I'm going up again."

Eric skied every day on that trip. In fact, when he finished skiing one day, he told us, "Stephanie didn't take me up the mountain today."

"Oh," said Nancy, "then who skied with you?"

"Some one-legged guy," answered Eric.

"What!" screeched Nancy. "What do you mean some one-legged guy?"

"Yep," said Eric, "a one-legged guy." And then Eric smiled mischievously and said, "Want to know how he lost his leg? Avalanche!"

Eric has been skiing every year since then, and his life hasn't been the same. He now has confidence that he never had before, and he is willing to try just about anything. He swims three days a week, works out with weights, plays power soccer, and does other sorts of things. I guess you could say that he has adopted the motto of the National Ability Center as his own: "If I Can Do This, I Can Do Anything!"

If they had done things Jim's way, Eric never would have gotten the chance to experience what he did on that mountain in Utah five years ago. Jim loves Eric with all his heart, but he tends to want to play it safe. Putting your faith in others involves taking a chance. But the rewards outweigh the risks. Robert Louis

Stevenson said, "To be what we are, and to become what we are capable of becoming, is the only end of life." When you put your faith in others, you help them reach their potential. And you become an important influencer in their lives.

Influence Checklist
HAVING FAITH IN PEOPLE

❏ **Find a strength.** Think about someone you'd like to encourage. Find a strength that the person has, and point it out to him or her. Use your interaction as an opportunity to express confidence in the person.

❏ **Build on past successes.** If you have to give someone a difficult assignment in the near future, take some time to recall his or her past successes. Then when you meet with the person, review those past successes. (If you go through this process and can't recall any past successes, that's a sign you've spent too little time getting to know the person. Plan to spend some time together to get better acquainted.)

❏ **Help others overcome defeat.** If you have colleagues, friends, employees, or family members who have recently experienced a defeat of some kind, take time to chat with them about it. Let them tell you the whole story, and when they're done, make it clear that you value them and still believe strongly in them.

❏ **Start off right.** The next time you recruit new people for your organization, start the relationships right. Instead of waiting until after they prove themselves to praise them, make it a point to repeatedly express your faith in them and their ability *before* they give you results. You'll be pleased by their desire to live up to your positive expectations.

A Person of Influence . . .

LISTENS TO PEOPLE

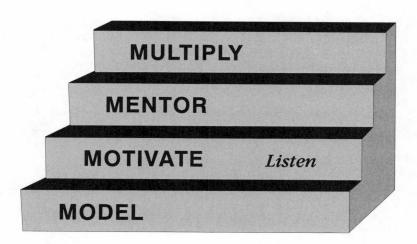

If you were going on a job interview today, what would you say is the most important skill you would need? Is it writing, to create a knockout résumé? Or maybe salesmanship? After all, isn't that what you do on an interview, sell yourself? Or how about charisma? If you're charismatic, you're sure to get the job you want, right?

Or let's say that instead of going on an interview, you were going to spend your day recruiting, whether for business prospects, ministry workers, or people to play on your softball team. What skill would you need as a recruiter? Discernment? An eye for talent? The ability to cast vision and get people excited? Or maybe it would be hard-nosed negotiation skills?

Better yet, let's say your job today was to supply new ideas for your organization. What qualities would you need? Creativity? Intelligence? Would you need a good education? What is the number one ability you would need?

No matter which one of these three tasks you were to take on today, you would need one skill over all others, more than talent, discernment, or charm. It is the one skill that all great leaders recognize as indispensable to their ability to influence others and succeed. Have you guessed what it is? It's the ability to listen.

Not everyone is quick to learn the lesson of the importance of listening. Take, for example, Jim's experience:

Fresh from Purdue University's engineering school, I started out in the corporate environment at McDonnell-Douglas where they had about 40,000 employees. I was working in the advanced design group for the DC-10 doing wind-tunnel analyses and computer simulations of the airplane's performance.

But it didn't take me long to realize that I wasn't going to be there for my whole career. Some of the guys I worked with had been there two decades, and nothing had changed in them for those twenty years. They were in a holding pattern, waiting for the gold watch. But I wanted to make a greater impact on my world.

That's when I started to pursue other business opportunities, and when I found the right one, I began trying to recruit others to join me. Back then my strategy was to meet people in the huge employee cafeteria. After waiting in line to get my lunch, I'd look for a seat next to a sharp-looking guy who was sitting by himself, and I'd strike up a conversation with him. The first chance I got, I'd bombard him with information and try to persuade him with impressive facts and irrefutable logic. I managed to intimidate a few people with the force of my convictions, but I was unsuccessful in building a productive relationship with anyone.

I'd been doing this for several months, with very little success, when one day I was just talking with a guy from another department. He was telling me about the frustrations he was having with his boss, and about some problems he was having at home. He just found out his oldest child needed braces, their old clunker of a car was on its last legs, and he wasn't sure how he was going to make it. I really felt for the guy, and I wanted to get to know him better. Then suddenly, I realized that I could help him out. He was feeling powerless on the job, and he had money problems—two things that could be helped by being in business for himself. So I started to tell him about my business and explain how it might solve some of his problems. And to my shock he was actually very interested.

That day it hit me: *What an idiot I've been! I can't succeed with others by dumping information on them. If I want to help them or have a positive impact on people, I need to learn how to listen to them!*

THE VALUE OF LISTENING

Edgar Watson Howe once joked, "No man would listen to you talk if he didn't know it was his turn next." Unfortunately, that accurately describes the way too many people approach communication—they're too busy waiting for their turn to really listen to others. But people of influence understand the incredible value of becoming a good listener. For example, when Lyndon B. Johnson was a junior senator from Texas, he kept a sign on his office wall that read, "You ain't learnin' nothin' when you're doin' all the talkin'." And Woodrow Wilson, the twenty-eighth American president, once said, "The ear of the leader must ring with the voices of the people."

The ability to skillfully listen is one key to gaining influence with others. Consider these benefits to listening that we've found:

Listening Shows Respect

Psychologist Dr. Joyce Brothers said, "Listening, not imitation, may be the sincerest form of flattery." Whenever you don't pay attention to what others have to say, you send them the message that you don't value them. But when you listen to others, you communicate that you respect them. Even more, you show them that you care. German-born philosopher-theologian Paul Tillich commented, "The first duty of love is to listen."

A mistake that people often make in communicating is trying very hard to impress the other person. They try to make themselves appear smart, witty, or entertaining. But if you want to relate well to others, you have to be willing to focus on what they have to offer. Be *impressed and interested,* not *impressive and interesting.* Poet-philosopher Ralph Waldo Emerson acknowledged, "Every man I meet is in some way my superior, and I can learn of him." Remember that and listen, and the lines of communication will really open up.

Listening Builds Relationships

Dale Carnegie, author of *How to Win Friends and Influence People,* advised, "You can make more friends in two weeks by becoming a good listener than you can in two years trying to get other people interested in you." Carnegie was incredibly gifted at understanding relationships. He recognized that people who are self-focused and who talk about themselves and their concerns all the time rarely develop strong relationships with others. David Schwartz noted in *The Magic of Thinking Big,* "Big people monopolize the listening. Small people monopolize the talking."

By becoming a good listener, you are able to connect with others on more levels and develop stronger, deeper relationships because you are meeting a need. Author C. Neil Strait pointed out that "everyone needs someone who he feels really listens to him." When you become that important listener, you help that person. And you take a significant step toward becoming a person of influence in his or her life.

Listening Increases Knowledge

Wilson Mizner said, "A good listener is not only popular everywhere, but after a while he knows something." It's amazing how much you can learn about your friends and family, your job, the organization you work in, and yourself when you decide to really listen to others. But not everyone clues in to this benefit. For example, we heard a story about a tennis pro who was giving a lesson to a new student. After watching the novice take several swings at the tennis ball, the pro stopped him and suggested ways he could improve his stroke. But each time he did, the student interrupted him and gave his opinion of the problem and how it should be solved. After several interruptions, the pro began to nod his head in agreement.

When the lesson ended, a woman who had been watching said to the pro, "Why did you go along with that arrogant man's stupid suggestions?"

You'll never know how close you are to a million-dollar idea unless you're willing to listen.

The pro smiled and replied, "I learned a long time ago that it is a waste of time to try to sell real *answers* to anyone who just wants to buy *echoes*."

Beware of putting yourself into a position where you think you know all the answers. Anytime you do, you'll be putting yourself in danger. It's almost impossible to think of yourself as "the expert" and continue growing and learning at the same time. All great learners are great listeners.

One common problem as people gain more authority is that they often listen to others less and less, especially the people who report to them. While it's true that the higher you go, the less you are required to listen to others, it's also true that your need for good listening skills increases. The farther you get from the front lines, the more you have to depend on others to get reliable information. Only if you develop good listening skills early, and then continue to use them, will you be able to gather the information you need to succeed.

As you proceed through life and become more successful, don't lose sight of your need to keep growing and improving yourself. And remember, a deaf ear is evidence of a closed mind.

Listening Generates Ideas

Fresh, innovative ideas help us to find new ways to solve old problems, to generate new products and processes to keep our organizations growing, and to continue growing and improving personally. Plutarch of ancient Greece asserted, "Know how to listen, and you will profit even from those who talk badly."

When we think about innovative companies that never seem to run out of ideas, 3M immediately comes to mind. That company seems to develop new products faster than just about any other manufacturer. The organization has a reputation for being open to employees' ideas and for listening to customers. In fact, a representative of 3M said the number one resource for product ideas was customer complaints.

Good companies have a reputation for listening to their people. Chili's restaurants, one of the nation's best-run food service chains according to *Restaurants and Institutions* magazine, is known for that quality too. Almost 80 percent of its menu has come from suggestions made by unit managers.

What's good for effective companies is good for individuals. When you consistently listen to others, you never suffer for ideas. People love to contribute, especially when their leader shares the credit with them. If you give people opportunities to share their thoughts, and you listen with an open mind, there will always be a flow of new ideas. And even if you hear ideas that won't work, just listening to them can often spark other creative thoughts in you and others. You'll never know how close you are to a million-dollar idea unless you're willing to listen.

Listening Builds Loyalty

A funny thing happens when you don't make a practice of listening to people. They find others who will. Anytime employees, spouses, colleagues, children, or friends no longer believe they are being listened to, they seek out people who will give them what they want. Sometimes the consequences can be disastrous: the end of a friendship, lack of authority at work, lessened parental influence, or the breakdown of a marriage.

Nobody ever **listened** *himself or herself out of a sale.*

On the other hand, practicing good listening skills draws people to you. Karl Menninger, psychiatrist, author, and one of the founders of the Menninger Foundation, said, "The friends who listen to us are the ones we move toward, and we want to sit in their radius." Everyone loves a good listener and is attracted to him or her. And if you consistently listen to others, valuing them and what they have to offer, they are likely to develop a strong loyalty to you, even when your authority with them is unofficial or informal.

Listening Is a Great Way to Help Others and Yourself

Roger G. Imhoff urged, "Let others confide in you. It may not help you, but it surely will help them." At first glance, listening to others may appear to benefit only them. But when you become a good listener, you put yourself in a position to help yourself too. You have the ability to develop strong relationships, gather valuable information, and increase your understanding of yourself and others.

COMMON BARRIERS TO LISTENING

Few people have reached their potential when it comes to listening. If you aren't as skilled at listening as you would like to be, then the first thing to do to improve your ability is to be aware of common barriers to listening:

Overvaluing Talking

A comic once described listening as being "composed of the rude interruptions between my exclamations." Many people's attitudes about listening agree with that statement more than they would like to admit. For example, if you asked six people how they could improve their communication skills, most of them would describe the need to become more persuasive or sharpen their public speaking skills. Few would cite a desire to listen better.

Most people overvalue talking and undervalue listening, even those in people-related jobs, such as sales. But the truth is that effective communication is not persuasion. It's listening. Think about it: Nobody ever *listened* himself or herself out of a sale.

Good communicators know to monitor their talking-to-listening ratio. President Abraham Lincoln, considered one of the most effective leaders and communicators in our nation's history, said, "When I'm getting ready to reason with a man, I spend one third of my time thinking about myself and what I am going to say— and two thirds thinking about him and what he is going to say." That's a good ratio to maintain. Listen twice as much as you speak.

Lacking Focus

For some people, especially those with high energy, slowing down enough to really listen can be challenging. Most people tend to speak about 180 words a minute, but they can listen at 300 to 500 words a minute. That disparity can create tension and cause a listener to lose focus. Most people try to fill up that communication gap by finding other things to do, such as daydream, think about their daily schedule or mentally review their to-do list, or watch other people. It's similar to what we do when we drive a car. We rarely just watch the road and do nothing else. Usually we look at the scenery, eat and drink, talk, or listen to the radio.

If you want to become a better listener, however, you need to learn to direct that energy and attention positively by concentrating on the person you're with. Observe body language. Watch for changes in facial expression. Look into the person's eyes. Management expert Peter Drucker remarked, "The most important thing in communication is to hear what isn't being said." If you expend your extra energy by observing the other person closely and interpreting what he or she says, your listening skills will improve dramatically.

Experiencing Mental Fatigue

Former president Ronald Reagan told an amusing story about two psychiatrists, one older and one younger. Each day they showed up at work immaculately dressed and alert. But at the end of the day, the younger doctor was frazzled and disheveled while the older man was as fresh as ever.

"How do you do it?" the younger psychiatrist finally asked his colleague. "You always stay so fresh after hearing patients all day."

The older doctor replied, "It's easy. I never listen."[1]

Whenever you listen to others for extended periods of time, the effect can be exhausting. But any kind of mental fatigue can negatively affect your ability to listen.

We heard a story about an eighty-nine-year-old woman with hearing problems. She visited her doctor, and after examining her, he said, "We now have a procedure that can correct your hearing problem. When would you like to schedule the operation?"

"There won't be any operation because I don't want my hearing corrected," said the woman. "I'm eighty-nine years old, and I've heard enough!"

If you're tired or facing difficult circumstances, remember that to remain an effective listener, you have to dig up more energy, concentrate, and stay focused.

Stereotyping

Stereotyping others can be a huge barrier to listening. It tends to make us hear what we expect rather than what another person actually says. Most of us may think that we don't fall into this trap, but we all do to some degree. Read the following humorous list of stereotype breakers from a piece called "Things I'd Like to Hear—But Won't" created by David Grimes. If you never expect to hear any of these things from the people listed, then you may be guilty of stereotyping:

From my auto mechanic:

"That part is much less expensive than I thought."

"You could get that done more cheaply at the garage down the street."

"It was just a loose wire. No charge."

From a store clerk:

"The computerized cash register is down. I'll just add up your purchases with a pencil and paper."

"I'll take a break *after* I finish waiting on these customers."

"We're sorry we sold you defective merchandise. We'll pick it up at your home and bring you a new one or give you a complete refund, whichever you prefer."

From a contractor:

"Whoever worked on this before sure knew what he was doing."

"I think I came in a little high on that estimate."

From the dentist:

"I think you're flossing too much."

"I won't ask you any questions until I take the pick out of your mouth."

From a restaurant server:

"I think it's presumptuous for a waiter to volunteer his name, but since you ask, it's Tim."

"I was slow and inattentive. I cannot accept any tip."[2]

These statements are clever. And they are also a reminder that it's a bad idea to stereotype others. Whenever you treat people strictly as members of a group rather than as individuals, you can get into trouble. So watch out. If you talk to people and find yourself thinking of them as computer geeks, typical teenagers, ditsy blondes, stiff engineer types, or some other representative of a group instead of as individual people, beware. You may not really be listening to what they have to say.

Carrying Personal Emotional Baggage

Nearly everyone has emotional filters that prevent him or her from hearing certain things that other people say. Your past experiences, both positive and negative, color the way you look at life and shape your expectations. And particularly strong experiences, such as traumas or incidents from childhood, can make you tend to react strongly whenever you perceive you are in a similar situation. As Mark Twain once said, "A cat who sits on a hot stove will never sit on a hot stove again. He'll never sit on a cold stove either. From then on, that cat just won't like stoves."

If you've never worked through strong past emotional experiences, you may be filtering what others say through those experiences. If you're preoccupied with certain topics, if a particular subject makes you defensive, or if you frequently project your point of view onto others, you may need to work through your issues before you can become an effective listener.

Sigmund Freud stated, "A man with a toothache cannot be in love," meaning that the toothache doesn't allow him to notice anything other than his pain. Similarly, anytime a person has an ax to grind, the words of others are drowned out by the sound of the grindstone.

Being Preoccupied with Self

Probably the most formidable barrier to listening is preoccupation with self. Many years ago we saw a TV sketch that illustrates this point really well. A husband was watching television, and his wife was trying to engage him in conversation:

WIFE: Dear, the plumber didn't make it in time to fix the leak by the hot water heater today.

HUSBAND: Uh-huh.

WIFE: So the pipe burst and flooded the basement.

HUSBAND: Quiet. It's third down and goal to go.

WIFE: Some of the wiring got wet and almost electrocuted Fluffy.

HUSBAND: Oh, no, they've got a man open. Shoot! Touchdown.

WIFE: The vet says he'll be better in a week.

HUSBAND: Can you get me something to eat?

WIFE: The plumber finally came and said that he was happy our pipe broke because now he can afford to go on vacation.

HUSBAND: Aren't you *listening?* I said I'm hungry!

WIFE: And, Stanley, I'm leaving you. The plumber and I are flying to Acapulco in the morning.

HUSBAND: Can't you please stop all that yakking and get me something to eat? The trouble around here is that nobody ever listens to me.

If you don't care about anyone but yourself, you're not going to listen to others. But the ironic thing is that when you don't listen, the damage you do to yourself is ultimately even greater than what you do to other people.

HOW TO DEVELOP LISTENING SKILLS

According to Brian Adams, author of *Sales Cybernetics,* during the average waking day, we spend most of it listening. He offers the following statistics:

9 percent of the day is spent writing
16 percent of the day is spent reading
30 percent of the day is spent speaking
45 percent of the day is spent *listening*[3]

So you probably agree that listening is important. But what does it mean to listen? We heard a story about a high school music appreciation class that provides a meaningful answer to that question. The teacher of the class asked for a volunteer to explain the difference between listening and hearing. At first no one wanted to answer, but finally, a student raised his hand. When the teacher called on him, he said, "Listening is *wanting* to hear."

That answer is a great start. To become a good listener, you have to want to hear. But you also need some skills to help you. Here are nine suggestions to help you become a better listener:

1. Look at the Speaker

The whole listening process begins with giving the other person your undivided attention. As you interact with someone, don't catch up on other work, shuffle papers, do the dishes, or watch television. Set aside the time to focus only on the other person. And if you don't have the time at that moment, then schedule it as soon as you can.

2. Don't Interrupt

Most people react badly to being interrupted. It makes them feel disrespected. And according to Robert L. Montgomery, author of *Listening Made Easy,* "It's just as rude to step on people's ideas as it is to step on their toes."

People who tend to interrupt others generally do so for one of these reasons:

- They don't place enough value on what the other person has to say.
- They want to impress others by showing how smart or intuitive they are.

- They're too excited by the conversation to let the other person finish talking.

If you are in the habit of interrupting other people, examine your motives and determine to make a change. Give people the time they need to express themselves. And don't feel that one of you has to be speaking all the time. Periods of silence give you a chance to reflect on what's been said so that you can respond appropriately.

3. Focus on Understanding

Have you ever noticed how quickly most people forget the things they hear? Studies at institutions such as Michigan State, Ohio State, Florida State, and the University of Minnesota indicate that most people can recall only 50 percent of what they hear immediately after hearing it. And as time passes, their ability to remember continues to drop. By the next day, their retention is usually down to about 25 percent.

One way to combat that tendency is to make your goal understanding rather than just remembering facts. Lawyer, lecturer, and author Herb Cohen emphasized, "Effective listening requires more than hearing the words transmitted. It demands that you find meaning and understanding in what is being said. After all, meanings are not in words, but in people."

To increase your understanding of others as you listen, follow these guidelines offered by Eric Allenbaugh:

1. Listen with a head-heart connection.
2. Listen with the intent of understanding.
3. Listen for the message and the message behind the message.
4. Listen for both content and feelings.
5. Listen with your eyes—your hearing will be improved.
6. Listen for others' interest, not just their position.
7. Listen for what they are saying and not saying.
8. Listen with empathy and acceptance.
9. Listen for the areas where they are afraid and hurt.
10. Listen as you would like to be listened to.[4]

As you learn to put yourself in the other person's place, your ability to understand will increase. And the greater your ability to understand, the better listener you will become.

4. Determine the Need at the Moment

The ability to discern the other person's need at the moment is part of becoming an effective listener. People talk for so many different reasons: to receive comfort, to vent, to persuade, to inform, to be understood, or to relieve nervousness. Often people talk to you for reasons that don't match your expectations.

A lot of men and women find themselves in conflict because they occasionally communicate at cross-purposes. They neglect to determine the need of the other person at the moment of interaction. Men usually want to fix any problems they discuss; their need is resolution. Women, on the other hand, are more likely to tell about a problem simply to share it; they often neither request nor desire solutions. Anytime you can determine the current need of the people you're communicating with, you can put whatever they say into the appropriate context. And you will be better able to understand them.

5. Check Your Emotions

As we've already mentioned, most people carry around emotional baggage that causes them to react to certain people or situations. Anytime that you become highly emotional when listening to another person, check your emotions—especially if your reaction seems to be stronger than the situation warrants. You don't want to make an unsuspecting person the recipient of your venting. Besides, even if your reactions are not due to an event from your past, you should always allow others to finish explaining their points of view, ideas, or convictions before offering your own.

6. Suspend Your Judgment

Have you ever begun listening to another person tell a story and started to respond to it before he or she was finished? Just about everyone has. But the truth is that you can't jump to conclusions and be a good listener at the same time. As you talk to others, wait to hear the whole story before you respond. If you don't, you may miss the most important thing they intend to say.

7. *Sum Up at Major Intervals*

Experts agree that listening is most effective when it's active. John H. Melchinger suggests, "Comment on what you hear, and individualize your comments. For example, you can say, 'Cheryl, that's obviously very important to you.' It will help keep you on track as a listener. Get beyond, 'That's interesting.' If you train yourself to comment meaningfully, the speaker will know you are listening and may offer further information."

A technique for active listening is to sum up what the other person says at major intervals. As the speaker finishes one subject, paraphrase his or her main points or ideas before going on to the next one, and verify that you have gotten the right message. Doing that reassures the person and helps you stay focused on what he or she is trying to communicate.

8. *Ask Questions for Clarity*

Have you ever noticed that top reporters are excellent listeners? Take someone like Barbara Walters, for example. She looks at the speaker, focuses on understanding, suspends judgment, and sums up what the person has to say. People trust her and seem to be willing to tell her just about anything. But she practices another skill that helps her to gather more information and increase her understanding of the person she is interviewing. She asks good questions.

If you want to become an effective listener, become a good reporter—not a stick-the-microphone-in-your-face-and-bark-questions-at-you reporter, but someone who gently asks follow-up questions and seeks clarification. If you show people how much you care and ask in a nonthreatening way, you'll be amazed by how much they'll tell you.

9. *Always Make Listening Your Priority*

The last thing to remember when developing your listening skills is to make listening a priority, no matter how busy you become or how far you rise in your organization. A remarkable example of a busy executive who made time for listening was the late Sam Walton, founder of Wal-Mart and one of the richest men in America. He believed in listening to what people had to say, especially his employees. He once flew his plane to Mt. Pleasant, Texas, landed, and gave instructions to his copilot to meet him about one hundred miles down the road. He then rode in a Wal-Mart truck the rest of the way just so that he could chat with the driver. We should all give listening that kind of priority.

> *If you show people how much you care and ask questions in a nonthreatening way, you'll be amazed by how much they'll tell you.*

Many people take for granted the ability to listen. Most people consider listening to be easy, and they view themselves as pretty good listeners. But while it's true that most people are able to hear, fewer are capable of really listening.

In our careers, we have done a lot of speaking. Between the two of us, we speak to several hundred thousand people every year. Jim's wife, Nancy, does a lot of speaking—and believe us, she is a great talker! But she is also a wonderful listener, and sometimes when she speaks, she talks about communication and the importance of listening. Not long ago she gave a talk about listening that emphasized giving other people the benefit of the doubt and trying to see things from their point of view.

In the audience that day was a man named Rodney. Though he was happily married and had a young son, he had been previously married and had two daughters with his first wife. And he was having problems with her. She was constantly calling him and asking for more money for herself and the two girls. They argued continually, and she was driving him so nuts that he had already hired an attorney and was preparing to sue her.

But when Rodney heard Nancy speak about listening that day, he realized how insensitive he had been to his ex-wife, Charlotte. A couple of days later he called her and asked if they could meet. She was suspicious of Rodney and even asked her attorney to call him to find out what he was up to. But eventually, Rodney convinced them that he just wanted to talk, and finally, Charlotte agreed to see him.

They met at a coffee shop, and Rodney said, "Charlotte, I want to listen to you. Tell me what your life is like. I do care about you and the kids."

"I didn't think you cared about the girls at all," she said as she began to cry.

"I do," he said. "I'm sorry. I've only been thinking of myself, and I haven't been thinking of you. Please forgive me."

"Why are you doing this?" she asked.

"Because I want to make things right," he answered. "I've been angry for so long that I couldn't see straight. Now, tell me how things are going for you and the girls."

For a while, Charlotte could only sob. But then she started telling him about her struggles as a single parent and how she was doing her best to bring up the girls, but that it didn't seem like enough. They talked for hours, and as they did, the beginning of a new foundation of mutual respect formed. In time, they believe they will be able to become friends again.

Rodney is probably not alone. Can you think of people you haven't been listening to lately? And what are you going to do about it? It's never too late to become a good listener. It can change your life—and the lives of the people in your life.

Influence Checklist
LISTENING TO PEOPLE

❑ **Measure your listening skills.** Have someone who knows you well use the following questions to evaluate your listening skills according to the nine qualities of good listening discussed in this chapter. Ask him or her to explain any no answers. And don't interrupt or defend yourself as you receive the explanation.

1. Do I usually look at the speaker while he or she is talking?
2. Do I wait for the speaker to finish talking before I respond?
3. Do I make understanding my goal?
4. Am I usually sensitive to the speaker's immediate need?
5. Do I make it a practice to check my emotions?
6. Do I regularly suspend my judgment until I get the whole story?
7. Am I in the practice of summing up what the speaker says at major intervals?
8. Do I ask questions for clarity when needed?
9. Do I communicate to others that listening is a priority?

❑ **Strategy for improvement.** Based on the answers received, list three ways you could improve your listening skills:
1._____
2._____
3._____

Commit yourself to making those improvements during the coming weeks.

❑ **Schedule a listening occasion.** Make an appointment with the most important person in your life this week, and plan to spend an hour together just communicating. Give that person your undivided attention, and spend at least two-thirds of the time just listening to him or her.

A Person of Influence . . .

UNDERSTANDS
PEOPLE

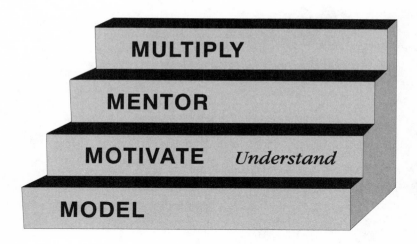

T he other night over dinner, the two of us were talking, and we started to explore some questions. How does a person build an organization? What does it take? What is the key to being successful? For example, what did it take for a person like Jim to build a business organization that's active in twenty-six countries and impacts the lives of hundreds of thousands of people? Or in the case of John, what did it take to triple the size of his church—making it the largest in its denomination—and in the process increase its budget from around $800,000 to more than $5 million, and raise active involvement by volunteers from just 112 to more than 1,800 people?

It doesn't matter whether your business is creating computer software, selling books, serving food in a restaurant, building houses, or designing airplanes. The key to success is understanding people. Jim says,

I'm not like John. I didn't grow up with an orientation toward people. He took Dale Carnegie courses while he was still in high school and went off to college knowing he would be in a people job. I went to Purdue University and studied aeronautical engineering. By the time I finished with my bachelor's degree, I thought there were two keys to success in any job: hard work and technical skills. It never even occurred to me that people skills had any value.

I entered my first job ready to work and loaded with technical knowledge. Purdue had given me a first-rate education, and I had always believed in working hard. But it didn't take me long to realize that success in business means being able to work with people. In fact, all of life is dealing with people. I found that to be true not only professionally as an engineer, a consultant, and an entrepreneur, but in every aspect of living, whether I was interacting with my family, working with one of my kids' teachers, or socializing with friends.

If you can't understand people and work with them, you can't accomplish anything. And you certainly can't become a person of influence.

UNDERSTANDING PEOPLE
PAYS GREAT DIVIDENDS

In *Climbing the Executive Ladder,* authors Kienzle and Dare said, "Few things will pay you bigger dividends than the time and trouble you take to understand people. Almost nothing will add more to your stature as an executive and a person. Nothing will give you greater satisfaction or bring you more happiness."

> *When we understand the other fellow's viewpoint— understand what he is trying to do—nine times out of ten he is trying to do right.*
> *—Harry Truman*

The ability to understand people is one of the greatest assets anyone can ever have. It has the potential to positively impact every area of your life, not just the business arena. For example, look at how understanding people helped this mother of a preschooler. She said,

> Leaving my four-year-old son in the house, I ran out to throw something in the trash. When I tried to open the door to get back inside, it was locked. I knew that insisting that my son open the door would have resulted in an hour-long battle of the wills. So in a sad voice, I said, "Oh, too bad. You just locked yourself in the house." The door opened at once.

Understanding people certainly impacts your ability to communicate with others. David Burns, a medical doctor and professor of psychiatry at the University of Pennsylvania, observed, "The biggest mistake you can make in trying to talk convincingly is to put your highest priority on expressing your ideas and feelings. What most people really want is to be listened to, respected, and understood. The moment people see that they are being understood, they become more motivated to understand your point of view." If you can learn to understand people—how they think, what they feel, what inspires them, how they're likely to act and react in a given situation—then you can motivate and influence them in a positive way.

WHY PEOPLE FAIL TO UNDERSTAND OTHERS

Lack of understanding concerning others is a recurrent source of tension in our society. We once heard an attorney say, "Half of all the controversies and conflicts that arise among people are caused not by differences of opinion or an inability to agree, but by their lack of understanding for one another." If we could reduce the number of misunderstandings, the courts wouldn't be as crowded, there would be fewer violent crimes, the divorce rate would go down, and the amount of everyday stress most people experience would drop dramatically.

If understanding is such an asset, why don't more people practice it? There are many reasons:

Fear

Seventeenth-century American colonist William Penn advised, "Neither despise or oppose what thou dost not understand," yet many people seem to do exactly the opposite. When they don't understand others, they often react by becoming fearful. And once they start fearing others, they rarely try to overcome their fear in order to learn more about them. It becomes a vicious cycle.

Unfortunately, fear is evident in the workplace when it comes to employees' reactions toward their leaders. Laborers fear their managers. Middle managers are intimidated by senior managers. Both groups are sometimes afraid of executives. The whole situation causes undue suspicion, lack of communication, and reduced productivity. For example, according to Dr. M. Michael Markowich, vice president of human resources at United Hospitals, Inc., employees are reluctant to suggest ideas. Here are some reasons why:

- They think their ideas will be rejected.
- They feel co-workers won't like the ideas.
- They think they won't get credit if the ideas work.
- They're afraid the boss will be threatened by the ideas.
- They're concerned that they'll be labeled as troublemakers.
- They're afraid of losing their jobs if they suggest ideas that don't work.[1]

The common thread in all of these reasons is fear. Yet in a healthy work environment, if you give others the benefit of the doubt and replace fear with understanding, everyone can work together positively. All people have to do is follow the advice of President Harry Truman, who said, "When we understand the other fellow's viewpoint—understand what he is trying to do—nine times out of ten he is trying to do right."

Self-Centeredness

When fear isn't a stumbling block to understanding, self-centeredness often is. Someone remarked, "There are two sides to every question—as long as it doesn't concern us personally." That's the way too many people think. Everyone is not self-centered on purpose; it's just in the nature of people to think of their own interests first. If you want to see an example of that, play with a two-year-old child. He naturally chooses the best toys for himself and insists on his own way.

One way to overcome our natural self-centeredness is to try to see things from other people's perspectives. Talking to a group of salespeople, Art Mortell shared this experience: "Whenever I'm losing at chess, I consistently get up and stand behind my opponent and see the board from his side. Then I start to discover the stupid moves I've made because I can see it from his viewpoint. The salesperson's challenge is to see the world from the prospect's viewpoint."[2]

That's the challenge for every one of us, no matter what our profession. There is a quote that John filed away years ago called "A Short Course in Human Relations." You may have already heard it because it's been around for a while. But it reminds us of what our priorities should be when dealing with other people:

The least important word: I
The most important word: We
The two most important words: Thank you.
The three most important words: All is forgiven.
The four most important words: What is your opinion?
The five most important words: You did a good job.
The six most important words: I want to understand you better.

Changing your attitude from self-centeredness to understanding requires desire and commitment to always try to see things from the other person's point of view.

Failure to Appreciate Differences

The next logical step after leaving behind self-centeredness is learning to recognize and respect everyone else's unique qualities. Instead of trying to cast others in your image, learn to appreciate their differences. If someone has a talent that you don't have, great. The two of you can strengthen each other's weaknesses. If others come from a different culture, broaden your horizons and learn what you can from them. Your new knowledge will help you relate not only to them, but also to others. And celebrate people's differences in temperament. Variety makes for interesting dynamics between people. For instance, John has a choleric-sanguine temperament, which means he loves to have fun and enjoys making decisions in the blink of an eye. On the other hand, Jim is a melancholy-phlegmatic. He is a great thinker and processor of information, and when he needs to make decisions, he gathers as much data as he can to make wise choices. Separate, we do well. But we're even more effective when the two of us are together.

Once you learn to appreciate other people's differences, you come to realize that there are many responses to leadership and motivation. Joseph Beck, the president of the Kenley Corporation, recognized that truth when he said that an influencer "must realize that different people are motivated in different ways. A good basketball coach, for example, knows when a player needs encouragement to excel and when a player needs a 'kick in the pants.' The main difference is that all players need encouragement and only some need a 'kick in the pants.'"

Failure to Acknowledge Similarities

As you learn more about people and get to know others well, you soon begin to realize that people have a lot in common. We all have hopes and fears, joys and sorrows, victories and problems. Probably the time when people are least likely to recognize their common ground with others is during adolescence. We came across a story that illustrates this:

> A teenage girl was talking to her father about all of her problems. She told him of the terrible peer pressure she faced, about conflicts with friends, and difficulties with schoolwork and teachers. In an attempt to help her put everything in perspective, he told her that life was not as dark as it might seem and, in fact, much of her worry was perhaps unnecessary.
>
> "That's easy for you to say, Dad," she replied. "You already have all your problems over with."

All people have an emotional reaction to what's happening around them. To foster understanding, think of what *your* emotions would be if you were in the same position as the person you're interacting with. You know what you would want to happen in a given situation. Chances are that the person you're working with has many of the same feelings.

We found a wonderful example of a person who understands this approach. A candy store sold its exotic chocolates only by the pound. In the store was one particular salesclerk who always had customers lined up waiting while other salesclerks stood around with nothing to do. The owner of the store noticed how the customers flocked to her and finally asked for her secret.

"It's easy," she said. "The other girls scoop up more than a pound of candy and then start taking away. I always scoop up less than a pound and then add to it. The customers feel that I'm looking out for them and getting them their money's worth."

Things Everybody Needs to Understand About People

Knowing what people need and want is the key to understanding them. And if you can understand them, you can influence them and impact their lives in a positive way. If we were to boil down all the things we know about understanding people and narrow them down to a short list, we would identify these five things:

1. Everybody Wants to Be Somebody

There isn't a person in the world who doesn't have the desire to be someone, to have significance. Even the least ambitious and unassuming person wants to be regarded highly by others.

John remembers the first time these feelings were stirred strongly within him. It was back when he was in the fourth grade:

> I went to my first basketball game when I was nine years old. I can still see it in my head. I stood with my buddies in the balcony of the gym. The thing that I remember most wasn't the game; it was the announcement of the starting lineups. They turned all the lights out, and then some spotlights came on. The announcer called out the names of the starters, and they ran out to the middle of the floor one by one with everybody in the place cheering.
>
> I hung over the balcony that day as a fourth-grade kid and said, "Wow, I'd like that to happen to me." In fact, by the time the introductions were over, I looked at my friend Bobby Wilson, and I said, "Bobby, when I get to high

school, they're going to announce my name, and I'm going to run out in the spotlight to the middle of that basketball floor. And the people are going to cheer for me because I'm going to become somebody."

I went home that night and told my dad, "I want to be a basketball player." Soon afterward, he got me a Spalding basketball, and we put a goal on the garage. I used to shovel snow off that driveway to practice my foul shots and play basketball, because I had a dream of becoming somebody.

It's funny how that kind of dream can impact your life. I remember in sixth grade we played intramural basketball, and our team won a couple of games, so we got to go to the Old Mill Street Gym in Circleville, Ohio, where I'd seen that basketball game in the fourth grade. When we got there, instead of going out onto the floor with the rest of the players as they were warming up, I went over to the bench where those high school players had been two years before. I sat right where they had, and I closed my eyes (the equivalent of turning the lights out in the gym). Then in my head I heard my name announced, and I ran out in the middle of the floor.

It felt so good to hear that imaginary applause that I thought, *I'll do it again!* So I did. In fact, I did it three times, and all of a sudden I realized that my buddies weren't playing basketball; they were just watching me in disbelief. But I didn't even care because I was one step closer to being the person I'd dreamed about becoming.

Everybody wants to be regarded and valued by others. In other words, everybody wants to be somebody. Once that piece of information becomes a part of your everyday thinking, you'll gain incredible insight into why people do the things they do. And if you treat every person you meet as if he or she were the most important person in the world, you'll communicate that he or she *is* somebody—to you.

2. Nobody Cares How Much You Know Until He Knows How Much You Care

To be an influencer, you have to love people before you try to lead them. The moment that people know that you care for and about them, the way they feel about you changes.

Showing others that you care isn't always easy. Your greatest times and fondest memories will come because of people, but so will your most difficult, hurting, and tragic times. People are your greatest assets and your greatest liabilities. The challenge is to keep caring about them no matter what.

We came across something called "Paradoxical Commandments of Leadership." Here's what it says:

People are illogical, unreasonable, and self-centered—love them anyway.

If you do good, people will accuse you of selfish ulterior motives—do good anyway.

If you're successful, you'll win false friends and true enemies—succeed anyway.

The good you do today will perhaps be forgotten tomorrow—do good anyway.

Honesty and frankness make you vulnerable—be honest and frank anyway.

The biggest man with the biggest ideas can be shot down by the smallest man with the smallest mind—think big anyway.

People favor underdogs but follow only hot dogs—fight for the few underdogs anyway.

What you spend years building may be destroyed overnight—build anyway.

People really need help but may attack you if you help them—help them anyway.

Give the world the best that you have and you will get kicked in the teeth—give the world the best that you have anyway.[3]

If better is possible, then good is not enough.

If you want to help others and become a person of influence, keep smiling, sharing, giving, and turning the other cheek. That's the right way to treat people. Besides, you never know which people in your sphere of influence are going to rise up and make a difference in your life and the lives of others.

3. Everybody Needs Somebody

Contrary to popular belief, there are no such things as self-made men and women. Everybody needs friendship, encouragement, and help. What people can accomplish by themselves is almost nothing compared to their potential when working with others. And doing things with other people tends to bring contentment. Besides, Lone Rangers are rarely happy people. King Solomon of ancient Israel stated the value of working together this way:

> **Two are better than one,**
>   **because they have a good return for their work:**
> **If one falls down,**
>   **his friend can help him up.**
> **But pity the man who falls**
>   **and has no one to help him up!**
> **Also, if two lie down together, they will keep warm.**
>   **But how can one keep warm alone?**
> **Though one may be overpowered,**
>   **two can defend themselves.**
> **A cord of three strands is not quickly broken.**[4]

People who try to do everything alone often get themselves into trouble. One of the wildest stories we've ever seen on this subject came from the insurance claim form of a bricklayer who got hurt at a building site. He was trying to get a load of bricks down from the top floor of a building without asking for help from anyone else. He wrote:

It would have taken too long to carry all the bricks down by hand, so I decided to put them in a barrel and lower them by a pulley which I had fastened to the top of the building. After tying the rope securely at ground level, I then went up to the top of the building, I fastened the rope around the barrel, loaded it with bricks, and swung it over the sidewalk for the descent. Then I went down to the sidewalk and untied the rope, holding it securely to guide the barrel down slowly. But since I weigh only 140 pounds, the 500 pound load jerked me from the ground so fast that I didn't have time to think of letting go of the rope. As I passed between the second and third floors I met the barrel coming down. This accounts for the bruises and the lacerations on my upper body.

I held tightly to the rope until I reached the top where my hand became jammed in the pulley. This accounts for my broken thumb.

At the same time, however, the barrel hit the sidewalk with a bang and the bottom fell out. With the weight of the bricks gone, the barrel weighed only about 40 pounds. Thus my 140 pound body began a swift descent, and I met the empty barrel coming up. This accounts for my broken ankle.

Slowed only slightly, I continued the descent and landed on the pile of bricks. This accounts for my sprained back and broken collar bone.

At this point I lost my presence of mind completely, and I let go of the rope and the empty barrel came crashing down on me. This accounts for my head injuries.

And as for the last question on your insurance form, "What would I do if the same situation rose again?" Please be advised I am finished trying to do the job all by myself.

Everybody needs somebody to come alongside and help. If you understand that, are willing to give to others and help them, and maintain the right motives, their lives and yours can change.

4. Everybody Can Be Somebody When Somebody Understands and Believes in Her

Once you understand people and believe in them, they really can become somebody. And it doesn't take much effort to help other people feel important. Little things, done deliberately at the right time, can make a big difference, as this story from John shows:

> For fourteen years I was privileged to pastor a very large congregation in the San Diego area where we did a wonderful Christmas program every year. We used to do twenty-eight performances, and altogether about thirty thousand people saw it each year.
>
> The show always included a bunch of kids, and one of my favorite parts of the show several years ago was a song in which three hundred kids dressed like angels sang while holding candles. Toward the end of the song, they walked off the stage, came up the aisles, and exited out of the lobby in the front of the church.
>
> During the first performance, I decided to wait for them back in the lobby. They didn't know I was going to be there, but as they went by I clapped, praised them, and said, "Kids, you did a great job!" They were surprised to see me, and they were glad for the encouragement.
>
> For the second performance, I did the same thing again. And I could see as they started to walk up the aisles, they were looking back expectantly to see if I was standing there to cheer them on. By the third performance of the night, as they turned the corner to come up the aisle, they had smiles on their faces. And when they got to the lobby, they were giving me high fives and having a great time. They knew I believed in them, and it made all of them feel that they were somebody.

When was the last time you went out of your way to make people feel special, as if they were somebody? The investment required on your part is totally overshadowed by the impact it makes on them. Everyone you know and all the people you meet have the potential to be someone important in the lives of others. All they need is encouragement and motivation from you to help them reach their potential.

5. Anybody Who Helps Somebody Influences a Lot of Bodies

The final thing you need to understand about people is that when you help one person, you're really impacting a lot of other people. What you give to one person overflows into the lives of all the people that person impacts. The nature of influence is to multiply. It even impacts you because when you help others and your motives are good, you always receive more than you can ever give. Most people are so genuinely grateful when another person makes them feel that they're somebody special that they never tire of showing their gratitude.

CHOOSE TO UNDERSTAND OTHERS

In the end, the ability to understand people is a choice. It's true that some people are born with great instincts that enable them to understand how others think and feel. But even if you aren't an instinctive people person, you can improve your ability to work with others. Every person is capable of having the ability to understand, motivate, and ultimately influence others.

If you truly want to make a difference in the lives of others, then make up your mind to possess . . .

The Other Person's Perspective

Mark McCormack, author of *What They Don't Teach You at Harvard Business School,* wrote about an amusing story for *Entrepreneur* magazine. It illustrates the value of recognizing other people's perspectives. He said, "A few years ago I was standing in an airport ticket line. In front of me were two children fighting over an ice cream cone. In front of them was a woman in a mink coat. I could see this was an accident waiting to happen. Should I interfere? I was still pondering this when I heard the girl tell the boy, 'If you don't stop, Charlie, you'll get hairs from that lady's coat on your cone.'"

Most people don't look beyond their own experience when dealing with others. They tend to see other people and events in the context of their own position, background, or circumstances. For example, Pat McInally of the NFL's Cincinnati Bengals said, "At Harvard they labeled me a jock. In the pros they consider me an intellectual." Though he had not changed, other people's perceptions of him had.

Whenever you look at things from the other person's perspective, you'll receive a whole new way of looking at life. And you'll find new ways of helping others. A story from the book *Zadig* by Voltaire shows the value of looking at people and situations in a new way.

A country's ruler was upset because his favorite horse was missing. The king sent couriers throughout the land to look for it, but to no avail. In desperation, the king offered a great reward. Many came hoping to win it and searched for the horse, but they all failed. The horse had disappeared.

A simpleton at the king's court sought an audience with the monarch, and told him that he could find the horse.

"You!" exclaimed the king. "You can find my horse when all others have failed?"

"Yes, sire," answered the simpleton.

"Then do it," said the king, who had nothing to lose.

Within hours the horse was back at the palace, and the king was astounded. He immediately had his treasurer issue a handsome reward to the man, and asked him to explain how he had found it when many men considered wise had not.

"It was easy, sire," said the simpleton. "I merely asked myself, 'If I was a horse, where would I go?' And putting myself in his place, I soon found him."

Personal Empathy

Another quality that you need if you want to understand and help others is personal empathy. Not everyone is naturally empathetic, as is evident in this story about a Kansas preacher. It seems that the preacher was returning home after a visit to New England, and one of his parishioners met him at the train station.

"Well," asked the preacher, "how are things at home?"

"Sad, real sad, Pastor," answered the man. "A cyclone came and wiped out my house."

"Well, I'm not surprised," said the unsympathetic parson with a frown. "You remember I've been warning you about the way you've been living. Punishment for sin is inevitable."

"It also destroyed your house, Pastor," added the layman.

"It did?" the pastor said, momentarily surprised. "Ah, me, the ways of the Lord are past human understanding."

Don't wait for your house to be blown down to have feelings about people's troubles and shortcomings. Reach out to others with a strong hand but a soft heart, and they'll respond to you positively.

A Positive Attitude About People

Author Harper Lee wrote, "People generally see what they look for and hear what they listen for." If you have a positive attitude about people, believe the best of them, and act on your beliefs, then you can have an impact on their lives. But it all starts with the way you think of others. You can't be a positive influencer if your thinking is like this:

When the other fellow takes a long time, he's slow.
　When I take a long time, I'm thorough.
When the other fellow doesn't do it, he's lazy.
　When I don't do it, I'm busy.
When the other fellow does something without being told, he's overstepping his bounds.
　When I do it, that's initiative.
When the other fellow overlooks a rule of etiquette, he's rude.
　When I skip a few rules, I'm original.
When the other fellow pleases the boss, he's an apple polisher.
　When I please the boss, it's cooperation.
When the other fellow gets ahead, he's getting the breaks.
　When I manage to get ahead, that's just the reward for hard work.

Your attitude toward people is one of the most important choices you'll ever make. If your thinking is positive, you can really make an impact on them. Pastor Robert Schuller, a strong proponent of positive thinking, tells the following story in *Life Changers:*

"I'm the greatest baseball player in the world," the little boy boasted as he strutted around his backyard. Shouldering his bat, he tossed a baseball up, swung, and missed. "I am the greatest ball player ever," he reiterated. He picked up the ball again, swung, and missed again. Stopping a moment to examine his bat, he stooped and picked up his ball. "I am the greatest baseball player who ever lived!" The momentum of his swing nearly knocked him down. But the ball plopped, unscathed, at his feet. "Wow!" he exclaimed. "What a pitcher!"[5]

If you want to become a person of influence, have an attitude toward others similar to the attitude that little boy had about himself.

> *If you treat every person you meet as if he or she were the most important person in the world, you'll communicate that he or she* **is somebody—** *to you.*

Jim was reminded of the importance of understanding people and seeing things from their perspective when visiting his aging parents in New York recently:

> My parents are in their upper eighties, and they worked hard all their lives. My dad was the city editor of the Niagara Falls *Gazette,* and my mother was the night supervising nurse at Niagara Falls Memorial Hospital. She worked many years from 11 P.M. to 7 A.M. when I was young so that she could be home to get me up for school, make breakfast, and pack my lunch. And then she was there when I got home from school each afternoon. I hardly realized she

worked. Growing up we always lived in a very small house. After they retired, they sold it and moved to a small apartment to live on their modest pensions.

Like most people who have been blessed financially, Nancy and I are always looking for ways to help our parents and repay them in some small way for the positive things they have done for us over the years. Recently, we thought we could help them by leasing them a penthouse unit in the most prestigious apartment building in the city. It was incredible and even had a view of Niagara Falls.

But after about six months, my parents asked if they could move out. My mother's eyesight was now so poor that she couldn't see the Falls. Dad, on the other hand, could see the Falls fine but was made extremely uncomfortable by being up so high. We were disappointed that they didn't like it, but we readily agreed to move them back into their small apartment.

My desire to help them was still strong, so one day after we got them squared away in their place, I took Mom to the store. Though she claimed she didn't need anything, I did manage to talk her into letting me get her a few items: a new trash can, some flatware, a small radio, and a new toaster—the old one had *shot* the toast out like a cannon when it was done. And it made me feel good when I overheard her showing the toaster to a neighbor and saying, "My *son* bought this for us!"

Nancy and I had wanted to get them big things, but that's not what was important to them. They were happy with a toaster. Oh, yes, there was one other item they finally admitted that they could use: a small tree for the front of their apartment. They thought it would be nice to have some shade in the summer when they sat outside. "But they're so expensive," my mother said. "Just get us a sapling."

We wanted them to have shade *today,* not fifteen years from now. So we went out and got them the biggest tree we could find. It didn't take a lot of money to make them happy, just a little understanding.

Not everyone learns that lesson. Lots of people try to push their own agenda—and then they wonder why they have no pull with others. To make an impact on others, find out what people want and then help them get it. That's what motivates them. And that's what makes it possible for you to become a person of influence in their lives.

Influence Checklist
UNDERSTANDING PEOPLE

❏ **Rate your understanding.** Use the following scale to rate your ability to understand people (circle the rating that applies to you):

Superior | I can nearly always anticipate how people will feel and react in any given situation. Understanding is one of my strongest abilities.

Good | Most of the time what people do and want makes sense to me. I consider my ability to understand people an asset.

Fair | I'm surprised by people just as often as I'm able to anticipate their thinking. I consider my ability to understand others to be average.

Poor | Most of the time people's feelings and motivations are mysteries to me. I definitely need to do better in this area.

❏ **Understanding action plan.** If you rated yourself superior, then you should be sharing your skill by teaching others how to better understand people. If you rated yourself good, fair, or poor, keep striving to learn and improve. You can improve your ability immediately by asking yourself these four questions each time you meet new people:

1. Where did they come from?
2. Where do they want to go?
3. What is their need now?
4. How can I help?

❏ **Activate your positive attitude.** If your ability to understand people isn't as good as you'd like it to be, the root cause may be that you don't value others as highly as you could. As you interact with people remember the words of Ken Keyes, Jr.: "A loving person lives in a loving world. A hostile person lives in a hostile world: Everyone you meet is your mirror."

A Person of Influence . . .

ENLARGES
PEOPLE

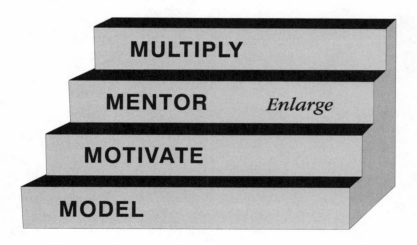

Once you have been a model of integrity with others and successfully motivated them, you're ready to take the next step in the process of becoming a person of influence in their lives. Jim has a story that will give you an idea of what that next step looks like:

Over the years, Eric has been through more than thirty individual brain operations, but that has never stopped him from being mentally sharp and full of optimism. And his great sense of humor keeps all of us entertained.

During one of his many surgeries, Eric experienced an interoperative stroke. The resulting loss of muscle balance has limited the use of his right hand and given him severe curvature of the spine. After a couple of years, that required another surgery in which the doctors performed spinal fusion and implanted steel rods from the base of his neck to his pelvis. He spent three months in a full body cast during his long recovery, and as a result, many of his previous abilities were reduced dramatically. But Eric came through it all with characteristically positive spirits.

After Eric's spinal surgery, Nancy could no longer handle him alone, so we decided it was time to employ a full-time home attendant to lift him, help with his daily life, and assist him with his ongoing rehabilitation. We knew the type of person we wanted to hire, but we had no idea where or how to locate him.

One day while Nancy was talking to one of our medical contacts, she heard about a person named Fernando. He sounded great. "He's the perfect person," our friend had said, "but you'll never get him."

Nancy's response was, "Just give us his number, and let us worry about whether or not we can get him."

A few weeks later we hired him, and he has been wonderful. Fernando had been a life skills trainer for Sharp Hospital, and though he was only five years older than Eric, he had already been a manager of a group home for abused kids and had worked in the field of rehab for seven years. He and Eric bonded immediately. Fernando provided a perfect combination of professional skills and companionship.

It's difficult to describe what a wonderful gift God has provided to Eric and our family in the person of Fernando. He sees his mission as that of enlarging Eric, to keep him growing toward his full potential. Fernando constantly learns new information and techniques in his field, and he seeks ways to expose Eric to new experiences and to challenge him to grow. As a result, Eric's life hasn't been the same. In the time that the two of them have been doing things together, Eric has done a lot more than go skiing every year. He has learned to jet ski—I never could have visualized Eric going forty miles per hour on the water, but Fernando believed Eric could do it, and so he did it. Eric also volunteers as a tutor with second graders, studies German, works in our office two days a week, swims a couple of days a week, and has begun to work out with weights. It's hard for us to remember that Eric is severely limited physically, because his life is full, challenging, and expanding every day.

One of Eric's greatest experiences since teaming with Fernando has been his involvement in power soccer. It's a new sport played by people using power wheelchairs. They meet in gymnasiums where they compete as teams and score goals using a large ball. Eric loves it and usually prefers to play goalie.

Not long ago Fernando took Eric to Vancouver, Canada, to compete in a power soccer tournament. It was quite an experience for Eric. They flew together, rented a car, got their hotel room, and got around town—just the two of them. Eric loved it, especially competing in the five-day tournament where he scored two goals. And best of all, his team won the gold medal!

We had never seen Eric so excited as he was when he returned from the tournament. He wore his gold medal home on the plane, and I don't think he touched the ground for days. Since then, his confidence has been so strong that he's willing to tackle just about any kind of challenge. And for that, Fernando deserves a lot of the credit.

> **Without his belief in Eric and his desire to expand his world, none of this would ever have happened.**

To become a person of influence and to make a positive impact on people, you have to come alongside them and really get involved in their lives. That's what Fernando did and continues to do with Jim's son Eric. And that's what you need to do with the people for whom you want to make a difference. Modeling a life of integrity is an important first step in becoming an influencer because it creates a strong foundation with others. And the next natural step is motivating people. As you nurture people, show your faith in them, listen to their hopes and fears, and demonstrate your understanding of them, you build a strong relational connection and give them incentive to succeed—and to be influenced by you. But if you want people to be able to *really* grow, improve, and succeed, you have to take the next step with them. You have to become a mentor to them.

THE MEANING OF MENTORING

Giving people the *motivation* to grow without also providing them the *means* of doing it is a tragedy. But the mentoring process offers people the opportunity to turn their potential into reality, their dreams into destiny. Mentors impact eternity because there is no telling where their influence will stop.

Nineteenth-century British statesman William Gladstone asserted, "He is a wise man who wastes no energy on pursuits for which he is not fitted; and he is wiser still who from among the things he can do well, chooses and resolutely follows the best." Most people don't have a natural knack for spotting their greatest areas of potential. They need help doing it, especially as they begin growing and striving to reach their potential. And that's why it's important for you to become a mentor in the lives of the people you desire to help. You need to lead them in their areas of personal and professional growth until they are able to work in these areas more independently.

The authors of *The Leadership Challenge,* James M. Kouzes and Barry Z. Posner, offer insights on leadership that pertain to the subject of mentoring: "Leaders are pioneers. They are people who venture into unexplored territory. They guide us to new and often unfamiliar destinations. . . . The unique reason for having leaders—their differentiating function—is to move us forward. Leaders get us going someplace."

Mentors impact eternity because there is no telling where their influence will stop.

Leading mentors move the people they are developing into growth and areas of strength. In this chapter and in the next three, we'll focus on four ways of accomplishing the task of mentoring others: enlarging people, helping them navigate through life's problems, connecting with them on a deeper level, and empowering them to reach their potential.

ENLARGING OTHERS IS AN INVESTMENT

Author Alan Loy McGinnis observed, "There is no more noble occupation in the world than to assist another human being—to help someone succeed." Helping others enlarge themselves is one of the most incredible things you can ever do for them. As John says in his book *The Success Journey,* growing to reach your potential is one of the three components to being successful (along with knowing your purpose and sowing seeds that benefit others).

Robert Gross, former president of Lockheed Aircraft Corporation, once explained to his supervisors, "It's one thing to build a product; it's another thing to build a company, because companies are nothing but men, and the things that come out of them are no better than the people themselves. We do not build automobiles, airplanes, refrigerators, radios, or shoestrings. We build men. *The men build the product.*"

When you enlarge others, you do several things:

Raise Their Level of Living

Denis Waitley said, "The greatest achievements are those that benefit others." Anytime you help people to enlarge themselves in any area of their lives, you benefit them because you make it possible for them to step up to a new level of living. As people develop their gifts and talents, learn new skills, and broaden their problem-solving abilities, their quality of living and level of contentment improve dramatically. No one can grow and remain unaffected in the way he lives his life.

When you enlarge others, you seize an opportunity to help them reach their potential.

Increase Their Potential for Success

Businessman George Crane claimed that "there is no future in any job. The future lies in the man who holds the job." When you enlarge other people, you brighten their future. When they expand their horizons, improve their attitudes, increase their skills, or learn new ways to think, they perform and live better. And that increases their potential.

Increase Their Capacity for Growth

When you help people enlarge themselves, you aren't giving them only a temporary, short-term shot in the arm or tools that will help them only today. Enlarging has long-term benefits. It helps them become better equipped, and it increases their capacity to learn and grow. After being enlarged, whenever they receive a resource or opportunity, they are better able to use it to its greatest benefit. And their growth begins to multiply.

Increase the Potential of Your Organization

If the people you are working to enlarge are a part of a group—no matter whether it is a business, church, sports team, or club—then the whole group benefits from their growth. For example, if many people in your organization improve themselves even slightly, the quality of your whole organization increases. If a few people improve themselves a lot, the potential for growth and success increases due to the increased leadership of these people. And if both kinds of growth occur as the result of your enlarging, hang on because your organization is about to take off!

Fred Smith, a friend of John, is an excellent leader, entrepreneur, and business consultant. Fred had been advising a group of twenty young CEOs and meeting with them monthly for about three years when he decided that they needed to spend some time on their own. So he told them he would not be coming back to see them for a while. They continued to get together without him, but eventually, they asked him to come back for a visit. When he did, they presented him with a piece of Baccarat crystal. On it were etched the words *He stretched us.*

Fred has been stretching and enlarging others for decades because he realizes the incredible value added not only to the people being stretched, but also to all the people they influence. Most people are funny; they want to get ahead and succeed, but they are reluctant to change. They are often willing to grow only enough to accommodate their *problems;* instead, they need to grow enough to achieve their *potential.* That's why they need help from you. Authors Helen Schucman and William Thetford aptly said, "Every situation, properly perceived, becomes an opportunity." When you enlarge others, you seize an opportunity to help them reach their potential.

French essayist Michel Eyquem de Montaigne wrote, "The value of life lies not in the length of days, but in the use we make of them; a man may live long yet live very little." When you enlarge others, you help them make the most of the time they have and raise their quality of life.

MAKE YOURSELF AN ENLARGER

For many people, just because they want to enlarge others doesn't necessarily mean they are ready for the task. They usually need to do some work on themselves first. As in most instances, if you want to do more for others, you have to become more yourself. That's never more valid than in the area of mentoring. You can teach what you know, but you can reproduce only what you are.

Leadership experts Warren Bennis and Bert Nanus spoke to this issue: "It is the capacity to develop and improve their skills that distinguishes leaders from their followers." In your preparations to take on the task of helping others enlarge themselves, the first thing you need to do is improve and enlarge yourself because only when you are growing and enlarging yourself are you able to help others do the same. Just as people will not follow a person whose leadership skills are weaker than their own, they will not learn to grow from someone who isn't growing. Not only must you be on a higher level in your personal growth, but you must continue to grow on an ongoing basis. (You can probably remember how little you respected one of your high school teachers or college professors who had obviously stopped learning and growing decades earlier—possibly the day he received his degree!)

Albert Schweitzer maintained that "the great secret of success is to go through life as a man who never gets used up." When you make it a goal to continually learn and enlarge yourself, you become the kind of person who can never be "used up." You're always recharging your batteries and finding better ways to get things done. To determine whether you are still growing, ask yourself what you're still looking forward to. If you can't think of anything or you're looking back instead of ahead, your growth may be at a standstill.

It has been said, "The greatest obstacle to discovery is not ignorance. It is the illusion of knowledge." Many people lose sight of the importance of personal growth once they finish their formal education. But don't let that happen to you. Make your growth one of your top priorities starting today. There is no time to waste. As Scottish writer and thinker Thomas Carlyle put it, "One life; a little gleam of time between two eternities; no second chance for us forever more." Any day that passes without personal growth is an opportunity lost to improve yourself and to enlarge others.

CAREFULLY CHOOSE
PERSONS TO ENLARGE

Once you've done some growing and you're ready to help others enlarge themselves, you need to start thinking about the people you will choose to work with. You have to be selective. You should try to be a model of integrity to all people, whether they're close to you or total strangers. And you should make it your goal to motivate all of the people you have a relationship with—family members, employees, fellow church volunteers, colleagues, and friends. But you can't take the time to enlarge everybody in your life; it's too involved a process. That's why you need to work first with the most promising people around you, the ones most likely to be receptive to growth.

In *Killers of the Dream,* Lillian Smith wrote, "We in America—and men across the earth—have trapped ourselves with that word equality, which is inapplicable to the *genus* man. I wish we would forget it. Stop its use in our country: Let the communists have it. It isn't fit for men who fling their dreams across the skies. It is fit only for a leveling down of mankind." We certainly desire for all people to have equal access to opportunities and justice, but we know that everyone doesn't respond equally to his environment or advantages. And that's true for the people you will have the opportunity to develop. Some people are eager to be enlarged. Others don't care about personal growth or won't grow under your care. It's your job to figure out which is which.

As you think about the people you want to enlarge, keep the following guidelines in mind:

- **Select people whose philosophy of life is similar to yours.** The underlying values and priorities of the people you desire to enlarge need to be similar to yours. If you and they don't have the basics in common, you may end up working at cross-purposes, and you won't experience the effectiveness you would like. Roy Disney, Walt's brother and partner, said, "It's not hard to make decisions when you know what your values are." And if you and the people you mentor have similar values, you will be able to make harmonious decisions as you work together.

- **Choose people with potential you genuinely believe in.** You can't help people you don't believe in. Give your best mentoring effort to people who have the greatest potential—the ones for whom you can see a promising future—not the ones for whom you feel sorry. Nurture, love, and motivate hurting people. But pour yourself into the people who will grow and make a difference.

- **Select people whose lives you can positively impact.** Not everyone you are capable of developing would benefit from what you have to offer. Look for a fit between their potential and your strengths and experience.

- **Match the men and women to the mountains.** We would like all the people we mentor to reach their full potential and develop into stars. After all, the greatest mentors develop people to a level beyond their ability. But the truth is that while all people can move to a higher level than they currently occupy, not everyone is capable of climbing to the highest levels. A successful enlarger evaluates the potential of others and places them in a position to succeed.

- **Start when the time is right.** Start the process at the right time in the lives of others. You've probably heard the expression "strike while the iron is hot." It means to act on a situation at the right time. We've heard that the saying goes back to the fourteenth century. It comes from the practice of blacksmiths who needed to strike metal when it was exactly the right temperature in order to mold it into the precise shape desired. You have to do the same thing with the people you want to enlarge. Start too soon, and they don't yet see the need to grow. Start too late, and you've missed your best opportunity to help them.

Once you've found the right people, keep in mind that you need to get their permission before you start enlarging them. People love to be encouraged and motivated, so you don't need their consent to do either one. But the mentoring process really works only when both parties know the agenda, agree to it, and give it 100 percent effort.

MAKE IT A PRIORITY TO TAKE THEM THROUGH THE ENLARGING PROCESS

Enlarging others can be rewarding and fun, but it also takes time, money, and work. That's why you have to commit yourself to the process and make it a top priority. John's friend Ed Cole says, "There is a price to pay to grow. Commitment is the price." Once you've made the commitment, you're ready to go. The following suggestions will help you maximize the enlarging process:

See Their Potential

Composer Gian Carlo Menotti forcefully stated, "Hell begins on that day when God grants us a clear vision of all that we might have achieved, of all the gifts we wasted, of all that we might have done that we did not do."[1] Unrealized potential is a tragic waste. And as an enlarger, you have the privilege of helping others discover and then develop their potential. But you can't do that until you *see* their potential.

Olympic gold medal swimmer Geoffrey Gaberino sums it up this way: "The real contest is always between what you've done and what you're capable of doing." Whenever you look at people you desire to enlarge, try to discern what they are capable of doing. Look for the spark of greatness. Watch and listen with your heart as well as your eyes. Find their enthusiasm. Try to visualize what they would be doing if they overcame personal obstacles, gained confidence, grew in areas of promise, and gave everything they had. That will help you to see their potential.

Cast a Vision for Their Future

Former presidential speechwriter Robert Orben urged, "Always remember there are only two kinds of people in this world—the realists and the dreamers. The realists know where they're going. The dreamers have already been there." To add value to the people you enlarge, travel ahead of them in your mind's eye and see their future before they do. You become able to cast a vision for their future that helps to motivate and enlarge them.

Someone once said, "Don't let yourself be pressured into thinking that your dreams or your talents aren't prudent. They were never meant to be prudent. They were meant to bring joy and fulfillment into your life." That's great advice. People will never succeed beyond their wildest dreams unless they have some pretty wild dreams. When you cast a vision for others, you help them see their potential and their possibilities. And when you add to that vision your faith in them, you spark them to action. The great British statesman Benjamin Disraeli declared, "Nurture great thoughts for you will never go higher than your thoughts." Help people have great thoughts about themselves, and they will begin to live like the people they can become.

Tap into Their Passion

As an enlarger of people, you are to help people want to grow, and one way to do that is to tap into their passion. Everybody— even the quietest, least demonstrative person—has a passion for something. You just have to find it. As scientist Willis R. Whitney pointed out, "Some men have thousands of reasons why they cannot do what they want to, when all they need is one reason why they can."

As you look for others' passions, go beyond the surface of their daily wants. Look deep within them. Harold Kushner perceptively wrote, "Our souls are not hungry for fame, comfort, wealth, or power. Those rewards create almost as many problems as they solve. Our souls are hungry for meaning, for the sense that we have figured out how to live so that our lives matter, so that the world will at least be a little bit different for our having passed through it."

Once you discover their passion, tap into it. Show them how it can activate their potential to the point that they will be able to realize their vision for their lives. Passion can help them make their dreams come true. And as U.S. President Woodrow Wilson said, "We grow by dreams. All big [individuals] are dreamers. They see things in the soft haze of a spring day, or in the red fire on a long winter's evening. Some of us let those great dreams die, but others nourish and protect them; nourish them through bad days until they bring them to the sunshine and light which comes always to those who sincerely hope that their dreams will come true." Passion is the fuel that helps people nourish and protect their dreams.

Address Character Flaws

As you explore how you can help others enlarge themselves, you need to address any character issues they may have. As we mentioned in Chapter 1, integrity is the foundation upon which everything else must stand in people's lives. No matter how much enlarging you do, if the foundation isn't solid, there's going to be trouble.

When examining the character of others, remember to look beyond their reputation. Abraham Lincoln made this distinction: "Character is like a tree and reputation like its shadow. The shadow is what we think of it; the tree is the real thing." Take time to really get to know the people you're enlarging. Observe them in various situations. If you get to know people well enough to know how they react in most situations, you'll have an idea of where any character shortcomings might be.

Martin Luther King, Jr., said, "The ultimate measure of a man is not where he stands in moments of comfort and convenience, but where he stands at times of challenge and controversy." Your goal should be to help the people you're developing to stand strong in the midst of challenges. But you have to start with the little things. Author and corporate leader Joseph Sugarman observed, "Every time you are honest and conduct yourself with honesty, a success force will drive you toward greater success. Each time you lie, even with a little white lie, there are strong forces pushing you toward failure." Help others learn to conduct themselves with integrity in every situation, and they will be ready to grow and reach their potential.

Focus on Their Strengths

When some people begin to work with others on their development, they often gravitate to weaknesses rather than strengths. Maybe that's because it's so easy to see others' problems and shortcomings. But if you start by putting your energies into correcting people's weaknesses, you will demoralize them and unintentionally sabotage the enlarging process.

We recently heard a baseball story that addresses the subject of people's weaknesses. One afternoon in St. Louis, Stan Musial was having a great game against Chicago pitcher Bobo Newsom. Stan first hit a single, then a triple, and then a home run. When Stan came up to bat for the fourth time, Chicago manager Charlie Grimm decided to yank Bobo and take a chance on a rookie relief pitcher. As the young rookie went to the mound from the bull pen and received the ball from Newsom, he asked, "Say, has this guy Musial got any weaknesses?"

"Yeah," replied Newsom, "he can't hit doubles."

Instead of focusing on weaknesses, pay attention to people's strengths. Sharpen skills that already exist. Compliment positive qualities. Bring out the gifts inherent in them. Weaknesses can wait—unless they are character flaws. Only after you have developed a strong rapport with them and they have begun to grow and gain confidence should you address areas of weakness. And then handle them gently one at a time.

Enlarge Them One Step at a Time

Ronald Osborn noted, "Unless you try to do something beyond what you have already mastered, you will never grow." To enlarge others, help them take growth steps that stretch them regularly without overwhelming or discouraging them.

For each person, that process will look different. But no matter where people are from or where they are going, they need to grow in certain areas. We suggest that you include the following four areas in the development process:

1. *Attitude.* More than anything else, attitude determines whether people are successful and able to enjoy life. And attitude impacts not only every area of their own lives, but it also influences others.

2. *Relationships.* The world is made up of people, so everybody has to learn to interact effectively with others. The ability to relate to others and communicate with them can affect marriage, parenting, occupation, friendships, and more. If people can get along, they can get ahead in just about any area of life.

3. *Leadership.* Everything rises and falls on leadership. If the people you're developing plan to work with others, they have to learn to lead them. If they don't, they'll be carrying the whole load themselves in everything they do.

4. *Personal and professional skills.* You may be surprised to see that we're listing this last. But the truth is that if thinking isn't positive and skills at working with people are missing, all the professional skills in the world are of little benefit. As you help people grow, work from the inside out. It's not what happens *to* people that makes a difference; it's what happens *in* them.

Put Resources in Their Hands

To help people grow, no matter what area you're addressing, put resources in their hands. Whenever either one of us meets with someone we're developing, we always try to take something with us to give to them—books, tapes, magazine articles, anything uplifting or instructive that we can get our hands on. Nothing gives us greater joy than to know that we've helped someone take another step in growth. That's one reason both of us are constantly creating resources for people's growth. If you can't find exactly what you're looking for to help people, you may want to give from your experience.

The next time you're ready to meet with people whom you want to enlarge, take an active hand in the process. Clip articles written on one of their areas of interest. Give them copies of a book that impacted your life. Or put into their hands tapes that will teach and inspire them. If you keep doing that, not only will the people you develop love the time they spend with you, but each time you meet you'll see that they've grown just a little more toward their potential.

Expose Them to Enlarging Experiences

Implementing a plan for growth enlarges people. But sometimes they need something more to give them a fresh burst of energy and inspiration. Author and champion for the blind Helen Keller said, "One can never consent to creep when one feels an impulse to soar." When you expose people to enlarging experiences, you plant within them that desire to soar.

Conferences and seminars, meetings with outstanding men and women, and special events have made a tremendous impact on us. They always take us out of our comfort zone, move us to think beyond ourselves, or challenge us to go to new levels of living. But remember that events and meetings don't make people grow. They *inspire* people to make important decisions that can change the direction of their lives. The growth itself comes from what people do daily after they have made a decision.

Teach Them to Be Self-Enlargers

According to Philip B. Crosby, "There is a theory of human behavior that says people subconsciously retard their own intellectual growth. They come to rely on clichés and habits. Once they reach the age of their own personal comfort with the world, they stop learning and their mind runs on idle for the rest of their days. They may progress organizationally, they may be ambitious and eager, and they may even work night and day. But they learn no more."

Once you've gotten people to value growth enough to start enlarging themselves, you've broken through a strong barrier. But the next step is to get them to keep growing on their own. It has been said that the goal of all teachers should be to equip students to get along without them. The same can be said of people who seek to enlarge others. As you work with others and help them to enlarge themselves, give them what they need so that they learn to take care of themselves. Teach them to find resources. Encourage them to get out of their comfort zone on their own. And point them toward additional people who can help them learn and grow. If you can help them to become lifelong learners, you will have given them an incredible gift.

> # *A successful enlarger evaluates the potential of others and places them in a position to succeed.*

We've heard it said, "No one becomes rich unless he enriches another." When you enrich others by helping them grow and enlarge themselves, you not only bring joy to them and yourself, but you also increase your influence and their ability to touch others' lives.

At the beginning of this chapter we told you about how Fernando has enriched the life of Jim and Nancy's son Eric. But there is more to the story:

> **Since Eric played in that power soccer tournament, he has really changed. He has become more assertive, and he is pursuing his goals with more enthusiasm. For example, Eric has now decided that he wants to try to play tennis, so Fernando has started working with him to get him ready. As I mentioned earlier, Eric has begun weight training. But he has also taken another step to help make tennis possible, a step that at first scared Nancy and me.**
> **Since his stroke, Eric's right hand is extremely limited in what it can do, so he really has full use of only his left hand.**

But to play tennis, he would have to use his good left hand to hold the racket. What was Fernando's solution? He waited until Nancy and I were out of town and switched Eric's wheelchair controls over to his bad hand. We didn't think it was possible, but it was. Eric now drives right-handed, and as soon as he is ready, he is going to take up tennis.

Eric also does other things that simply astound us. For example, he works in the office, and he puts himself into bed at night. But that's nothing compared to some of his goals: someday Eric wants to be able to drive a car.

Fernando's mentoring and coaching of Eric have been fantastic. We always wanted the best for Eric, but we discovered that we were overly protective. The whole process has enlarged us and broadened our horizons. And of course, it's incredible to see Eric grow and change as he has. But he, Nancy, and I are not alone in that. Even the enlarger has become enlarged. Fernando is changing and growing too. He has always been the consummate professional, but we're now seeing a softer, more loving side that was previously hidden. And recently he told Nancy, "I'm learning that I have to really give to have joy in my life."

What nineteenth-century American philosopher-poet Ralph Waldo Emerson said is true: "It is one of the most beautiful compensations of this life that no man can sincerely try to help another without helping himself." If you give yourself to enlarging others and assisting them in reaching their potential, the rewards you reap will be almost as great as the ones of the people you help.

Influence Checklist
ENLARGING PEOPLE

❑ **Whom will you enlarge?** Write down the names of the top three candidates for you to enlarge. Remember to pick people whose philosophy of life is similar to yours, whose potential you believe in, whose lives you can positively impact, and who are ready for the process.

1. _____
2. _____
3. _____

❑ **Enlargement agenda.** Use the following grid to develop your strategy for enlarging the three persons you selected:

	Person 1	Person 2	Person 3
Name	_____	_____	_____
Potential	_____	_____	_____
Passion	_____	_____	_____
Character Issue(s)	_____	_____	_____
Greatest Strength	_____	_____	_____
Next Step in Development	_____	_____	_____
Resource for Current Need	_____	_____	_____
Next Enlarging Experience	_____	_____	_____

A Person of Influence . . .

NAVIGATES FOR OTHER PEOPLE

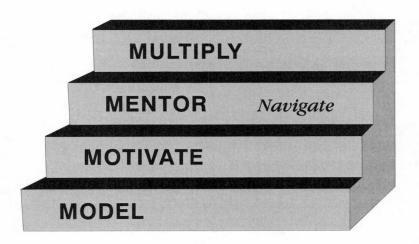

Helping people enlarge themselves and develop their potential makes it possible for them to go to a whole new level of living. But no matter how much they grow and learn, they will still face obstacles. They will make mistakes. They will run into problems in their personal and professional lives. And they will encounter circumstances that they won't be able to get through well without some help.

John tells a story about a time when he decided to help a whole planeload of people get through a tough day together:

> I travel a lot because of the speaking I do around the country, and sometimes that leads to unusual situations. I remember one particular evening when I was in the airport in Charlotte, North Carolina, getting ready to fly to Indianapolis, Indiana. I was on the phone up to the last minute, and then I dashed up to my gate and met Dick Peterson, the president of INJOY, expecting to run onto the plane just before the doors closed. But to my surprise, the waiting area had about fifty or sixty people moping around in it.
>
> I looked at Dick and said, "What's going on?"
>
> "Well," said Dick, "it looks like we won't get to fly out for a while yet."
>
> "What's the problem?" I asked.
>
> "I don't know," he said.
>
> So I went up and talked to the agent at the gate, and he told me, "The flight attendants aren't here yet, and we can't allow anyone to board until they come." Then he announced the same thing over the PA system, and I could see everyone in the waiting area kind of deflate. They looked miserable.
>
> I looked at Dick, and I said, "You know, let's see if we can help these people out." So we went to a snack counter close by, and I told the woman there, named Denise, "I'd like sixty Coca-Colas, please."
>
> She stared at me a moment and finally said, "You want sixty?"

Then I explained to her, "There are a whole bunch of passengers down at that next gate who are disappointed, and they need something to boost their morale."

"You're not kidding? You're going to buy one for everybody?" she asked.

"You bet."

She paused for a moment, then said, "Can I help?"

She, Dick, and I took those drinks down to the people at the gate, and I could see that they weren't sure what to think. So I said, "May I have your attention, please? My name is John Maxwell. Since we're not going to leave for thirty to forty-five minutes, I thought I would at least get you something to drink. It's on the house."

We started passing out the Cokes, and I could tell they thought I was weird. So did the airline personnel. But after a while I began to develop rapport with them, and when they found out the flight attendants were on the ground and would be at the gate soon, I was finally able to talk them into letting us get on the plane.

As soon as we all got on the plane, I saw a large basket of peanuts, granola bars, and goodies in the galley, and I thought to myself, *Hey, they ought to have something to eat with that Coca-Cola.* So I went down the aisle giving out the goodies. In only five minutes I had served them all something to eat, and they were drinking their Cokes. About this time the flight crew rushed aboard. They were very apologetic. They got on the plane's PA system right away and said, "Ladies and gentlemen, we're going to get started right away. As soon as we can, we'll begin the beverage service."

Well, they could hear a lot of laughter and chattering in the cabin, and one of the flight attendants said to the other, "What's going on here?"

"Hi, my name's John," I said. "They're not too worried about your service right now. I've already given everybody something to drink and some snacks to eat. In fact, would it be all right if I talked to everybody a moment?" They laughed and said, "Sure. Why not?"

As we taxied out to the runway, they let me talk. "Hi, folks," I said, "this is your friend, John Maxwell. Please buckle up. We'll be airborne in a few moments, and as soon as we're in the air, I'll be back again to serve you."

We had a great time on that flight. I talked to everybody and helped serve drinks. When we landed, I asked if I could talk to everybody one last time. "Gang," I said, "this is John. I'm so glad you were on this flight today. Didn't we have a wonderful time?" Everyone clapped and cheered. "Now when we get off, I'm going to go down to the baggage claim area. If any of you have any problems, please see me, and we'll immediately take care of the situation."

While I was down in the baggage area helping people find their luggage, a man came up to me and said, "This has been great. I'm from Florida, and I've got some grapefruit with me. Here, have a grapefruit."

"Thank you very much," I said. "You know, I've got a brother who lives in Florida—in Winterhaven."

"That's where I live!" he said. "What's your name again? John Maxwell? Wait! Is your brother's name Larry and his wife, Anita?"

"That's correct."

"I know them!" he said. "Anita serves on a board with me. I'm going to call them right now. They won't believe it." He hurried off toward a bank of phones. "I've traveled for years," he said, "and nothing like this has ever happened before!"

What could have been a miserable plane ride of tired, grumpy people turned out to be an experience that nobody on that flight will ever forget. Why? Because one person decided to take others under his wing and help them through a potentially unpleasant situation. It's a process that we call *navigating*.

Most people need help working through some of life's difficulties. That plane flight probably wasn't more than an inconvenience for most of those passengers, but they still enjoyed being coached through the experience by someone with a good attitude. That kind of assistance is needed and appreciated by most people, especially when life's complicated problems hit closer to home, and people have a tougher time with them.

A person well known for trying to help people work through their problems is Ann Landers. Talking about what she has learned from people through the letters she has received for her column, Ann Landers said,

> I've learned plenty—including, most meaningfully, what Leo Rosten had in mind when he said, "Each of us is a little lonely, deep inside, and cries to be understood." I have learned how it is with the stumbling, tortured people in this world who have nobody to talk to. The fact that the column has been a success underscores, for me at least, the central tragedy of our society, the disconnectedness, the insecurity, the fear that bedevils, cripples, and paralyzes so many of us. I have learned that financial success, academic achievement, and social or political status open no doors to peace of mind or inner security. We are all wanderers, like sheep, on this planet.[1]

The people in your life with whom you have influence need your help, especially the ones who are trying to go to a new level, start a new venture, or enter a new phase of life. They need someone to lead and guide them. Mel Ziegler, founder of Banana Republic, outlined a leader's ability to navigate when he wrote: "A leader discovers the hidden chasm between where things are and where things would better be, and strings up a makeshift bridge to attempt the crossing. From the other side he guides those who dare to cross his rickety traverse until the engineers can build a sturdier span for all."[2]

A leader is one who sees more than others see, who sees farther than others see, and who sees before others do.
—Leroy Eims

Ziegler painted a vivid picture. But for most people, the leadership they need isn't just a one-time event, a single chasm to cross. Most people need guidance on a fairly continual basis until they can get their lives together, and then they can be encouraged to make the trip under their own power. It's more like an ocean voyage that you have to navigate them through than a chasm you have to coax them to cross. You've got to help them find their way, spot icebergs, and weather stormy seas, and you've got to take the trip with them—at least until they are on the right course and can learn to navigate on their own.

A NAVIGATOR IDENTIFIES
THE DESTINATION

A good navigator helps people identify their destination. In *Be the Leader You Were Meant to Be,* Leroy Eims wrote, "A leader is one who sees more than others see, who sees farther than others see, and who sees before others do." In the previous chapter, we talked about the importance of casting a vision of people's future so that they are encouraged to grow. The next step is to show them their destination in a more concrete way. Most people who are dissatisfied and discouraged feel that way because they haven't grabbed hold of a vision for themselves. It has been said, "To bury our dreams is to bury ourselves, for we are really 'such stuff as dreams are made on.' God's dream for us is to reach our potential." You have to help others discover their dream and then get them moving toward it. If there is no movement, then there can be no navigation. And any movement will be progress only if it's in the direction of the destination.

You may already recognize much of the potential of the people you're trying to mentor, but you need to know more about them. To help them recognize the destination they will be striving for, you need to know what really matters to them, what makes them tick. To do that, find out these things:

- **What do they cry about?** To know where people truly want to go, you need to know what touches their hearts. Passion and compassion are compelling motivators. It has been said that the great men and women of history were great not for what they owned or earned, but for what they gave their lives to accomplish. Listen with your heart and you are likely to discover the things for which others are willing to give themselves.

- **What do they sing about?** Frank Irving Fletcher observed, "No man can deliver the goods if his heart is heavier than his load." There is a big difference between the things that touch people's hearts and the things that weigh them down. In the long run, people need to focus a lot of energy on what gives them joy. Looking for enthusiasms in the people you mentor will give you another clue concerning their intended destination.

- **What do they dream about?** Napoleon Hill said, "Cherish your visions and your dreams as they are the children of your soul; the blueprints of your ultimate achievements." If you can help people discover their dreams and truly believe in them, you can help them become the persons they were designed to be.

A NAVIGATOR PLOTS THE COURSE

When you consider people's passions, potential, and vision, you are better able to see where they really want to go because you view them with more depth and discernment. Often, people say that their goal is happiness or success, but if they identify such a surface thing as their destination, they're sure to be disappointed. As John Condry emphasized, "Happiness, wealth, and success are by-products of goal-setting; they cannot be the goal themselves."

Once you as the navigator assist others in identifying a vision for their lives, you need to help them find a way to make it a reality. And that means plotting a course and setting goals. J. Meyers said, "A #2 pencil and a dream can take you anywhere." No doubt he understood the value of planning and putting goals in writing. That doesn't mean that things always go as you expect, but you have to start with a game plan. A good rule of thumb is to set your goals in concrete and write your plans in sand.

To help people plot their course, give attention to these areas:

Where They Need to Go

You would be amazed by how far off track some people can get when trying to reach their goals. As E. W. Howe wrote in *Success Is Easier Than Failure,* "Some people storm imaginary Alps all their lives, and die in the foothills cursing difficulties that do not exist." People who have not yet experienced success often have no idea what it takes to get from where they are to where they want to go. They throw themselves into a labyrinth of activity because they don't recognize that they can take an easier path. As the navigator, you are to show them the best course.

What They Need to Know

We heard an amusing story about a husband who wanted to help his wife because he suspected she had a hearing problem. One night he positioned himself across the room from her with her back to him, and softly he said, "Can you hear me?" He didn't get an answer from her, so he moved closer and repeated, "Can you hear me now?" Still nothing. He moved closer and asked, "Can you hear me?" He heard no response, so finally he repeated the question from directly behind her. She turned to face him and said, "For the fourth time, *Yes!*"

Too many people out there are similar to that husband. They want to succeed and help others, but their misunderstanding or lack of knowledge hinders them. A good navigator recognizes the blind spots in others, gently identifies them, and helps people overcome them.

How They Need to Grow

When you are navigating for others, remember that they can't make the whole trip in a day. They have to grow into their goals and take things one step at a time. An experiment performed by Alfred J. Marrow, a company president with a Ph.D. in psychology, illustrated this fact. He was interested in finding a way to help new unskilled employees reach optimum performance and match the standards of his skilled, experienced employees as quickly as possible.

Marrow decided to divide some new employees into two groups. With the first, he asked the unskilled workers to match the production of the skilled ones by the end of twelve weeks. With the second group, he established escalating weekly goals. Each week's goal was slightly more ambitious than the one from the week before.

> *A #2 pencil and a dream*
> *can take you anywhere.*
> *—J. Meyers*

In the first group with the single goal, only 66 percent of the workers were able to meet his expectations. But the second group with the intermediate goals performed significantly better and was able to match the production averages of the company's experienced laborers more quickly.[3]

As you work with people, help them to figure out not only their long-term destination, but also the smaller steps along the way. Help them identify attainable goals that will give them confidence, and they'll make progress.

A NAVIGATOR THINKS AHEAD

Few things are more discouraging than being blindsided, especially when someone who could have helped you stands by and watches it happen. That's why thinking ahead for others is part of your task as a navigator. As people's leader and mentor, you have been places they have not yet gone, had experiences they have not been through, and gained insights they have not yet developed. You have the ability to prepare them for what they are going to face. If you don't, you're not helping them the way you should, and you are no longer performing one of your most important functions as a leader. American humorist Arnold H. Glasow saw the significance of this: "One of the tests of leadership is to recognize a problem before it becomes an emergency." That's something the less-experienced persons you're helping cannot at first do on their own.

Here are four things you should help them understand as they get under way:

1. Everybody Faces Problems

Someone quipped, "If you keep your head when all about you are losing theirs, you just don't understand the problem." As you mentor people and help them grow, you may find that they expect to someday reach a point in their lives when their problems disappear. But they need to realize that everybody has problems. No matter how far they go or how successful they become, they will continue to face difficulties. Or as writer and artists' advocate Elbert Hubbard said, "The man who has no more problems to solve is out of the game."

The Barna Research Group surveyed more than twelve hundred people to gather information on the problems they faced. They were asked to identify their single most serious need or problem. Here are their answers along with the percentage of people who ranked the problems most pressing:

39%	Financial
16%	Job-Related
12%	Personal Health
8%	Time and Stress
7%	Parenting
6%	Educational Attainment
3%	Fear of Crime
3%	Personal Relationships[4]

As you can see, people face a variety of problems, with money being the greatest. Be prepared to give them assistance. And remember to settle your own issues before trying to help others with theirs.

2. Successful People Face More Problems Than Unsuccessful People

Another common misconception is that successful people have achieved because they didn't have problems. But that isn't true. In his book *Holy Sweat,* Tim Hansel tells this story:

> In 1962, Victor and Mildred Goertzel published a revealing study of 413 famous and exceptionally gifted people. The study was called *Cradles of Eminence.* These two researchers spent years trying to understand the source of these people's greatness, the common thread which ran through all of these outstanding people's lives. The most outstanding fact was that almost all of them, 392, had to overcome very difficult obstacles in order to become who they were. Their problems became opportunities instead of obstacles.[5]

Not only do people overcome obstacles to become successful, but even after they have achieved a level of success, they continue to face problems. The bad news is that the higher people go—personally and professionally—the more complicated life gets. Schedules get tighter, money issues increase, and greater demands are put on successful people. But the good news is that if they continue to grow and develop themselves, their ability to deal with problems will also increase.

3. Money Doesn't Solve Problems

Another faulty belief is that money solves all problems. The opposite is actually true—people with money tend to be less content and have additional problems. For example, Ernie J. Zelinski cites a recent survey showing that a higher percentage of people making more than $75,000 a year are dissatisfied with their incomes than of those making less than $75,000 a year. He also noted:

> A larger percentage of the rich have alcohol and drug problems than the general population. I have a theory about how well off we will be with a lot of money. If we are happy and handle problems well when we are making $25,000 a year, we will

be happy and handle problems well when we have a lot more money. If we are unhappy and don't handle problems well on $25,000 a year, we can expect the same of ourselves with a lot of money. We will be just as unhappy and handle problems as ineffectively, but with more comfort and style.[6]

The bottom line is that you should try to help people understand that money is no substitute for the basic problem-solving skills they need to develop. Financial problems are usually a symptom of other personal problems.

4. Problems Provide an Opportunity for Growth

As you look ahead and help people, realize that while problems can cause pain, they also provide an excellent opportunity for growth. Or as author Nena O'Neill put it, "Out of every crisis comes the chance to be reborn."

The people of Enterprise, Alabama, understand that idea. In their town stands a monument to the Mexican boll weevil, erected in 1919. The story behind it is that in 1895, the insect destroyed the county's major crop, cotton. After that disaster, local farmers began to diversify, and the peanut crop of 1919 far exceeded the value of even the best ones comprised of cotton. On the monument are the following words: "In profound appreciation of the boll weevil and what it has done as the herald of prosperity. . . . Out of a time of struggle and crisis has come new growth and success. Out of adversity has come blessing."

As you have certainly observed, not everyone approaches life's problems in the same way. Historian Arnold Toynbee believed that all people react in one of four ways under difficult circumstances:

1. Retreat into the past
2. Daydream about the future
3. Retreat within and wait for someone to rescue them
4. Face the crisis and transform it into something useful

As you help others, let them know there may be rough waters ahead. Show them that it's wise to plan ahead as best they can.

And when trouble comes, encourage them to face it and try to become better as a result.

A NAVIGATOR MAKES
COURSE CORRECTIONS

We've heard that back before the time of sophisticated electronic navigational equipment, the ship's navigator used to take a reading of the stars at a particular time in the middle of the night, determine how far off course the vessel was, and make adjustments to its course. No matter how accurately the original course had been laid out or how carefully the helmsman had followed his orders, the ship always got off course and needed adjustments.

People are the same way. No matter how focused they are or how well they plan, people will still get off course. The problem comes when they have difficulty making course corrections— either because they don't know they're off course, or because they don't know what they should do to fix things. Not everyone is a natural problem solver. For most people, it's a skill they must learn. John Foster Dulles, secretary of state during the Eisenhower administration, proposed that "the measure of success is not whether you have a tough problem to deal with, but whether it's the same problem you had last year." As the navigator, you can help people avoid that situation.

Teach Them Not to Listen to Doubting Critics

In the book *Principle-Centered Leadership,* Stephen Covey tells how Columbus was once invited to a banquet where he was given the most honored place at the table. A shallow courtier who was jealous of him asked abruptly, "Had you not discovered the Indies, are there not other men in Spain who would have been capable of the enterprise?"

Columbus made no reply but took an egg and invited the company to make it stand on end. They all attempted to do it, but none succeeded, whereupon the explorer tapped it on the table, denting one end, and left it standing.

"We all could have done it that way!" the courtier cried.

"Yes, if you had only known how," answered Columbus. "And once I showed you the way to the New World, nothing was easier than to follow it."

> *When you are navigating for others, remember that they can't make the whole trip in a day.*

The truth is that it's a hundred times easier to criticize others than to find solutions to problems. But criticism gets you nowhere. Alfred Armand Montapert summed it up this way: "The majority see the obstacles; the few see the objectives; history records the successes of the latter, while oblivion is the reward of the former." Help the people within your influence to ignore the critics and keep their eyes on the big picture. Show them that the best way to silence critics is to solve the problem and move on.

Coach Them Not to Be Overwhelmed by Challenges

A rookie major-league baseball player faced pitcher Walter Johnson for the first time when Johnson was in his prime. The batter took two quick strikes and headed for the dugout. He told the umpire to keep the third strike—he had seen enough.

When faced with tough problems, just about anybody is likely to get discouraged. That's why it's a good idea to coach people through their problems, especially early on in the mentoring process while you're first helping them to navigate. Encourage them to maintain a positive attitude, and give them strategies for problem solving.

Management expert Ken Blanchard recommends a four-step problem-solving process that includes (1) thinking about the problem in order to make it specific, (2) forming theories for solving it, (3) forecasting the consequences of carrying out the theories, and (4) then choosing which method to use based on the big picture. Blanchard says, "Whether you choose a vacation or a spouse, a party or a candidate, a cause to contribute to or a creed to live by—think!" There are no impossible problems. Time, thought, and a positive attitude can solve just about anything.

Encourage Them to Seek Simple Solutions

There are a couple of keys to the most effective method of problem solving. The first is recognizing that the simple way to solve a problem is better than the most clever one. An example from the life of Thomas Edison illustrates this point well. It's said that Edison had a unique way of hiring engineers. He would give the applicant a lightbulb and ask, "How much water will it hold?" There were two ways the engineers usually went about solving the problem. The first way was to use gauges to measure all the angles of the bulb, and then use those figures to calculate the surface area. That approach sometimes took as long as twenty minutes. The second way was to fill the bulb with water and then pour the contents into a measuring cup, which usually took about one minute.[7] Edison never hired the engineers who used the first method. He didn't want the engineers to impress him—he wanted them to provide simple results.

The second element in effective problem solving is the ability to make decisions. Thomas J. Watson, Jr., former head of IBM, believed that solving problems quickly was essential to making progress. "Solve it," he declared. "Solve it quickly, solve it right or wrong. If you solve it wrong, it will come back and slap you in the face, and then you can solve it right. Lying dead in the water and doing nothing is a comfortable alternative because it is without risk, but it is an absolutely fatal way to manage a business." And it's also a terrible way for people to manage their lives. Help others to realize when they need to make course adjustments, find simple solutions that they think will work, and then execute them without delay. Don't let them continue traveling off course for any length of time.

Instill Confidence in Them

One pitfall of helping others with their problems and mistakes is that they can doubt themselves. Continually encourage the people you help. George Matthew Adams said, "What you think means more than anything else in your life. More than what you earn, more than where you live, more than your social position, and more than what anyone else may think about you." The size of the persons and the quality of their attitude are more important than the size of any problem they may face. If your people remain confident, they will be able to overcome any obstacle.

A NAVIGATOR STAYS WITH THE PEOPLE

Finally, a good navigator takes the trip with the people he is guiding. He doesn't give directions and then walk away. He travels alongside his people as a friend. Author and conference speaker Richard Exley explained his idea of friendship this way: "A true friend is one who hears and understands when you share your deepest feelings. He supports you when you are struggling; he corrects you, gently and with love, when you err; and he forgives you when you fail. A true friend prods you to personal growth, stretches you to your full potential. And most amazing of all, he celebrates your successes as if they were his own."

As you come alongside some of the people within your influence and mentor them, you and they may experience difficult times together. You won't be perfect and neither will they, but just keep in mind Henry Ford's words: "Your best friend is he who brings out the best that is within you." Do your best to follow that objective, and you will help a lot of people.

Once people learn to become effective problem solvers and can navigate for themselves, their lives begin to change dramatically. No longer do they feel powerless in the face of life's difficult circumstances. They learn to roll with the punches—and even to duck a few. And once problem solving becomes a habit, no challenge seems too large.

Jim is an excellent thinker and problem solver. He has navigated through some pretty interesting situations over the years. Recently, he recounted a story that you will undoubtedly enjoy:

A couple of years ago while Nancy and I were hosting a business seminar aboard a large cruise ship in the Caribbean, we were called away to an important business meeting in Michigan. We had no problem getting to the meeting because arrangements had been made for us to be picked up by a private jet at the airport in San Juan, Puerto Rico. But leaving Michigan and getting back turned out to be quite another story.

Our plan was to return on the same jet the next day and meet the ship at its next port. From there the ship would return to Miami, and we could continue teaching our seminar. But in Michigan when we began to depart, our aircraft developed a problem and had to return to the hangar. That caused a serious problem for us. There were no commercial flights to our destination, nor were there any private planes with enough range to get us down to St. Martin, which is some fifteen hundred miles off the coast of Florida.

Missing the seminar simply was not an option for us, so we looked at other possibilities. The best we could do was take an available private jet to Atlanta and work on finding another plane to take us the rest of the way.

By the time we touched down in Atlanta, we had managed to arrange for another plane, and it was ready and waiting for us. As soon as our plane came to a stop, we gathered up our things and scrambled over to the other jet. You can imagine how relieved we were to get on board and get in the air.

We weren't on our way for very long before we found out that our current flight was going to get us on the island exactly fifteen minutes after the ship was scheduled to depart. "We've got to get them to delay the ship," I said.

The pilot started working on the problem via radio and managed to contact the ship's captain from the cockpit. He agreed to a twenty-minute delay. Then the pilot worked on getting us a quick clearance through customs. And when word came back that we would be able to do it, we started getting optimistic.

We dashed to the first taxi we could find and headed out, but almost immediately, we hit a huge traffic jam.

"How far is it to the ship?" Nancy asked.

"On the other side of the island," the driver answered.

"How long will that take?'

"Fifteen, maybe twenty minutes."

"We need to make it in less than ten," I said, offering him a really good tip.

He looked at me, looked at the money, and said, "Yes, sir." He pulled the cab over onto the sidewalk and made a quick turn up an alley. We went over curbs, through lights, and weaved down alleys and side streets in a blur. We felt as if we were on Mr. Toad's Wild Ride at Disneyland. It seemed like we saw the back of every building on the island. But then we shot through a narrow opening between two buildings and careened out into the sunlight onto a pier—and the ship was in sight, its horn sounding its imminent departure.

As we screeched to a halt at the end of the pier, we piled out of the cab. That's when we began to hear the cheering. Evidently, word had gotten to our people on the ship that we were fighting to make our way back to them. And when we finally had a second to look up, we could see more than five hundred people on deck whooping and clapping and cheering to celebrate our arrival.

"Who are you anyway?" our driver asked. I just handed him the money and said, "Thanks for your help." Then Nancy and I ran for the gangway. It hadn't been easy, but we had made it.

The ability to navigate problems and overcome obstacles is a skill that anyone can learn, but it takes practice. If Jim and Nancy had faced that same situation twenty years before, they probably would not have made it to that ship. But over the years, they've developed an incredible ability to make things happen, not only in their own lives, but also in the lives of others.

You can have that same ability. Become a navigator in the lives of others. You will be able to use your influence to help them move up to the next level in their lives, and if you assist them during their darkest hours, you will make friends of them for life.

Influence Checklist
NAVIGATING FOR OTHER PEOPLE

❏ **Identify their destination.** Think about the three people you've decided to enlarge. What are their destinations? Observe what makes them cry, sing, and dream. Write those things down here:

Person 1: _____
Cry: _____
Sing: _____
Dream: _____

Person 2: _____
Cry: _____
Sing: _____
Dream: _____

Person 3: _____
Cry: _____
Sing: _____
Dream: _____

❏ **Look ahead.** Based on your experience and knowledge of these people, list the difficulties you think they are likely to face in the near future:

1. _____
2. _____
3. _____

❏ **Plan ahead.** How can you help them navigate through these potential problems? Write down what you can do and when you should do it.

1. _____
2. _____
3. _____

A Person of Influence . . .

CONNECTS
WITH PEOPLE

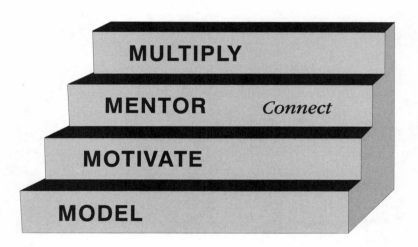

Have you ever been to a family or school reunion? It can be fun because it gives you a chance to connect with people you haven't seen in a long time. John recently went to a reunion of sorts, and he had an incredible time. Let him tell you about it:

My first job out of college in 1969 was at a little church in Hillham, Indiana. I was the senior pastor there for three years. The church really grew during the short time Margaret and I were there, so much so that we had to construct a new church building in 1971 to hold all the people. We look back on those three years as a crucial growing time in our lives that we really enjoyed and benefited from.

Recently, I got a phone call from that little country church. The person on the phone excitedly explained they were getting ready to celebrate the twenty-five-year anniversary of the building we constructed. They were preparing to have a big service and invite everybody for miles around to come celebrate with them. And then the person on the other end of the phone paused and cleared his throat. And he finally asked, "Dr. Maxwell, would you be willing to come back and preach that Sunday service for us?"

"I would love to come back and preach at your service," I told him. "It would be an honor. You just tell me the day, and I'll be there."

During the next few months, I spent some time thinking about how I could make their anniversary a great day for them. The last thing I wanted to do was come back as some kind of conquering hero. I knew I needed to find ways to connect with them.

The first thing I did was get them to send me a copy of their church directory with the pictures and names of all the people in their congregation. There in the book were many faces I recognized. Some people had less hair than I remembered, and much of that hair was now gray, but I knew the faces behind those twenty-five years of wrinkles. And there were many others who were new to me. Sons and daughters of the people I loved, and some new names

I didn't recognize. I spent many hours poring over those pictures and memorizing those names.

Then I prepared the best message I could, one filled with stories of our common experiences. I shared some of my mistakes and recounted all of their victories. I wanted them to know that they shared in my success. They were king makers, and I felt very privileged to have served them for three years and benefited from their loving support and care for me.

But I knew that more important than the message I preached or anything else I could do would be the time I was able to spend with the people. So when the time came, Margaret and I flew in early, and we spent Saturday afternoon with some of the old-timers who had been such a vital part of our ministry twenty-five years before. We shared a lot of wonderful recollections. I talked to them about some of my fondest memories, and they surprised me with a few stories of their own. For instance, there was one man in a wheelchair who had been a teenager when I was the pastor there. He had been in an accident that left him in a coma. I had visited him and his family several times in the hospital, and one night I shared my faith with him as he lay unconscious in his bed. I left Hillham soon after that to go to my next church, and until my current visit, I hadn't known he had ever awakened from the coma.

"Do you remember coming into the hospital and talking to me twenty-five years ago?" he asked.

"I sure do," I answered.

"So do I," he told me. "I remember that day as clear as can be. I wasn't able to answer you, but I heard every word you said. That's the day I became a believer." And he told me about how his faith had impacted other people in the community. It was a very special time.

The next day, I got to the church early to shake the hands of the people as they came into the sanctuary. It was wonderful to get to meet so many of the people and be able to greet them by name. And I preached a message of affirmation to them. Even though they had done some wonderful things since I had last seen them, I told them that I could see that in the next twenty-five years lay their greatest potential. Their best days were still ahead of them. And when I left, I felt as though I had not only renewed some old acquaintances, but also had made a lot of new friends.

The time John spent with the people in Hillham was brief, but in that short time, he was able to do something that was important to them and him. He was able to connect with them.

CONNECTING ENABLES OTHERS TO TRAVEL TO A HIGHER LEVEL

Connection is a very important part of the process of mentoring others. And it's absolutely critical if you want to influence people in a positive way. When you navigate for others, you come alongside them and travel their road for a while, helping them handle some of the obstacles and difficulties in their lives. But when you connect with them, you are asking them to come alongside you and travel your road for your and their mutual benefit.

When we think of connecting with people, we compare it to trains and what happens to them in a train yard. The cars sitting on the tracks in a train yard have a lot of things going for them. They have value because they're loaded with cargo; they have a destination; and they even have a route by which to get to that destination. But they don't have a way of getting anywhere on their own. To do anything of value, they have to hook up with a locomotive.

Have you ever been to a train yard and watched how unrelated and disconnected pieces of equipment come together to form a working train? It's quite a process. It all begins with the locomotive. First, it switches itself onto the same track as the car it's going to pick up. Then it moves to where the car is, backs up to it, makes contact with it, and connects. Once it's all hooked up, together they move toward their destination.

A similar thing must happen before you can get people to go with you on a journey. You have to find out where they are, move toward them to make contact, and connect with them. If you can do that successfully, you can take them to new heights in your relationship and in their development. Remember, the road to the next level is always uphill, and people need help to make it to that higher level.

Nine Steps for Connecting
with People

Fortunately, you don't have to be an engineer to connect with people, but it does take effort to make connection happen. You'll need communication skills, a desire to help people grow and change, and a sense of personal mission or purpose—after all, you have to know where you're going to take others along.

Take a look at the following steps, and use them to help you connect with the people you influence:

1. Don't Take People for Granted

You can connect with people and lead them only if you value them. Weak leaders sometimes get so caught up in the vision of where they're going that they forget the people they're trying to lead. But you can't take people for granted for any length of time before your leadership begins to fall apart. And you won't be able to connect with them.

A wonderful story from former Speaker of the House Tip O'Neill reveals what can happen when you take people for granted. He said that on one election day, an elderly neighbor came up to him after leaving the polls and said, "Tip, I voted for you today even though you didn't ask me."

O'Neill was surprised. "Mrs. O'Brien," he said, "I've known you all my life. I took your garbage out for you, mowed your lawn, shoveled snow for you. I didn't think I had to ask."

"Tip," she said in a motherly tone, "it's always *nice* to be asked." O'Neill said he never forgot that piece of advice.

Valuing people is the first step in the connection process, but it has additional benefits. When you let people know that you don't take them for granted, they turn around and do the same for you. John was reminded of this by his friend and colleague Dan Reiland. John will tell you the story:

> Margaret and I spent a long weekend with Dan and his wife, Patti, not too long ago. Dan has worked with me for fifteen years, first as my executive pastor at Skyline Church where I was the senior pastor, and now as a vice president at INJOY. We spent the weekend at a resort hotel in Laguna Beach. It was great. We enjoyed the pool and spa, ate some great meals, and had a wonderful time together.
>
> As Margaret and I were checking out, I went to the front desk to pay the bill and discovered that Dan had beaten me there and already taken care of everything. Later I talked to him and said, "Dan, you didn't have to do that. I wanted to treat you and Patti."
>
> "No, John," said Dan, "it was our pleasure. You do so much for us; I never want to take you for granted."

John's friend Coach Bill McCartney, former head football coach of the Colorado State Buffaloes, said, "Anytime you devalue people, you question God's creation of them." You can never tell people too often, too loudly, or too publicly how much you love them.

You can connect with people and lead them only if you value them.

2. Possess a Make-a-Difference Mind-Set

If you desire to accomplish something great and really want to see it happen, you need to possess a make-a-difference attitude. Anytime you don't believe you can make a difference, you won't. How do you cultivate a solid make-a-difference mind-set?

Believe you can make a difference. Every person on this earth—including you—has the potential to make a difference. But you can do it only if you believe in yourself and are willing to give yourself away to others. As Helen Keller said, "Life is an exciting business and most exciting when lived for others." You may not be able to help *everybody,* but you can certainly help *somebody.*

Believe what you share can make a difference. The two of us spend a large part of our lives connecting and communicating with people. Between the two of us, we impact more than one million people every year. If we believed that what we share with others couldn't make a difference, we would quit tomorrow. But we know that we can help others change their lives. We believe that everything rises and falls on leadership. We're certain that people's attitudes make or break them. And we know that there is no joy, peace, or meaning in life without faith.

You have to believe that what you have to offer others can make a difference in their lives. No one wants to follow a person without conviction. If you don't believe, neither will other people.

Believe the person you share with can make a difference. We've read about something called a reciprocity rule in human behavior. It states that over time, people come to share similar attitudes toward one another. In other words, if we hold a high opinion of you and continue to hold that opinion, eventually, you will come to feel the same way about us. That process builds a connection between us, and it opens the way for a powerful partnership.

Believe that together you can make a big difference. Mother Teresa is a living example of a truth she once expressed: "I can do what you can't do, and you can do what I can't do. *Together* we can do great things." No one ever achieves alone what he can do when partnering with others. And anybody who doesn't recognize that falls incredibly short of her potential.

There is a story about a famous organist in the 1800s that illustrates the importance of recognizing valuable partnerships. The musician traveled from town to town giving concerts. In each town, he hired a boy to pump the organ during the concert. After one particular performance, he couldn't shake the boy. He even followed the organist back to his hotel.

"We sure had us a great concert tonight, didn't we?" said the boy.

"What do you mean *we?*" said the musician. "*I* had a great concert. Now why don't you go home?"

The next night when the organist was halfway through a magnificent fugue, the organ suddenly quit. The organist was stupefied. Then suddenly, the little boy stuck his head around the corner of the organ, grinned, and said, "We ain't having a very good concert tonight, are *we?*"

If you want to connect with people and take them with you to a higher level, recognize the difference you can make as a team, and acknowledge it at every opportunity.

3. Initiate Movement Toward Them

According to Tom Peters and Nancy Austin, "The number one managerial productivity problem in America is, quite simply, managers who are out of touch with their people and out of touch with their customers."[1] Lack of contact and communication is a problem that affects many people, not just managers in organizations. Maybe that's why sales expert Charles B. Ruth says, "There are many cases of salesmen who have nothing to offer a prospect except friendship out-selling salesmen with everything to offer—except friendship."[2]

We believe there are many reasons why people don't connect with one another more than they do. A primary reason, especially within organizations, is that many leaders believe that it is the follower's responsibility to initiate contact with them. But the opposite is true. To be effective, leaders must be initiators. If they don't go to their people, meet them where they are, and initiate the connection, then 80 percent of the time no connection will be made.

4. Look for Common Ground

Anytime you want to connect with another person, start where both of you agree. And that means finding common ground. If you have developed good listening skills, as we talked about in Chapter 4, you'll probably be able to detect areas where you have common experience or views. Talk about hobbies, where you've lived, your work, sports, or children. What you discuss isn't as important as your attitude. Be positive, and try to see things from the other person's point of view. Being open and likable is half the battle. As it's sometimes said, "All things being equal, people will do business with people they like. All things not being equal, they still will."

Sometimes even when you find common ground, you can face obstacles in the communication process. If you detect that people you're trying to connect with are tentative about your approaching them, then try to meet them on emotional common ground. An excellent way to do that is to use something called *feel, felt, found* to help them relate to you. First, try to sense what they *feel,* and acknowledge and validate the feelings. If you've had similar feelings in the past, then share with them about how you've also *felt* the same way before. Finally, share with them what you've *found* that has helped you work through the feelings.

Once you make it a regular practice to look for common ground with others, you'll find that you can talk to just about anybody and meet her where she is. And when you can do that, you can make a connection.

5. *Recognize and Respect Differences in Personality*

We are capable of finding common ground with others, but at the same time we need to acknowledge that we're all different. And that's one of the great joys of life, though we didn't always see it that way. An excellent tool for understanding other people is a book by John's friend Florence Littauer called *Personality Plus.* In it, she describes four basic personality types:

- **Sanguine:** desires fun; is outgoing, relationship oriented, witty, easygoing, popular, artistic, emotional, outspoken, and optimistic.

- *Melancholy:* desires perfection; is introverted, task oriented, artistic, emotional, goal oriented, organized, and pessimistic.
- *Phlegmatic:* desires peace; is introverted, unemotional, strong-willed, relationship oriented, pessimistic, and purpose driven.
- *Choleric:* desires power or control; is strong-willed, decisive, goal oriented, organized, unemotional, outgoing, outspoken, and optimistic.[3]

Just about everyone you try to connect with falls into one of these categories (or has characteristics from two complementary categories). For example, John is a classic choleric-sanguine. He loves to have fun, he is decisive, and he naturally takes charge in just about any situation. Jim, on the other hand, is melancholy-phlegmatic. He is an analytical thinker who's not driven by emotion, and he generally keeps his own counsel.

As you connect with others, recognize and respect their differences in motivation. With cholerics, connect with strength. With melancholics, connect by being focused. With phlegmatics, connect by giving assurance. And with sanguines, connect with excitement.

Playwright John Luther understood this point: "Natural talent, intelligence, a wonderful education—none of these guarantees success. Something else is needed: the sensitivity to understand what other people want and the willingness to give it to them." Pay attention to people's personalities, and do your best to meet them where they are. They'll appreciate your sensitivity and understanding.

6. Find the Key to Others' Lives

Industrialist Andrew Carnegie had an uncanny ability for understanding people and what was important to them. It's said that when he was a boy in Scotland, he had a rabbit that had a litter of bunnies. To feed them, Carnegie asked the neighborhood boys to collect clover and dandelions. In return, each boy got to name a bunny after himself.

Carnegie did something similar as an adult that showed his understanding of people. Because he wanted to sell his steel to the

Pennsylvania Railroad, when he built a new steel mill in Pittsburgh, he named it the J. Edgar Thompson Steel Works after the president of the Pennsylvania Railroad. Thompson was so flattered by the honor that he thereafter purchased all his steel from Carnegie.

You don't have to be a Carnegie to connect with people. You just need to know what's important to them. Everybody has a key to his or her life. All you need to do is find it. Here are two clues to help you do it: To understand a person's mind, examine what he has already achieved. To understand his heart, look at what he aspires to do. That will help you find the key, and once you do find it, use it with integrity. Turn the key only when you have the person's permission, and even then use that key only for his benefit, not your own—to help, not to hurt.

7. *Communicate from the Heart*

Once you've initiated a connection with others, found common ground, and discovered what really matters to them, communicate to them what really matters to you. And that requires you to speak to them from your heart.

A young man with a brand-new degree in psychology was asked to deliver a speech to a group of senior citizens. For forty-five minutes he talked to them on how to live your twilight years gracefully. When the speech was over, an eighty-year-old woman came up to the young speaker and said, "Your vocabulary and pronunciation were excellent, but I must tell you one thing that you'll come to understand as you get older, you don't know what you're talking about!"

Being genuine is the single most important factor when communicating with others, whether one-on-one or before large audiences. No amount of knowledge, technique, or quick-wittedness can substitute for honesty and the genuine desire to help others.

Abraham Lincoln was well known for communicating well with others, and at the heart of that skill was his ability to speak from the heart. In 1842, Lincoln addressed members of the Washington Temperance Society. During his speech titled "Charity in Temperance Reform," he made the following observation: "If you would win a man to your cause, first convince him that you are his sincere friend. . . . Assume to dictate to his judgment, or to command his action, or to mark him as one to be shunned and despised, and he will retreat within himself. . . . You shall no more be able to pierce him than to penetrate the hard shell of a tortoise with a rye straw."[4]

As you communicate with others to build connections with them, share from your heart and be yourself.

8. Share Common Experiences

To really connect with others, you have to do more than find common ground and communicate well. You need to find a way to cement the relationship. Joseph F. Newton said, "People are lonely because they build walls instead of bridges." To build bridges that connect you to people in a lasting way, share common experiences with them.

No one ever achieves alone what he can do when partnering with others.

The two of us have enjoyed sharing experiences with others for years. For example, whenever John hires a new member of his executive staff, he always takes that person on the road with him to several of his conferences. He does that not only because he wants the new staff member to become familiar with the services the company offers to its customers, but also because they can travel together and get to know each other in a wide variety of settings. Nothing bonds people together like racing through impossible traffic in an unfamiliar city to get to the airport and then running with your bags down the concourse to scramble onto a plane at the last minute!

The common experiences you share with others don't have to be that dramatic (although adversity definitely brings people together). Share meals with people. Go to a ball game together. Take people out on a call or visitation with you. Anything you experience together that creates a common history helps to connect you to others.

A wonderful story of connection comes from the career of Jackie Robinson, the first African-American to play major-league baseball. Robinson faced jeering crowds, death threats, and loads of abuse in just about every stadium he visited while breaking baseball's color barrier. One day in his home stadium in Brooklyn, he committed an error, and immediately, his own fans began to ridicule him. He stood at second base, humiliated, while the fans jeered. Then shortstop Pee Wee Reese came over and stood next to him. He put his arm around Robinson and faced the crowd. The fans grew quiet. It's said that Robinson later claimed that Reese's arm around his shoulder saved his career.

Look for ways to build bridges with people within your influence, especially during times when they experience adversity. The connections you make will strengthen your relationships incredibly and prepare you for the journey you can take together.

9. Once Connected, Move Forward

If you want to influence others, and you desire to get them moving in the right direction, you must connect with them before you try to take them anywhere. Attempting to do it before connecting is a common mistake of inexperienced leaders. Trying to move others before going through the connection process with them can lead to mistrust, resistance, and strained relationships. Always remember that you have to share yourself before you try to share the journey. As someone once observed, "Leadership is cultivating in people today, a future willingness on their part to follow you into something new for the sake of something great." Connection creates that willingness.

A challenge for any influencer is connecting with people from another culture. Jim has had a lot of experience in this area since he works with people in twenty-six countries. He found it particularly interesting working with people in the Eastern bloc countries formerly controlled by the Soviet Union:

> **When we first started working with people in Eastern Europe, it was really a unique experience. We had experienced very little exposure to their culture and values, and**

we found that things we accept in everyday business were foreign to people who had endured fifty years of Communist rule.

Most people in America have been raised on Judeo-Christian ethical and moral values. We often take that for granted, along with the benefits of free enterprise and capitalism. Our new friends in countries like Poland, Hungary, and the Czech Republic, however, were used to surviving in a corrupt world of oppressive government, propaganda, and little-to-no-ethical teaching as we know it. Their environment led them to believe that success comes only to those who work *around* the rules and beat the cheaters at their own game. We found that many people embraced a success-at-any-cost mind-set and almost a pride in how cleverly they could break the rules.

We believed it was important to show these wonderful people that real success was possible only when a person behaved ethically and stood on the principles of integrity and trust. It seemed like a big job, but the people were smart, and we were working with some great young professionals who were hungry to learn the secrets of true success.

We began the process by doing everything we could to connect with people in those countries. In some ways, that has been one of our greatest challenges as influencers. But we were able to find a few key people, and we came alongside them as friends and mentors. We began navigating them through this new paradigm of ethical living and principle-centered business. And we invested a lot of time in getting to know them better and connecting with them on this worthwhile journey. Our goal was to give them tools to positively impact the people in their country.

This is still an ongoing journey for us. But whether we are working with people in Eastern Europe, mainland China, or another part of the world, we recognize that people are basically the same. Everyone wants to be successful and happy and is eager to learn from others who have gone ahead of them. But you can't make a significant impact in people's lives until you personally connect with them. Only then can you take them on a journey and really make a difference.

Jim and Nancy are making an impact that is being felt around the world. They understand that influence means relating to people, raising them up, and then turning them loose to reproduce themselves in others' lives. Connecting is a fundamental step in that process. But before people can go to the highest level and reproduce their influence in others, there is one more step they need to take: They need to be empowered. And that is the subject of the next chapter.

Influence Checklist
CONNECTING WITH PEOPLE

❏ **Measure your current connection.** How strong is your connection with the top people whose lives you are influencing? Do you know the key to each person's life? Have you established common ground? Are there common experiences that bond you together? If your connection is not as strong as it could be, remember that it's your role to be the initiator. Schedule time in the coming week to have coffee, share a meal, or just chat with each person.

❏ **Connect at a deeper level.** If you've never spent any kind of meaningful time with your top people in a nonprofessional setting, schedule a time to do so in the coming month. Plan a retreat or a getaway weekend, and include your spouses. Or take them to a seminar or conference. The main thing is to give yourselves opportunities to connect on a deeper level and share common experiences.

❏ **Communicate your vision.** Once you've made a strong connection with your people, share your hopes and dreams. Cast vision for your common future, and invite them to join you on the journey.

A Person of Influence . . .

EMPOWERS
PEOPLE

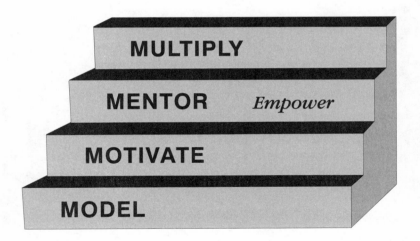

A big part of Jim's business includes meeting fairly often with some of his key leaders, and because they come from around the country and all over the world, he makes it a goal to schedule meetings in various locations. One place that has become a favorite of his and Nancy's over the years is Deer Valley near Salt Lake City, Utah. Recently, when they were there with some of their leaders, something interesting happened. Jim will tell you about it:

Deer Valley is really a beautiful setting. In the winter it's great for skiing, and in the summer it's got gorgeous forested mountains and meadows full of wildflowers. We really enjoy vacationing there and using it as a place to meet with some of our people.

This past year we spent time with a group of about ten couples at some condos in Deer Valley right on the ski slopes. We all had a wonderful time.

When we were ready to leave, we packed up our belongings and swung by the rental office to check out on the way to the airport. But as we worked to get our bill squared away, we discovered that one couple in our party had inadvertently left their room key in their condo.

"I'm going to have to charge you $25 for the lost key," the desk clerk said.

I have to admit I was a little surprised. We had been their customers for eight years. And we had spent thousands of dollars with them in the past week. "Look," I said, "I appreciate that you have a policy about missing keys, but the key is in their room. And if we were to go back and get it, we'd miss our flight. Can't you just forget the charge?"

"No," he said, "the rule is that I have to add the charge to your bill." Even when I reminded him of our history with their company and told him that I didn't feel good about the extra charge, he wouldn't budge. In fact, he got more rigid, and I got really irritated. As I stood there waiting, I calculated in my mind how much money we had spent there over the years, and I figured out that he was jeopardizing our $100,000 history with their company for a $25 key!

We finally left and paid the fee. On the way to the airport, Nancy and I talked about the incident, and I thought about how it really wasn't the desk clerk's fault. The problem was with the owner who had failed to train him properly.

"That kind of thing drives me crazy," she said. "Some people just don't get it. You know who's just the opposite of that?" she asked. "Nordstrom. They're unbelievable. I didn't tell you about what happened the other night before we left for Deer Valley. I went down to Nordstrom to get Eric a pair of pajamas. I picked out some that I knew he'd like, but I told the salesgirl that I needed the pants hemmed and that we were leaving on a trip early the next morning. She didn't blink and offered to have them done that night and drive them out to us at home.

"And that was the only thing I bought!" added Nancy. "It's not like I had spent a lot of money. She did that just for a pair of pajamas."

Stories of the excellent service at Nordstrom department stores have become legendary. Anyone who shops there can attest to it. Their employees are exceptional because the company is built on the principle of *empowerment*. That philosophy of empowering employees is capsulized in the following brief statement that every employee receives when he or she begins working for the company:

Welcome to Nordstrom
We're glad to have you with
our Company.
Our number one goal is to provide
outstanding customer service.
Set both your personal and
professional goals high.
We have great confidence in your ability to achieve them.
Nordstrom Rules:
Rule #1: Use your good
judgment in all situations.
There will be no additional rules.
Please feel free to ask
your department manager,

store manager, or division general
manager any question
at any time.[1]

Nordstrom stores emphasize people, not policies. They believe in their people, they encourage them to achieve excellence, and they release them to do it. As Tom Peters said, "Techniques don't produce quality products or pick up the garbage on time; people do, people who care, people who are treated as creatively contributing adults." The managers and staff at that rental office in Deer Valley would benefit greatly from learning that lesson.

WHAT IT MEANS TO
EMPOWER OTHERS

An English artist named William Wolcott went to New York in 1924 to record his impressions of that fascinating city. One morning he was visiting in the office of a former colleague when the urge to sketch came over him. Seeing some paper on his friend's desk, he asked, "May I have that?"

The act of empowering others changes lives, and it's a win-win situation for you and the people you empower.

His friend answered, "That's not sketching paper. That's ordinary wrapping paper."

Not wanting to lose that spark of inspiration, Wolcott took the wrapping paper and said, "Nothing is ordinary if you know how to use it." On that ordinary paper Wolcott made two sketches.

Later that same year, one of those sketches sold for $500 and the other for $1,000, quite a sum for 1924.

People under the influence of an empowering person are like paper in the hands of a talented artist. No matter what they're made of, they can become treasures.

The ability to empower others is one of the keys to personal and professional success. John Craig remarked, "No matter how much work you can do, no matter how engaging your personality may be, you will not advance far in business if you cannot work through others." And business executive J. Paul Getty asserted, "It doesn't make much difference how much other knowledge or experience an executive possesses; if he is unable to achieve results through people, he is worthless as an executive."

When you empower people, you're not influencing just them; you're influencing all the people they influence.

When you become an empowerer, you work with and through people, but you do much more. You enable others to reach the highest levels in their personal and professional development. Simply defined, empowering is giving your influence to others for the purpose of personal and organizational growth. It's sharing yourself—your influence, position, power, and opportunities—with others with the purpose of investing in their lives so that they can function at their best. It's seeing people's potential, sharing your resources with them, and showing them that you believe in them completely.

You may already be empowering some people in your life without knowing it. When you entrust your spouse with an important decision and then cheerfully back him up, that's empowering. When you decide that your child is ready to cross the street by herself and give her your permission to do so, you have empowered her. When you delegate a challenging job to an employee and give her the authority she needs to get it done, you have empowered her.

The act of empowering others changes lives, and it's a win-win situation for you and the people you empower. Giving others your authority isn't like giving away an object, such as your car, for example. If you give away your car, you're stuck. You no longer have transportation. But empowering others by giving them your authority has the same effect as sharing information: You haven't lost anything. You have increased the ability of others without decreasing yourself.

QUALIFICATIONS OF AN EMPOWERER

Just about everyone has the potential to become an empowerer, but you cannot empower everyone. The process works only when certain conditions are met. You must have:

Position

You cannot empower people whom you don't lead. Leadership expert Fred Smith explained, "Who can give permission for another person to succeed? A person in authority. Others can encourage, but permission comes only from an authority figure: a parent, boss, or pastor."

You can encourage and motivate everybody you meet. You can enlarge or help navigate for anyone with whom you have built a mentoring relationship. But to *empower* people, you have to be in a position of *power* over them. Sometimes that position doesn't have to be formal or official, but other times it does. For example, if we went to a restaurant to have lunch with you one day, and we weren't happy about how long it was taking to get our food, we could never empower you to go into the kitchen to fix our meal for us. We don't have that authority, so we certainly can't give it away to you. The first requisite of empowerment is having a position of authority over the people you want to empower.

Relationship

The second requirement for empowering people is having a relationship with them. Nineteenth-century writer Thomas Carlyle said, "A great man shares his greatness by the way he treats little men." Although the people you empower are not "little," they can be made to feel that way if you don't value your relationship with them.

It has been said that relationships are forged, not formed. They require time and common experience. If you have made the effort to connect with people, as we talked about in the previous chapter, by the time you're ready to empower them, your relationship should be solid enough for you to be able to lead them. And as you do, remember what Ralph Waldo Emerson wrote, "Every man [or woman] is entitled to be valued by his [or her] best moments." When you value people and your relationships with them, you lay the foundation for empowering others.

Respect

Relationships cause people to want to be with you, but respect causes them to want to be empowered by you. Mutual respect is essential to the empowerment process. Psychiatrist Ari Kiev summed it up this way: "If you wish others to respect you, you must show respect for them. . . . Everyone wants to feel that he counts for something and is important to someone. Invariably, people will give their love, respect, and attention to the person who fills that need. Consideration for others generally reflects faith in self and faith in others." When you believe in people, care about them, and trust them, they know it. And that respect inspires them to want to follow where you lead.

Commitment

The last quality a leader needs to become an empowerer is commitment. USAir executive Ed McElroy stressed that "commitment gives us new power. No matter what comes to us—sickness, poverty, or disaster, we never turn our eye from the goal." The process of empowering others isn't always easy, especially when you start doing it for the first time. It's a road that has many bumps and sidetracks. But it is one that's worth traveling because the rewards are so great. As Edward Deci of the University of Rochester stated, "People must believe that a task is inherently worthwhile if they are to be committed to it." If you need a reminder of the value of empowering others, remember this: When you empower people, you're not influencing just them; you're influencing all the people they influence. That's impact!

If you have authority in people's lives, have built relationships with them, respect them, and have committed yourself to the process of empowerment, you're in a *position* to empower them. But one more crucial element of empowering needs to be in place. You need to have the right attitude.

Many people neglect to empower others because they are insecure. They are afraid of losing their jobs to the people they mentor. They don't want to be replaced or displaced, even if it means that they would be able to move up to a higher position and leave their current one to be filled by the person they mentor. They're afraid of change. But change is part of empowerment— for the people you empower and for yourself. If you want to go up, there are things you have to be willing to give up.

If you're not sure about where you stand in terms of your attitude toward the changes involved with empowering others, answer these questions:

QUESTIONS TO ASK
BEFORE YOU GET STARTED

1. Do I believe in people and feel that they are my organization's most appreciable asset?
2. Do I believe that empowering others can accomplish more than individual achievement?
3. Do I actively search for potential leaders to empower?
4. Would I be willing to raise others to a level higher than my own level of leadership?
5. Would I be willing to invest time developing people who have leadership potential?
6. Would I be willing to let others get credit for what I taught them?

7. Do I allow others freedom of personality and process, or do I have to be in control?
8. Would I be willing to publicly give my authority and influence to potential leaders?
9. Would I be willing to let others work me out of a job?
10. Would I be willing to hand the leadership baton to the people I empower and truly root for them?

If you answer no to more than a couple of these questions, you may need an attitude adjustment. You need to believe in others enough to give them all you can and in yourself enough to know that it won't hurt you. Just remember that as long as you continue to grow and develop yourself, you'll always have something to give, and you won't need to worry about being displaced.

How to Empower Others to Their Potential

Once you have confidence in yourself and in the persons you wish to empower, you're ready to start the process. Your goal should be to hand over relatively small, simple tasks in the beginning and progressively increase their responsibilities and authority. The greener the people you're working with, the more time the process will take. But no matter whether they are raw recruits or seasoned veterans, it's still important to take them through the whole process. Use the following steps to guide you as you empower others:

1. Evaluate Them

The place to start when empowering people is to evaluate them. If you give inexperienced people too much authority too soon, you can set them up to fail. If you move too slowly with people who have lots of experience, you can frustrate and demoralize them.

Sometimes when leaders misjudge the capabilities of others, the results can be comical. For example, we read about an incident from the life of Albert Einstein that illustrates this point. In 1898, Einstein applied for admittance to the Munich Technical Institute and was rejected because he would "never amount to much." As a result, instead of going to school, he worked as an inspector at the Swiss Patent Office in Bern. And with the extra time he had on his hands, he worked at refining and writing his theory of relativity.

Remember that all people have the potential to succeed. Your job is to see the potential, find out what they lack to develop it, and equip them with what they need. As you evaluate the people you intend to empower, look at these areas:

- **Knowledge.** Think about what people need to know in order to do any task you intend to give them. Don't take for granted that they know all that you know. Ask them questions. Give them history or background information. Cast a vision by giving them the big picture of how their actions fit into the organization's mission and goals. Knowledge is not only power; it's empowering.

- **Skill.** Examine the skill level of the people you desire to empower. Nothing is more frustrating than being asked to do things for which you have no ability. Look at what people have done before as well as what they're doing now. Some skills are inherent. Others need to be learned through training or experience. Your job as the empowerer is to find out what the job requires and make sure your people have what they need to succeed.

- **Desire.** Greek philosopher Plutarch remarked, "The richest soil, if uncultivated, produces the rankest weeds." No amount of skill, knowledge, or potential can help people succeed if they don't have the desire to be successful. But when desire is present, empowerment is easy. As seventeenth-century French essayist Jean La Fontaine wrote, "Man is made so that whenever anything fires his soul, impossibilities vanish."

2. Model for Them

Even people with knowledge, skill, and desire need to know what's expected of them, and the best way to inform them is to show them. People do what people see. A little parable about a farm boy who lived in a mountainous region of Colorado illustrates this point. One day the boy climbed to a high place and found an eagle's nest with eggs in it. He snatched one of the eggs while the eagle was away, took it back to the farm, and put it under a sitting hen who had a brood of eggs.

The eggs hatched one by one, and when the eaglet came out of his shell, he had no reason to believe he was anything other than a chicken. So he did everything that the other chickens did on the farm. He scratched around the yard looking for grain, he tried his best to cluck, and he kept his feet firmly planted on the ground, even though the fence around the pen wasn't more than several feet high.

That went on until he towered over his would-be siblings and his adopted mother hen. Then one day an eagle flew over the chicken yard. The young eagle heard its cry and saw it swoop down on a rabbit in the field. And at that moment, the young eagle knew in his heart that he wasn't like the chickens in the yard. He spread his wings, and before he knew it, he was flying after the other eagle. Not until he had seen one of his kind flying did he know who he was or what he was capable of doing.

The people you desire to empower need to see what it looks like to fly. As their mentor, you have the best opportunity to show them. Model the attitude and work ethic you would like them to embrace. And anytime you can include them in your work, take them along with you. There is no better way to help them learn and understand what you want them to do.

3. Give Them Permission to Succeed

As a leader and influencer, you may believe that everyone wants to be successful and automatically strives for success, probably as you have. But not everyone you influence will think the same way you do. You have to help others believe that they can succeed and show them that you want them to succeed. How do you do that?

- **Expect it.** Author and professional speaker Danny Cox advised, "The important thing to remember is that if you don't have that inspired enthusiasm that is contagious—

whatever you do have is also contagious." People can sense your underlying attitude no matter what you say or do. If you have an expectation for your people to be successful, they will know it.

- **Verbalize it.** People need to hear you tell them that you believe in them and want them to succeed. Tell them often that you know they are going to make it. Send them encouraging notes. Become a positive prophet of their success.

- **Reinforce it.** You can never do too much when it comes to believing in people. Leadership expert Fred Smith has made it a habit to give people plenty of positive reinforcement. He says, "As I recognize success, I try to stretch people's horizons. I might say, 'That was terrific!' but I don't stop there. Tomorrow I might return, repeat the compliment, and say, 'Last year, would you have believed you could do that? You may be surprised at what you can accomplish next year.'"

Once people recognize and understand that you genuinely want to see them succeed and are committed to helping them, they will begin to believe they can accomplish what you give them to do.

4. Transfer Authority to Them

The real heart of empowerment is the transfer of your authority—and influence—to the people you are mentoring and developing. Many people are willing to give others responsibility. They gladly delegate tasks to them. But empowering others is more than sharing your workload. It's sharing your power and ability to get things done.

Management expert Peter Drucker asserted, "No executive has ever suffered because his subordinates were strong and effective." People become strong and effective only when they are given the opportunity to make decisions, initiate action, solve problems, and meet challenges. When you empower others, you're helping them develop the ability to work independently under your authority. W. Alton Jones offered this opinion: "The man who gets the most satisfactory results is not always the man with the most brilliant single mind, but rather the man who can best co-ordinate the brains and talents of his associates."

As you begin to empower your people, give them challenges you know they can rise to meet and conquer. It will make them confident and give them a chance to try out their new authority and learn to use it wisely. And once they've begun to be effective, give them more difficult assignments. A good rule of thumb is that if someone else can do a job 80 percent as well as you do, delegate it. In the end, your goal is to empower others so well that they become capable of meeting nearly any challenge that comes their way. And in time, they will develop their own influence with others so that they no longer require yours to be effective.

5. *Publicly Show Your Confidence in Them*

When you first transfer authority to the people you empower, you need to tell them that you believe in them, and you need to do it publicly. Public recognition lets them know that you believe they will succeed. But it also lets the other people they're working with know that they have your support and that your authority backs them up. It's a tangible way of sharing (and spreading) your influence.

John is especially talented at empowering people and publicly showing them his confidence, and he has an interesting story about one of his greatest successes in empowerment:

> I mentioned in the last chapter that Dan Reiland has worked with me for fifteen years. When Dan first started with me, he was an intern, fresh out of graduate school. He had a lot of talent, but he still had some rough edges. I worked with him quite a bit—modeling, motivating, and mentoring him—and in a short time he grew to be a first-rate pastor.
>
> In just a few years, he became one of my key players. When we had a new program that needed to be created and implemented, I frequently looked to Dan, empowered him to take on the task, and gave him my full confidence and authority. And he took care of it. Time after time, I'd give him a major project, he would work through the whole process, implement it, raise up leaders to run it,

then come to me for another task. He continually worked himself out of a job.

In 1989, about six or seven years after Dan began working for me, I came to a point where I realized I needed to hire an executive pastor, a kind of chief administrative officer. And I knew right away that I wanted Dan to fill the position.

Now I knew that when you raise up a leader from within the ranks, there are often resentment and resistance from some of that person's colleagues. But I had a strategy. As I began to transfer my authority to Dan, I tried my best not to miss an opportunity to publicly praise him, show my confidence in him, and remind everyone that Dan spoke with my authority. As a result, the rest of the staff quickly rallied around him, and he was empowered as their new leader.

As you raise up leaders, show them and and their followers that they have your confidence and authority. And you will find that they quickly become empowered to succeed.

6. Supply Them with Feedback

Although you need to publicly praise your people, you can't let them go very long without giving them honest, positive feedback. Meet with them privately to coach them through their mistakes, miscues, and misjudgments. At first, some people may have a difficult time. During that early period, be a grace giver. Try to give them what they need, not what they deserve. And applaud any progress that they make. People do what gets praised.

7. Release Them to Continue on Their Own

No matter who you are working to empower—your employees, children, colleagues, or spouse—your ultimate aim should be to release them to make good decisions and succeed on their own. And that means giving them as much freedom as possible as soon as they are ready for it.

President Abraham Lincoln was a master at empowering his leaders. For example, when he appointed General Ulysses S. Grant as commander of the Union armies in 1864, he sent him this message: "I neither ask nor desire to know anything of your plans. Take the responsibility and act, and call on me for assistance."

That's the attitude you need as an empowerer. Give authority and responsibility, and offer assistance as needed. John and I have been fortunate to have been empowered by key people in our lives since we were kids. Probably the person who has been the most empowering in John's life is his father, Melvin Maxwell. He always encouraged John to be the best person he could be, and he gave him his permission and his power whenever he could. Years later as they talked about it, Melvin told John his philosophy: "I never consciously limited you as long as I knew what you were doing was morally right." Now that's an empowering attitude!

THE RESULTS OF EMPOWERMENT

If you head up any kind of organization—a business, club, church, or family—learning to empower others is one of the most important things you'll ever do as its leader. Empowerment has an incredibly high return. It not only helps the individuals you raise up by making them more confident, energetic, and productive, but it also has the ability to improve your life, give you additional freedom, and promote the growth and health of your organization.

Farzin Madjidi, program liaison for the city of Los Angeles, has expressed his beliefs concerning empowerment: "We need leaders who empower people and create other leaders. It's no longer good enough for a manager to make sure that everybody has something to do and is producing. Today, all employees must 'buy in' and take ownership of everything they're doing. To foster this, it's important that employees should make decisions that most directly affect them. That's how the best decisions are made. That's the essence of empowerment." When it comes down to it, empowering leadership is sometimes the only real advantage one organization has over another in our competitive society.

As you empower others, you will find that most aspects of your life will change for the better. Empowering others can free you personally to have more time for the important things in your life, increase the effectiveness of your organization, increase your influence with others and, best of all, make an incredibly positive impact on the lives of the people you empower.

Jim recently received a letter from someone he has spent several years motivating, mentoring, and empowering. His name is Mitch Sala, and here's his letter:

Dear Jim,

I know you are in the process of writing a book on influence, and I feel the need to put pen to paper to express my deep respect and love for you and Nancy and tell you about the profound impact you've had on my life.

Your influence on me started before we even met when I listened to one of your tapes for the first time. Your vision, positive attitude, and committed faith were inspiring, and Nancy's ability to put life and its obstacles in proper perspective helped me to see my world in a new way.

As I observed you, I sensed an incredible depth of character in you. I admired that and wanted it myself. And it made me want to get to know you better, to develop our relationship. I had never really developed close friendships before, so that was new for me. You see, I grew up in Africa where my father ran a large sawmill in the forest. My older brother and sister were away at school, so I pretty much grew up without other kids around. I was kind of a loner. When I was eight, they sent me to traditional [boarding] school. It was good for my education, but bad for my self-image. It left me feeling like a loser.

As an adult, those feelings drove me to work hard and try to prove myself, but I still felt empty no matter what I did. And I was failing at the things that mattered to me most: being a good husband and father.

But you became an influence in my life at just the right time. You understood me and made me feel accepted despite my mistakes and failings. You've helped me to grow in my family life, financially, and spiritually. Everything has changed in my life.

Jim's positive influence has helped Mitch Sala change his life. Jim has taken him through the entire process. He has modeled a life of integrity to him. He has motivated and mentored him. He has empowered him. And over the years, Mitch has become a world-class influencer. Through his business enterprises and public speaking, Mitch touches the lives of hundreds of thousands of people every year in more than twenty countries around the world. And best of all, he is using his influence to raise up more leaders who are learning how to positively impact the lives of many more people. He has reproduced his influence in others, which is the subject of the final chapter of this book.

Influence Checklist
EMPOWERING PEOPLE

❑ **Give others more than just something to do.** If you lead a business, a department, a family, a church, or any other kind of organization, you are probably preparing to hand off some responsibilities to others. Before you officially start the process, carefully plan your strategy for passing the baton by using the following checklist:

Describe the task: _____

Name the person to whom you will give it: _____

What knowledge does the task require? _____
_____

Does the person have the required knowledge? ❑ Yes ❑ No

What skills does the task require? _____
_____

Does the person have the skills required?   ❑ Yes ❑ No

Have you modeled how you want the job done? ❑ Yes ❑ No

Have you given the person the authority and permission to succeed?   ❑ Yes ❑ No

Have you publicly given the person your confidence?
                                                              ❑ Yes ❑ No

Have you privately supplied the person with feedback? ¨
                                                              ❑ Yes ❑ No

Have you set a date to release the person to continue on his or her own?   ❑ Yes ❑ No

Repeat this process with every task you intend to delegate until it becomes second nature. Even when someone you empower is successful and established in performance, continue praising, encouraging, and showing your confidence publicly.

A Person of Influence . . .

REPRODUCES OTHER INFLUENCERS

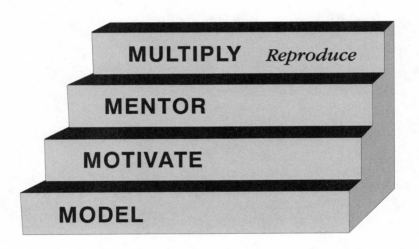

At the beginning of this book, we told you about influencers and specifically about some of the people who have made an impact on our lives, people like Glenn Leatherwood, who was John's Sunday school teacher in seventh grade—and Jerry and Patty Beaumont, who took Jim and Nancy under their wing around the time Eric was born. Our lives have been filled with wonderful people of influence. But the greatest value has been added to our lives by people who not only influenced us, but also made influencers of us. In John's case, his father, Melvin Maxwell, has shaped and molded him the most, helping him to become an outstanding leader. And in the case of Jim, that place is probably held by Rich DeVos:

> I grew up in a great family. We had lots of love, even though there wasn't much money. My father's views on politics and economics were pretty liberal, and his advice to me was to go to college and get a good job. But when I was in my twenties, I heard Rich DeVos speak for the first time, and I was mesmerized. He introduced me to a whole new paradigm. He talked about free enterprise, the worth of the individual, dreams, freedom, and "compassionate capitalism." He also talked about his faith in God and encouraged people to live with integrity and passion. I had never before heard any philosophy that made so much sense as his simple message of personal achievement. I was forever changed.

Today, of course, Rich DeVos is one of the most influential businessmen in the world. He is a founder and past president of Amway; he owns the NBA's Orlando Magic; he is the president of Gospel Films and the DeVos Foundation; and he is frequently asked to give advice on business matters to presidents and other influential leaders. Jim has looked up to him as a leader and mentor, and over the years, he has come to call Rich his friend.

Rich DeVos understands the value of raising up leaders, people who are able to become influencers in their own right. In some ways, teaching others to become leaders is like handing off the baton in a relay race. If you run well but are unable to pass the baton to another runner, you lose the race. But if you run well, recruit and train other good runners, and learn to hand off the baton smoothly, you can win. And when it comes to influence, if you can do that process repeatedly, you can multiply your influence incredibly.

THE POWER OF MULTIPLICATION

In the work with people that the two of us have done, we've had to learn to hand off the baton. We never could have been successful if we hadn't. And now we want to hand it off to you. If you've moved successfully through the influence process, you've learned how to run the race. You understand how important it is for you to model integrity. You've learned to motivate people by nurturing them, having faith in them, listening to them, and giving them understanding. You understand that people really grow only when you mentor them. They have to be enlarged, navigated through life's difficulties, connected with, and empowered. Right now, you're running a good race. And if you've mentored others, you've got them running now too. But it's time to pass the baton, and if you don't get it into their hands, the race is over. They will have no reason to keep running, and the momentum will die with them.

That's why the reproduction phase of becoming a person of influence is so significant. Take a look at some benefits of creating leaders in your organization who are able to not only follow you but also influence others and raise them up:

- **Reproducing leaders raises your influence to a new level.** Anytime you influence people who either do not or cannot exercise influence with others, you limit your influence. But when you influence leaders, you indirectly influence all the people they influence. The effect is multiplication. (This idea is treated in greater depth in John's book *Developing the Leaders Around You*.) The greater your influence, the greater the number of people you can help.

- **Reproducing leaders raises the new leaders' personal potential.** Whenever you help others become better leaders, you raise the bar on their potential. Leadership is the lid on a person's ability to perform and influence. A person acting independently who doesn't practice leadership can accomplish only so much, personally or professionally. But as soon as people understand leadership and start practicing leadership principles, they blow the lid off personal potential. And if they lead people who lead others, the potential for what they can achieve is almost limitless.

- **Reproducing leaders multiplies resources.** As you develop leaders, you'll find that your resources increase in value. You have more time because you can share the load and increasingly delegate authority. As the people on your staff learn leadership, they become wiser and more valuable as advisers. And as an added bonus, you receive personal loyalty from just about everyone you raise up.

- **Reproducing leaders ensures a positive future for your organization.** G. Alan Bernard, president of Mid Park, Inc., put the issue of raising up leaders into perspective: "A good leader will always have those around him who are better at particular tasks than he is. This is the hallmark of leadership. Never be afraid to hire or manage people who are better at certain jobs than you are. They can only make your organization stronger." Not only does it make an organization stronger when you develop leaders, but it gives that organization a strong future. If only a couple of people in the organization are capable of doing the leading, the organization can't flourish when they retire or anything happens to them. It may not even be able to survive.

John had the opportunity in 1995 to see exactly how an organization reacts when its leader leaves after equipping and empowering many strong leaders within it. Following fourteen years of leading and reproducing leaders at Skyline Wesleyan Church, John resigned from his position as senior pastor. He left so that he could devote himself full-time to INJOY, his organization that offers seminars and materials for leadership growth and personal development. And the result of his move? Skyline is doing very well. In fact, about a year after John left, he received a note from Jayne Hansen, an INJOY employee whose husband, Brad, was on staff at Skyline.

Dear John,

I was just thinking about Skyline and how it is really thriving since you've left. . . . It's such an absolute TRIBUTE to the kind of leadership and lay ministry that you developed. We have a living example of the saying "practice what you preach" unfolding as we see the fruit of your labor. I can tell anyone without question that the principles you teach work. I can think of no greater honor than that a man pour his life into something, leave, and have it flourish! What a shame it would be to have a ministry die on the vine when one man leaves.

Thank you for pouring your life into us.

Your friend,
Jayne

Mentoring people and developing their leadership potential really can make a huge difference—for your organization, for your people, and for you.

Awaken the Reproducer in You

Everyone has the potential to multiply influence by developing and reproducing leaders. To awaken the reproducer in you, make the following principles a part of your life:

Lead Yourself Well

Being able to lead others begins with leading yourself well. You can't reproduce what you don't have. As entrepreneur and Chick-Fil-A restaurant chain founder Truett Cathy said, "The number one reason leaders are unsuccessful is their inability to lead themselves."

When we think about self-leadership, many qualities come to mind: integrity, right priorities, vision, self-discipline, problem-solving skills, a positive attitude, and so forth. Desire and a game plan for personal development can help you cultivate these qualities, but the greatest obstacle to becoming a leader may be yourself. Psychologist Sheldon Kopp remarked about this problem: "All the significant battles are waged within the self."

If you haven't already put yourself on a program for growth and leadership development, start today. Listen to tapes. Go to conferences. Read enlightening books. (John's *Developing the*

Leader Within You is an excellent primer for leadership development.) If you make personal growth your weekly goal and daily discipline, you can become a reproducer of leaders. Nineteenth-century theologian H. P. Liddon clearly saw this connection when he stated, "What we do on some great occasion will probably depend on what we already are; and what we are will be the result of previous years of self-discipline." Personal development pays dividends.

Look Continually for Potential Leaders

Former Notre Dame head football coach Lou Holtz said of a subject he knew well: "You've got to have good athletes to win, I don't care who the coach is." The same thing is true in your personal and professional lives. You need good people with leadership potential if you're going to reproduce leaders. Industrialist Andrew Carnegie emphasized that "no man will make a great leader who wants to do it all himself or get all the credit for doing it." Effective developers of people are always on the lookout for potential leaders.

It's said that "when the student is ready, the teacher appears." But it's also true that when the teacher is ready, the student appears. If you keep developing yourself as a leader, you will soon be ready to develop others. And if you want to be a great reproducer of leaders, you need to seek out and recruit the best people possible.

Put the Team First

Great developers of leaders think of the welfare of the team before thinking of themselves. J. Carla Northcutt, who receives John's monthly INJOY Life Club tapes, stated, "The goal of many leaders is to get people to think more highly of the leader. The goal of a great leader is to help people to think more highly of themselves."

Bill Russell was a gifted basketball player. Many consider him to be one of the best team players in the history of professional basketball. Russell observed, "The most important measure of how good a game I played was how much better I'd made my teammates play." That's the attitude necessary to become a great reproducer of leaders. The team has to come first.

Do you consider yourself to be a team player? Answer each of the following questions to see where you stand when it comes to promoting the good of the team:

SEVEN QUESTIONS FOR A SUCCESSFUL TEAM ORIENTATION

1. Do I add value to others?
2. Do I add value to the organization?
3. Am I quick to give away the credit when things go right?
4. Is our team consistently adding new members?
5. Do I use my "bench" players as much as I could?
6. Do many people on the team consistently make important decisions?
7. Is our team's emphasis on creating victories more than producing stars?

If you answered no to a few of these questions, you may want to reevaluate your attitude toward the team. It has been said, "The ultimate leader is one who is willing to develop people to the point that they eventually surpass him or her in knowledge and ability." That should be your goal as you multiply your influence by developing leaders.

Commit Yourself to Developing Leaders, Not Followers

We believe that our country is experiencing a leadership crisis today. Not long ago, we saw an article in the *New Republic* that addressed the issue. In part it read, "Two hundred years ago, a little republic on the edge of the wilderness suddenly produced people like Jefferson, Hamilton, Madison, Adams, and others. Yet the total population was only 3,000,000 people. Today, we have over 200 million. Where are the great people? We should have 60 Franklins in a cover story on leadership. The search was in vain."

Ralph Nader, consumer advocate and founder of the Center for Responsive Law, declared, "The function of a leader is to produce more leaders, not more followers." Maybe two hundred years ago, people understood that better. But today, producing leaders isn't a priority for many people. Besides, developing other leaders isn't always easy or simple, especially for people who are natural leaders. As management expert Peter Drucker observed, "People who excel at something can rarely tell you how to do it."

That's why it's important for a person who wants to raise up other leaders to be committed to the task. We've said it before and we'll repeat it here: Everything rises and falls on leadership. When you raise up and empower leaders, you positively impact yourself, your organization, the people you develop, and all the people their lives touch. Reproducing leaders is the most important task of any person of influence. If you want to make an impact, you have got to be committed to developing leaders.

MOVING FROM MAINTENANCE TO MULTIPLICATION

Many people live in maintenance mode. Their main goal is to keep from losing ground rather than trying to make progress. But that's the lowest level of living when it comes to the development of people. If you want to make an impact, you must strive to become a multiplier. Take a look at the five stages that exist between maintenance and multiplication, starting with the lowest:

1. Scramble

About 20 percent of all leaders live on the lowest level in the development process. They are not doing anything to develop people in their organization, and as a result, their attrition rate is off the charts. They can't seem to keep anyone they recruit. That's why we say they're in the scramble stage—they spend most of their time scrambling to find people to replace the ones they lose. You may know some small business owners who seem to stay in scramble mode. The morale in their organization stays low, and it doesn't take long for them to burn out from exhaustion.

2. Survival

The next stage in the development ladder is survival mode. In it, leaders do nothing to develop their people, but they do manage to keep the people they have. About 50 percent of all organizational leaders function this way. Their organizations are average, their employees are dissatisfied, and no one is developing personal potential. No one really benefits from this approach to leadership. Everyone merely survives from day to day without much promise or hope for the future.

3. Siphon

About 10 percent of all leaders work at developing their people into better leaders, but they neglect to build their relationships with their people. As a result, their potential leaders leave the organization to pursue other opportunities. In other words, they are siphoned off from the organization. That often leads to frustration on the part of the leader because other people benefit from their effort, and they must devote a lot of time to looking for replacements.

4. Synergy

When leaders build strong relationships, develop people to become good leaders, empower them to reach their potential— and are able to keep them in the organization—something wonderful happens. It's often called synergy, meaning that the whole is greater than the sum of its parts because the parts interact well together and create energy, progress, and momentum. An organization on the synergy level has great morale and high job satisfaction. Everyone benefits. Only about 19 percent of all leaders reach this level, but those who do are often considered the very best there are.

5. Significance

Many people who reach the synergy level never try to go any farther because they don't realize they can take one more step in the development process, and that's to the significance level. Leaders on that level develop and reproduce leaders who stay in the organization, work to reach their potential, and in turn develop leaders. And that's where influence really multiplies. Only about 1 percent of all leaders make it to this level, but the ones who do are able to tap into almost limitless growth and influence potential. A handful of leaders continually functioning on the significance level can make an impact on the world.

How to Raise Up Leaders
Who Reproduce Leaders

In an article published by the *Harvard Business Review,* author Joseph Bailey examined what it took to be a successful executive. In conducting his research, he interviewed more than thirty top executives and found that every one of them learned firsthand from a mentor.[1] If you want to raise up leaders who reproduce other leaders, you need to mentor them.

We've been told that in hospital emergency rooms, nurses have a saying: "Watch one, do one, teach one." It refers to the need to learn a technique quickly, jump right in and do it with a patient, and then turn around and pass it on to another nurse. The mentoring process for developing leaders works in a similar way. It happens when you take potential leaders under your wing, develop them, empower them, share with them how to become persons of influence, and then release them to go out and raise up other leaders. Every time you do that, you plant seeds for greater success. And as novelist Robert Louis Stevenson advised, "Don't judge each day by the harvest you reap but by the seeds you plant."

Now you know what it takes to become a person of influence, to positively impact the lives of others. Being an influencer means . . .

- modeling *integrity* with everyone you come into contact with.
- *nurturing* the people in your life to make them feel valued.
- showing *faith* in others so that they believe in themselves.
- *listening* to them so that you can build your relationship with them.
- *understanding* them so that you can help them achieve their dreams.
- *enlarging* them in order to increase their potential.
- *navigating* them though life's difficulties until they can do it themselves.
- *connecting* with them so that you can move them to a higher level.
- *empowering* them to become the person they were created to be.
- *reproducing* other leaders so that your influence continues to grow through others.

Over the years, Jim and I have worked hard to make this process more than a mere set of principles or method of working. We have sought to make investing in others a way of living. And as time goes by, we keep working to become better developers of people. Our reward is seeing the impact we make on the lives of other people. Listen to this story from Jim:

One of the greatest things about becoming a person of influence is that you actually get to see the lives of others change before your eyes. I told you in the previous chapter about Mitch Sala, whom I got to see blossom into a person of impact. But what I didn't tell you is that Mitch has became more than just an influencer. He has gone through the entire development process himself and now is a great *reproducer* of influencers too.

One of his greatest success stories is a man named Robert Angkasa. Robert is from Indonesia, holds an MBA from Sydney University, and used to work for Citibank, where he had risen to become a vice president in Jakarta by the time he was thirty years old.

Robert has always worked hard. He put himself through school driving a taxi, working in restaurant kitchens, and cleaning stadiums after concerts. But a few years ago, he met Mitch Sala. Mitch took Robert under his wing, motivated him, mentored him, and empowered him to become a person of influence.

Robert says, "The turning point in my life came when I met Mitch. At first, all I noticed was that he was a kind person. But the more time I spent with him, the more I realized that I wanted to be like him while still being myself. Mitch taught me that the way to success was through integrity and hard work. Today I am tasting the sweetness of a new life. I enjoy the financial security that's come from hard work, but more than that, I am becoming a better person. The pleasure that I get from helping others is enormous and gives me great satisfaction. I am a better person, husband, and family man. I owe a lot of who I am today to Mitch. He is a mentor, a friend, and a parent. I thank God every day for all his blessings that I've received through Mitch. And what I am trying to do now is be to others what he's been to me. I want to help others have a better life. The words *Thank you* don't seem sufficient, but they're the best words I can find."

Today Robert impacts the lives of thousands of people throughout Indonesia, Malaysia, China, and the Philippines. He is one of several key business leaders whom Mitch is now mentoring. And Robert's influence is continuing to increase daily.

My friend, you have the same potential as Robert Angkasa, Mitch Sala, or Jim Dornan. You can become a person of influence and impact the lives of many people. But the decision is yours. You can either develop your influence potential or let it remain unrealized. Jim gave the baton to Mitch. Mitch found Robert and taught him to run. He has successfully given the baton to Robert, and now he is running. There is one more leg—and the baton is ready. Now is your chance. Reach out your hand, take the baton, and finish the race that only you can run. Become a person of influence, and change your world.

Influence Checklist
REPRODUCING OTHER INFLUENCERS

❏ **Develop your own leadership potential.** The way to be prepared to teach others leadership is to continue developing your own leadership potential. If you haven't already put yourself on a personal plan for growth, start today. Select tapes, books, and magazines that you will review weekly for the next three months. Growth comes only if you make it a habit.

❏ **Find people with leadership potential.** As you continually enlarge and empower the people around you, some will emerge as potential leaders. Choose the person with the greatest potential for special mentoring, and talk to him or her about developing greater leadership skills. Proceed only if the person wants to be developed and agrees to mentor others in leadership in the future.

❏ **Teach the person to be a leader, not just perform tasks.** Give the person complete access to you, and spend lots of time modeling leadership. Devote time each week to increasing the person's leadership potential by teaching, sharing resources, sending him or her to seminars, and so forth. Do everything in your power to help that person reach his or her leadership potential.

❏ **Multiply.** When the person becomes a good leader, help him or her select someone to mentor in the area of leadership. Release them to work together, and find yourself a new potential leader so that you can keep repeating the process.

Notes

Introduction

1. John C. Maxwell, *Developing the Leader Within You* (Nashville: Thomas Nelson, 1993), 5–12.
2. Brad Herzog, *The Sports 100: The One Hundred Most Important People in American Sports History* (New York: MacMillan, 1995), 7.

Chapter 1

1. Stephen R. Covey, *The Seven Habits of Highly Effective People: Restoring the Character Ethic* (New York: Simon and Schuster, 1989).
2. Proverbs 22:1 NIV.
3. Donald T. Phillips, *Lincoln on Leadership: Executive Strategies for Tough Times* (New York: Warner Books, 1992), 66–67.
4. Bill Kynes, "A Hope That Will Not Disappoint," quoted in *Best Sermons 2* (New York: Harper and Row, 1989), 301.

Chapter 2

1. Everett Shostrom, *Man the Manipulator.*
2. *Bits and Pieces.*
3. Jack Canfield and Mark Victor Hansen, "All the Good Things," in *Chicken Soup for the Soul* (Deerfield Beach, Fla.: Health Communications, 1993), 126–28.
4. Arthur Gordon, "The Gift of Caring," in *A Touch of Wonder.*
5. Greg Asimakoupoulos, "Icons Every Pastor Needs," *Leadership,* fall 1993, 109.
6. Dennis Rainey and Barbara Rainey, *Building Your Mate's Self-Esteem* (Nashville: Thomas Nelson, 1993).

Chapter 3

1. 1 Samuel 17:32–37 NIV.

Chapter 4

1. Quoted by Fred Barnes in the *New Republic.*
2. David Grimes, (Sarasota, Florida) *Herald-Tribune.*
3. Brian Adams, *Sales Cybernetics* (Wilshire Book Co., 1985), 110.
4. Eric Allenbaugh, *Wake-Up Calls* (Austin: Discovery Publications, 1992), 200.

Chapter 5
1. M. Michael Markowich, *Management Review,* cited in *Behavioral Sciences Newsletter.*
2. Art Mortell, "How to Master the Inner Game of Selling," vol. 10, no. 7.
3. Kent M. Keith, *The Silent Revolution: Dynamic Leadership in the Student Council,* (Cambridge, Mass: Harvard Student Agencies) 1968.
4. Ecclesiastes 4:9–12 NIV.
5. Robert Schuller, ed., *Life Changers* (Old Tappan, N.J.: Revell).

Chapter 6
1. Quoted in Og Mandino, *The Return of the Ragpicker.*

Chapter 7
1. *Saturday Review.*
2. Quoted in advertisement, *Esquire.*
3. Mortimer R. Feinberg, *Effective Psychology for Managers.*
4. "The Top Problems and Needs of Americans," *Ministry Currents,* January–March 1994.
5. Tim Hansel, *Holy Sweat* (Waco: Word, 1987), 134.
6. Ernie J. Zelinski, *The Joy of Not Knowing It All* (Edmonton, Alberta, Canada: Visions International Publishing, 1995), 114.
7. David Armstrong, *Managing by Storying Around,* quoted in *The Competitive Advantage.*

Chapter 8
1. Tom Peters and Nancy Austin, *A Passion for Excellence.*
2. Charles B. Ruth, *The Handbook of Selling* (Prentice-Hall).
3. Florence Littauer, *Personality Plus* (Grand Rapids: Revell, 1983), 24–81.
4. Carl Sandberg, *Lincoln: The Prairie Years.*

Chapter 9
1. *The Nordstrom Way,* 15–16.

Chapter 10
1. Joseph Bailey, "Clues for Success in the President's Job," *Harvard Business Review* (special edition), 1983.